Social Life,
Local Politics,
and Nazism

Social Life, Local Politics, and Nazism

MARBURG, 1880–1935

Rudy Koshar

The University of North Carolina Press

Chapel Hill and London

94 93 92 91 90   6 5 4 3 2

Library of Congress Cataloging-in-Publication Data
Koshar, Rudy.
  Social life, local politics, and Nazism.

  Bibliography: p.
  Includes index.
  1. Marburg (Germany)—Politics and government.
  2. Marburg (Germany)—Social life and customs.
  3. National socialism.   4. Middle classes—Germany
  (West)—Marburg—Political activity.   I. Title.
  DD901.M283K67 1986   943'.41   85-28958
  ISBN 0-8078-1694-9
  ISBN 0-8078-4287-7 (pbk.)

Publication of this book has been aided by a subvention
from the University of Southern California.

Designed by Ron Maner

For Judy, Drew, and Annelise

Contents

Tables

Illustrations

Preface

This book discusses the organizational fabric of politics and the rise of the National Socialist party in a single German city. Its goal is to embed a discussion of the Nazi movement in a broad social and chronological framework while avoiding a teleological interpretation that makes of this framework a simple prehistory of German fascism. The setting is Marburg an der Lahn, a Hessian university town where the Nazi party received early and above-average electoral support. I became interested in the topic partly because I thought that most case studies of the 1930s suggested the importance of a longer time frame in understanding the genesis and evolution of the NSDAP (Nationalsozialistische Deutsche Arbeiterpartei) but treated developments prior to 1918 and large parts of Weimar history superficially—as general background rather than as integral chapters in the rise of Hitler's violent politics. Moreover, I thought that studies of the organizational genealogy of the Nazi movement captured only a narrow range of social ties based on national political parties, economic pressure groups, and protofascist associations. Although I recognized the importance of these groups, I thought that the majority of Nazi party members also received a political education from mundane social organizations of ordinary joiners. I became convinced that the everyday substructures of local politics were also the substructures of German fascism and that informal diffusion of Nazi ideology through quotidian organizational networks was as important to the NSDAP as were propaganda, the personality cult of Hitler, and conspiratorial infiltration of voluntary groups by activists.

I wanted to reconstruct that part of a town's organizational ecology in which the Nazi party gained success. I aimed to study apparently unpolitical social clubs as well as pressure groups and local parties. Although many groups in which the NSDAP gained support claimed that they shut out contentious party politics, they also gave Germans a chance to talk about political events, form contacts, and gain parliamentary skills. In my view, the "apoliticism" of many voluntary associations—a much discussed though insufficiently analyzed aversion to mass parties and the political marketplace that produced them—was not based on a misunderstanding of power relations but rather contained the raw materials of an ideology, of a particular mode of political practice, and of a common sense with diverse origins and textures. Rejecting mass parties as the sole or dominant instruments of national political representation, many voluntary organizations used apoliticism after the late nineteenth century to build an antisocialist movement, an effort which Nazi agitators eventually exploited by mobilizing diverse social networks. The small-town bourgeoisie—a community of sentiment including the Protestant, nonsocialist upper middle, lower middle, and working classes—was a leading force in such processes. Yet scholars of modern Germany have devoted more attention to working-class milieus than to local bourgeois groups. My study will, I hope, fill part of this gap.

I am interested in the nexus formed by bourgeois voluntary associations, party politics, and the National Socialist movement between the late nineteenth century, when a surge of organization building occurred throughout Germany, and late 1935, when the first stage of Nazi "coordination" of voluntary group life was completed. Readers who are looking for a blow-by-blow history of local associations or political events will be disappointed. Similarly dissatisfied will be those who want a full discussion of the diverse motivations and interests nested in one city's voluntary groups. These are important issues, but tackling them would have made this an unmanageable and overly long project. My study assumes that at particular historical junctures dissimilar groups experience similar stresses and confront similar issues. The goal is therefore to discuss a greater range of voluntary associations than most previous studies of German political history have, to watch different organizations interact in the dance of local power relationships, and to trace those groups in the evolution of the Nazi party. In the latter task I place particular emphasis on the organizational roots of Nazi mobilization and the cross-affiliations of Nazi party members. I think the advantages of this approach outweigh the disadvantages, and it is hoped that this book will encourage further discussion of how to study Germany's fascinating maze of local clubs and associations.

Other readers may be unhappy with my discussion of apoliticism. It is a contentious and difficult term that covers a wide field of practices and sentiments. The goal here is to tease out various manifestations of a general distrust of mass political parties in an age in which such parties began to dominate the national and local polity in Western Europe. If my handling of the problem leads to more systematic treatment of the social location and forms of expression of anti-party sentiment, then I will have accomplished a part of my task.

I have written about a mainly Protestant university and administrative city that, like all localities, captures only part of an elusive national average. Marburg was a peculiar city, more singular than most communities perhaps, but it was not an island. For reasons I will make clear in the Introduction, Marburg is well suited to stimulate further thinking about the interaction of social and political life in modern German history.

The kernel of this book is my doctoral thesis, "Organizational Life and Nazism: A Study of Mobilization in Marburg/Lahn, 1918–1935," which was generously funded by the German Academic Exchange Service and the Alvin M. Bentley Foundation. Since completing the dissertation, I have extended the chronological scope of my work, gathered much more information on social organizations and political parties, added to quantitative evidence on Nazi party members' cross-affiliations, and generally reshaped the entire study. A postdoctoral grant from the Center for Western European Studies at the University of Michigan, a Fellowship for Recent Recipients of the Ph.D. from the American Council of Learned Societies, a semester of financial support from the Department of History at the University of Southern California, and a Haynes Foundation Summer Faculty Fellowship made possible the additional research and writing. Most of the new material appears in chapters 2, 3, 4, and 6. Only chapters 1, 5, and 7 retain something of their thesis form, but these also contain much new information. All this makes the present study an older and hopefully more mature second cousin, rather than a sibling, of my doctoral thesis.

One ultimately writes the book one wants to. Nonetheless, academic studies are collective enterprises. Throughout the preparation of this work, I have benefited from the encouragement and criticism of my dissertation codirectors, Charles Tilly and Michael Geyer, who have helped me keep faith in the project. Additionally, Geoff Eley has played an instrumental role in encouraging my revisions and forcing me to rethink portions of an earlier version of the manuscript. I have gained much from his support, criticism, and commentary. Thomas Childers, Mary Nolan, and Walter Struve likewise offered valuable advice during my revisions. I am grateful to Lewis Bateman, my editor at the University of North Carolina Press, who never lost interest in the manuscript. Thanks also go to Ron Maner, who copyedited the manuscript with great care. And I thank my colleagues in the Department of History at the University of Southern California, who besides the financial support already mentioned, offered time and encouragement.

I could not have conducted my research without the help of many West German friends and acquaintances. The staff members of the Hessisches Staatsarchiv, university library, Landratsamt, and photo archive in Marburg were extremely helpful and patient, as were those of the Universitätsarchiv Würzburg, the Bundesarchiv, and the Berlin Document Center. Many Marburgers—Hermann Bauer, Prof. Dr. Luise Berthold, and others—made special efforts to teach me something about local politics. Prof. Dr. and Frau Dr. Ulrich Cappeller; Herr Dr. and Frau Max Schönenberger; and Paul Knowlton, Ursula Wenzel, and Max helped my wife and me to learn from and eventually enjoy the Federal Republic. I would also like to thank Bernhard vom Brocke and Hellmut Seier, who kept me informed of their research on Marburg.

My greatest debt is to my family—to Drew, whose anticipated arrival hurried an earlier version of the manuscript toward completion; to Annelise, whose beginning accompanied the last major revisions of the study; and to Judy, who understands how difficult it would have been to complete this book without her.

Abbreviations

The following party and organization abbreviations are used in the text.

AMSt Allgemeine Marburger Studentenschaft (General Marburg Student Government)
AStA Allgemeiner Studentenausschuß (student government)
BDM Bund Deutscher Mädchen (League of German Girls)
BK Bekennende Kirche (Confessing church)
CNBLP Christlich-Nationale Bauern- und Landvolkpartei (Christian National Peasants' and Rural People's party)
CSV Christlich-Sozialer Volksdienst (Christian Social People's Service)
DC Deutsche Christen (German Christians)
DDP Deutsche Demokratische Partei (German Democratic party)
DHV Deutschnationaler Handlungsgehilfenverband (German National Commercial Employees' Association)
DNVP Deutschnationale Volkspartei (German National People's party)
DT Deutsche Turnerschaft (German Gymnastics Association)
DVLP Deutsche Vaterlandspartei (Fatherland party)
DVP Deutsche Volkspartei (German People's party)
Gestapo Geheime Staatspolizei (secret state police)
GVG Großdeutsche Volksgemeinschaft (Greater German Folk Community)
HDA Hochschulring Deutscher Art (German University Ring)
KPD Kommunistische Partei Deutschlands (Communist party)
KVP Konservative Volkspartei (Conservative People's party)
MDSB Mitteldeutscher Sängerbund (Central German Song Club)

NSDAP Nationalsozialistische Deutsche Arbeiterpartei
(National Socialist German Workers' party)
NSDStB Nationalsozialistischer Deutscher Studentenbund (Nazi
Student League)
SA Sturmabteilung (Nazi storm troops)
SPD Sozialdemokratische Partei Deutschlands (Social
Democratic party)
SS Schutzstaffel (Nazi elite guard)
Stuko Studentenkorps (Student Corps)
USPD Unabhängige Sozialdemokratische Partei Deutschlands
(Independent Social Democratic party)
VF Vaterländischer Frauenverein (Patriotic Women's
Association)
VfB Verein für Bewegungsspiele 05 (Athletic Association)
VFV Volksbund für Freiheit und Vaterland (People's League for
Freedom and Fatherland)
VSB Völkisch-Sozialer Block (an election coalition of the
Nazi party and the German-Völkisch Liberation party)
WP Wirtschaftspartei (Economic party)

For source abbreviations used in tables, appendix, and notes see
pages 301–2.

Social Life,
Local Politics,
and Nazism

Introduction

"When I ask if the German *Bürgertum* is mature enough today to be the leading political class of the nation," Max Weber stated in his Freiburg inaugural address of 1895, "I am *presently* unable to answer the question affirmatively." German unification in 1871 generated an " 'unhistorical' and unpolitical spirit" in the bourgeoisie, the famous sociologist argued. This left parts of the upper middle classes (*Großbürgertum*) longing "for the coming of a new Caesar" and both the upper middle and lower middle classes (*Kleinbürgertum*) foundering in "political philistinism" (*Spießbürgerei*).[1] Weber had sounded these themes before. A year earlier he wrote that Germany was in danger of being ruled by political philistines who shared a "lack of developed instincts for national power, the limitation of political endeavors to material goals or even the interests of one's own generation, [and] the lack of any consciousness of the measure of responsibility vis-à-vis our heirs."[2] These characteristics applied to bourgeois groups as well as the socialist working classes. Weber was convinced that Germany remained "a nation without any and all political inclinations."[3] He viewed this alleged political immaturity as a tragedy and agonized over Germany's inability to realize national and imperialist goals after Bismarck's downfall in 1890.

From Weber's perspective the problem was sociopolitical rather than economic or cultural. He argued that Germany possessed some of the same social underpinnings that supported the English and American parliamentary systems but that in Germany the substance needed to make parliament an effective advocate of national aims was lacking. Weber's remarks about the relationship between voluntary organizations and politics illustrated what he had in mind: he saw a close connection between individual personality development and club (*Verein*) membership, on the one hand, and between club membership and public life, on the other. Nowhere was the importance of organizational life clearer than in the United States, where "a maze of exclusive sects, associations, and clubs" existed. Weber thought the religious sect, for which there was no true equivalent in the institutionalized church life of twentieth-century Germany, was the purest example of an American voluntary group. He stressed the positive effects of membership in religious sects, student fraternities, or even English sports clubs. Participation in such groups supposedly toughened individuals, made them think for themselves, and ultimately created a society in which large parts of the population were self-directed. Consequently, the United States and England developed traditions of responsible citizenship and popular support for the leadership of a coherent national elite.[4]

Weber knew that Germany possessed a rich, complex undergrowth of voluntary groups. Addressing his colleagues at the 1910 Frankfurt Sociological Conference, he stressed the need to study German organizational life in the broadest sense of the term—"starting with the bowling club . . . and continuing to the political party or the religious, artistic or literary sect." He noted that modern man had become "organizational man [*Vereinsmensch*] to a frightful and never before anticipated degree" and that in this respect Germany had attained "a very high standard." He invited the audience to peruse city address books listing names of local clubs and associations (*Verbände*). Significantly, he used a middle-sized German city to illustrate his point. He estimated that in cities of 30,000 people, there was one voluntary association for every one hundred people, or one for every twenty householders.[5]

But Weber was skeptical that German voluntary associations were as politically advanced as their Anglo-American counterparts. "The quantitative spread of organizational life [*Vereinswesen*]," he said, "does not always go hand in hand with its qualitative significance." Weber criticized the most active joiners of German voluntary organizations—the upper, upper middle, and lower middle classes. He felt they were unprepared for autonomous citizenship. He made his point bluntly at the Frankfurt conference, and in keeping with his belief that many associations played a role in politics, Weber chose a song club as an example. "A man who is accustomed to use his larynx in voicing powerful sentiments on a daily basis without, however, finding any connection to his actions," he said of the singing club member, ". . . that is a man who, to be brief, easily becomes a 'good citizen' [*Staatsbürger*] in the passive sense of the word."[6] Here was the essence of Weber's view of the political nature of social organizations in Germany: grass roots associations failed to promote active, creative involvement of the *Bürgertum* in the polity.

The effects of this failure were allegedly most apparent in the political parties led by the upper and middle classes. Weber likened the bourgeois parties to solipsistic guilds. He said they failed to develop parliamentary skills, bureaucratic structures, wide constituencies, and autonomous political personalities because they had the opportunity only to attack rather than to initiate government policy. "In a parliament where one only criticizes . . . and whose political leaders are never forced to show what they can produce politically," Weber wrote in May 1918, "mindless demagogy or routinized impotence, or both, carry the day."[7] Demagogy or impotence—for Weber, these were possible results of the interplay of German social and political life.

But Weber left an opening. If Anglo-American sects, clubs, and associations promoted responsible citizenship, he asked the Frankfurt audience, "how do matters look here? In what form and to what degree do analogues exist?" Inclined to leave open the question of how voluntary associations and political institutions interacted, he was equally willing to consider whether a close relationship between them had developed in the first place. "I simply maintain," he said by way of closing the issue, "that a connection of the kind I have intimated can exist, possibly—I don't know to what degree, perhaps I have exaggerated."[8] The variegated texture of German organizational life led the circumspect Weber to caution against quick answers when discussing links between voluntary groups and political life.

This study examines the interplay of three elements suggested by Weber's thought: organizational life in the widest sense of the term, the relationship of voluntary organizations to party politics, and the rise of unexampled demagogy in the form of Adolf Hitler's National Socialist German Workers' party. Because this book concentrates on a range of organizations, its geographical focus is a single town, the Protestant university city Marburg/Lahn. Between 1880 and 1935 this Hessian community featured a rich organizational life that expanded dramatically after the late nineteenth century, a bourgeoisie actively involved in local associations, and a seemingly irresponsible and contentious political scene that gave rise to a powerful National Socialist movement with electoral support well above the national average. Despite its peculiarities, which are discussed subsequently, the city provides a useful social location for exploring Weber's ideas about the supposed passivity of German voluntary groups, the political impotence of the middle classes, and the anticipated popular authoritarianism that followed.

This study also takes Weber's caution seriously, arguing that the result of participation in voluntary organizations was not political immaturity or philistinism, in the sense in which the sociologist used these terms. Instead, a contradictory relationship developed between voluntary associations, political conflict, and nazism. The ideological product of this relationship for the *Bürgertum* was "apoliticism."[9]

Apoliticism can be a misleading concept if we equate it with unpolitical sentiment or naiveté about the realities of power, both allegedly typical of the German view of public life and the state.[10] I will later argue that "political" refers to the realm of general societal interests. But many Germans thought of politics as national *party* politics, and the notion of apoliticism takes account of this narrower perspective. Just as "amoral" describes something to which moral judgments are inapplicable, "apoliticism" describes a desire to make party political concerns, practices, and structures inapplicable to public life. The desire was multiform, appearing in efforts to muffle party conflict by eliminating political discussion from social life, in practices of keeping economic pressure groups from committing themselves fully to a single party trajectory, in active resistance to the increasing influence of mass parties, and in systematic attempts to create forms of political representation alternate to mass parties. Apoliticism encompassed diffuse and fragmented prejudices as well as more systematic thought and practices; it was common sense and ideology. The lowest common denominator of all its component traditions and activities was a deep distrust of bureaucratized parties linked to large constituencies in the national political marketplace.

Germans were not alone in reacting to popular politics in this way. Antiparty sentiment was present in all advanced parliamentary systems, though it varied in social location and form. The crucial point is that Weber's bourgeois associational and party members were not without political instincts. Rather, they were convinced that the Social Democratic and Catholic Center parties—both representatives of a new mass politics in Imperial and Weimar Germany—upset a precarious balance of power, created open conflict, and damaged the moral and political fiber of town, region, and nation.

In any specific historical period, voluntary associations may share "a common situation or context . . . rather than a series of discrete situations for different subject-areas."[11] This is an important assumption for the following study. German groups that endorsed apoliticism were hardly unanimous in proposing alternatives to a polity increasingly shaped by big parties. But they seemed to favor parties that were weak in comparison with Social Democratic and Catholic political groups. Moreover, they formed economic and social organizations that were more loosely tied to political parties than were social clubs and trade unions in the Social Democratic and Catholic movements. One inspiration for all this was the small-town polity, where unevenly organized bourgeois parties were nested in a wide field of clubs and associations.

This study concentrates partly on local branches of national parties and economic *Verbände*—entities that scholars have studied mainly in the national sphere—but primarily on bourgeois gymnastics, sharpshooting, women's, religious, veterans', and student associations. These mundane local clubs swallowed large amounts of leisure time and participated, consciously or unconsciously, in the political life of their communities; they linked sociability and power. Motivations for joining club life varied. Some individuals wanted to promote their professional interests; some wanted to raise prizewinning Alsatian dogs; some just wanted to smoke cigarettes, drink beer, and gossip. Through numerous personal ties, however, social organizations in many urban settings became "substructures" of more visible parties, pressure groups, and city governments. From Bismarck's demise to Hitler's rise to power, urban bourgeois social organizations hardly escaped political conflict. But their responses to conflict facilitated precisely the things Weber thought German *Vereinswesen* prevented: concern for general political issues, a collective resolve to control sectional divisions and party fragmentation, and, in the Weimar Republic, an autonomous grass roots movement from which national socialism eventually issued.

German organizational life failed to encourage the polity Weber wanted: a bureaucratized, imperialist state led by charismatic elites who emerged from the competition of parliamentary politics. But if voluntary associations faltered at this task, they created some of the conditions of popular politics that Anglo-American groups did —albeit in a different environment. Seemingly unpolitical associations had an impact on power relationships, as Weber suggested, but the results of that impact differed from what he anticipated. By studying the organizational fabric of local bourgeois politics over a long chronological sweep we can see what those results were. This book undertakes such a study, analyzing the interaction of *Verein*, party, and nazism.

How have contemporary scholars of German history addressed the problem of interaction between voluntary associations, political power, and the rise of the Nazi movement? Many elements compatible with Weberian thought have precipitated into a transatlantic consensus about the alleged political immaturity of Germany's upper and middle classes. Developed mainly in the last two decades, and aided by the migration of European intellectuals to the United States since the 1930s, the argument presupposes that social and political life were radically separated in modern Germany. Though influenced by a specifically West German Marxism, Hans-Ulrich Wehler's work is homologous with Weber's critique of German politics. For Wehler, German history after 1871 was a process in which "the necessary synchronization of socioeconomic and political development was frustrated until the very last." He argued that many factors—rapid economic modernization, tardy national state formation, the continued presence of reactionary landholding Junkers in government and the military, and the manipulation or repression of social groups in the interests of agrarian and industrial elites—caused this lack of synchronization. More recently, the American scholar John R. Gillis adopted a compatible view when he wrote that modern Germany, unlike other countries, was incapable of solidifying "the bond of state and nation that marked political modernity." There was, argued Gillis, a "unique dualism between state and nation (or society)." Whereas central government developed and expanded its capabilities for rule, "little in the way of complementary change either in society at large or in those mediating institutions, the parliament and the parties," followed.[12] In the Second Empire, state and military elites thus imposed political consensus on a society that postponed its entrance into modernity.

Historians argue that the failure of German liberalism was both cause and effect of the separation of social and political experience and the absence of popular consensus. There can be little doubt that by the last decades of the nineteenth century the liberal movement was fragmented and dispersed.[13] But the central question for this study is, what replaced it? A volatile mix of ideological notions created by power elites of the Second Empire allegedly streamed in to fill the vacuum left by liberalism. Fearing Social Democratic advances as well as wider political participation, elites reinforced "pre-industrial norms and institutions" in party politics, the school system, the courts, local government, churches, the army, the media, and voluntary associations.[14] This was said to encourage authoritarianism, antimodernism, glorification of the state, anti-Semitism, and aggressive nationalism—all supposedly incompatible with the workings of a mature industrial society.

These attitudes allegedly extended throughout the class structure and polity. Within the independent lower middle classes (the "old" *Mittelstand* of craftsmen and shopkeepers), urban master artisans of the late nineteenth century rejected "all aspects of modern life."[15] White-collar employees—the largest group of a "new" *Mittelstand* that also included petty professionals and minor officials—succumbed to "preindustrial, precapitalist and prebourgeois traditions" in the clash of capitalist development and traditional society.[16] The custodians of culture and education, Germany's *Bildungsbürgertum*, compensated for political impotence by retreating into "vulgar idealism."[17] Even socialist workers were touched by an authoritarian consensus imposed from the political center. The so-called negative integration of the working classes allowed for partial realization of legal and actual equality and for some economic improvement but denied workers recognition as full citizens.[18] The appropriate label for Germans from many different class positions seemed to be that provided by Ralf Dahrendorf, "unmodern men in a modern world."[19] Here was the Weberian philistine, now reshaped by modernization theory and presented without Weber's doubts about the caricature.

Like the Weberian ideas that inspired them, such arguments made a lasting contribution to the historiography of modern Europe by directing scholarly attention to the social background of German politics. But they have come under fire in the past decade. The debate has been more than a product of generational revolt or ideological critique; historians of different generations and with diverse methodological and political viewpoints have joined in.[20] In particular, however, the work of younger Anglo-American scholars suggests that Germans were seen as politically immature partly because their history was compared with idealized versions of the British and North American past, an idealization typical of Weber's thought.[21] These historians also point out that recent scholarship has overlooked significant failures, inconsistencies, and contradictions in elite politics.[22] Most importantly, and without fully explicating this view, the critics suggest that previous arguments focused too exclusively on political parties and big associations at the national level. The implication is that earlier works glossed over a bewildering array of parties, clubs, and associations at the grass roots, assuming that these local structures were either politically irrelevant or easily absorbed in the imposed consensus of the Reich. And the critics are right: the argument regarding Germany's un-modern men and women can be substantiated or challenged only when the local community—the fabric of marketplace, workshop, school, family life, and social club—is incorporated into historical discussion.

Yet even younger Anglo-American critics have failed to explore fully grass roots politics and social life. There is a real need for exploring the political workings of the organizational fabric, the "public sphere," of a single town or city. There is, moreover, a need to extend the time frame of such research to include a broader interplay of organizational and political processes. Weber's views suggest the utility of studying the period from the organizational explosion of the late nineteenth century through the rise of the National Socialist party. Regardless of specific chronologies, however, longer-term grass roots research is essential. For many Germans the local polity has been a primary focus of involvement in the larger society throughout the nineteenth and twentieth centuries.[23] We need a mosaic of studies concentrating on local public life over longer blocks of time. This book aspires to contribute to the shape and content of that mosaic.

If arguments about the causes, social location, timing, and even the existence of German political philistinism deserve rethinking, we also need to reconsider relationships between prior traditions and the rise of nazism. Many scholars see an unbroken arc of authoritarianism, like a sustained discharge of energy between two electrodes, that connects the dominance of Imperial elites to the Nazi seizure of power. According to Gillis, whereas the state bureaucracy and military controlled "the course of change" in the nineteenth century, "insurgent groups, first of the left and then of the right," shaped events in cooperation with state elites in the Republic. In both eras, "revolution from above" dominated.[24] Such continuities must not be overlooked. But this argument reduces the Second Empire to a background for the ultimate triumph of the Nazi party.[25] Moreover, it underestimates the unique and original qualities of German fascism by arguing that the Nazis performed the same function as Imperial elites, that is, they forced a template of unity onto a fragmented and unmanageably backward society. Although this study emphasizes continuities between developments in the Second Empire and the rise of nazism, it also portrays Hitler's party as an unprecedented and syncretic popular movement that transformed German political traditions.

David Schoenbaum was one of the first historians to stress the originality of the Nazi "social revolution." In this view, nazism lifted people from their narrow social milieus and created an alternative racist community from fragments of the old society.[26] Valuable as it was, this view overlooked the cohesion of communities and local organizations before and during the rise of the Nazi party. It distorted the dynamic interpenetration of nazism into prior social networks, a process involving independent local activity over which the NSDAP had less control than is usually assumed.[27] If local associations were capable of more than philistinism, they could also develop relatively independent political opinions. Thus, unable to shape local groups without struggle, the Nazi party grappled, negotiated, and clashed with them to gain support. Interactions between the Nazi party and its followers require much more attention than they have received so far.[28]

The empirical and theoretical background necessary for research in this area already exists in part.[29] But most recent sociographical work has concentrated on the occupations of NSDAP adherents rather than associational membership or other social ties. In view of this, it is useful to recall that older "mass society" interpretations, though riveted on social breakdown and deracination as causes of fascism, drew attention to the importance of voluntary group structures in political strife.[30] Providing a contrast to arguments that emphasized the atomization of German groups before Hitler, William Sheridan Allen discussed voluntary associations in his classic study of Northeim, stressing that intact social networks gave the local "middle class" a sense of solidarity that served it well in its support of nazism and its offensive against the local Social Democratic party.[31] Other case studies stressed compatible points.[32] They began to sketch "the process by which the intermediary structure was taken over by the Nazis."[33] "The conquest of the bourgeois infrastructure," in combination with Nazi propaganda and bureaucratic party organization, came to be viewed as "one of the most important social preconditions" for the success of the NSDAP.[34]

But these studies have not gone far enough. Most research on National Socialist infiltration of social life has concentrated on single organizations or single types of organizations. There are informative works on Nazi agitation within occupational associations of white-collar employees, peasants, women, and industrial workers. In addition, valuable research has been done on the relationship between the NSDAP and other racist (*völkisch*) parties and associations. With the exception of limited evidence for various social organizations, however, other groups have escaped scholarly attention in studies of Nazi social conquest just as they have been overlooked in the question of bourgeois political maturity.[35] Group life was a product of many different solidarities, most of them ostensibly divorced from political life, and a wider organizational map of Nazi mobilization needs to be charted. Additionally, the issue of the form of Nazi infiltration of social groups has never been thoroughly considered. Without offering the necessary detail, Zdenek Zofka has argued that Nazi successes depended more substantially on "group formation within the community [and] conversation at the Stammtisch, on the town square, and in voluntary associations" than on party propaganda and direct agitation.[36] We need a more finely textured discussion that addresses not only infiltration of parties and pressure groups by activists but less visible processes of quotidian organizational life and informal or unauthorized Nazi social penetration as well. Thus a central concern of this work is to analyze the form, scope, timing, and contradictions of National Socialist diffusion in local associations.

This study began with a long search for local organizational affiliations of Marburg Nazi party members, a project that then led me to consider the broader political workings of voluntary groups.[37] The result was a group of 428 Nazi "joiners," NSDAP and Nazi Student League (Nationalsozialistischer Deutscher Studentenbund) members who belonged to at least one non-Nazi voluntary association. The joiners constituted a subsection of the Nazi movement that overlapped with but remained distinct from the diverse party membership and electorate. They were distinguished by their simultaneous involvement in Hitler's party and in non-Nazi voluntary associations and, hence, by their importance in the drive to fold National Socialist ideology into local culture. Marburg Nazi joiners came mainly from the bourgeoisie, or *Bürgertum*. Since scholars justifiably emphasize the social diversity of the Nazi following, and because the notion of the *Bürgertum* is central to this book, it is necessary to discuss briefly who belonged to Marburg's bourgeoisie.

The *Bürgertum* was hardly a single, coherent entity. It included varied groups whose only real point of identification in the late nineteenth and twentieth centuries was their antisocialism. As Charles Maier has noted, "bürgerlich," or "bourgeois," came to denote anyone—East Elbian landholder, Ruhr industrialist, Schleswig-Holstein peasant, Hessian storeowner, or Saxon skilled worker —who opposed socialism.[38] However, I use the term here to refer to a local bourgeoisie consisting of Protestant, nonsocialist groups who lived in smaller towns and cities.[39] Influenced by notions of medieval urban citizenship, the small urban *Bürgertum* espoused not only opposition to the socialist working class but also economic thrift, a commitment to hard work, economic group interests, resistance to unfettered large-scale industrial capitalism, Protestant faith, community pride, participation in local club life, devotion to the family, and apoliticism. The small-town bourgeoisie is an ideological rather than economic category; hence it is a broader grouping than the classic "bourgeoisie," a term that referred to a national class that owned and/or managed the means of production. The small urban *Bürgertum* was socially complex and politically divided. It ranged from manual workers to middling merchants or industrialists, from left-wing liberals to conservatives. The idea of a nonsocialist moral community thus became more important for calming sociopolitical tensions within the small urban bourgeoisie than for fighting socialism. By fostering apoliticism, social organizations in cities like Marburg claimed with some justification that they smoothed the way for a tenuous bourgeois solidarity.

Marburg was a university and service city with little large-scale industrial development, and its disaggregated local bourgeoisie consisted mainly (though not exclusively) of groups that in the national society were referred to as "the middle classes" or "middle strata."[40] From my point of view a class is a cluster of individuals who share a common socioeconomic standing and awareness of their collective economic and political interests in relation to other classes in a given geographical setting. In contrast, I refer to strata as groups that share a particular socioeconomic location or layer in a population. Unlike the Social Democratic working class or the industrial bourgeoisie in Germany, middle strata possessed no awareness of being a class. But their more perspicacious representatives realized that they shared a negative feature, namely, "separation from the dominant relations of production."[41] Additionally, groups within the middle strata gained an awareness of common interests vis-à-vis other groups at particular historical junctures. In terms of my definition there was at least one bourgeois class in

Marburg, the local upper middle class, or elite. Additionally, there were five strata (identified below), at least two of which worked toward a sense of class under particular conditions. Each class and stratum in turn consisted of various occupational subgroups.

The Marburg elite or upper middle class was an amalgam perhaps typical of cities touched but not transformed by industrialization, population growth, and intense social conflict.[42] It consisted of university professors, some university students, well-to-do free professionals such as lawyers and medical doctors, a handful of small industrialists and building contractors, the most powerful city officials—such as the lord mayor (*Oberbürgermeister*) and vice-mayor —clergy, military officers from the small local garrison, and wives of these individuals. Though increasingly differentiated and politically divided, the Marburg elite maintained a tenuous solidarity for most of the period between Bismarck and Hitler. A tiny group of individuals within this circle could be described as notables (*Honoratioren*), those who enjoyed a feeling of social influence and political leadership as well as substantial economic well-being. The Marburg upper middle class denied being a class, stressing that apoliticism and devotion to community service lifted it above economic self-interest. But this negative attitude toward class also created the awareness of being an automatic elite, and it legitimized notables' attempts to organize local strata in an apolitical, moralistic community of sentiment—an attempt driven by contradictions to be discussed in subsequent chapters.[43]

Two nonelite strata of the local bourgeoisie possessed relatively coherent notions about their traditions, economic standing, and political location. They were self-employed, middling independents and minor civil servants. They may be considered as two separate lower middle classes when each pursued their perceived interests in relatively systematic ways. The former consisted of self-employed artisans and retailers, the old *Mittelstand* or independent lower middle class.[44] Contemporaries rather simplistically associated these people with preindustrial practices and mentalities. It is nevertheless true that many self-employed artisans worked in crafts that had existed in Marburg for centuries. Moreover, many Marburg storeowners looked back on long histories of family involvement in the same or similar commercial undertakings. The development of guilds, participation in clubs and associations, and strong mobilization in city politics during the Republic all suggested a sense of shared economic and political interest among self-employed craftsmen and shopkeepers. Like the upper middle class, most independents rejected class referents, seeking their own niche in the wider town *Bürgertum*. Like the elite also, most Marburg artisans and retailers tried to paper over economic and political differences with antisocialism and apoliticism.

Minor civil servants consisted of state, county, and local government officials plus petty professionals such as elementary school teachers. They were a large group in this administrative center. Whereas independents were identified with long-standing Marburg traditions, local observers regarded the civil servants as relative newcomers "imported" after Prussia's annexation of the Marburg region in 1866–67.[45] In the Empire government employment was the backbone of this group's sense of collective interest. In the Republic the activities of the local Civil Servants' Association, which ran its own slates for city parliament in opposition to those of the independents, also reflected officials' awareness of shared economic and political concerns. But, again like elites and independents, civil servants denied the connotations of class even when they acted like one. They supported an apolitical, bourgeois community morally opposed to Social Democracy and mass politics.

The local bourgeoisie included three other strata—white-collar workers, nonsocialist blue-collar workers, and nonelite individuals without professions (that is, nonstudent *Berufslosen*)—that never attained the structural or political coherence of the other three *bürgerlich* elements. Like civil servants, white-collar workers were employed in what can be regarded as middle-class occupations that required little manual effort, but they lacked the independence of self-employed individuals.[46] Moreover, they enjoyed little of the security or prestige that government employment offered officials. Employees labored in shops and offices in Marburg and belonged to a number of occupational associations, including antisocialist groups like the German National Commercial Employees' Association (Deutschnationaler Handlungsgehilfenverband) and, by 1917, a socialist white-collar organization. It has been commonplace to include white-collar employees with civil servants in the new *Mittelstand*. The present study continues this convention for analytical purposes, grouping officials and white-collar workers not organized in socialist *Verbände* in a service stratum of nonelite bourgeoisie. For the most part, however, this work stresses the differences in status, level of organization, and degree of solidarity between minor civil servants and white-collar employees.

Non-Marxist craft, skilled, and unskilled laborers could also be found in the bourgeois community of sentiment. Often coming from "better sorts" of workers who possessed property, these blue-collar workers enter the purview of this investigation through membership in organizations such as the city's largest gymnastics club, the Turnverein 1860. Finally, Marburg's *Rentner*—mainly nonelite pensioners and other individuals who lived off savings, rents, and investments—must be considered. Although in times of crisis, such as the hyperinflation of 1922–23, these groups belonging to the strata of nonelites without professions could make their dissatisfaction heard, they never developed solid organizations or a strong awareness of group interests locally. But, like the other two groups, they could be encouraged to support an apolitical order led by elites of the town bourgeoisie.[47]

The Marburg bourgeoisie was a shifting coalition of local classes and strata aimed against socialism, the language of class, and mass political parties. Seeking to unify what was socially disparate, the grass roots bourgeoisie defined itself according to what it was not— and, in Marburg at least, discovered a hazy solidarity in the process. By mobilizing joiners with these class, group, and organizational roots, the Marburg NSDAP became a bourgeois movement. But bourgeois diversity gave nazism a wide following in the upper middle, lower middle, and working classes. In short, the Nazi party became a bourgeois people's party (*Volkspartei*).

Most historians work with eclectic, patterned arguments in mind, though they are often reluctant to explicate the theoretical roots of those patterns. The following remarks underscore the most important building blocks of my research on local politics and Nazi joiners. They are not an attempt to "apply" a model—that would take a very different book—but a device whereby I can place my research on a fairly wide conceptual map.

This study takes its inspiration from concepts of "resource management" and Gramscian categories. The resource management approach straddles Weberian, Millian, and Marxist thought.[48] Its most important assumption is that groups struggle to achieve their collective goals through mobilization. Mobilization is a process in which organized groups acquire collective control over votes, sports equipment, loyalties, more members, and many other things.[49] Mobilizing groups assemble and invest these resources and compete with other groups over limited stocks of resources in specific settings. From my point of view mobilization is not a solely quantitative process; one must also read specific events to determine if groups are gaining collective control of loyalties, organizational contacts, and the like. All groups, from a political party of notables (*Honoratiorenparteien*) locked in a struggle for the Hessian farm vote to sharpshooting clubs engaged in membership drives, mobilize to secure their goals and interests.[50] Though members of leisure-time groups (and often parties and pressure groups) were interested in sociability (*Geselligkeit*), their organizations needed resources to maintain such social interchange. The concern of *Verein* leaders for the machinery of club life—collecting membership fees, maintaining contacts with innkeepers who opened their establishments to club functions, renting halls and equipment at favorable rates, keeping up attendance at meetings—attests to the importance of group mobilization in local organizational culture.

Significantly, the approach assumes that all individual mobilizers face similar requirements of resource management.[51] Despite peculiarities of German history, therefore, we need not treat German voluntary associations differently from their British or North American counterparts with regard to the mechanics of group mobilization. Analytically, German singularity fades in resource management thinking. Thus before pinpointing the particular nature of local politics or the unprecedented qualities of national socialism, this study presupposes an essential likeness between Nazi party agitators and the mobilizers of economic pressure groups, sharpshooting societies, gymnastics clubs, community service organizations, and bourgeois political parties.

In the mobilization literature power relationships are the result of competition for resources; power is achieved by assembling resources and raising the costs of access to resources for other groups through the application of material force. But the struggle for material power takes place within specific cultural settings that are not exclusively products of resource management. There is a moral as well as material result of mobilization. For instance, nineteenth-century Marburg notables gained collective control over the means of administration, culture, and organization. At the same time they elicited active popular consent as they pursued what they perceived to be the general good of the town. How do we move conceptually from groups using material force to the broader conditions for this moral authority?[52]

A broadly Gramscian perspective is appropriate here. Briefly summarized, the value of Gramsci's thought for the present study is twofold. First, Gramsci conceptualized power relationships as products not only of coercion and force—mobilization and repression—but of negotiated and active consent of the ruled as well.[53]

Power stems from "reconstitution" of hegemony, the potentially and sometimes actually contested preservation of moral authority of leaders over led. For most of the period covered here, Marburg elites enjoyed this moral authority and occasionally shared it with select members of nonelite classes. In party politics, however, local elites failed to maintain a similar leadership, a disparity I discuss presently.

A similar mix of coercion and consent characterizes relationships between actors in social movements. Gramsci distinguished "leadership" from "domination." He thought of the former in terms of moral *and* material force used with allies and sometimes with hostile groups. He contrasted this with domination, the subjugation or even elimination of antagonistic groups.[54] Gaining control over resources, the Marburg Nazi party dominated Social Democrats when it attacked their neighborhoods during the Republic and destroyed their voluntary organizations in the Third Reich. But it led the local bourgeoisie when it represented specific interests and gained authority to speak for the good of the town. The Nazi goal was to replace an eroding bourgeois hegemony with popular, *völkisch* leadership in social and political life.

Second, Gramsci assumed that struggle for leadership will take place not only in the state but also in what the Italian thinker referred to as "civil society." We need not explore the difficulties of this term.[55] The insight is most useful for arguing that seemingly unpolitical institutions that facilitate the moral authority of leaders can also be foci of negotiation and conflict. Voluntary organizations, churches, the press, and educational institutions thus become arenas in a struggle for hegemony. This facet of Gramscian thought points up the centrality of everyday organizational life in understanding *bürgerlich* hegemony and Nazi mobilization.

It is now possible to define more specifically organizational and political life. By organizational life I mean social activities through which voluntary organizations mobilize to pursue or defend their specific interests—whether they are trying to get one of their members elected to public office, socializing, singing, sharpshooting, or taking care of disabled war veterans. In this study organizational life is considered a formal expression of social life, the entire range of activities that constitute society. Political life is a subsection of social life in which group mobilization issues into discussion of and competition over general interests.[56] The words associated with general interests were nebulous and numerous—"the people" (*Volk*), "the commonweal" (*Gemeinwohl*), "the public good" (*Ge-*

meinnutz). Such concepts are never fixed; there exists no single general good. Particular groups derive meaning from such notions as they look beyond immediate interests. Specific group interests and political life are separate but may also be connected in the activities and thoughts of different historical actors. The crucial measure of hegemony is whether a group of individuals, from elites to Nazi party activists, can make this connection between social concerns and the political sphere. A group is hegemonic when it uses material force to claim convincingly that it pursues both special interests and the general good but achieves a moral authority qualitatively different from power achieved by material force alone.

Connections between voluntary organizations, the struggle for power, and nazism can be understood by studying a wide assortment of groups over a considerable stretch of time. But this necessitates a concentrated geographical scope, a relatively "closed" environment where one can grapple with such historical interactions. Why is Marburg an appropriate focus for this study?

I have said that Marburg contained some of the elements Weber would have expected to find in a medium-sized city of bourgeois joiners. A more mundane reason for my choice of Marburg, however, is that I wanted a locality neither so small that it lacked the complexity of larger urban centers nor so big that it made the project of reconstructing organizational life immense. Though its population numbered only 28,439 in the early 1930s, Marburg was a surprisingly diverse community. It had an established Social Democratic movement, a growing university, and a rich and perplexing party political scene known throughout Germany for its variety and contentiousness. The city was much more volatile politically than its structural analogue, the Swabian university town of Tübingen.[57] But in view of this diversity, Marburg's specific makeup—its lack of heavy industry, dependence on trade and administration, attractiveness for retirees, social and economic reliance on the university, overwhelming Protestantism, and history of political experimentation—should not mislead us into seeing the city as an exception bearing little relation to the national society. Marburg was peculiar, but it was not an island. Despite the idiosyncrasies of the city, the experiences of its people spoke to broader German developments. Finally, my selection was determined by an even more practical concern. A respectable amount of secondary literature on Marburg's political history has now accumulated, and the availability of such sources allowed me to devote more time to the still unmapped detail of one town's bourgeois clubs and associations than would otherwise have been possible.[58]

The analysis presented here moves from broader interactions of organizational and political life to more detailed discussion of Nazi mobilization. Part I examines relationships between economic structure, party politics, and social organizations from the late nineteenth century to the early 1930s. Chapter 1 provides an introduction by discussing how local economic structure and patterns of hardship—factors which at first glance appear to have disrupted local politics—favored the organization and social resilience of the bourgeoisie from 1880 to 1935. Chapter 2 takes a similarly long view of Marburg history by exploring the interaction of national and local politics over five decades. In chapters 3 and 4 I discuss the response of bourgeois associations to the rise of sectional interests and political conflict from Bismarck to Hitler. More specifically, chapter 3 concentrates on the weaving of a complex organizational fabric in the Second Empire, a fabric that often muffled party strife. Chapter 4 discusses changes in leadership, membership, and political involvement of social organizations during World War I and the Republic.

In Part II, I focus on Nazi attempts to recast the relationship between social and political life. Chapter 5 discusses the emergence of nazism from local organizational milieus and analyzes the transformation of the NSDAP into a popular movement before Hitler's seizure of power. Chapter 6 examines the organizational, residential, and occupational roots of NSDAP joiners and members. Chapter 7 follows the contradictions of Nazi coordination in Marburg in the crucial first three years of Hitler's rule. The conclusion reconsiders the argument, suggests theoretical and historical implications, and sketches a partial agenda for further studies of German organizational and political life.

part one

Economics, Party Politics, and Social Organizations

one

Economic Structure and Hardship: Bases for Radicalism?

*L*ike a good actor, Marburg wore different faces for different audiences. It was a quiet town of national loyalties and rural beauty for conservatives, the home of a "Fascist university" from the point of view of socialist critics, and either a "citadel of reaction" or a "city of philistines" in the eyes of Nazi activists. But this multiform character was based on a single socioeconomic fact: Marburg was a university and service city. Its population of 28,439 in 1933 was dominated by students, professionals, civil servants, white-collar employees, teachers, storeowners, craftsmen, and pensioners. Working-class people were underrepresented in the local labor force compared with the Reich as a whole and with cities of comparable size. Historians—whether they think of Marburgers as quiet patriots, reactionaries, or yokels—contend that this socioeconomic structure, so skewed by the absence of industry and by dependence on trade and service, made the city more susceptible to economic crisis and political "radicalization" in the form of nazism.[1]

I have a contrasting view of the relationship between Marburg's economic makeup and politics. The decision of local notables to build an administrative city narrowed possibilities for responding to the economic challenges caused by war, inflation, and depression, yet it also made the city less susceptible than more industrial towns to sudden, devastating economic hardship. The structural potential for radicalization of the populace was lower than historians have assumed. Indeed, local economic structure facilitated the social resilience rather than the economic devastation of the Bürgertum, a resilience of great importance for everyday organizational life. The general economic development of Marburg after the late nineteenth century is outlined in the following pages, prior to a discussion of the two most important moments of economic hardship locally, the inflation of 1916–23 and the Depression of 1929.

Rise and Partial Fall of the University City

The foggiest of German cities, Marburg is located in a "cold air sea" formed by the narrow Lahn valley and *Amöneburg* basin of *Oberhessen*. Standing in this misty north Hessian valley, the city appeared isolated to contemporaries and later scholars. But Marburg's history always intersected with regional, national, and international events, as the architectural face of the city in the Weimar Republic suggested. The castle (*Schloß*), which was built by Thuringian nobles in the thirteenth century, recalled Marburg's role as a military stronghold and center of religious controversy, having been the site of the Luther-Zwingli debates in 1529. The elegant Gothic *Elisabethkirche*, architectural counterpoint to the castle, reminded one that more than 86 percent of the town's population in 1932 was Protestant—well above the Reich average of 64.1 percent. The cult of St. Elisabeth, after whom the church was named, had drawn medieval pilgrims from German lands, France, Austria, and Hungary. Classroom buildings and modern medical clinics traced the growth of the university, founded by the Thuringian Philipp the Great in 1527. The first Protestant institution of higher learning in Germany, the university was mirror and motor in German religious life.[2]

The market square in front of the city hall and many small shops of the upper city (*Oberstadt*) recalled the town's economic ties to the larger society. The city lay 2.5 kilometers east of an older trade route that facilitated north-south connections between Frankfurt/Main and northern Germany and east-west ties between the Rhine and Thuringia. Sources list Marburg markets in which salt, wood, cattle, geese, corn, and leather goods were bought and sold. Although the majority of Marburg's artisanal trades relied only on the local market, the linen, wool, and leather crafts possessed regional trade links that persisted into the nineteenth century. These trades were important sources of commercial employment in the city until the modern era. The pottery trade, which still employed ninety people in 1843 and produced articles that one anonymous local poet described as "so very fine," sold wares in the Rhineland, Franconia, Thuringia, and Hamburg.[3]

Marburg's regional economic ties eroded before the late nineteenth century, partly because of the policies of Electoral Hessian officials, who feared the social consequences of industrialization and, unlike Prussian bureaucrats, rejected any presumption of being modernizers or reformers. These officials did little to encourage manufacturing or protect small-scale export industries against foreign competition. International competition was especially disastrous for vulnerable north Hessian textile producers. When English and Scottish machine-made textile goods flooded world markets in 1816 and the United States and Spain erected protective tariffs in the same year, Hessian linen production and export collapsed. These problems were exacerbated by a general agricultural crisis in northern Hesse that lasted from 1816 to 1818. Linen producers recouped their losses somewhat in subsequent decades, but the Hessian linen industry would never again achieve the high point it had reached in the earliest years of the nineteenth century. The Marburg linen trade could not escape these economic developments, and the expansion of rail networks in midcentury completed the collapse of weaving in the city. Between 1866 and 1914 the city's once-lively tanning and pottery trades also declined precipitously. Emigration from Marburg was higher than in surrounding Hesse, and this alleviated some economic hardship. Nonetheless, autocratic government policy and large-scale socioeconomic change had combined to intensify a centuries-long development that weakened Marburg's ties to nonlocal markets. Meanwhile, most Marburg artisans remained dependent on the home market, as they had been for centuries.[4]

Prussian intervention in 1866–67 brought about the sharpest break with the past. Prussia annexed a number of Hessian duchies and principalities, including the city of Frankfurt/Main, and combined them into the new province of Hesse-Nassau. The "stagnant, patriarchal government of Electoral Hesse," one historian wrote, had now given way to the "most efficient, rationally directed administration in Europe, that of the Prussian state."[5]

Prussia concentrated on the university. The Prussian university budget for Marburg doubled from 1890 to 1910. Between 1870 and 1914 fifteen university buildings, institutes, and clinics were constructed or renovated. The physical plant of the university "achieved a level of quality comparable to that of the great majority of other middle-sized universities" in Germany in the view of a Marburg professor in 1904.[6]

Student enrollment grew from under three hundred in 1861 to one thousand in 1897 and two thousand a dozen years later. Between 1831 and 1914 the number of university students for every thousand inhabitants in the city increased from 52 to 113.9. Not only more students but different kinds of students came to Marburg. In the mid-nineteenth century, a Marburg professor said his mainly Hessian students were "a bit phlegmatic" yet full of "goodwill." The Marburg student body became more varied and, presumably, more lively once the proportion of students from regions other than the surrounding province increased from one-tenth of all students in 1866 to over two-thirds in 1900 and nearly four-fifths in 1926. The university lost its provincial character as an expanding student population became indispensable to local economic life. At the same time, Marburg began to be a stepping-stone university for upwardly mobile academics, attracting more talented faculty members. Though the university functioned as an economic resource base for the town prior to 1866, Prussian policy isolated this sinew of economic life, abstracted it from its previous relationships, and exaggerated its role in providing for local people's livelihoods.[7]

Three other factors combined with the expansion of the university and the decline of local export trades to shape Marburg's economic development. First, large-scale factory production made no inroads in Marburg. Some townspeople hoped that Marburg's annexation to industrializing Prussia would facilitate the growth of local manufacturing, but their hopes proved vain.[8] Industrialization was hampered in part because the city started from a very low economic base after 1880. The largest factory in Marburg, which manufactured wallpaper, employed two hundred workers before World War I, and a handful of other plants employed more than one hundred people. Up to the late nineteenth century, the humanistic character of the university hindered technological spinoff activities like the specialized optics industry in Göttingen.[9] Geographical location and shortage of space also discouraged industry. But by the end of the nineteenth century keeping Marburg nonindustrial became a pronounced goal of city policy. Local officials encouraged light industry, and the founding of the famous Behring chemical laboratories in Marbach, outside the city limits, was a measure of their success. Conversely, in 1885 Ludwig Schüler, the lord mayor, opposed efforts of the city building commissioner Louis Broeg and Karl Benz to establish what reputedly would have been the world's first automobile factory.[10] In addition, city officials promoted tourism, tried to attract wealthy retirees, and emphasized a "medieval and villagelike impression" the city made on visitors.[11] Prussian practice and the interests of local notables thus merged to shape the university city.

Second, although the proportion of individuals employed in local artisanal industries declined, crafts and trade remained important to the city's economy. Printing and construction expanded in direct response to university growth. Despite fluctuations, more bakers, butchers, tailors, seamstresses, tinsmiths, coppersmiths, carpenters, and painters worked in the city in 1914 than in 1867. Industry and crafts still employed nearly one-third of all working townspeople after World War I.[12]

Third, the tertiary sector became the dominant source of employment. Retail trade, heavily dependent on students and tourists, was among the most important pursuits in this area. In 1914 there were 19.8 independent shopkeepers (*Krämer*) per thousand town dwellers, possibly a higher ratio than at annexation.[13] These individuals and independent craftsmen made up the majority of the city's resilient old *Mittelstand*. Marburg also became an administrative center, with university clinics, state and county government offices, elementary and secondary schools, and vocational training institutes. After World War I, civil servants and white-collar employees made up the largest single occupational group in Marburg. Two-thirds of all employed townspeople earned a living from the tertiary sector. No other local development illustrated more succinctly that the medieval balance between production and consumption had been altered in favor of the latter.[14]

German urban history is regional history, as J. J. Lee has suggested, and it is important to note how the rise of the university city affected its hinterland. Rural northern Hesse had been transformed in the nineteenth century from an open-field manorial system to one of capitalist exploitation based on small single-family farms. Hessian officials did little to improve agriculture in the region, one of the poorest in the Reich, and Prussianization intensified rather than lessened differences between Marburg and rural *Oberhessen*, strengthening intraregional disparities in German society.[15]

In contrast to the situation in Marburg, population growth in the Kassel administrative district and *Oberhessen* was well below the national rate between 1867 and 1914. But it was higher than in Württemberg, where unemployment and underemployment in the countryside were correspondingly less serious.[16] Railroads enhanced transportation between city and countryside. Yet economic ties between Marburg and the hinterland ran toward the former; they were hardly reciprocal in any meaningful sense of the term. North Hessian farmers traveled to Marburg to shop or to sell their goods. Manual laborers worked in city factories and construction trades but lived in "industrial" villages such as Ockershausen (which was consolidated with Marburg in 1931). The sons and daughters of farmers often left their homes to settle in Marburg or other cities, exacerbating chronic shortages of farmhands and milk-maids in the countryside.[17]

A relative scarcity of land for small-scale gardening and farming in the city—a consequence of Marburg's location in the narrow Lahn valley—diminished town dwellers' daily physical contact with the countryside but simultaneously increased the city's dependence on foodstuffs from the hinterland. In contrast, the university town of Tübingen enjoyed a more substantial reciprocity with its hinterland, due in part to town-based viniculture and to hop growing in the hills surrounding the city.[18] The Hessian community's unbalanced links with the countryside were formalized in the Republic when the city government had Marburg declared "county-free" (*kreisfrei*) even though its population fell below legal limits for implementing this administrative device.[19] Although Marburg became a shopping center for the countryside after World War II, its differences with rural *Oberhessen* increased in the late nineteenth and twentieth centuries. This one-sided economic relationship with rural Hesse proved to have political implications. Liberal and conservative party leaders from Marburg often ignored surrounding towns until elections. As a result, the anti-Semitic and populist Böckel movement was able to exploit Marburg's arrogance to win a Reichstag seat in 1887, and the Nazis similarly capitalized upon it to mobilize the hinterland in the Republic.

Reshaping Marburg in this way created a narrow range of alternatives for municipal policymakers. But the disadvantages of the administrative city were never seriously exposed before World War I. Marburg city officials knew they had to compensate for a relatively weak tax base by depending more than other communities on income and property taxes, unorthodox financial measures, a high level of borrowing, and wealthy patrons. Officials were aware of their obligations to retirees and pensioners who were attracted to the community, but they could hardly imagine the economic difficulties that war and inflation would bring for these groups. Overcrowding in artisanal and retail trades led to chronic underemployment, but the period of real crisis would come after 1914. A general inflationary tendency before the war and a cost of living higher than that in cities of comparable size caused little alarm. Impoverished Marburgers, such as the 350 homeless people who were sheltered in the city work house in November 1908, were relatively hidden from public view.[20] Though challenged in local Reichstag campaigns, the "politics of notables" (*Honoratiorenpolitik*) in city affairs suppressed conflict over economic policy. City officials were hardly blind to the human costs of remaining dependent on administration and the university. Before World War I, however, they were able to conduct policy without facing the consequences of this distribution of economic resources.[21]

The tragic conflagration of 1914–18 changed all that, as the war created unprecedented burdens for the local political economy. Marburg and Reich history intersected more intensely than ever before, producing social, political, and economic tensions. This illustrates a general characteristic: national political or economic penetration, by potentially raising questions about the local distribution of power, forces local elites to reshape their own hegemony in response to external challenges. It also suggests that Marburg, a town involved in Reich political affairs since the late nineteenth century, was far less provincial than some larger cities, such as Konstanz, which was pushed to the margins of national political and economic life.[22] The economic or political involvement of a town in national matters is not determined by community size alone.

In 1914 the Reich government enlisted the support of city administrations for the war effort. Reich and Land officials in Hesse-Nassau urged city authorities to "nurture and maintain the exemplary atmosphere and attitude of the entire population, regardless of social origins or political stance, which were shown in such an encouraging way during the mobilization for war." According to a 25 August 1914 letter sent by Prussian officials to the Kassel administrative district, of which Marburg was a part, upholding morale was the rationale of "all administrative measures." Subjects of particular concern for Prussian officials were "unemployment and the combating of its demoralizing consequences." Some cities had already implemented financial measures to support individuals thrown out of work by the war, but Prussia expected localities to create additional employment. Besides continuing previous programs, cities were to implement communal projects planned before the war, forbid employment of voluntary labor if it disadvantaged the unemployed, and favor the jobless for civil service posts vacated because of the military draft.[23]

New demands made by the national state tested the capacities of the local economy. Marburg's ability to create jobs was limited by an absence of industries integrated with the war effort. Important local industries, such as the building trades, fell on particularly difficult times. Construction and other craft industries experienced problems securing labor, raw materials, and credit. In addition, the city's most valuable economic resource, university students, was diminished by war mobilization. In 1914 2,529 students enrolled at the university; during the war 1,700 Marburg students went to the front. Their absence hurt local shopkeepers, artisans, tavern owners, and the many townspeople who rented rooms to students. In economic terms, this was the most drastic example of the state's seizure of resources from the local community.[24]

In addition to placing temporary burdens on the local economy, World War I set in motion three processes that continued into the Weimar Republic. First, city financial policy strengthened an inflationary spiral that had already begun as a result of the national state's conduct of the war. The city government expanded budgets to implement war-related projects, including care for households whose main income earner had gone to war, support for wounded veterans, and regulation of the price and supply of food and raw materials. To meet such obligations, city expenditures increased from 44.5 million marks in 1914 to 232.2 million in 1916 and 593.8 million in 1917. Like other cities, Marburg printed emergency money, and an additional 27,000 marks now chased increasingly unavailable goods. The inflation that resulted from these and similar measures throughout the Reich surged forward in fits and starts after the war until the mark was destroyed in 1923.[25]

Second, city government became increasingly vulnerable to group demands because World War I brought about the interpenetration of municipal authority with many different voluntary associations. The municipal administration demanded cooperation from townspeople, and organizational life became a vehicle for implementing official policy. Many city-sponsored wartime programs, including financial aid for needy families, clothing drives, soup kitchens, and first aid stations, depended on the help of local *Vereine*. Women's organizations were particularly important in these endeavors. Popular mobilization gave townspeople a feeling of participation in a patriotic effort, but it also increased their awareness of collective material interests vis-à-vis the city administration.[26]

This awareness was sharpened by the growth of general popular dissatisfaction with the city's wartime economic policy, the third process that carried over into the Republic. A Marburg war chronicler noted that the municipal Economic Bureau, which handled daily administrative tasks of the War Economy Commission, created rancor when the city intervened "in economic life in areas where it was not always prepared. The work was made more difficult," the chronicler wrote, "by the fact that there was little trust for some official measures."[27] Distrust of government regulation of the economy increased after 1918, when demobilization, inflation, and stabilization created new hardships. Moreover, the introduction of universal suffrage in municipal parliaments in 1919 exposed city policy to increased popular scrutiny and gave local groups a chance to voice their economic grievances more directly than ever before. Throughout the period of growing popular dissatisfaction, as always, the city government's maneuverability was limited by a narrow economic base.[28]

Centralization of Reich authority exacerbated matters once Marburg emerged from the war. Financial reforms during the Republic increased the Reich share of total government revenue from 30 to 39 percent while that of states decreased from 30 to 23 percent and that of localities from 40 to 38 percent. Urban financial autonomy virtually disappeared. For example, before 1918 cities determined the local surcharge to be added to the state income tax rate. But during the Republic the national government set the proportions of income and corporation taxes distributed to cities, making the latter passive recipients of revenues controlled by state and Reich administrations. These and other financial measures were constant sources of irritation for Marburg officials.[29]

At the same time, the national state expected more of German cities with regard to social welfare programs and the support of the unemployed. Implemented on 1 April 1924, the Reich Welfare Ordinance helped cities streamline local welfare agencies, but it also increased municipal government financial burdens by making cities responsible for the support of individuals who could no longer secure unemployment benefits or "crisis support" payments because of extended joblessness. Chronic joblessness had been a problem in Marburg throughout the 1920s, and prolonged periods of unemployment increased the number of people who moved from the two above-mentioned kinds of payments onto the roles of the welfare-aided unemployed. By the early 1930s Marburg had to pay proportionately more to local people eligible for these services than did other cities of comparable size. Between 1930 and 1932 the number of welfare-aided unemployed tripled, climbing from 273 to 815. Emergency Reich benefits for needy pensioners hardly offset such financial strains.[30] Thus, while the city lost power to a centralizing state in some areas, it was asked to carry out the national state's duties in others, and city policy was exposed to a twin dynamic of state centralization and scattering of state authority.

To meet these and other obligations, the city increased taxes on property and entertainment, cut back city building projects, reduced salaries of city employees, consolidated parts of outlying regions to generate more tax revenues, and declared itself to be an independent *Stadtkreis* free of the perceived tax burdens of the county. At the same time, universal suffrage opened city policy to widespread criticism and led many local groups to question the benefits of Marburg's nonindustrial structure. This signaled the end to an economic period that began with the emergence of the Prussianized university town.[31] The limited capacities of the city to manage economic crisis had become painfully clear.

National Socialist economic policy also grappled with the disadvantages of the nonindustrial local economy. Attempting to combat what Nazi officials referred to as overcrowding at German universities, the NSDAP began to reduce the number of students in Marburg soon after coming to power, depriving many landlords, storeowners, and publicans of an important source of income.[32] The city reached its lowest economic point since the early days of the Republic, but this forced officials to search for alternatives in the development of medium-sized industry, conference facilities, and other projects. The city received loans for regulation of the Lahn River, the building of work camps, and street construction. It increased revenues from taxes on business, income, and alcohol by 42 percent from 1935 to 1937. But Reich decrees in 1938 robbed local administration of the ability to collect certain tax revenues, social services became ever more costly, and the city abandoned plans for a new conference hall.[33] Like Marburg city officials in the Republic, Nazi leaders recognized that the limits of keeping Marburg nonindustrial had been reached. Yet the resources for acting on that realization were unavailable until after World War II.

Townspeople and Hardship

If Marburg's economic base gave the city administration little margin for maneuver, how were townspeople affected by this? Were they reduced to economic despair? Or did the local economic structure also contain resources that enabled townspeople to be resilient in times of material crisis? We work toward an answer by looking first at occupational makeup. The absence of census data for the city before World War I makes completely accurate statements difficult, but we do have Lord Mayor Paul Troje's 1911 estimates of how townsfolk earned a living. Troje estimated that 40 percent of all townspeople were dependent on small industry, crafts, and trade; 40 percent on civil service, military duty, and pension payments; 10 percent on support for university study; and a final 10 percent on other miscellaneous occupations. Although imprecise, Troje's data illustrate the general occupational outlines of a city based on service and trade rather than industrial production.[34]

Census data on occupations after World War I classified the largest single group of Marburgers as having no occupations (see table 1-1). This group consisted of university students (who accounted for 34 to 37 percent of the total), pensioners, small investors, and miscellaneous groups. The proportion of Marburgers without occupations in 1925 (25) exceeded that of the Reich by nearly three times. Marburg also had a higher share of *Berufslosen* in the population than did Tübingen, Bonn, Bad Godesberg, and Jena—all *"Rentner* cities" (*Rentnerstädte*) in which large parts of the population lived off rents, pensions, investments, and other personal assets. In 1925–33 the size of this category increased, partly because of a 59.4 percent increase in the number of university students. The share of students in the population decreased from 11.3 percent in 1914 to 8.6 percent in 1925, but it increased to more than 13 percent in 1933.[35]

The next largest occupational category was industry and crafts. Its percentage was well below those of the Reich (42.1) and other cities with 20,000 to 50,000 inhabitants (52.1) in 1925. This vividly expressed the nonindustrial nature of the city. The categories of trade and transport, civil service and administration, and domestic service were more important to townspeople than to the Reich as a whole and other cities of comparable size. The percentage of townspeople dependent on agriculture, forestry, and gardening in 1925 was smaller in Marburg than in cities of similar size (2.8), a consequence of limited available land in the narrow Lahn valley.[36]

Table 1-1 *Population in Marburg, by Major Economic Categories, 1925 and 1933*[a]

Category	1925			1933		
	Marburg N	%	Reich %	Marburg N	%	Reich %
Industry, crafts	5,680	24.4	42.2	6,607	23.2	39.0
Trade, transport	5,046	21.7	16.7	5,291	18.6	16.9
Civil service, administration	4,669	20.1	6.8	5,829	20.4	7.7
Domestic service, other	1,686	7.2	2.4	1,347	4.7	2.0
Without occupation	5,833	25.0	9.1	8,654	30.4	13.6
Agriculture, forestry, gardening	385	1.6	22.8	711	2.7	20.8
Totals	23,299	100.0	100.0	28,439	100.0	100.0

a. Includes unemployed and their dependents.
SOURCE: *SDR* 405 (1931): 26/82; 408 (1931): 121; 456 (1936): 25/41.

Evidence on the local labor force makes the importance of the tertiary sector clearer (see table 1-2). Civil servants and white-collar employees were the largest group in the work force in 1925. Their share of the employed population was nearly two times larger in the Hessian university town than it was in the Reich and 29.5 percent larger than in cities of comparable size in the same year. The share of craft, skilled, and unskilled workers increased, but it remained small in both 1925 and 1933 in comparison with the share on the national scene and in other middle-sized cities (44.3). In 1933, 26.4 percent of Marburg workers were unemployed.[37]

The proportion of Marburgers who worked as independent craftsmen and shopkeepers decreased from 1925 to 1933, but it was still larger than in the Reich or in cities with more than 20,000 inhabitants (14.8 percent). There were eighty-nine fewer individuals in the category in 1933 than in 1925, but the size of the difference in the share of independents is due in part to a 16 percent expansion

Table 1-2 *Major Groups in Marburg Work Force, 1925 and 1933*

Category	1925[a] Marburg N	1925[a] Marburg %	1925[a] Reich %	1933[b] Marburg N	1933[b] Marburg %	1933[b] Reich %
Independent	1,884	19.7	15.6	1,795	16.3	16.1
Employed family	432	4.7	17.0	612	5.5	16.5
Civil servants				1,333	12.1	4.7
	3,133	32.9	17.3			
White-collar				2,559	23.2	12.7
Craft, skilled, unskilled workers	2,826	29.6	46.1	3,554	32.1	46.4
Domestic servants	1,243	13.1	4.0	1,192	10.8	3.6
Total work force	9,518	100.0	100.0	11,045	100.0	100.0
(Women)	3,468	36.4	35.4	4,336	39.3	34.1

a. The 1925 census combined civil servants and white-collar.
b. Includes unemployed.
SOURCE: *SDR* 405 (1931): 26/82; 456 (1936): 25/41.

in the total work force.[38] Independents retained a relatively stable presence in the local work force during the Republic.

Domestic service was important in Marburg, partly because of the large number of women who were employed as cleaning ladies in student apartments, and partly because university professors and other better-off *Bürger* favored having servants as a social distinction. Though the percentage of people in domestic service declined, it too was well above that for the Reich and for cities of Marburg's size in 1925 (3.1). The overall share of women in the work force was higher in Marburg than in the Reich as a whole. This reflected not only the importance of the service sector generally, but also the need of many wives and daughters to supplement the incomes of household heads.[39]

The evidence reveals continuing patterns of employment in which independent artisanry and retail trade slowly declined while industrial activity inched forward and services remained dominant. Local occupational makeup in the Republic bore the marks of Marburg's transformation into a modern university city in the late nineteenth century. No sudden break with the past occurred in this area of everyday life.

An equally durable aspect of economic life was a gross disparity in income. In 1910, 192 Marburgers had annual incomes of more than 9,500 marks. They paid 51 percent of the total income tax revenues in the city although they and their family members accounted for only 3.7 percent of the population. In the late nineteenth century, this income category included some university professors, factory owners, merchants, wealthy retirees, and, after 1912, the lord mayor. The other 49 percent of income tax revenues was paid by an array of townspeople accounting for 45.3 percent of the population and consisting of the majority of professors, small-scale merchants, artisanal masters, pensioners, middle-level city officials and employees, and elementary and secondary school teachers. At the base of the income pyramid was 51 percent of the population. Living in households with incomes of less than nine hundred marks per year, this group included many pensioners, low-level city employees, workers, some independent craftsmen and shopkeepers, clerks, and domestic servants. There was a long-term movement out of the lowest income category. The share of the population living in households that paid no income taxes decreased from 57 percent in 1892 to 51 percent in 1910 and 43 percent in 1930. Despite this improvement, many Marburgers shared a negative economic homogeneity based on very low annual earnings.[40]

These figures hint at widespread hardship in the city, but other information drives the point home. In 1916 the city War Credit Commission estimated that one-half of all households in the town had yearly incomes of less than 1,500 marks. Anyone with an income below this line was needful of special assistance in acquiring foodstuffs and raw materials. In 1930, the *Oberhessische Zeitung* reported that 71 percent of the city's population belonged in this income category. Compared with all citizens of the Reich, for whom the figure was 72.6 percent, Marburgers were slightly better off.[41] However, townspeople had to face a more inflated cost of living. Data assembled by the Housewives' Association indicated that meat and baked goods were more expensive in Marburg than in other German cities. Dairy products, fruit, and vegetables were also dearer there than in larger urban centers. The liberal *Hessisches Tageblatt* blamed the situation on local shops that catered to tourists and students who paid higher prices "in full" rather than on credit. Though it was addressing only a surface manifestation of the local political economy, the *Tageblatt* was correct in saying that Marburg was an "unspeakably expensive town" for the majority of people who lived there.[42]

Many people with incomes below 1,500 marks annually belonged to the heterogeneous *Bürgertum*. City-size differentials in income for particular occupational groups were quite large, and Marburg city employees, craft masters, white-collar workers, and shop-owners—to say nothing of blue-collar workers and domestic servants—probably had lower yearly incomes than their counterparts in other communities.[43]

But there is reason to be cautious about the specific relationship between earnings and cost of living as well as the implications of that relationship for economic and political life. First, the evidence presents a partial and discontinuous picture that fails to reflect significant fluctuations in both wages and living costs in the Republic, a subject to be discussed below. Second, low earnings and high living costs were ingrained patterns of everyday life. Marburgers suffered, but they were familiar with hardship and possessed other resources that counterbalanced or at least cushioned their suffering. Although the economic pressures of living in the city became greater in the war and the Republic, this hardly surprised, confused, or uniformly devastated townspeople. The durability and intensification of hardship called up resiliency and caution in the face of crisis; perhaps Hessian stolidity, a recurrent theme of local lore, was more than a myth. Finally, despite some of the uniformities stressed above, the impact of economic hardship varied from group to group, and no single characterization of the scope or intensity of economic difficulty suffices, especially for the differentiated local bourgeoisie.

What happened during the German inflation illustrates these points. There can be no doubt that Marburgers experienced considerable hardship in this period. There was a 96 percent drop in the number of savings accounts, a 99 percent decline in the total value of deposits, and an 87 percent decrease in the average size of deposits in the municipal savings bank between 1922 and 1924. This was an unprecedented expropriation of capital, a radical tax on the livelihoods of many townspeople. Additionally, local artisans experienced difficulties paying inflationary prices for raw materials. Shopkeepers could not maintain inventories and complained that the high price of paper and postage stamps made the most fundamental business activities impossible. Marburg's small industrial enterprises operated at a fraction of their capacities in the worst part of the hyperinflation. City employees experienced a growing gap between salaries and living costs. Unemployment hurt craft workers, white-collar employees, and unskilled laborers. But did this suffering justify the response of local historian Walter Kürschner, who wrote that inflation had suddenly "made previously comfortable people into beggars"?[44]

Kürschner's statement was an exaggeration. Indeed, he made points in the same publication in which the quote appeared that hinted at the existence of local, built-in counterbalances to devastating economic crisis.[45] Let us first examine the offsetting tendencies that helped to cushion suffering. For one thing, the inflation was not a sudden crisis that overtook townspeople in a moment of unpreparedness. The inflation began in World War I and lasted nearly a decade. Although there was a major trough from March 1920 until June 1921, in which a "sustained abatement of mark depreciation" occurred, the inflation was a "long-term experience," as Gerald Feldman has perceptively observed.[46] In Marburg the city magistrate said that by the summer of 1920 a decline in buying power had made beef, butter, fat, milk, and potatoes too expensive for "a growing number" of consumers.[47] By the time of the most serious stage of the inflation from the middle of 1921 into late 1923, therefore, Marburgers were all too familiar with the hardships created by the crisis. Of course, familiarity did not decrease suffering. But if the suddenness of suffering could increase the potential for radicalization of townsfolk, this factor was absent in the early 1920s.

What of the loss of savings, a catastrophic effect of the hyperinflation? Though townspeople's losses were serious, the effects of the expropriation were uneven. The majority of Marburgers did not live solely from savings. Losing these assets did not produce immediate poverty or great hardship; it was a setback, to be sure, but it was more important for its effect on future plans than on immediate living conditions. Indeed, recent research suggests that the differentiated *Mittelstand*, a large part of the local bourgeoisie, emerged from war and inflation in a stronger position relative to other classes in terms of income. This partially offset the loss of savings.[48]

Conversely, for creditors—those who relied completely on savings, pensions, and investments—the hyperinflation was much more serious. The proportion of the population that relied solely on such income, the nonstudent *Berufslosen*, was no doubt larger in Marburg than in the Reich. But some of these individuals were still capable of helping themselves, either by relying on relatives or sending sons and daughters into the work force. Increases in the number of retailers and women in the labor force suggest that the latter was an option. Some Marburgers could rent rooms to students, for although enrollments declined in 1919–23, the low point in absolute numbers of students did not occur until two years after the stabilization of the mark. Still, some townspeople were completely dependent on outside help; the city administration, local businesses, and charitable organizations helped these elderly, disabled, and needy persons.[49]

Even if these means failed to counterbalance the economic suffering of nonstudent *Berufslosen*, there is another important factor that diminishes the importance of such groups as possible agents of political radicalization. Many retirees, pensioners, and small investors were not actively engaged in the public life of the community: many were elderly; an indeterminate number had moved to Marburg from elsewhere and were not intimately involved in local family networks; the oldest or most impoverished did not join the town's clubs and associations as often as other parts of the *Bürgertum* or socialist working class did; and the *Berufslosen* did not play a dominant part in the local party political scene. In short, these were the individuals in the local adult population least able to respond to economic suffering with organized and collective effort. There were *Rentner* associations in the city, though they never coordinated their actions fully and never avoided having their political voices scattered among many different parties and special interest slates. Ostensibly organized to fight for pensioners, *Rentner* associations often featured pleasant lectures, music, and other entertainments rather than agitation. Members of an often silent minority, the city's *Berufslosen* could on occasion make their dissatisfaction clear, as they did in the May 1924 Reichstag elections. Moreover, throughout the Republic several municipal electoral slates addressed pensioners' concerns, although this was often part of a wider and very successful appeal to consumer groups rather than a singular championing of the interests of the *Berufslosen*. As a rule, however, differentiated small investors, pensioners, and retirees remained disgruntled recipients of government policy rather than becoming independent political actors.[50]

Other factors mitigated or balanced suffering in the inflation. The inflation gave some artisans and farmers an opportunity to liquidate debts by the end of 1923. This was a significant development for groups burdened by chronic indebtedness. Homeowners who took advantage of a trend toward concentration of ownership in the inflation liquidated mortgage liabilities and strengthened their overall position in the capital market. Civil servants enjoyed the relative security of a government position and benefited from the stability of their pension programs, which, unlike private programs, escaped destruction in the inflation. Moreover, incomes of most lower-level and some middle-level public employees, who made up the great majority of administrative personnel in Marburg, improved during the war and inflation relative to highly paid civil servants. Students benefited from university cafeteria prices that did not rise as fast as the inflation, donations of food from Hessian farmers, and increased social welfare measures engineered by the student government. Fraternity students could not hold the usual number of beer parties during the inflation, but they obtained relatively inexpensive meals while their organizations liquidated debts and their alumni associations helped them invest in new buildings, silverware, and boats. The groups that benefited least from offsetting tendencies were manual laborers and white-collar employees in the private sector, who, unlike lower middle class independents and civil servants, faced high unemployment during the inflation. Conversely, manual laborers in public employment improved their incomes relative to the best-paid civil servants.[51]

Finally, it is impossible to tell how effectively other informal devices softened economic difficulties. Finely textured detail would no doubt reveal employers providing inexpensive meals, shopkeepers accepting payment in kind, and family and friends helping people in emergencies. Unfortunately this kind of evidence is not attainable through quantitative analyses or government documents and newspapers. These "data" live on in the memories and feelings of participants—and disappear with their passing.

Even winners could think of themselves as losers in the inflation, as Robert Moeller has demonstrated.[52] But a minimum of economic well-being was required to express a sense of loss and mobilize opinion. Current research suggests this relative well-being existed for the small-town bourgeoisie in the war and inflation, despite the suffering these events caused.[53] In Marburg, the hyperinflation made the everyday machinery of local voluntary organizations difficult to sustain. It accelerated dissolution of the liberal and conservative parties. It failed, however, to tear permanently the intricate weavings of the bourgeois organizational fabric.[54] Those who are economically devastated do not sustain the kind of effective, long-term social and political activity that the Marburg *Bürgertum* sustained. The tradeoffs of the local economic structure provided the resilience that such activity required.

Stabilization also counterbalanced hardships. After an upsurge in consumer goods prices in the hyperinflation, prices rose more gradually until 1929, after which they dropped. The cost of renting accommodations peaked in the middle 1920s in Marburg and then declined. Though many townspeople would never recoup their losses from savings, the number of accounts in the municipal savings bank in 1932 rose to 52 percent of the 1913 total. Restaurant owners, hoteliers, and innkeepers benefited from an expanding tourist industry and increasing student enrollments. After a low point in 1924/25, when 1,803 students attended the university, enrollments grew steadily, reaching more than 3,800 in summer 1931. State and local funding of construction projects in the city and university helped the building trades. Compared to their counterparts at other German universities, Marburg students were relatively well off. In 1924/25, 78.1 percent of students at sixteen universities and technical colleges responding to a questionnaire reported that they had escaped having to discontinue their studies for economic reasons; in Marburg, where 1,012 students responded to the survey, the number was 83.5 percent. The high cost of living in the city appeared to affect townspeople more than it did students. The average weekly expenditure for food, accommodations, clothing, and other costs was higher for students at eleven of sixteen universities and technical colleges than it was for Marburg students in 1924/25.[55]

There were signs not just of stabilization but even of well-being. In 1934 there was one motorized vehicle for every 65.4 inhabitants in Marburg, a ratio better than that in almost three-quarters of all German cities with 20,000 to 50,000 townspeople. And in 1929 Marburg had forty "domestic employees" (*Hausangestellten*) for every thousand inhabitants, considerably more than Kassel with twenty-four and Bonn with twenty-one, a partial reflection of local wealth.[56]

The conservative *Oberhessische*, which rarely missed a chance to criticize conditions in the Republic, declared in 1927: "Recently, circumstances in all areas of life have once again begun to move forward slowly despite the stagnation and impoverishment of the people in general. Health conditions have improved, golden wedding anniversaries and birthday celebrations for those eighty years old and up are not infrequent."[57] Marburgers suffered; but we shall have to seek some explanation other than sudden or uniform economic hardship to account for the social and political mobilization that occurred in the 1920s.

The same can be said for the Depression of 1929. To understand why, we must first take a backward look at the issue of unemployment, the most visible consequence of the worldwide economic crisis. Inherited from pre–World War I days, unemployment and underemployment were constant features in Marburg during the war and the Republic.[58] In 1918–23 the Labor Bureau (*Arbeitsamt*) serving Marburg and several adjoining counties reported that there were rural construction workers, craft workers, and salesclerks who were unemployed. In the past many construction workers from Hessian villages had traveled to the Rhineland or Westphalia for work. But the building trades suffered badly from shortages of material and credit in the early postwar years, and these outlets were therefore reduced after 1918. Other workers had found employment in smelting works in the Siegerland, Lollar, and Frankfurt, but they had fewer opportunities after the war. In 1921 the Labor Bureau reported that there were two hundred unemployed people in Marburg, many of them younger unskilled laborers or craft workers, but that an even greater number of jobless individuals went unreported. In February 1922, 80 to 160 persons had been unemployed "for months" as Marburg factories operated at a fraction of their capacity.[59]

After 1923, when observers noted the city's rebound from the inflation, unemployment persisted. In October 1925 local newspapers reported that employment opportunities had deteriorated again after a mild improvement. The number of jobseekers and recipients of unemployment benefits increased, while reported job openings decreased. In Kassel administrative district, which included Marburg, over 10,000 men and women sought jobs when less than two hundred new openings were reported. In Marburg, layoffs and shortened work time plagued the building trades, a local machine shop, and the metal works. The Labor Bureau reported that the employment situation for retail clerks was "bad, as usual." The number of people seeking jobs in the district had more than doubled in late 1925, from 671 in November to 1,524 in mid-December. Younger rural people, who continued in their prewar pattern of seeking employment in Marburg, increased the number of jobless. In the hinterland, conversely, a labor shortage prompted farmers to consider importing Polish laborers.[60]

The number of unemployed fluctuated. In 1927 the Marburg Labor Bureau and Kassel Chamber of Industry and Crafts reported real improvement. Conditions in the labor market were more favorable than at any time since the war, and the number of unemployed fell steadily through the autumn. However, a serious frost in December brought seasonal labor to a standstill in agriculture, construction, and the gravel and basalt industry. Of 1,140 people seeking work in the Marburg district in April 1928, 620 were construction laborers and craft workers. By this time overall unemployment reached 1926 levels.[61]

Serious unemployment was not a shock of unprecedented scope when the worldwide Depression struck. Rather, it was a weakening of an already depressed labor market in Marburg and the hinterland. Many who worked seasonally, who hovered on the margins of the labor force, now slipped into the ranks of the permanently unemployed. Of 4,736 individuals seeking jobs in the Marburg district in September 1931, 37 percent were construction workers, and 16 percent were day laborers who had previously worked in the building trades or the gravel and basalt industry in Dreihausen, Niederoffleidin, or Giessen.[62] Workers in those economic areas where labor demand had fluctuated in preceding years were the ones who suffered most when the Depression arrived. And people did suffer. However, Marburg fared better than more industrial cities, where drastic declines in production led to mass unemployment. In Marburg "only" 11.8 percent of the work force was jobless by mid-1933; just 9 of 163 German cities with populations of 20,000–50,000 had lower proportionate unemployment.[63] This was one of the most fortunate results of Marburg's nonindustrial structure.

Like pensioners and retirees, unemployed townspeople were not only economically disadvantaged but also less capable than other local groups of making their plight known. This was especially true of unskilled laborers, younger craft workers, and white-collar employees. Unemployed blue-collar or white-collar employees found it difficult to participate in local trade unions or employees' associations. Not surprisingly, free trade union membership in Marburg declined in the late 1920s after rising significantly in the early Republic.[64] The local unemployed joined elderly Marburg pensioners in the growing ranks of the suffering, disgruntled, but usually silent strata.

Relatively low unemployment rates were matched by business declines that were comparatively less serious in the city than in the Reich. Marburg saw a 34 percent drop in tourists in 1929–34, but the biggest part of the decline did not begin until 1932. Moreover, though 1932 was the worst year of the Depression for local hotels, the total number of tourists visiting the city that year was only slightly below that of 1925. The number of students began to drop, and by winter 1932 enrollment at the university failed to reach three thousand for the first time since 1928. However, the number of enrolled students in 1929–33 never fell below the low point of 1925, when only 1,704 students attended Marburg university. The townspeople most directly dependent on trade with students—landlords, restaurant and tavern owners, shopkeepers—thus experienced significant but certainly not devastating declines in income. This was reflected in per capita income, which declined somewhat less sharply in Marburg than in the Reich during the Depression.[65] After discussing Marburg's economic troubles, Walter Kürschner, no friend of the Republic, expressed his view of local conditions in the early 1930s: "Nonetheless, in many ways things were more bearable in Marburg than in pure industrial communities. The relative lack of industry, which earlier was often a source of such complaining, hindered a deeper decline. The great mass of civil servants, officials' widows, and pensioners were no doubt weakened by emergency decrees and cuts in income, but they nevertheless always helped to keep up the buying power of townspeople."[66]

The university city faced narrow economic and fiscal limits, but it also shielded townspeople from devastating crisis. Everyone suffered in the inflation and Depression, but suffering was mitigated by numerous local circumstances. Moreover, townspeople's economic conditions varied so greatly that no single characterization suffices to convey the reality of economic life. Those groups who suffered most—unemployed workers and service personnel, impoverished pensioners, and other creditors—were often less able than other townspeople to voice their grievances effectively in local politics. Rather than creating an environment for panicky radicalism, the local economy fostered social resilience for most of the bourgeoisie. More important as a spur to subsequent events than economic hardship, this resiliency facilitated organizational activity, political contention, and nazism. We turn to the workings of the local polity and organizational life in the next three chapters.

two

No-man's-land: The Intersection of National and Local Politics

The party is not only the characteristic form of modern political organization," wrote Geoffrey Barraclough, "but also its hub." Unlike the elite parties of early European liberalism, the new political associations relied on mass electorates, permanent bureaucratic structures, party discipline, and popular control of party policy. They were attuned to national political marketplaces of advanced capitalist countries in the late nineteenth century. But adaptations to the rise of mass politics varied from country to country and group to group. Barraclough noted that whereas the Social Democratic working class in Germany was the first beneficiary of new party organization, the German middle classes were too divided socially to build a mass party.[1]

Though Barraclough underestimated middle-class adaptation, he was correct in pointing out different responses to the new age. In Germany neither the national parties respresenting Protestant, urban upper middle and lower middle classes nor those representing agrarian elites and peasants became hubs of their respective constituencies in the same way that the Social Democratic and Catholic Center parties did. Nonsocialist and non-Catholic constituencies were disengaged from national parties. They were situated in a net of economic pressure groups, patriotic societies, and social organizations that mobilized mass audiences in conjunction with, or at times in opposition to, the parties. A sociopolitical asymmetry characterized this net: nonparty associations galvanized political followings more successfully than did liberal and conservative parties. For these constituencies there were many hubs of political adaptation to the new age, many loci of moral and material power. Thus bourgeois apoliticism, which tried to control, counterbalance, or even reject mass political parties, had its origin in this polycentric response to the new age. Strengthened by institutions limiting development of mass parties, local bourgeois hegemony was one of the hubs of this many-centered political universe. But the reliability of such grass roots bulwarks against mass parties lessened dramatically when universal suffrage was introduced locally in the Republic. The result was a profound challenge to apoliticism.

The university heightened interactions between national and local politics in Marburg because it provided leaders, agitators, and traditions of political mobilization and experimentation oriented toward national issues. Marburg party politics became an unusually contentious variant of politics on the national scene. Although a socialist movement already existed in the city, a regional, anti-Semitic protest movement, which was led by a former Marburg student and university employee and aided by student agitators, introduced mass politics to Marburg during the Second Empire. Moreover, in contrast to many local polities, Marburg saw no single party establish a hold in local Reichstag politics until late in the Weimar Republic. After World War I the Marburg municipal party scene was equally fractious, allowing nonparty economic coalitions to gain extraordinary support. The city's political conflicts convinced more than one observer that, in the words of the left liberal politician Hellmut von Gerlach, Marburg was a political "no-man's-land."[2] These conditions increased bourgeois antipathy to mass parties and heightened the importance of bourgeois social organizations in stabilizing political rule. By discussing the intersection of national and local party politics after 1880, this chapter lays the groundwork for subsequent analysis of the politics of social organizations. The first section discusses liberal and conservative parties in the Reich and the changing relationship between national and local politics. The second section concentrates on Marburg bourgeois adaptation to fractious party politics in the Reich and community.

Disengagement, Asymmetry, and Apoliticism

Demographic change, heightened capitalist industrialization, urbanization, and growing state intervention reshaped German public life in the late nineteenth century. These intertwined processes prompted organization of all classes and strata, resulting in an age of social organization even more imposing than another great surge of voluntary association a century earlier.[3] "All relationships," wrote democrat Friedrich Naumann in describing the early twentieth century, "are now permeated with the idea of organization, of the rule of the mass."[4] Social mobilization in turn placed new pressures on political life. Universal manhood suffrage, which had been introduced by Bismarck, opened the national polity to an increasingly organized population conscious of group interests. Voting participation increased from 50.7 percent of the eligible electorate in 1871 to 77.2 percent in 1887. From 1887 until 1912 participation averaged more than 75 percent in Reichstag elections.[5]

The Social Democratic and Catholic Center parties were in the vanguard of the new politics.[6] We take the Social Democrats first. Unlike bourgeois groups, socialist workers could hardly rely on the state, parliament, or other civic organizations and institutions to defend their interests. Instead, workers depended on the Social Democratic party (Sozialdemokratische Partei Deutschlands), realizing that there would be no workers' movement without a central political apparatus. The party needed strong grass roots structures in which leaders determined strategy, organized social activities, and put together lists of candidates for political office. Strong local branches were in part products of socialist adaptation to *Verein* legislation that prohibited wider coalitions until 1900. In addition, the centrality of the party to working-class life necessitated bureaucratic mechanisms instead of the ad hoc conventions that characterized early bourgeois politics. Finally, there was a dense substructure of organizations supporting the party. It included electoral associations (*Wahlvereine*), trade unions, and sports and cultural clubs. Though they often diminished interest in general political issues, social clubs could mobilize workers for strikes, demonstrations, and elections. Due in part to the pariah status of Social Democrats in national society, these organizational features enhanced a party discipline that was unprecedented in German political history. The SPD became the largest political organization in Wilhelmine Germany, with a million members, more than one-third of the total vote, and more than one-quarter of 397 Reichstag seats in the 1912 elections.[7]

The Catholic Center (Zentrum) was the only party to match SPD efforts at building a wide political audience. In the Second Reich its share of the total national vote varied from 16.4 to 27.9 percent and its share of all Reichstag seats from 22.9 to 26.7 percent. The Center was loosely organized compared to the SPD. The party Reichstag delegation enjoyed paramount authority in a field of affiliated social organizations, the most important of which was the German Catholic People's Association (Volksverein für das katholische Deutschland), which listed nearly 900,000 members before World War I. Situated in a tangle of social networks, the Zentrum became increasingly less "confessional" after 1880, as it appealed more to peasants and the middle classes than to clerics and Catholic nobles. Unlike the Social Democrats, Center party representatives participated in national government coalitions in Imperial Germany, anchoring parliamentary majorities in all governments after 1890 except that of 1906–9.[8]

Though Social Democrats and Catholics built mass parties, there were other political adaptations to social reorganization. One of the most important nonparty organizations with political power was the Bund der Landwirte, or Agrarian League, organized in 1893 by East Elbian landholders (Junkers) who opposed Chancellor Caprivi's policies for reduced tariffs on wheat and rye. The league achieved a mass membership in 1913 of 328,000, consisting mainly of family peasants from west of the Elbe River. It incorporated grass roots anti-Semitism as part of a potentially integrative nationalist ideology of antisocialist "productive estates," worked against progressive tariff policies that would have lowered the price of foodstuffs for working classes, and once Social Democratic electoral gains in 1908 revealed the decreasing effectiveness of Junker and government antisocialist strategies, championed "corporative" (berufsständisch) principles stressing the primacy of sectional interests in national political life. The league's East Elbian leaders were closely tied to the Deutschkonservative Partei (German Conservative party or simply Conservative party), though some Bund representatives also belonged to the more moderate Free Conservative and National Liberal parties, especially in Hanover. The league's close ties to the German Conservative party ensured that the latter would benefit from the former's mass base in the countryside. But this also kept the German Conservatives from developing a more autonomous party organization.[9]

What of the constituencies outside socialist, Catholic, and agrarian organizations? These groups were geographically splintered, culturally diverse, and economically disparate. They were represented most often by right-wing or left-wing liberalism. The former found expression in the National Liberal party and the latter, by 1910, in the Progressive People's party. James Sheehan has argued that the typical liberal voter was

a Protestant who belonged somewhere in the middle range of
the class and status hierarchies. It was from these groups that
the bulk of the two parties' 3.15 million voters came in the
elections of 1912. And it was districts where these groups
were best represented which elected a majority of the liberals'
eighty-seven delegates. In size and social composition, these
districts tended to fall in between the small, agrarian *Wahl-
kreise* dominated by the Conservatives and the huge, urban,
and/or industrial districts controlled by the SPD. Characteris-
tically, the liberals' districts were touched but not transformed
by the social, economic, and cultural changes at work in German society. They were composed of small and medium-sized
towns, not great cities or distended industrial suburbs; when
liberals did win in large cities, it was most often in the relatively stable central districts where the urban middle strata
still predominated. Similarly, their rural support came in
places where agriculture was carried on by a large number of
proprietors, not by a few big landowners.[10]

The National Liberal party was the largest and most important
political representative of the Protestant middle classes in Germany until just before World War I, when left and right liberalism
became about equal in national electoral support. In Reichstag elections of 1871, the National Liberals had the largest following, receiving 30.1 percent of the total vote and 32.7 percent of all Reichstag seats. Though their electoral success fluctuated, a long-term
decline then set in. The last year in which the National Liberals
had more than a 20 percent share of the national electorate was
1887, when they held 99 Reichstag seats, one more than the Center.
In 1890 the absolute number of National Liberal votes declined by
one-quarter from the previous election. By 1912, despite a gain of
500,000 votes over 1890 totals, the National Liberal share of the
Reich vote diminished to 13.6 percent, compared with 12.3 percent
for a left liberal coalition of three parties. The German Conservative and Free Conservative parties also achieved 12.3 percent of the
vote between them in national elections that year.[11]

The electoral decline of the National Liberal party was due in
part to organizational weaknesses. Between 1892 and 1910 the
party began transforming itself from an exclusive party of notables
into a more popular "member party" (*Mitgliederpartei*). But National Liberal leaders never constructed strong ties between the

central party apparatus and grass roots satellites. Contacts between national and local power brokers were inconsistent; and contacts between local party leaders and their constituents were disorganized, uneven, and often based one-sidedly on personal relationships rather than bureaucratic mechanisms.[12]

National Liberal provincial organizations assumed more power after the turn of the century, but this influence was never institutionalized. Nor was any mechanism found for facilitating popular involvement in National Liberal politics. Although the power of the regions ensured some popular influence on policy, the National Liberal organization remained loose and uncoordinated; as Nipperdey has suggested, it was "constantly threatened with dissolution."[13] National Liberal leaders complained that in 1890 only one-third of the districts in which they nominated candidates had strong local party associations. The party press at times compensated for shortcomings in grass roots organization, but editorializing was an unsatisfactory substitute for tireless campaigning. One cost of such weaknesses was illustrated even in rural areas where National Liberal decline was less serious than in cities with large socialist electorates after 1890. In these country regions National Liberal candidates mortgaged their power by relying on the electoral apparatus of the Bund der Landwirte.[14]

National Liberal decline left a large block of mainly Protestant voters from middle strata without a coherent national political organization. This was a major problem in an age in which, as one contemporary said, disciplined party mobilization was a "skilled trade."[15] The National Liberals failed to integrate the social claims of their followers in a broader political vision represented by a strong national party. National Liberal adherents were therefore always relatively disengaged from party structures, and the resources party members held were never fully available for the national organization. Unlike the Social Democratic and Catholic Center parties, the National Liberal party never enjoyed moral and material dominance over its followers.

Left liberals were financially and electorally weaker than National Liberals. A number of parties represented the left liberal cause—the Progressive party (Fortschrittspartei) up to 1880, the German Liberal party (Deutschfreisinnige Partei) from 1884 to 1893, and the Progressive People's party (Fortschrittliche Volkspartei) after 1910. All of these groupings shared common political styles and organizational practices, and they often drew on similar constituencies. Aside from the German People's party (Deutsche

Volkspartei) of southern Germany, left liberal parties followed a single trajectory during most of the Second Empire. Despite some disorganization, left liberals were collectively more unified and coherent than their right-wing counterparts. Left liberals received the support of a relatively homogeneous group of urban upper-middle-class and lower-middle-class voters, and contacts between national party leadership and local constituencies were more developed in the left liberal than in the National Liberal camp. Moreover, left liberal followers were less divided than right liberals by political disagreements and factions. In spite of such advantages, the transformation of left liberal parties into coherent member parties had just begun in the Second Empire, and the left liberal networks were also disengaged from their national parties.[16]

To the right of these organizations, the Free Conservative party depended on parliamentary representatives and local power brokers in Silesia, the province of Saxony, and cities such as Marburg/Lahn, Halle, and Freiburg/Breisgau. The German Conservatives meanwhile possessed no significant mass organization, although in the western provinces the influence of local leaders played a role in party organization and the selection of candidates for political office. But there was little wider popular influence in the party, and parliamentary representatives as well as the party leadership were dependent on Agrarian League functionaries. The presence of the latter organization gave conservative groupings a marked advantage over liberals by funneling mass support toward the Conservative party. Yet this also caused disengagement. In contrast to liberal groups, conservative constituencies found a single, powerful organizational focus for their distance from the party.[17]

Relationships between the Agrarian League and the Conservatives dramatized the general situation of nonsocialist and non-Catholic parties in the Reich. Saddled with constitutional provisions hindering parliamentary sovereignty, liberal and conservative parties relied on associations that either supplemented or posed alternatives to party activity. Besides the Agrarian League, these associations included a tangle of economic pressure groups, ranging from big business organizations like the Central Association of German Industrialists and the Hansa League, to national artisans', white-collar employees', and retailers' associations. Additionally, liberal and conservative parties relied on noneconomic associations such as the nationalist *Verbände*. These patriotic societies included pressure groups like the Pan-German League, cultural associations such as the Society for Germandom Abroad, paramilitary formations like the Young Germany Union, and antisocialist organizations such as the Imperial League against Social Democracy. Naturally, the scope and intensity of involvement in party politics varied among all of these groups.[18]

Special interest organizations, nationalist associations, and other groups added up to a mirror image of the prepolitical networks of Social Democratic and Catholic parties. But there was no single, coherent political force to act as a center for this shifting, diverse, and unstable jumble of organizations. A polycentric constellation of organizations and institutions drew upon the political potential of this wider network. Resources shifted and moral leadership passed from one organization to another. Within the asymmetry created between these networks and liberal and conservative parties, *bürgerlich* groups invented a tradition of apoliticism.[19]

Apoliticism comprised common sense and ideology. For Gramsci common sense consisted of shifting, mutating layers of tradition that were built on a "chaotic aggregate of disparate conceptions" and drawn from centuries-old elements as well as contemporary ideas.[20] The Italian theorist saw common sense as an everyday thumbnail philosophy constructed, maintained, and reshaped daily from the raw materials of community custom and "outside" influences. In this form German apoliticism was a traditional, virtually unquestioned disdain for political parties and parliaments.[21] But the divisions between common sense and more systematic forms of thought are fluid, and the former can contain the building blocks of the latter. After 1880 apoliticism became more ideological in the sense that it enabled groups to rationalize, define, and make meaning of their interests in the national political marketplace. Ideological apoliticism found expression in many different venues. Bismarck strengthened it when he referred to political parties in 1884 as "the ruin [*Verderb*] of our constitution and of our future." It was certainly present in social organizations, where disdain for political parties' "brawling and strife"—as a veterans' club publication put it—became widespread in the last quarter of the nineteenth century.[22]

Such sentiments reflected the core assumption of apoliticism: that public life could operate without permanent party bureaucracies and discipline, special interest lobbying, and grass roots organization—all features that characterized the biggest vote-getters of the Second Empire. Apoliticism was an ideology of disengagement from the national party system. This was especially crucial for the *Bürgertum*, which rejected Social Democracy and the Center as models of political organization in favor of polycentric arrangements de-emphasizing party hegemony. Most importantly, apoliticism was hardly the manifestation of a timeless German cultural trait, as Thomas Mann argued; it was instead a functional response to mass politics.[23]

Disengagement, asymmetry, and apoliticism had appeal as responses to the new politics partly because they were based on tensions between the national and local scene, between fragmented and multifaceted bourgeois participation in the Reich polity and a more coherent political experience for the bourgeoisie at the grass roots. Such tensions were especially well developed in mainly Protestant towns and cities where liberalism was strong. For many liberal politicians, local government power provided "refuge for those excluded or alienated from national party politics."[24]
Had these urban constituencies become strongly attached to powerful national parties in the 1880s, as had liberal social groups in England twenty years earlier, the German *Bürgertum* might have accepted the limited democracy of English liberalism.[25] But a number of factors—recent national unification, an accelerated tempo of capitalist modernization, the rapid rise of large-scale industrial organization, the quick growth of a united working-class movement, the adoption by Bismarck of universal manhood suffrage in Reichstag elections, the whole of the Bismarckian constitutional system, and strong state penetration—ensured that Germany would not be England. The urban bourgeoisie was suspicious of national politics and tried to channel and deflate national conflict in local arenas. This attachment to local power bases was not a sign of political philistinism but a practical response to power relationships in the late Second Empire. Dependent on local circumstances, the tension between Reich and community that defined those relationships, like the tension of a rope stretched beyond its capacity, would collapse in the Weimar Republic.
World War I set in motion events that upset the precarious relationship between Reich and local polities. For one thing, the war furthered disengagement of bourgeois constituencies. The Kaiser set the tone by proclaming that he no longer recognized parties or classes, an idea that reinforced the image of public life without modern political groups. From the beginning of the war, proponents of an aggressive war-aims policy used economic *Verbände* and nationalist associations to discuss and propose plans for a "popular outbreak" (*Volksausbruch*) in support of the war effort, an outbreak

over which the political parties would presumably have little control. The industrialist Emil Kirdorf pointed out to his colleagues that only widespread patriotism could "pull the *Volk* . . . away from the incitement [*Verhetzung*] of the parties and loyally bind them to the German fatherland." Kirdorf had been discussing the SPD in particular, but his words reflected a distrust of parties in general. Directly supported by military, agricultural, and industrial elites, the Fatherland party (Deutsche Vaterlandspartei) strengthened such sentiments by organizing local party branches and extolling "suprapolitical" [*überparteilich*] coalitions. These were aimed against the supporters of the peace resolution in the Reichstag and against the influence of political parties generally. Boasting of more than one million members in July 1918, the "party of those without parties" galvanized mass support.[26]

Such efforts were of obvious danger to already weakened liberal and conservative parties. A fault line existed in the National Liberal party as it entered the war. Younger National Liberals such as Gustav Stresemann wanted to broaden the party's influence among workers, the lower middle classes, and peasants, whereas older leaders emphasized National Liberal links to heavy industry and East Elbian landholders. Though internal differences lessened when the party supported aggressive territorial annexation, National Liberals faced the prospect of being swallowed up by war-aims agitation fostered by economic *Verbände* and nationalist associations. Additionally, domestic political issues such as Prussian electoral reform served to intensify party divisions. By January 1918 National Liberal *Vereine* were virtually inactive, and the national leadership found it impossible to enlist local constituencies for party work.[27] The party dissolved.

The Progressive People's party and both conservative parties experienced similar problems in the war. Hampered by their national leadership's indecision over war aims, Progressives struggled against being engulfed by what a party spokesman described as a "radical wave, which breaks over workers as well as middle classes" (*Bürgerkreisen*). This radical wave included agitation for electoral reform and local responses to the German state's wartime social policies. The latter produced widespread hardship and sharpened differences between economic classes.[28] Due to its unrelenting support of aggressive territorial gains and opposition to internal political reform, the German Conservative party became increasingly isolated from its peasant and lower-middle-class base. Meanwhile, the previously weak popular foundations of the Free Conservative party splintered. "During the *Burgfrieden*," the 1916 annual report of the Breslau local branch (*Ortsgruppe*) stated, "political activity did not take place. Accordingly, there were not many meetings of the party membership or leadership."[29]

Bourgeois party leaders tried hesitantly to modernize their organizations before World War I, and these efforts continued after 1918.[30] Though right and left liberals failed to unify under a single party umbrella, all bourgeois parties worked to tighten contacts with their constituencies. The German Democratic party (Deutsche Demokratische Partei), which represented left liberal constituencies in the Republic, emphasized strong links with its voters and members. But after successes in the 1919 National Assembly elections, the DDP quickly lost its initial momentum and a mass following. Meanwhile, the national coherence of the German People's party (Deutsche Volkspartei), the successor of the National Liberals, was damaged by powerful district electoral organizations in Westphalia, Hanover, Osnabrück-Oldenburg, and Saxony. Local groups remained disengaged from the DVP central organization. The German National People's party (Deutschnationale Volkspartei)—a coalition of conservative, Christian social, and anti-Semitic associations—relied on a loosely consolidated front of agrarian pressure groups (the Reichslandbund), the German National Commercial Employees' Association, Protestant churches, homeowners' associations, and other groups for mass support. These networks did not, however, prevent serious electoral fluctuations for the DNVP in the Republic.[31]

Ongoing disengagement led to a dissolution of bourgeois constituencies starting with the May 1924 Reichstag elections. Prior to this, the liberal parties, the DVP and DDP, gained a combined total of 22.9 percent of the vote for the National Assembly and 22.2 percent for the first Reichstag in 1920; both totals were lower than but roughly comparable to the combined share of their liberal Wilhelmine predecessors in 1912 (25.9 percent). But in May 1924 the DVP-DDP share dropped 7 percentage points, to 14.9. This was the largest decrease during the Republic until Reichstag elections in July 1932, when the DVP managed only 1.2 percent and the Staatspartei, housing the reorganized remnants of the DDP, only 1 percent of the national vote.[32]

The May 1924 elections came in the wake of popular disaffection with hyperinflation and stabilization. The DVP and DDP were vulnerable to popular disgruntlement because they had participated in government cabinets in 1922–24. But liberal party losses were attributable to something more than temporary outpourings of economic dissatisfaction. As Thomas Childers has argued, a realignment of voter sympathies began in 1924, exacerbating liberal fragmentation and furthering voter disengagement. A drastic crumbling of the organizational and geographical bases of popular support for the liberal parties had started.[33]

Conversely, the 1924 elections signaled temporary electoral dominance for the DNVP in *bürgerlich* circles. The German Nationals received 19.5 percent of the national vote in May 1924 and 20.5 percent in December of that year. A large part of their success can be attributed to the DNVP's courting of pensioners, retirees, small investors, and others who sought a more equitable revalorization scheme from the government after sustaining losses in the inflation.[34] It was this impressive DNVP showing that made the total bourgeois share of the 1924 vote comparable to that of earlier elections. Indeed, the combined DNVP-DVP-DDP share in May and December 1924 (34.4 and 36.9 percent respectively) was higher than in the 1919 National Assembly elections (33.2 percent). The DNVP's share eventually shrank to 7 percent in 1930. Nevertheless, the DNVP occupied a more stable social space than the DVP or DDP; in March of 1933 the party was still able to hold 8 percent of the electorate.

Another important feature of the 1924 elections was increased influence for splinter parties. Regional parties had existed on the national scene before 1914, but the introduction of proportional representation after the war gave limited electoral influence to a wider variety of splinter groups. After 1919, when the Economic party (Wirtschaftspartei) was organized to represent homeowners, splinter parties were established in the Weimar electoral landscape. Appealing to the same disgruntled creditor groups that supported DNVP candidates in 1924, two revalorization parties appeared in that year. The WP and the revalorization parties were mobilized to represent specific economic groups, although the Economic party later tried to assemble a broad middle-class following and all three parties voiced some general ideological themes. In contrast, splinter groups such as the Christian Social People's Service (Christlich-Sozialer Volksdienst) and, later, the Conservative People's party (Konservative Volkspartei) were founded with the goal of reorganizing voters around wider ideological issues. Support for such parties reached a new plateau in the May 1924 elections: regional, special interest, and splinter parties received 8.3 percent of the national vote, compared with 3.7 percent in the June 1920 elections. While the number of voters increased by 3.9 percent between the two elections, the absolute number of voters for these political organizations increased by 208 percent. The small parties' share of the vote declined to 7.8 percent in November 1924 but reached 14 percent in 1928 and 13.6 percent in September 1930.[35]

The NSDAP emerged from the first 1924 Reichstag election with 6.5 percent of the vote. It also benefited from widespread disillusionment resulting from hyperinflation and stabilization. In view of the party's disarray, its vote total represented a significant gain.[36] But the Nazi party quickly sank into insignificance in national, state, and local elections. For voters who were disillusioned with liberal and conservative parties, the NSDAP was less viable as an alternative than the special interest parties of the 1920s.

While the national party system dissolved, grass roots bourgeois parties also began to crumble. In the pre–World War I era, liberal and conservative weakness was softened by institutional devices such as the three-class electoral system. Although the situation varied from city to city, the Prussian three-class system slowed the growth of Social Democratic power and hindered development of political parties in municipal elections. But in the Republic universal suffrage made local politics just as threatening as national politics for bourgeois classes and strata. "Having always upheld and stamped communal self-government," Helmuth Croon wrote, "the liberal *Bürgertum* now became a minority" in the cities.[37]

Held before the full effects of the Depression were felt, municipal elections in November 1929 illustrated what had happened after one decade of democratic city politics in Prussia. The SPD earned 26.5 percent of all municipal seats in cities with 20,000 or more inhabitants, giving that group the largest block of seats for any party contesting Prussian city elections. The Center received 16.8 percent of all seats, and the three principal bourgeois parties 13.1 percent. The remaining 43.6 percent went to the NSDAP (just 4.4 percent), Communists (Kommunistische Partei Deutschlands), CSV, joint slates (*Einheitsliste*), and special interest parties.[38]

Joint slates and special interest parties illustrate the complexities of bourgeois city politics. Gaining 13.5 percent of all seats, the joint slates comprised parties representing "essentially the right-wing *Bürgertum*."[39] There was an inverse correlation between town size and success of the *Einheitsliste*. Cities of 50,000 or fewer inhabitants elected about two-thirds of all municipal parliament seats held by joint list representatives even though they elected only 44.1 percent of all city council seats. In many of these cities the unified lists were more than footnotes to local power struggles. They occupied 17 of 37 city parliament seats in Stolp, 13 of 31 in Wittenberge, and 13 of 28 in Küstrin.[40] The *Einheitsliste* were temporary coalitions; by 1933 their total share of municipal seats in Prussia sank to 1.2 percent. But because they rested on alliances of local bourgeois parties and constituencies in the 1920s, they promoted collective protest rather than undirected fragmentation. Above all, they were militantly local, designed to meet immediate hometown needs. They were signs of a continuing disengagement of grass roots constituencies from the national sphere and hence updated variations on the tradition of bourgeois apoliticism.

Garnering 11 percent of the vote in 1929 city elections, special interest slates also furthered voter disengagement. They were least successful in cities with more than 200,000 inhabitants, where they gained less than 9 percent of all seats. But they managed 12.6 percent in cities with 100,000–200,000 inhabitants, 11.5 percent in communities with 50,000–100,000, and 11.8 percent in towns of 20,000–50,000. Most special interest parties described themselves as unpolitical alliances. They mobilized not only upper-middle-class and lower-middle-class voters but also some working-class people, particularly where there were viable renters' coalitions. Their interests were diverse: the voters were confronted with the Alcohol Opponents' slate in Flensburg, the Sport party in Oberhausen, the Partyless party of Fürth, the Land Reformers' ticket in Breslau, the Renters' party in Augsburg, and the Trade, Commerce, and Landed Property party of Potsdam.[41]

Municipal special interest parties represented the narrowest of local concerns and often appeared slightly absurd. However, by mobilizing sectional interests, the slates adapted to grass roots power politics. Moreover, like special interest parties in the nation, the local coalitions possessed general political conceptions. They strongly criticized the party system in community and Reich, championing an apoliticism more compatible with local bourgeois ideology than with the formal party programs of national liberal and conservative parties. In some cities, they attracted large parts of the local electorate. In Wittenberg, 11 of 30 seats were held by such alliances in 1929; in Dinslaken, 9 of 30; and in Marburg, 14 of 30. Marburg special interest parties influenced city politics and played an important role in the political education of Nazi party members.[42]

Disengagement weakened national bourgeois parties in the Empire and shattered them in the Republic. Disengagement was ultimately feasible because of local bourgeois hegemony, but during the Republic conflict in the cities assaulted this last reliable source of political power. The assault gained momentum in 1924–29, before the onset of the Depression. For the bourgeoisie, the useful tension between national and local power was dissolving, and energies released in the process fueled unprecedented political conflict. Disengaged from national party structures but now also challenged in the local sphere, the urban bourgeoisie explored new political forms. Could recast apoliticism stabilize asymmetry, facilitate a workable bourgeois presence in the national polity, and ensure bourgeois hegemony at home? Or would political activists reshape urban constituencies, creating new modes of moral authority in national and local spheres?

Local Politics

National and regional conflict set the boundaries of grass roots struggles. But local people shaped these struggles on their own terms, making national party politics an "average" of diverse local activities. Crucial for our understanding of Marburg politics were town notables, individuals "who possessed both a secure position in local society and a sense of belonging to a leadership group."[43] For these *Bürger* leaders, political parties in the 1880s were rather more like nonspecialized social clubs of the early nineteenth century than present-day political organizations; they were loose assemblages of notables rather than disciplined, bureaucratized associations. More importantly, like national bourgeois parties, they were nested in a wider ecology of local organizations. Unlike their Reich equivalents, however, these local parties were often based on everyday social networks rather than bureaucratized patriotic societies, economic pressure groups, and the like.

A fundamental building block of this ecology of local organizations was the *Stammtisch*, a table reserved by the same group of people at regularly scheduled intervals in a favorite restaurant. Lord Mayor Ludwig Schüler, who served in Marburg from 1884 to 1907, headed a well-known *Stammtisch* at the Seebode restaurant, and a Weidenhausen pub was host to Stammtisch Drallia.[44] Members of the large and influential Stammtisch Käsebrod understood their role in quietly shaping local politics. "It's pleasant at the Käsebrod, and there a lot takes place," they sang, "of which in local government you never hear a trace."[45] The men who sat at these *Stamm-*

tische also interacted in other ways. Some served together on the city council (*Stadtrat*), which in 1898 consisted of the lord mayor, three craft masters, two university professors, two merchants, two *Rentner*, two brewery owners, and one city building official. Many notables also joined the elite social club Museum, and others belonged to the Philipps House, the "St. Jacob" Charity Association, the Library Club, the Antiquities and Art Society, and the Concert Association.[46]

The most broadly based elite political group in Marburg was the Liberal Association. The common ground of association members was a broad philosophical attachment to liberalism—an ideology designed to bring about and justify social and political conditions favorable to capitalist property relations—rather than to a specific party program.[47] Formed in 1874 by Marburg's eminent law professor Ludwig Enneccerus, the Liberal Association initially encompassed much of the city elite, because until January 1885 National Liberals, Free Conservatives, and Progressives were members. The association's membership list from 1874 contains, out of 140 members, 22 university professors, 5 unsalaried university instructors (*Privatdozenten*), 15 upper-level officials, 9 free professionals, and 3 students.[48] Thus nearly 40 percent of Liberal Association members came from the *Bildungsbürgertum*, individuals whose social status and collective interests were based on a notional custodianship over "culture."[49] In addition, 35 craft masters, 26 retailers and bankers, and 8 "industrialists"—a group of 69 self-employed *Bürger* —made up almost 50 percent of the members. Eleven minor civil servants and a miscellaneous group of 8 others rounded out the association's membership. Later, elite political loyalties would be split between a conservative association (the Konservativer Verein), left liberal parties, and anti-Semitic organizations. But for a time Liberal Association membership indicated that many elites as well as nonelite townsfolk were willing to be grouped together under the liberal mantle.

The fortunes and development of liberal and conservative parties varied depending on whether local, state, or national offices were being contested. In city politics there were no strong political parties throughout the period of the Second Empire, as voters chose candidates from unified lists representing neighborhood and civic associations. In terms of the recruitment of political leaders and suffrage, local representative structures institutionalized political closure. The city council consisted of twelve individuals and the lord mayor while the city parliament included twenty-four standing and twenty-four extraordinary members. Age and gender restrictions, property requirements, and income qualifications ensured that people serving in these bodies would be drawn from the narrowest of social circles. When the Prussian municipal ordinance was enacted in 1897 and implemented in the following year, a city magistrate and parliament consisting of thirty representatives selected by an expanded three-class electorate replaced older institutions. But these changes did not substantially widen the local polity. In 1894 city elections, the last held under the Kurhessian municipal ordinance, less than two-thirds of 6.8 percent of townspeople eligible to vote cast ballots. After the introduction of the three-class voting system in Prussian cities, the potential electorate was expanded 85 percent in 1898 elections. But the three-class system categorized voters according to the amount of direct taxes paid, devaluing ballots as one moved "down" the class and status structure. In Marburg 85.7 percent of all eligible voters elected just one-third of the city parliament. Despite some Marburg notables' misgivings about the three-class system and despite increases in the electorate and voter participation, the closure of municipal politics in Marburg continued until the Republic, when universal suffrage was extended to city elections.[50]

Underlying this closure was an assumption that city administration had little to do with electoral power and mobilization of public opinion. More important were the balanced actions of individuals whose exalted position in social life supposedly equipped them to exercise moral and material power over the local polity. Marburg's experience parallels that of many dissimilar urban centers before 1914, in that the *Bürgertum* found a relatively stable political anchor for social hegemony. It therefore seems inaccurate to argue that there was little relationship between "culture" and "politics" in German towns before World War I.[51] In many municipal polities the two spheres intersected through private relationships and public organizations.

In voting for the Prussian state house, the Landtag, the Marburg district was a "citadel of the conservatives with National Liberal coloring." This was the case because the countryside, in which two-thirds of all voters lived, elected mainly conservative candidates in state elections, while Marburgers opted for National Liberals.[52] But the three-class system in Prussian state elections also diminished chances for a fuller venting of public opinion.

The Landtag was the site of competition over financial resources indispensable to the university city. But the Reichstag is more important for this study because it was the locus of a clash between alternative political forms. Here universal suffrage enabled all males aged twenty-five or older to vote. Reichstag politics in Marburg was more contentious than city or state politics, more capable of having unanticipated results. Indeed, observers referred to the Marburg Reichstag district as the "most unpredictable electoral district in Germany."[53] The 1880s opened a struggle between liberal and conservative parties on one side and prototypical mass parties on the other. Notionally backward and sleepy, Marburg was the scene of a vigorous clash between competing modes of political mobilization.

Why Marburg? Numerous factors—rapid economic and demographic growth, occupational structures, mounting antagonism between city and countryside—merit consideration. But more important than these was the capacity of the town population to mobilize politically. Two factors heightened this capacity. The first and most fundamental was the relationship between the university and city.[54] Marburg university, a growing institution in a small city that depended on students and educators for its economic livelihood, was integrated into the fabric of local life and therefore capable of influencing political conflict. Perhaps only in Göttingen and Tübingen did similar conditions exist. Members of a national and local elite, most professors and many students possessed leadership abilities, contacts, and social advantages in the Hessian university town. They wove strands of interaction between Reich politics and local power struggles. Second, local bourgeois classes and strata maintained and developed strong voluntary organizations after the 1880s. Without appropriate comparative evidence, it is difficult to tell whether organizational life was more strongly developed in Marburg than in other cities. But the absence of large-scale industry in the city undoubtedly had an effect on the scope and form of voluntary structures. Shielded from the disruptive and transformative effects of industrialization, older organizational networks persisted, widened, and prompted new voluntary groups. All they needed was the opportunity to act politically.[55]

Bourgeois parties were no weaker in Marburg than in comparable cities, but they faced more organized and potentially more volatile social groups over which no single party could gain control. This allowed for the rapid appearance of new political challengers, and it enabled nonparty associations to influence political life. Industrialization and state penetration politicized national society in the Second Empire; but Prussian state-making and the strengthening of traditional institutions and social organizations were more important in politicizing Marburgers.[56]

The Social Democratic party was the oldest of Marburg's modern political organizations. A Lassallean General German Workers' Association was formed in Marburg in 1869, five years before the Liberal Association and well before the German Conservative party. Its earliest leaders were the factory worker and later shopkeeper Volpertus Heinrich Schneider and the farmer Heinrich Lauer. They gave the party a potential urban and agrarian base. Before the enactment of antisocialist legislation, the party occasionally supported a nonsocialist candidate in runoff elections, as it did in 1874 when Social Democratic votes helped a National Liberal candidate defeat a German Conservative. Partly because of disagreement within the national leadership over policy toward peasants and the *Mittelstand*, the base of the Marburg party remained narrow in the Second Empire. In 1903–6 local party membership was concentrated among unionized skilled and craft workers (such as printers and woodworkers), with only marginal participation from day laborers and *Mittelständler* (see table 2-2). Among Marburg university teachers, Social Democracy attracted only the iconoclastic Robert Michels, who belonged to the SPD for several years prior to 1907 but later saw in the workings of the party a typical manifestation of the "Iron Law of Oligarchy."[57]

Yet electoral returns suggested that local Social Democrats were not entirely doomed to isolation. Indicative of the porousness of the repression resulting from antisocialist legislation in 1878–90 is the fact that the Marburg Social Democrats received 254 votes, or one-quarter of the total ballots cast, in 1884 Reichstag elections (see table 2-1). Though they never again gained this share in the next six decades, they obtained 20.5 percent in 1903 and 21.5 percent in 1919 elections for the National Assembly. These local totals were well below the national average, but they were substantial for a community of services and trade. In view of these results, Marburg Social Democracy potentially represented the kind of broad social movement to which local notables were ideologically committed but practically opposed. Nonetheless, in part because of Marburg's small working-class population, local socialists were unable to build on these modest beginnings.

More consequential as a motor of popular politics in Marburg before World War I was political anti-Semitism.[58] The leader of the anti-Semitic movement in northern Hesse was Otto Böckel, a former Marburg university student, university librarian, and collector

Table 2-1 *Reichstag Voting (by Percentage) in City of Marburg, 1871–1912, First Ballots (I) and Runoffs (II)*[a]

	Cons.	FC	NL	Z	Lib-NS	SPD	AntiS	GS-EA	Other
1871–I	50.4		39.5			10.1			
1871–II	61.4		38.0						
1874–I	35.8		39.1			20.1			0.5
1874–II	43.0		56.0						1.0
1877		72.4				15.2			14.3
1878		87.6		4.0		7.8			0.5
1881	29.9		61.5			8.3			
1883[b]	41.9		57.7						
1884	38.3		36.2			25.0			0.2
1887	41.7				10.9		42.1		
1890		45.2		2.0		10.0	41.7		
1893–I	18.9		21.0	1.3	13.2	8.6	35.4		1.5
1893–II	26.9						70.8		2.3
1898–I	36.0			7.7	16.5	12.9	12.9		13.7
1898–II	73.0						26.5		0.4
1903–I	21.6			4.9	38.6	20.5	13.8		0.7
1903–II	31.2				66.5				
1907–I			22.2	4.4	34.0	17.9		22.7	0.5
1907–II					68.7			31.0	0.3
1912–I			34.7		40.1	10.7	6.6	7.6	0.3
1912–II					63.8			35.6	0.6

KEY:
Cons. = Old and New Conservatives (1872); German Conservative party (1876)
FC = Reichs- und Freikonservative Partei, or Free Conservative party
NL = National Liberal party
Z = Catholic Center party (Zentrum)
Lib-NS = Progressive party (1884); Progressive Association (1893); National Social Association (1896); Democratic Association (after 1908)
SPD = Social Democratic party
AntiS = Anti-Semitic People's party (1890); German Reform party (1893); German Social Reform party (1903)
GS-EA = German Social party, in Economic Alliance with Christian Socials and Agrarian League (1907, 1912)
Other = Hessische Rechtspartei, miscellaneous, and invalid ballots

a. Blank spaces indicate that the party did not run; vom Brocke's percentages do not always add up to 100.
b. By-election.
SOURCE: Vom Brocke, "Marburg im Kaiserreich," pp. 478–79.

of Hessian folk tunes. Böckel came to politics circuitously: he became interested in political questions through his contact with Hessian people during searches in the countryside for folklore materials. In this respect he was a sociopolitical rather than party political person, a characteristic important for understanding his attitude toward the parliamentary system.

Before Böckel's appearance, National Liberal candidates had won the Marburg–Frankenburg–Kirchhain–Vöhl Reichstag seat in 1867, 1871, and 1874, while Free Conservative and Conservative representatives had won it in an 1871 special election and in 1877, 1881, and 1883. But in 1887 Böckel became the first political anti-Semite and the youngest candidate ever elected to the German lower house. He continued to occupy a seat there until 1903. Böckel gained 42.1 percent of the vote in the city in 1887 and 56.6 percent in the electoral district (Wahlkreis) as a whole. His most commanding victory occurred in 1893. In that year he received 35.4 percent of the vote in the city and 48.6 percent in the district in the initial balloting; he then managed to increase his percentage to 70.8 in Marburg and 68.5 in the Wahlkreis in the runoff elections.[59]

Dubbed the "peasant king" by contemporaries, Böckel exploited widespread anti-Semitic prejudice in the Marburg hinterland. Anti-Jewish feeling was strong in northern Hesse partly because Jews enjoyed visible and controversial influence at the center of financial and trade networks in small towns and rural areas of the region. But anti-Semitism was also fired by popular identification of Jews with Prussianization. Böckel linked racial prejudice with appeals to the material interests of local people hurt by Prussian policy, chronic economic difficulties, capitalist penetration, and urbanization. Urging potential constituents to free themselves "from the Jewish middle man," Böckel endorsed an anti-Semitism oriented toward social and economic issues. This was compatible with but also different from the more ideological or cultural anti-Semitism of university students and the city-dwelling bourgeoisie, who constructed fine arguments to legitimize doctrines of racial inferiority but paid little attention to the material interests of nonelite groups.[60]

Böckel anchored his movement in local life by building special interest associations and social clubs. The Central German Peasants' Association (Mitteldeutscher Bauernverein), formed after Böckel's first electoral victory, boasted 15,000 members. It offered members twice-weekly editions of the Reichsherold, Böckel's personal newspaper, as well as cheap insurance schemes, expert agricultural information, and arbitration services. Böckel also revived versions of medieval "Jew-free" markets in Lang-Göns, Rheinheim, Gemünden a. d. Mohra, and elsewhere. Youth groups and other social clubs provided sociability and indoctrination. Böckel's motto was "Against Junker and Jew," a phrase he concretized in his support of the small-town *Mittelstand* and peasants against Prussia, big-city capital, large landowners, lavish military expenditures, disadvantageous credit arrangements, and restrictions on voluntary organization and assembly. Notwithstanding Böckel's racial prejudice, Hellmut von Gerlach was correct in referring to him as a "thoroughly democratic anti-Semite." This separated Böckel from the Hessian Nazi movement, which later incorporated specific parts of the Böckelian heritage.[61]

No political contender held the Marburg Reichstag seat without competition. The Social Democrats were among Böckel's bitterest opponents in the Marburg hinterland, even though their electoral gains were higher in the city than in the Wahlkreis. In contrast to their national leaders, who patiently awaited proletarianization of the peasants and lower middle classes, Marburg Social Democrats made an active effort to address the interests of country and small-town groups. They realized that in agricultural north Hesse there was little to be gained from ignoring the *Mittelstand*, farmers, or rural laborers. Social Democratic organizers and agitators confronted anti-Semitic competitors throughout the countryside, a strategy more effective in districts of non-Prussian Hesse such as Giessen–Grünberg–Nidda, where after 1887 the SPD vote total increased steadily. Philipp Scheidemann, a printer in Marburg and a leading figure of the Social Democratic party there, wrote that he became a nuisance to Hessian anti-Semites, who expected to have a row with socialists on the hustings. But socialist agitation remained on the margins of the rural polity in the Marburg area. In 1893, for instance, the Social Democrats rarely held their own campaign assemblies, attending instead speeches by the Progressive party candidate and Böckel in order to debate campaign issues. Social Democrats received less than 10 percent of the total district vote in every Reichstag election after 1887 except in 1903.[62]

Böckel was hampered even more by government, local bourgeois organizations, and his own incompetence. Government agents enrolled the support of local tavern owners in an effort to keep Böckel from holding assemblies and prohibited demonstrations once they had begun. More indirectly, by encouraging agricultural cooperatives, the government competed with the anti-Semites in appealing to farmers' material concerns. Named after Friedrich Wilhelm Raiffeisen, the organizer of a national agricultural cooperative movement, Raiffeisen cooperatives appeared in the Kurhessian region in the 1880s, and in 1888 a Raiffeisen cooperative was founded in Marburg County. It listed 2,256 members in 1895. Organizations such as the Association to Combat Anti-Semitism, led in 1890 by Professor Edmund Stengel, Böckel's former teacher, also counterbalanced the spread of anti-Semitism. Furthermore, Böckel incurred the disfavor of his supporters by refusing to ally with other anti-Semitic parties, fathering an illegitimate child, and importing what country people saw as "alien" Prussian administrators for his Hessian anti-Semitic movement. Though the votes of country people kept him in the Reichstag until 1903, Böckel lost his leadership over the Mitteldeutscher Bauernverein (later, Hessischer Bauernbund) by 1894.[63]

Most important for the present analysis is the legacy of Böckel's activity. Anti-Semites altered the repertoire of Hessian politics by relying more than previous parties on popular rituals and hectic campaigning. In contrast to liberal and conservative candidates, Böckel engineered campaign tours that featured speeches at local taverns or atop makeshift platforms at county fairs. He employed marching bands and torchlight processions in which participants sang Lutheran hymns and patriotic songs. Böckel's wagon was usually guarded by mounted youths, while others, each wearing a single blue cornflower, walked behind. Hoisting their children to see the Marburg librarian pass, mothers reportedly cried, "Look at that man, that's our savior!"[64]

Although Böckel imported Prussian administrators and tried to give the Bauernverein a central German rather than narrowly Hessian focus, his movement was obviously influenced by Hessian folk traditions. Indeed, Böckel's campaigns appear regional and primitive when compared to later Nazi activity. Conversely, Hessian anti-Semitism developed an activist political style directed against both bourgeois and Social Democratic parties, and to this extent the movement was part of a larger family tree in Reich politics that eventually produced the Nazi party. Still, Böckelian agitation was not uniformly prototypical of NSDAP activity, as chapter 5 will demonstrate.

Scholars too often assume that imagery and theater gradually displaced rational discourse in Germany's popular anti-Semitic movements of the late nineteenth century. But the new style is best described as a combination of mass symbolism and an appeal to sectional interests. Obviously, taking electoral campaigns to the hustings and injecting politics with emotional fervor created opportunities for imagery and symbolism. But observers claimed that anti-Semitic candidates' speeches were "objective" and evenhanded. Hellmut von Gerlach, who gained experience dealing with Hessian country people in local Reichstag contests, noted that one had to address farmers, not simply shout at them. Audiences were aware of their interests and were not likely to be swayed by panic and outbursts of emotion. Open appeals to special interests coexisted with the rise of symbolic form in German mass politics, making people more aware of what they were seeing and hearing on the political stage. More than thirty years later, Nazi agitators working in Marburg and the towns of the hinterland would remark on the rationality of the people they addressed.[65]

Böckel's original program rejected the party system of the Second Empire. In 1887 Böckel lashed out against "party and fraction haggling," which he identified as "Germany's greatest misfortune." "Conservative, ultramontane, liberal, progressive, all these parties must depart the scene," he insisted; all of them worked only for their "egotistical goals." In their place, Böckel envisioned a "true people's party of the middle and lower strata" (*Mittelstands- und Volkspartei*). Shared by other anti-Semites, these ideas were variations on well-known antipathies toward existing party cleavages. Böckel's supporters rejected the class basis of German politics, arguing that the "worker question" and "peasant question" were inseparable. Otto Kirchel predicted in 1891 that German politics would be reshaped into two camps, one represented by an "anti-Semitic German national people's party" and the other by "social democracy, without a fatherland and allied with international Jewry."[66]

Böckel and his followers identified "the" *Mittelstand* as a coherent socioeconomic constituency, although they never bothered to define the term. But anti-Semitic agitators also attributed coherent sectional interests to "the people" (*Volk*). A traditional theme of anti-Semitic thought, this notion was endorsed through Böckel's frenetic campaign style. The *Volk* rather than specific classes, strata, or occupational subgroups came to challenge elites and government in the political marketplace. In the ideology of Böckel and his allies, the people were more than an object of policy; they were autonomous, critical political actors capable of altering power relationships. Insofar as Böckel used such notions, he can be considered to have been the leader of a populist movement. The evidence does not conclusively indicate whether Böckel achieved a broader populist constituency. But his agitators, who usually consisted of university students and respectable (though not notable) Marburgers, reinforced the image of his wide social appeal by operating in more venues—university, city, small town, village, and countryside—than were traditionally covered by local notables at election time.[67]

The general impulse of Böckelian populism was therefore to mobilize a syncretic following that rejected the legitimacy of all existing parties. This was a popular, specifically local refinement of a national trend toward disengagement from the Reich party universe. More than an agrarian protest movement headed by a "peasant king," Hessian political anti-Semitism contained the *idea* of a broad populist constituency divorced from the national party system. If disengagement were to lead to a new mass party, the latter would have to be different from the Social Democratic party. The socialist movement represented a class, whereas the anti-Semitic party would rely on the *Volk*. Given the available models, this party of the people would necessarily be an anti-party. It would reject all previous party cleavages, save that between the Social Democrats and a broader antisocialist community of sentiment.

The Böckel movement was too regional and disorganized to be likened to other challengers to the party system, such as nationalist associations, the Fatherland party, and the NSDAP. But without Böckel there would have been less potential for popular backing of these groups in Marburg and the hinterland. The eventual flagging of Böckel's critical initiatives, the growing cooperation between populist anti-Semites and the Agrarian League, and the clumsiness with which anti-Semites represented themselves locally and nationally should not obscure the significant impact that Böckel had on local political culture. However, to reiterate the important point, one should be equally wary of thinking of Böckel as a direct ancestor of Marburg's later nationalist groups.

Political anti-Semitism was also a stronger solvent of bourgeois politics locally than was the Social Democratic party. Böckelian politics widened existing disparities between countryside and city. In contrast to voting patterns in pre-1887 elections, electoral participation in the countryside after Böckel's first victory exceeded that in the city for the remainder of the Empire. Virtually ignored by Marburg liberal and conservative politicians in Reichstag campaigns, the small towns and countryside of the region were now exposed to "every conceivable electoral publication," as an 1893 police report on the Reichstag campaign in the district suggested.

Relying on National Liberal and conservative support in the Marburg hinterland, the Agrarian League promoted the new electoral style and undoubtedly encouraged greater voting participation in the district. Indeed, the league appeared to have cornered populist support in the countryside in 1904 by gaining an alliance with the Bauernbund. The Bund refused to become an adjunct of the league,[68] but Agrarian League activity pointed up a substantial adaptation to mass politics in the hinterland.

In 1903 Hellmut von Gerlach, once a supporter of the anti-Semitic Adolf Stöcker, became the only candidate of Friedrich Nauann's left liberal National Social party (Nationalsozialer Verein) to win a Reichstag seat when Böckel decided not to run. Though National Socials tried to unify conservatives, socialists, and liberals in a national party, von Gerlach's activity disengaged voters from bourgeois parties locally. Von Gerlach wrote in 1898 that his party "was equally divorced from Social Democracy on the one side and the *bürgerlich* parties on the other." After running unsuccessfully for the Reichstag in 1898, von Gerlach moved to Marburg, promoted civic associations (*Bürgervereine*) designed to increase his support in Hessian towns and villages, and in 1903 tailored a coalition of Social Democratic, anti-Semitic, and Catholic votes to win a Reichstag seat. His campaign used populist electoral techniques to disassemble party loyalties and recast them in new configurations. As the National Social candidate in the 1903 runoff elections, he won 66.5 percent of the vote in the city and 56.2 percent in the rest of the district. Thereafter, von Gerlach continued to do well in Reichstag contests in the city, gaining more than 60 percent of the vote in 1907 and 1912 runoffs but losing to right-wing candidates in the district.[69]

There were still other avenues of grass roots disengagement. In the three decades before World War I, Marburg earned a reputation as a "national city" because of its patriotic societies. There were branches of the Pan-German League, General German School Association, German Association, Colonial Society, Women's Colonial Society, Navy Association, Society for the Eastern Marshes, German Language Association, and Society for Germandom Abroad. The nationalist local historian Kürschner noted that patriotic associations appeared because of townspeople's loss of "secure faith in the political leadership of the nation" and opposition to "material istic international Marxism and materialistic liberal capitalist thinking."[70] The nationalist associations were political outlets for local elites who either despaired of the established parties or were entering political life for the first time. They strengthened a growing asymmetry between parties and social organizations in the local sphere. Though the patriotic *Verbände* gained some support from Marburg students before World War I, they never reached deeply into grass roots social life.[71]

After 1887 no member of the National Liberal, Free Conservative, or Conservative parties won the Marburg Reichstag seat. After Böckel and Hellmut von Gerlach, Karl Böhme occupied the Reichstag post in 1907 and Johann Heinrich Rupp in 1912. Böhme and Rupp were members of the anti-Semitic German Social party, which since 1907 belonged to the Economic Alliance, a Reichstag faction that, besides the German Socials, included the Agrarian League and the Christian Social party. Government officials were alarmed that Reichstag campaigns caused a "considerable fragmentation" of the party political scene in the electoral district. Unlike in Tübingen, where the left liberal and populist Friedrich Payer held power, in Marburg Reichstag politics were volatile and unsettled. Von Gerlach commented in 1896 that the Marburg district was a political no-man's-land; but this judgment applied to the Marburg polity during the entire time from Böckel to World War I.[72]

Throughout these changes, the National Liberal party was the biggest loser among nonsocialist parties in Marburg. This was an era of declining National Liberal strength in the city, just as it was in the Reich. The last time a National Liberal candidate won the Marburg Reichstag seat was 1874. In the ensuing elections, Free Conservative and Conservative politicians won the seat, often with National Liberal help. Starting in 1887, the National Liberals ran their own candidates in Reichstag elections only twice, gaining 21 percent of the city vote in 1893 and 22.2 percent in 1907, with 5.8 percent in the district in both years. The city percentages were well above the party's national average of 13 in 1893 and 14.5 in 1907. But in neither year did the National Liberal candidate enter runoff elections. In 1893 a Conservative candidate was defeated by Böckel in the runoff, and in 1907 the National Liberals were absorbed into a right-wing coalition that elected the German Social, Dr. Karl Böhme. The National Liberal party had become an adjunct to a broader right-wing coalition that elected German Social party and Economic Alliance candidates in 1907 and 1912.[73]

Conservative decline was less drastic. The Conservative party ran candidates in every election after 1881 except in 1890, 1907, and 1912; its candidates gained more than 40 percent of the vote in 1883 and 1887 and averaged more than 30 percent for the whole period. The Conservatives would have a persistent hold on part of the city electorate in the Republic also: in bitter 1932–33 Reichstag campaigns the German National People's party gained more support than either liberal party despite National Socialist gains. But by the last two elections of the Second Empire, the Conservatives were part of a right-wing coalition endorsing other candidates, just as the National Liberals were.[74]

The National Liberal party possessed a narrower social base than its bourgeois competitors, being more dependent on town elites than any other party (see table 2-2).[75] In 1908 and 1913 more than half (51.1 percent) of the party's 90 Landtag electors, individuals involved in the selection of candidates for state parliament, were from the elite, with 14 university professors making up the largest single elite group. Self-employed artisans and retailers (31.3 percent), nonelite employees (8.8 percent), and pensioners (8.8 percent) made up the other electors, whereas workers were absent. The social profile of other nonsocialist parties was more balanced. Of fifty-two Conservative party members, nineteen (36.5 percent) were part of Marburg's elite, though only two were professors. But the party also possessed a strong lower-middle-class character, having among its members twelve self-employed artisans and retailers and thirteen individuals from the employed bourgeoisie. Another eight Conservatives were miscellaneous pensioners. The 1906 National Social Association also drew significantly higher shares of lower-middle-class people than did National Liberals. Additionally, the National Socials had a small minority of working-class members. In 1908 the left liberal party had a considerable following from nonelite groups also; seventeen of its eighteen electors in 1908 were nonelite *Bürger*, and the remaining individual was a worker.

Yet the Marburg National Liberal party did change. The 1907 campaign of Friedrich Siebert illustrates how one important National Liberal notable accommodated himself to mass political mobilization. A retired assistant mayor and apothecary whose political career stretched back to 1872, Siebert was seventy-six years old in 1907. His supporters came from the local bourgeoisie. Of 146 signatories listed on a 1907 campaign handout, 26.1 percent were professors and 21.9 percent merchants. The rest were civil servants, craft masters, free professionals, and bankers and manufacturers.[76]

Siebert said he would represent the Marburg electoral district in a "strictly national sense and on the basis . . . of a moderate liberalism that politically sober conservatives could also support." He said he was a man of the middle who supported colonies, agriculture, higher wages for civil servants, and favorable legislation for small and middling artisans and retailers. But he saved his most passionate language for criticism of the new electoral style and the "clerical–social democratic Reichstag majority." He derided national politics, where "big parties were dominant." A campaign flyer dated 1 January 1907 claimed that Siebert's "name is a program; his life and work speak more eloquently for him than all excesses that public elections so freely pour out." In another handout Siebert promised that he would not assail voters by going "from village to village, in order to compete for votes." Instead his campaign would consist of "simple words, averted from all party wrangling [*Parteigezänke*]."[77]

Siebert's critique reflected personalistic traditions of local politics in which one's name was indeed one's program. But it also revealed that liberals could no longer stand by while the big national parties dominated the Reichstag. Instead they would emphasize bourgeois traditions by incorporating specific aspects of the new style. Siebert pledged not to campaign, but through his handouts he appealed to sectional interests and broader nationalist sympathies divorced from party strife, just as rabble-rousing anti-Semitic agitators did.[78] Marburg city notables were adapting to the new political era, extending older traditions into the widening political marketplace.

Yet Siebert's comments reflect an unusually strong antipathy to national politics. Such antipathy remained attractive to National Liberals and other nonsocialist candidates because of specific conditions in Marburg politics. For many liberal or conservative party leaders, disengagement from the national scene rested on party hegemony at home. This was not the case in Marburg, where no single *bürgerlich* party established and maintained hegemony in Reichstag politics after 1887. Apoliticism—in the form of active criticism of mass parties in favor of traditional, personalistic politics that was nevertheless expressed in modern forms of agitation— thus became an even more useful way of making sense of political life and of rationalizing political action. Exceptional political disarray in the Hessian town heightened the appeal of antiparty traditions; Marburg's peculiarities exaggerated a national tendency.

Institutional factors buttressed local apoliticism. It has already been noted that there were limitations on municipal suffrage before 1918. The Social Democrats did not run candidates for city parliament in Marburg in the third class of voters until 1906. In the lower house (Abgeordnetenhaus) of the Prussian Landtag, meanwhile, the

Table 2-2 *Occupations of Members of Five Political Parties in Marburg, 1906, 1908, and 1913*

Stratum	Subgroup	NL	Lib	C	SPD	NS
Elite						
	Professors	14	0	2	0	4
	Free professionals	9	0	2	1	1
	Clergy	0	0	0	0	0
	Entrepreneurs	7	0	4	0	0
	Civil servants	8	0	4	0	2
	Women without professions	0	0	0	0	0
	Military officers (including retired)	0	0	4	0	0
	Pensioners	0	0	1	0	1
	High school teachers	8	0	1	0	0
	Others[a]	0	0	1	0	3
	Subtotal	46	0	19	1	11
Nonelite independents						
	Craftsmen	10	9	5	0	7
	Retailers, innkeepers	18	1	6	3	16
	Gardeners	0	0	1	0	0
	Subtotal	28	10	12	3	23
Nonelite employees[b]						
	White-collar	7	6	12	0	9
	Civil servants	0	0	0	0	5
	Teachers	1	1	1	0	2
	Subtotal	8	7	13	0	16

three-class system also retarded the growth of opposition parties. Conservatives enjoyed an impressive hegemony over Landtag politics in Marburg, retaining the Marburg seat by themselves from 1879 to 1894 and in 1903, and keeping it with Agrarian League help in 1898 and 1908. Professor Viktor Bredt, a moderate Free Conservative, won the Landtag seat in 1911 and 1913, gaining National Liberal support in the process. Additionally, National Liberals took heart from knowing that their colleagues Professors Reinhold Pauli, August Ubbelohde, and Ernst Küster served as university representatives to the Prussian upper house (Herrenhaus) from 1866 to 1918.[79]

One reservoir of apoliticism was more fundamental than others

Table 2-2 continued

Stratum	Subgroup	NL	Lib	C	SPD	NS
Workers						
	Craft, skilled[c]	0	1	0	104	6
	Unskilled	0	0	0	6	2
	Subtotal	0	1	0	110	8
Nonelite Berufslosen						
	Retired	8	0	8	0	0
	No occupation	0	0	0	0	0
	Subtotal	8	0	8	0	0
Total numbers		90	18	52	114	58

KEY:
NL = National Liberals, 1908 and 1913
Lib = Left Liberals, 1908
C = Conservatives, 1908 and 1913
SPD = Social Democratic party, 1906
NS = National Social Association, 1906

a. For C: 1 estate owner; for NS: 3 students.
b. Civil servants and white-collar counted together for NL, Lib., and C.
c. Skilled and unskilled counted together for Lib.
SOURCES: see n. 75, this chapter.

to everyday relationships. This was the complex, changing organizational life of the city. Whereas patriotic associations or the Agrarian League counterbalanced the political weaknesses of liberal or conservative parties nationally, veterans', gymnasts', and singers' clubs performed this role locally. Though increasingly self-absorbed, social organizations provided a crucial political service for the local bourgeoisie. Nonstudent clubs as well as student Vereine absorbed and channeled party conflict after about 1880. They did so partly by emphasizing commitment to a general public good, supposedly unsullied by party rancor. Because this muffling effect strengthened bourgeois moral authority in social organizations, it made full party reorganization less urgent. Here apoliticism assumed a different form, more diffuse than Siebert's direct attack on mass parties, more reliant on unspoken resentments and common sense. Because party politics offered no reliable anchor for bourgeois social authority, the political functions of nonparty organizations assumed added significance in Marburg, as we shall see.[80]

Local apoliticism, whether manifested in Siebert's critique or in the burying of party rancor in the customs of daily social interchange, rested on an asymmetry between strong social organizations and weak parties. During most of the Second Empire, the state provided insurance for such power arrangements. However, once state power eroded, once political conflict intensified, and once local government was exposed to the uncertainties of universal suffrage the tensions of asymmetry became more pronounced.

Although economic and social stress mounted in Marburg from the beginning of the Kaiser's wartime truce, the peace resolution of 1917 touched off a new era of local political conflict. On 19 July 1917 a Reichstag majority passed a resolution that reaffirmed Germany's peaceful aims in the war and renewed the Kaiser's claim of August 1914 that the Reich was "not driven by a desire for conquest." Marburg notables debated the issue when the district Reichstag representative, Economic Alliance deputy Johann Heinrich Rupp, voted in favor of the majority resolution along with eleven Deutsche Fraktion colleagues. The Fraktion, which consisted of Economic Alliance representatives, some Free Conservatives, anti-Semites, and regionalists, announced that it wanted "to save Europe from further useless sacrifices." But the Fraktion also wanted to save itself from parliamentary impotence.[81]

The response from Rupp's supporters in the 1912 runoff elections—German and Free Conservatives, National Liberals, members of the Agrarian League, and German Socials—was swift and critical. The estate owner Klingelhöfer of Brückerhof, who chaired the county Agrarian League, criticized Rupp in local newspapers. The *Oberhessische* supported the Reichstag representative's critics, though it allowed Rupp to plead his case in the 27 August 1917 edition. Noting that Rupp now appeared to have aligned himself with Social Democrats and others "with whom he once wanted nothing to do," the *Oberhessische* stated that Rupp's voters did not share his support of the resolution.[82] The debate illustrated the contentious relationship between local notables and their Reichstag representative.

Supported by local notables, the Fatherland party was a response to the peace resolution. The *Oberhessische* gave prominent coverage to the founding of the DVLP in Berlin in September 1917. In early October in the Kaiserhof Inn prominent members of the Conservative, National Liberal, and German-Völkisch (Deutschvölkische) parties announced the organization of a Marburg DVLP branch. These people included Professors Viktor Bredt, Wilhelm

Busch, Walter Hassenpflug, and Hubo along with businessmen Schaefer, Gottlieb Braun, Piscator, and Stumpf. Stating in December that the party's goal was to achieve "a powerful movement against the Reichstag majority decision" and secure "peace through power, not violent politics," organizers wanted to mobilize townspeople for a peace of conquest. Party leaders encouraged people to register for membership at the headquarters of local parties or at select local shops—Elwert bookstore, Schwan and Trauben apothecary, the photographer Mauss's establishment, or the saddlemaker Heusser's business.[83]

Although national membership figures were inflated by corporate enrollment, evidence for Marburg suggests that the party attracted a large group of townsfolk. In November 1917 the Marburg DVLP claimed to have over 500 members; in the first half of 1918 it held more assemblies than any other political party in the city. The *Oberhessische* reported on 12 February 1918 that the DVLP student group attracted considerable interest, particularly from students serving in the field in World War I. The DVLP student group had 58 members, making it one of the largest student organizations in the city and the largest political group at the university.[84]

Was the DVLP "protofascist," as some scholars have argued?[85] The question is crucial for understanding the continuities and discontinuities of local political life. Claiming to appeal to those "who without party prejudice and selfish interests want to promote the prosperous future of Germany and all its citizens,"[86] the DVLP reiterated older themes of elite representation of general interests divorced from party intrigues and sectional divisions. Of course the DVLP message implied support for the economic interests of peasants, artisans, retailers, and even workers who supported the national cause. But the party's stated indifference to internal politics and concern for the general interest were functions of its opposition to all political reform, its support for the Kaiser, and its belief in the Bismarckian balance of power. The DVLP shrank from sustained political mobilization of nonelite as well as elite groups beyond the temporary crisis of wartime; its leaders resisted a permanent linking of social and political life on a mass basis. This made the DVLP program very different from national socialism. Though Nazi agitators used arguments superficially compatible with DVLP ideology, they tried to fuse social and political spheres in a national "folk community." It is essential not to obscure this difference between the Fatherland party and the NSDAP.

An important effect of DVLP activity was the deepening of political conflict among local elites. Students of the dueling fraternities disagreed as to whether they should join the quasi-political Student Lodge or the Fatherland party. The conflict also generated debate between fraternity alumni and their younger brothers. In a December 1917 assembly in Marburg, Reichstag deputy Julius Kopsch of the Progressive People's party characterized DVLP members as "Pan-Germans," a remark that drew an instant and critical response from the conservative *Oberhessische*. Opposition to the DVLP also spurred a counterorganization, the small People's League for Freedom and Fatherland (Volksbund für Freiheit und Vaterland). Led by liberal university professors Martin Rade, Walther Schücking, and Rudolf Otto, the organization called for a peace of negotiation and internal political reforms. Members of the VFV and supporters of the "moderate and left parties" in the city kept alive the issue of Prussian electoral reform and other social and economic concerns, problems the DVLP refused to discuss. But the VFV's national leadership remained ambiguous about German war aims, especially after the peace of Brest-Litovsk, and uneasy about the actions of Social Democratic workers within their organization. While causing debate among elites, the VFV also revealed disagreements in the coalition of moderate opponents of direct annexation. Elite conflict weakened the "infrastructure" (*innere Gefüge*) of established political parties, as one Center party opponent of the DVLP noted.[87]

Social Democrats appeared to assume state control in 1918. But signs of the new order in Marburg were superficial. The Workers' and Soldiers' Council occupied the Rathaus on the night of 10–11 November 1918. Council members placed a machine gun in the fountain overlooking the marketplace, and a small red flag found its way to the Rathaus steeple. Producing bad will but little violence, the Republic seemed to creep into Marburg, barely altering social life.[88]

In view of the Republic's uninspiring entrance into Marburg history, it is not surprising that Weimar Coalition successes in 1919 National Assembly elections were less substantial locally than nationally. The local Coalition (Social Democrats, Catholics, and Democrats) gained 59.4 percent of the vote, nearly 17 percentage points below the national average (see table 2-3). The Marburg Center and Social Democratic parties received below-average proportions of local votes. But the DDP—inheriting votes from prewar liberal, National Social, and some populist anti-Semitic groups—received 31.2 percent.[89] This exceeded the party's national share by almost 13 percentage points and made of the DDP the linchpin of the local coalition.

The Democratic party gave the Weimar Coalition an inroad into elite and nonelite bourgeois networks. Hermann Bauer, who in 1925 became publisher of the left liberal *Hessisches Tageblatt*, joined the party. Additionally, the liberal theologian Rudolf Otto, former university chancellor Walter Troeltsch, and left liberal Martin Rade, husband of Friedrich Naumann's sister, entered the DDP. Other elite members of the party included the dentist Heinrich Corell, who in 1921 became chair of a respected sports club, the Athletic Association 05 (Verein für Bewegungsspiele 05). DDP membership in early 1919 came largely from self-employed artisans and storeowners, though there were also elites, teachers, white-collar employees, and officials (see table 2-5).[90]

But Democratic party success was shortlived, and right-wing liberal and conservative forces soon recaptured some of the ground they had lost in National Assembly elections. In the June 1920 elections 29.9 percent of the vote went to the German People's party and 31.1 percent to the German National People's party. With 61 percent of the vote, the right-wing liberal and conservative parties in the city turned back the electoral successes that Weimar Coalition parties had gained eighteen months before. The latter parties' combined vote total was just 27.7 percent in 1920, a result of deep losses by the SPD to the Independent Social Democratic party and by the DDP to the USPD, DVP, and DNVP.[91]

Instead of having stabilized the political sphere with their victories, the DNVP and DVP added a new tone of vituperation to campaign debates preceding the June 1920 elections. The DNVP announced in a flashy advertisement in the *Oberhessische* that the DDP was an "appendage" of social democracy. Competing with the Democrats and German Nationals for the farm vote, the DVP attacked both parties. Its 3 June 1920 advertisement claimed that the DDP, a "representative of finance capital," had "given Jews a leading position in its ranks." Moreover, the DVP said, the Democrats were "hostile to peasants and were representatives of consumer interests." As for the DNVP, the DVP characterized it as the "successor of the old conservative parties that . . . carry responsibility for the unfortunate course of the war." The DDP was not above using insults and anti-Semitism. In responding to DVP charges of being representatives of finance capital, the Democratic party noted that the leading DVP candidate was "the Jew Rießer," a reference made

Table 2-3 Reichstag Voting (by Percentage) for Major Parties in Marburg, 1919–1933[a]

	KPD	USPD	SPD	DDP	Z	DVP	WP	CSV	KVP	DNVP	V-NS
1919		2.7	21.5	31.2	6.7	17.8				20.1	
1920	0.4	10.9	7.9	14.0	5.8	29.9				31.1	
1924(1)	6.1		7.9	8.6	6.1	15.1	5.6			30.3	17.7
1924(2)	4.5		13.9	11.2	6.6	18.1	5.3			33.1	6.2
1928	2.5		15.7	8.7	6.1	24.0	7.3	6.1		25.0	5.6
1930	5.3		14.7	7.3	5.8	10.7	4.1	1.6	4.7	11.1	28.8
1932(1)	5.5		16.2	1.3	6.5	3.4	0.2	1.8		11.6	53.3
1932(2)	8.0		13.3	1.2	6.1	4.8	0.2	1.9		15.0	49.2
1933	4.7		13.5	1.3	5.8	3.6				11.1	57.4

KEY:

KPD = Communist party

USPD = Independent Social Democratic party

SPD = Social Democratic party

DDP = Democratic party (DDP) up to 1930, thereafter State party

Z = Catholic Center party

DVP = German People's party

WP = Economic party, Reich party of the German Mittelstand

CSV = Christian Social People's Service

KVP = Conservative People's party

DNVP = German National People's party; Kampffront Schwarz-Weiß-Rot (1933)

V-NS = VSB (1924, 1 and 2); National Socialist party thereafter

a. Blank spaces indicate that the party did not run.

SOURCE: Computations based on Neusüß-Hunkel, Parteien und Wahlen, p. 35.

in block letters to the head of the prestigious Darmstädter Bank, Jakob Rießer. The DNVP was not to be outdone. In a subsequent advertisement the German Nationals pointedly asked Hessian farmers if they were aware "that the German People's party ticket is headed by the Jew Rießer." The DNVP said that "thousands of Democrats" had left the DDP and gained influence in the DVP, where democratic ideals were now certain to be influential. "So vote for the only party," the advertisement continued, "that opposes the Jews, the German National People's Party!" This vitriolic campaign rhetoric revealed how deeply anti-Semitism had penetrated daily political discourse in Marburg. Moreover, it manifested the growing contentiousness of local bourgeois parties at a time when nonparty organizations were restoring social calm in the city.[92]

The May 1924 Reichstag election produced a sharp electoral turn in Marburg, just as it did in the Reich. The DDP vote fell below the 10 percent mark, a hurdle it surmounted only once more in the Republic. The DVP vote total shrank from 29.9 percent in 1920 to 15.1 percent in the May election. Though the party recovered more effectively than did the DDP in the second 1924 and in the 1928 elections, its vote would decline precipitously from 1930 to 1933. Additionally, splinter parties began to make a showing in local Reichstag voting; the Economic party, for example, which was organized mainly by the local Property Owners' and Landlords' Association, gained 5.6 percent of the vote in 1924.[93]

More ominous in May 1924 were the electoral gains of a Nazi-conservative coalition, the Völkisch-Sozialer Block. The VSB received 17.7 percent of all votes in Marburg, a share well above the NSDAP's national average of 6.5 percent and higher than the 17.1 percent achieved by the Bavarian VSB. In city parliament elections the VSB and the Greater German Folk Community (Großdeutsche Volksgemeinschaft), which was the wing of the Nazi party unwilling to ally with conservatives in the bloc, ran separate slates. The latter gained 358 votes (3.5 percent) and placed the railway porter Arthur Alt in the municipal parliament, while the VSB received 289 votes.[94]

Dissatisfaction with the hyperinflation, which had ended just months previously, worked to the advantage of the VSB. But if the hyperinflation had had a truly profound impact, voter turnout should have been higher. With 75.4 percent of all eligible townspeople voting, participation in May 1924 was only one-tenth of a percentage point higher than in June 1920 and a full percentage point lower than in National Assembly voting in 1919. Moreover, significant fluctuations in support for the bourgeois parties occurred before the 1924 elections, and DDP, DVP, and DNVP defectors were no doubt divided between the VSB and the Economic party that year.[95] The inflation may have caused this fluctuation to be speedier than it would have been otherwise, but it was not the sole factor behind VSB success. Rather, a number of factors—among them the decline of the Coalition, heated anti-Semitic rhetoric by right-wing liberals and conservatives, and hyperinflation and stabilization—worked together in the spring of 1924. That Nazi electoral success was the product of a temporary confluence of tensions was shown six months later, when the VSB and NSDAP quickly declined in the second 1924 Reichstag election at a time of relative economic and political calm.

Copying the national drama but wearing local costumes, municipal special interest coalitions made the most significant impact on Marburg electoral politics in May 1924. The appearance of the coalitions was, once again, the result of a combination of elements—the introduction of universal suffrage in city elections, increased voting due to the holding of municipal and Reichstag elections on the same day, the direct impact of hardship caused by hyperinflation, and a continuation of activity by economic associations that had begun in the war. Formed in 1918, the local Civil Servants' Association ran its own slate in city elections a year later, gaining 16.6 percent of the vote. But in 1924, when participation in city elections was 20 percent higher than in 1919, special interest coalitions dominated the municipal vote. Three nonparty slates gained 54 percent of the vote, a percentage far higher than the average in municipal parliament elections in Prussia and higher than in any other city election in Marburg during the Republic (see table 2-4).[96]

The local special interest coalitions were hardly temporary aberrations. In November 1929, well before the worst effects of the Depression hit Marburg, special interest coalitions received 42.5 percent of the total municipal vote. This was almost four times the average for special interest slates in Prussian city elections. By 1933 a bewildering array of interest groups—civil servants, merchants, artisans, landlords and property owners, renters, white-collar employees, disabled war veterans and their dependents, land reformers, apartment hunters, restaurant and hotel operators, small investors, schoolteachers, and Lutheran women—had run slates for the city parliament. Yet 1924–29 was the crucial period for these

Table 2-4 *City Parliament Elections (by Voting Percentage) in Marburg, 1919–1933*[a]

	1919	1924	1929	1933
Parties				
DNVP[b]	39.3	15.9	13.2	10.2
DVP		6.1	10.7	2.0
DDP	23.9	3.9	4.4	
SPD	13.7	5.7	11.0	11.3
Catholic Center	6.5	3.8	5.5	5.4
KPD		4.2	2.0	3.5
Völkisch/NSDAP[c]		6.4	5.3	55.1
CSV			5.0	1.4
Special interest slates				
Civil Servants	16.6	11.6	7.3	
Working Alliance[d]		17.8	10.8	3.6
United Independents			7.5	2.3
Artisans and Businessmen			4.6	
Interest Alliance		24.6	12.4	2.2
Evangelical List				2.1
Women's List				0.9
Invalid votes[e]			0.3	
Total	100.0	100.0	100.0	100.0
Total votes	6,766	10,156	9,017	13,112

a. Blank spaces indicate that the party did not run.
b. With DVP in 1919; in 1933, Kampffront Schwarz-Weiß-Rot.
c. VSB and GVG vote combined in 1924.
d. Working Alliance of Economic Associations (1924); Bourgeois Working Alliance (1929, 1933).
e. OZ did not report invalid votes in 1919 and 1933 and reported that no invalid votes were cast in 1924.
SOURCE: Computations based on *OZ* 3 March 1919, 5 May 1924, 18 November 1929, and 13 March 1933.

groups: in 1933 they received less than 12 percent of the municipal vote.[97]

With nearly one-quarter of all votes in the 1924 town elections, the Interest Alliance was the most successful municipal ticket. Running candidates for city parliament seats in 1924 and 1929, it consisted of representatives of the Renters' Association, Organization of Disabled Veterans and Dependents, League of Land Reformers, League of Apartment and House Hunters, Pensioners' Association, Trade Union of White-Collar Workers (Gewerkschaftsbund der Angestellten), and League of Big Families. Appealing to "workers, civil servants, white-collar workers, and independents," the alliance stressed mainly consumer interests. Its candidates called for "maintenance of renters' protection, fair taxation of property and income, taxation of rents to be used exclusively for the construction of new housing, housing settlements for disadvantaged groups, more single-family housing, legally regulated rents, social 'living right', fair treatment of disabled veterans and programs for their occupational rehabilitation, the attraction of industry [to Marburg] and the consequent eradication of unemployment, [and] sound social conditions." Significantly, despite the fact that retirees were among its target constituencies, the alliance chose not to appeal overwhelmingly to this group, but nested retirees' interests in a wider field of demands. Nonetheless, most Interest Alliance planks —fair rent, equitable taxation, just housing, and programs for the disabled—touched on some aspect of the lives of nonstudent *Berufslosen*.[98]

Other slates appealed to a similarly broad range of material interests. The 1924 Civil Servants' Association slate called for fair rent policies, measures to protect the poor and disabled, "sound progress in city management," and "promotion of all cultural and educational questions." Here the interests of local officials mixed with those of elderly pensioners and others. The Working Alliance of Economic Associations—including representatives from artisans', retailers', landlords', homeowners', restaurant and hotel operators', and small investors' associations—wanted to "struggle against overburdening taxation, which leads to the ruin of the enterprising *Mittelstand* and especially small business." In 1929 the United Independents claimed to be a more effective representative of small business and artisanry than major economic associations, political parties, and city government.[99]

The coalitions reflected the social vitality and activism of many different local organizations. Moreover, they were logical vehicles for pursuing sectional interests in local politics. Traditions of popular involvement in the municipal parliament had been weak, and the old "city hall parties" of notables were unable to harness popular loyalties in an age of universal suffrage. The special interest coalitions stepped in to fill this need, mobilizing many different groups and educating them in the practices of city politics.

It would be a mistake to see the interest alliances as local expressions of a larger trend toward the end of ideology. By expressing strong antipathies to parties in the local arena, the coalitions promoted a grass roots apoliticism that created ideological alternatives to mass parties in city affairs. This went beyond mere criticism of mass parties or fragmented and often unspoken disillusionment with politics. The leaders of most special interest associations stated in 1919 that municipal politics should be "depoliticized." The Renters' Association appealed to other groups in the Interest Alliance by saying it wanted to "avert party political goals." The slates' leaders promoted apoliticism by example: they were often former liberal or conservative party members. The leading candidate of the Interest Alliance in 1924 was the nursery owner Franz Thiele, who in 1919 had run for city parliament for the DDP. The leading official of the Working Alliance was the building contractor Wilhelm Münscher, a member of the combined DNVP-DVP slate in 1919. The head of the United Independents was former Democratic party member Heinrich Ilk.[100]

Special interest coalitions gained a wider following than did liberal and conservative parties. This is reflected in the social makeup of the slates (see table 2-5).[101] Elite groups could be found in smaller proportions in special interest coalitions than in bourgeois parties. But with more than 17 percent of all coalition candidates coming from Marburg elite circles, it is impossible to argue that elites found the alliances unattractive. Even more interesting was the occupational makeup of nonelite coalition candidates. Larger shares of self-employed artisans and retailers appeared in special interest coalitions than appeared in other parties, indicating that the alliances were especially important as vehicles for antiparty protests by these groups. Significantly, the coalitions also mobilized larger shares of working-class people and nonelite *Berufslosen* than liberal and conservative parties did. More than any party in the *bürgerlich* camp, the economic interest coalitions represented an accessible outlet for the political ambitions of local people. The slates were not, however, a single, coherent party. Until the energies they aroused were harnessed and focused, the slates left the local bourgeoisie more disengaged politically than ever before.

Liberal and conservative parties possessed resources to respond to splinter groups, the VSB, and special interest coalitions. Even though the Democrats lost much of the support they had gained in 1919, they still had a wide following of elites, independent craftsmen and retailers, and teachers and civil servants. But the party remained an exclusive circle of liberal notables championed by university professors Martin Rade, Heinrich Hermelink, and others. Theodora Perino, an active DDP and Schoolteachers' Association member, referred to her party as a "closely knit circle."[102] Though hardly inaccurate as a description of emotional and intellectual bonds that united the leading figures of the organization, the statement is also suggestive of DDP inaccessibility to most townspeople.

The DVP's situation was somewhat different. Having inherited the social space previously occupied by the conservative National Liberals, the DVP was the most elitist of all local parties. More than 45 percent of its nonstudent members came from local elites, with university professors and well-to-do entrepreneurs constituting more than half of this group. As the largest nonelite groups in Marburg, self-employed artisans, independent retailers, and civil servants were also potential constituencies for the DVP. But the party's daily organizational and financial operations were too haphazard to effect useful contacts with these constituencies, as the fluctuating electoral totals of the party throughout the Republic indicated. The DVP walked a perilous road; after being the largest vote-getter in the city in 1920, it declined to the point of having less than 4 percent of the total vote in the first 1932 Reichstag election. Less than one year later, after the NSDAP gained more than 55 percent of the Marburg vote in the first and last Reichstag election of the Third Reich, the business manager of the Lahn–Eder DVP in Marburg wrote his national headquarters that "we will never capture the masses, but we should show more concern for youth."[103] It had taken this long for party leaders to learn this limited lesson.

The DNVP fared better but it still sustained serious losses. The name of the party suggested a renewed attention to popular forces despite the leadership's refusal to support a democratic republic. The DNVP received 20.1 percent of the total vote in the 1919 elections, a share it increased to 33.1 percent in the second Reichstag elections of 1924. This gave it the largest vote total of any Marburg party in Reichstag elections before July 1932, when the NSDAP received 53.3 percent of the vote. Though the DNVP was identified with the town elite—university professors, city officials, military officers, Protestant pastors—it also gained a popular following within the *Mittelstand*, particularly among churchgoing, self-employed artisans and storekeepers who relied on Protestant clergy for political cues.[104] Nevertheless, the German Nationals could get only 11.1 percent of the vote in September 1930 and 15 percent in November 1932.

Bourgeois party dissolution was evident in the countryside also. The *Landrat* warned on 12 January 1928 that economic problems in the Hessian countryside—low profits, high production costs, expensive credit, labor shortages—required immediate government attention, so that "radical elements within the rural population do not get the upper hand and make farmers behave in an unreasonable or destructive way." Expressing the hinterland's disaffection with liberal and conservative parties, the Christian National Peasants' and Rural People's party (Christlich-Nationale Bauern- und Landvolkpartei), received nearly one-quarter of all county votes in the 1928 Reichstag elections. In 1930 the NSDAP would get more than one-third of the county vote. The lessons of the Second Empire (when Agrarian League, anti-Semitic, and populist agitators stressed agitation and organization rather than the "simple words" of town notables) had still not been accepted by Marburg liberal and conservative candidates. The latter were unable to organize effective rural agitation in the crucial last elections of the Republic.[105]

Traditional power relationships dissolved in Marburg student government, just as bourgeois constituencies splintered in the town. Corporation Committee students and the German University Ring (Hochschulring Deutscher Art), which championed a "people's community [*Volksgemeinschaft*] on the basis of German race," dominated student government (Allgemeiner Studentenausschuß) in the early Republic. This ensured continued power for pure fraternities—student associations that dueled and wore symbolic colors—and modified fraternities—which selectively adapted pure fraternity traditions—despite the minority status of both groups in the student body. Having served in the military, many students in the immediate postwar period were older and therefore more willing to stress cooperation than previous generations of students. But

Table 2-5 *Percentage Distribution of Occupations of Nonstudent Members for Selected Party Categories in Marburg, 1919–1933*

Stratum	Subgroup	Bourgeois	Worker	Special Interest
Elite				
	Professors	11.6	1.4	0.9
	Free professionals	7.1	0.0	4.9
	Clergy	0.0	0.0	0.0
	Entrepreneurs	5.8	0.0	2.7
	Civil servants	1.9	0.0	1.3
	Women without professions	4.5	0.0	4.9
	Military officers (including retired)	2.6	0.0	0.9
	Pensioners	0.6	0.0	2.2
	High school teachers	7.1	0.0	0.0
	Subtotal	41.2	1.4	17.8
Nonelite independents				
	Craftsmen	21.9	4.3	27.1
	Retailers	12.9	0.0	14.2
	Subtotal	34.8	4.3	41.3
Nonelite employees				
	White-collar	5.8	20.0	10.7
	Civil servants	6.5	7.2	15.1
	Teachers	6.5	1.4	3.1
	Subtotal	18.8	28.6	28.9

the departure of these students and a return of internecine tensions inherited from Wilhelmine times made the maintenance of harmony increasingly difficult.[106]

In 1927 students reorganized the Marburg AStA on a private basis after refusing to bow to the demand of Prussian Minister of Education Carl Heinrich Becker to end anti-Semitic Austrian and Sudeten student governments' memberships in the Deutsche Studentenschaft, the central organization of all local German student governments. But the new General Marburg Student Government

Table 2-5 *continued*

Stratum	Subgroup	Bourgeois	Worker	Special Interest
Workers				
	Craft, skilled	2.6	45.7	6.2
	Unskilled	0.0	17.1	0.4
	Subtotal	2.6	62.8	6.6
Nonelite *Berufslosen*				
	Retired	1.3	2.9	3.6
	No occupation	1.3	0.0	1.8
	Subtotal	2.6	2.9	5.4
Total		100.0	100.0	100.0
Total numbers		155	70	225
Percent women		16.1	7.1	11.1

KEY:
Bourgeois = DNVP, DVP, DDP, Staatspartei
Worker = SPD, USPD, KPD
Special Interest = seven special interest coalitions in city parliament elections, 1919–33.

SOURCES: *MEB*, 1913, 1920, 1925, 1930, 1934/35; *OZ* 25 and 28 February, 2 and 3 March 1919, 26 April 1924, 9 November 1929, 2 March 1933; lists of *Wahlvorstände*, in HSAM 330, Mbg C, 2676–2678.

(Allgemeine Marburger Studentenschaft) did little to foster student solidarity. Critics charged that the AMSt, by organizing an "unpolitical" system of proportionate representation in student government and disallowing open elections, reflected the interests of fraternities rather than the general student body. Other critics attacked the German University Ring, saying it was an empty special interest organization that, like the liberal and conservative parties, had lost its educative functions and concern for general political reform. AMSt leaders and university professors finally gave in to a popular cry for elections, hoping that this would put student government on more solid ground. But the Nazi Student League— both cause and effect of "a greater interest in politics" among university students in the late 1920s—gained 49.6 percent of the vote when elections were held on 8 July 1931 and more than 50 percent of the vote the following summer. This was hardly the stabilizing force many students and instructors had wanted.[107]

Relying on numerous local social organizations and institutions, the urban bourgeoisie refused to give liberal and conservative parties the same power that Social Democratic and Center parties enjoyed in their constituencies. Apoliticism—expressed in personalistic traditions of local politics, in an unspoken and commonsensical distaste for mass parties, or in attempts to devise local alternatives to national parties—rationalized and gave meaning to this political choice. The Marburg bourgeoisie responded to political conflict in much the same way as other bourgeois groups. Yet unlike some of those groups, the Marburg *Bürgertum* was unable to establish stable party rule. In Reichstag voting the city was a no-man's-land in which populist and social liberal challengers exchanged blows with shifting alliances of National Liberal, conservative, and anti-Semitic groups. In city politics after 1918, economic interest alliances weakened liberal and conservative influence. Extraordinary political instability made apoliticism uncommonly practical and appealing for the Marburg bourgeoisie. It also increased the importance of social organizations in the local polity.

Insofar as nonparty groups played an important role in national politics for the local *Bürgertum*, Marburg again reproduced a general pattern in the Reich by giving so much political influence to social organizations. Still, local social clubs and associations were indeed different from large-scale, national pressure groups and patriotic societies: they were more demanding of members' time and loyalties and more deeply nested in everyday social relationships. They thus presented richer possibilities for mass political involvement by encompassing so much of the daily lives of their members. Though functional in the sense that it counterbalanced the evolution of mass parties, the local asymmetry between social and political organizations also contained hidden dangers for town elites, for the stabilizing effects of social associations could lead to unprecedented political mobilization. In order to understand more fully the operations and effects of these social associations in a local setting, we must now ask, What organizations were these? Who belonged to them? What were the political advantages and disadvantages of nonparty *Vereinsleben* for the Marburg bourgeoisie?

three
Resisting, Modifying, Reversing: Social Organizations, 1880–1914

tephen Yeo has theorized that "during any single phase in the development of capitalism there are hegemonic types of organization and dominant directions of change for organizations." But these forms and tendencies are not fixed; they may be "resisted, modified or reversed."[1] The history of Marburg organizational life from 1880 to 1914 reflects how town elites and their allies, by retaining material and moral leadership over social clubs and associations, resisted, modified, or reversed the direction in which local *Vereine* were being pushed. Responding to the rise of sectional interests and mass politics, many bourgeois social associations claimed that they blunted and absorbed political tension. The aim of their apoliticism was to suppress the contentious world of party politics rather than to criticize it or propose alternatives to it. Unable and unwilling to prevent polarization of the town into socialist and antisocialist camps, such apoliticism nonetheless reinforced the idea that social organizations lessened political divisiveness within the bourgeoisie. This in turn helped the organized bourgeoisie to uphold its social hegemony. But such resilience was by no means permanent, and some of the conditions for the later downfall of bourgeois hegemony were apparent even before World War I. This chapter outlines changes in Marburg social organizations from 1880 to 1914, and then concretizes the analysis by discussing the Gymnastics Club 1860, the Sharpshooting Club, and student organizations.

The Second Age of Organization

Not only in Marburg but in the Reich as well, the late nineteenth century was an era of explosive organization formation. But it was not unprecedented, having followed an equally powerful surge of association building in the late eighteenth and early nineteenth centuries. We need a brief understanding of earlier associational activity in order to discuss the foundations of the second great "age of organization."[2]

Marburg organizational life thrived partly because of the activity of two institutions, the university and the church. Based on the neohumanist reforms of Wilhelm von Humboldt, the German university claimed to prepare students for leadership roles, but it ignored the social and emotional needs of students outside the classroom, creating a gap between the requirements of culture (*Bildung*) and everyday life. Originating in their modern form in the early nineteenth century, student associations began to fill this space.[3] Later, expanding student enrollments, an increasingly differentiated faculty, and growing numbers of alumni caused the circle of voluntary organizations linked to the university to widen and generate still other concentric or overlapping circles of associational activity. Specialized student *Vereine*, fraternity alumni clubs, and academic support groups took their place alongside the earliest student associations—all nurtured in the rich organizational soil of the university.

Marburg Lutheran and Reformed congregations, both influenced by Hessian pietism, generated voluntary organizations that had links to the church but also led an independent existence. Lutheran churchgoers outnumbered their Reformed counterparts by two to one in Marburg in 1852, when Evangelical congregants made up 99.4 percent of the 7,704 church members in the city. Protestant religious associations included the Oberhessian Missionary Society, founded in 1834, the Elisabeth Club, and youth associations. Catholicism was virtually absent from the Marburg religious landscape in the first half of the nineteenth century, but in the last decades before World War I it fostered young adults' social clubs, a journeymen's association, and other groups. Catholic men's clubs used the local Kolping Haus, a product of social Catholicism, for their membership meetings and group functions in the twentieth century.[4] While the church ordinarily operated in the background of organizational life, as part of the furniture of local culture, it assumed a more direct role in times of crisis.[5] We will see that this was the case in the early years of the National Socialist dictatorship.

Encompassing parts of university and church networks, a bourgeois public sphere also nurtured voluntary organizations in Marburg. This public arena was home to groups of private individuals notionally independent of the economy and family, on the one hand, and governmental power, on the other. We turn to the ideology of such public activity shortly. The press and, above all, voluntary associations were the seedbeds of the new public sphere. Lasting from roughly 1765 to 1835, the first surge of voluntary organization formation in the German states started in big urban centers such as Hamburg, where in 1792 the Society "Harmony" had 500 members. In smaller towns and rural areas, this organizational activity occurred later. Significantly, the early nineteenth century word *Verein* was a depoliticized version of earlier designations—*Klub, Gesellschaft, Vereinigung, Bund*—formulated to make French occupation authorities less suspicious of German public life. Marburg's first significant wave of modern *Verein* formation—in the generic sense of the word—took place around the turn of the century.[6]

Vereine emphasizing sociability were dominant locally, just as they were nationally. Despite the appearance of narrower economic associations such as savings banks in the first half of the nineteenth century, the most widespread organizational form in Marburg was the *Gesellschaft*—literally, "society."[7] Particularly drawn to this associational style were town elites, who formed the social club Museum for professors, students, and city officials, and the social circle Sonntagsgesellschaft for the families of Hessian nobles, officers, city officials, pastors, and professors.[8]

General social interchange was also the bedrock of organizations with more specific purposes. Though drama, concert, and singing clubs dealt with specific cultural pursuits, they organized balls and festivals that promoted social life for members and nonmembers alike. University students helped to knit social bonds by building fraternities such as Corps Teutonia (organized in 1825), joining the Museum, and cooperating with military officers to form the nationalist organization Tugendbund, or League of Virtue. Reflecting its political concerns, the Tugendbund encouraged patriotic feeling. But its members were also committed to sociability, especially in the form of card games such as vingt-et-un and faro. Less well-off town dwellers, at least those who could afford the leisure time that voluntary associations presupposed, formed gymnastics clubs, sharpshooting societies, music clubs, and the like—many of them with elite participation and all of them founded on social interchange as the currency of specialized activities. Not only in the Hessian university town but across a broad range of dissimilar communities as well, *Verein* organizers placed greatest emphasis on sociability.[9]

A minority of townspeople was actively involved in voluntary organizations in this and subsequent eras. The clubs of the late eighteenth and early nineteenth centuries served partly to promote interaction between the upper middle classes and the nobility on a supposedly neutral social territory independent of existing status hierarchies and the state. Additionally, some voluntary associations provided chances for social interchange between town elites and better-off craft masters, storeowners, minor civil servants, and workers.[10] Embedded in this net of sociability were an important assumption and a revealing contradiction.

First, early *Verein* members assumed that they pursued general interests independent of government, family relationships, and the marketplace. Although organizations possessed specialized functions, they also had a public role, however that role was perceived. They made no radical distinctions between the general interest, their special interests, and sociability, even though these were separate spheres that could be emphasized at particular times. A Marburg *Gesellschaft* stressed "social entertainment" but also aimed for "collective discussions of political, belletristic, and scientific works in reading circles."[11] Despite the banality and apparent narrowness of early clubs, *Welt* remained *Pflicht*, that is, concern for the world outside one's town, region, or nation was a duty of every organization member.[12] In short, voluntary organizations were nonspecialized with regard to their internal workings and public interactions. This allowed club members to think of themselves as representatives of a general societal interest even as they were involved in small social circles and circumscribed cultural activities. Social and political life were separate but also closely connected in early bourgeois *Vereine*.

Second, a strong contradiction existed in early social clubs between members' intellectual commitment to egalitarianism and their practical attachment to exclusiveness.[13] Egalitarian impulses were apparent in the character of *Vereine*: they were voluntary assemblages of equal individuals reaching decisions through parliamentary procedure. Stamped by this assumption, *Vereine* theoretically put aristocracy and commoners on equal footing and established a cooperative relationship with the state. Equality, openness, freedom, and accessibility were the key ideas.[14] But egalitarian tendencies were contradicted by evolving traditions of exclusivity. Organizational form provides one example. Early organizational life possessed a strong secretive element that was particularly evident in groups such as lodges. These organizations were egalitarian insofar as secretiveness facilitated interchange between individuals who stepped out of existing social hierarchies. But exclusiveness could promote a castelike atmosphere. Moreover, in practice *Vereine* restricted membership on the basis of education and economic success, to say nothing of the limits that economic differences placed on leisure time activity for most Germans. "In terms of social access," David Blackbourn has written, "the rhetoric of universality became rather threadbare" in bourgeois organizational life.[15] Thus town notables ensured their exclusive position atop an expanding network of clubs and associations. Although they preached internal egalitarianism, early *Vereine* reinforced the external class structure, cementing local elite hegemony in the process.

The commitment of *Vereine* to serving some version of the public good and the contradiction between internal egalitarianism and social exclusivity marked local organizational life in the nineteenth and twentieth centuries. But such tendencies were not fixed; like all ideological and social relationships, they could be altered, and they could produce unexpected results.

A complex half-century of change separated organizational life in the first age of organization from its counterpart in the late nineteenth century.[16] Three processes were crucial in Marburg. First, economic and demographic growth enlarged the critical mass of townspeople available for organization. This enhanced social differentiation within the bourgeoisie and between classes and strata generally. It also facilitated the development of organizations that represented specialized interests.[17] Second, waves of political unrest such as those of the 1830s or 1848 prompted organization. At these times, local organizers and agitators—the "restless gents" (*unruhige Köpfe*) of the city mentioned in Kassel police official Bernhardi's comments in the 1830s—helped to extend *Verein* networks to more and more townsfolk. Successive swirls of protest left behind voluntary groups with traditions and rituals linked to the circumstances in which each association originated.[18] Third, after 1866–67 the Prussian state intervened in organizational life more than ever before, penetrating areas that had been wrested by society from absolutist governments of the past. This fostered organization as groups tried to defend their interests from and press their claims on the expanding state. Increasingly, the state encouraged veterans' clubs, nationalist associations, and other presumably "system-supporting" organizations.[19] This social expansion produced tensions that shaped local history after 1880.

What distinguished the new age of organization in Marburg from previous eras? Most obviously, there was a quantitative expansion of organizational life. Of 181 voluntary organizations for which I could determine founding dates between 1850 and 1919, 42.5 percent originated in the twenty years before 1900. In 1850–59, .4 voluntary organizations were formed for every thousand town dwellers. In the next two decades the number of new organizations increased, as the ratio reached 1.1 for the 1860s and 1.07 in the 1870s. But in 1880–89 there were 1.92 new organizations for every thousand inhabitants, and in 1890–99, 2.79. The ratio then declined to 1.42 in 1900–1909, but this was still higher than in the decades before 1880. The average rate of organization formation for the 1880s and 1890s (2.4) was higher than for 1910–19 (2.09). If we remember that the latter decade was marked by the organizational explosion of the first postwar year, then 1880–1899 becomes particularly important as an era of intense organizational activity. The data capture only part of the total number of organization formations, and they do not speak to the issue of participation, but they evoke a real quantitative explosion in local organizational life.[20]

Because it became the administrative and service center of the region, Marburg was a bellwether of the organizational surge. The city had some of the oldest, richest, and most influential voluntary associations of *Oberhessen*. Veterans' clubs provide examples. The Marburg Krieger- und Landwehrverein was the oldest and largest of forty-two clubs in the County Veterans' Association. Formed in September 1872, the Marburg club had 365 members directly after the turn of the century. The second largest and seventh oldest veterans' association in the county was the Marburg Krieger-Kameradschaft. It was founded in April 1879 and had 225 members in 1905. A third club, the Verein ehemaliger Gardisten, was founded in 1892 and had 39 members in 1905. In 1908 the city's three veterans' associations accounted for 37 percent of all veterans' club members in the county, a percentage equaling the city's share of county population. Compared to other county clubs, the Krieger- und Landwehrverein and Krieger-Kameradschaft possessed considerable financial resources. When six county clubs voluntarily donated money in a German Veterans' Association drive to build an orphanage in 1909, the two largest Marburg clubs donated nearly three-quarters of the sixty-five marks raised in the county.[21]

Nonspecialized *Vereine* based on seamless relationships between sociability, special interests, and general interests were the dominant type of voluntary organization until after 1850. Though economic pressure groups existed before the late nineteenth century, specialized occupational associations were much more prominent after 1880. They were products of a general expansion of public life. But they were also formative agents in the evolution of mass politics, because political success came to depend on appealing to these groups. Moreover, economic associations pointed up a growing independence of nonelite townspeople from notables' leadership in economic matters. Thirty-seven of forty-nine pre-1914 occupational associations for which I had data appeared in Marburg in the thirty years before World War I.[22]

The Marburg working class was particularly active in forming such associations. Between 1880 and 1913 construction workers, textile laborers, painters, woodworkers, metalworkers, bandsmen, and carpenters formed trade unions. They collectively followed the example of the printers' trade union. Founded in 1863, the printers' union reflected the importance of craft and skilled workers to the early socialist movement. In 1907 forty-eight of fifty printers who worked in Marburg belonged to the union. Because the small Hessian city offered increased chances for face to face contact and control over group membership, it is not surprising that the proportion of organized printers was much higher locally than it was in the Reich, where 68.1 percent of all printers were unionized. Nonetheless, the level of organization attained by Marburg printers remains impressive. The Social Democratic leader Philipp Scheidemann was chair of the Marburg union from 1889 to 1894. By 1902 all local trade unions were members of the Municipal Trade Union Commission. Working-class organization contributed to strike actions in 1891, 1904, 1908, 1910, and 1913.[23]

White-collar workers and peasants also formed occupational organizations. Although it emphasized its status differences with the working class, the local branch of the German National Commercial Employees' Association, founded in 1896, was a trade union of clerks and office workers. In the 1880s peasants joined a number of economic associations, including a Raiffeisen cooperative encouraged by state officials and the Böckel-inspired Central German Peasants' Association. Subsequently, the Agrarian League made deep inroads into the Hessian countryside, gaining leadership over

the Hessian Peasants' League (Hessischer Bauernbund), the successor of Böckel's association, but not bringing about a complete absorption of the organization.[24]

None of this suggests that workers, commercial employees, or
peasants failed to use economic associations for sociability. The
trade unions and Social Democratic party not only provided social
interchange but also facilitated the formation and growth of social
Vereine, such as the Workers' Song Club "Harmony," formed in
Marburg in 1900.[25] However, unlike early bourgeois clubs, the occupational associations routinely pursued the economic interests of
their members in the national polity: they were pressure groups.

The city's civil servants, independent retailers and craftsmen,
elite women, and some free professionals formed economic associations also, but the scope and influence of these groups were mixed.
Lower-level civil servants founded an Unterbeamtenverein in the
city in 1897, and city officials had their own *Verein* before the Republic, but no strong, national special interest organization for
Marburg officials appeared until 1918. Hansjoachim Henning has
found a similar reluctance to form occupational associations among
nonacademically trained officials in Hanover province, at least before the turn of the century.[26] As for civil servants with academic
training, besides enjoying corporate advantages of government employment, these individuals shared with other *Bildungsbürger*—
university professors, Protestant pastors, *Gymnasium* teachers,
doctors, lawyers—an ambivalence toward occupational associations. One exception in this regard was the Association of Health
Insurance Physicians, formed in 1912 to facilitate the work of
medical doctors involved in the Reich Health Service, promote
"collegial togetherness," and contribute to the "general health of
the people." Another exception was fraternity alumni clubs, of
which there were twenty in Marburg before 1914. Though they defended the economic interests of fraternities, the alumni clubs were
social extensions of individual fraternity chapters rather than pure
occupational associations.[27]

A female teacher and the wife of a university professor formed an
occupational association for women before World War I. They submitted a board of directors and bylaws to the Marburg Organization
Register in 1913. "Women's Work, Women's Study" of Marburg, as
the association was called, stated that it was interested in "helping
women to achieve both inward and outward independence by promoting general and professional education, by finding technical
jobs for women, by bettering women's economic situation, and by

helping women exercise their social and political duties and rights."[28] The largest and most active occupational association of local women, the Housewives' Association, also led by the wife of a university professor, would not be formed until the First World War. Significantly, it did not stress women's advancement in professional and technical employment but dealt with household economics and relations between housewives and servants.[29]

Artisans and retailers had occupational associations, but they were underdeveloped and ineffective compared with trade unions. Buoyed by state legislation in 1897, Marburg artisans formed twelve trade guilds in subsequent years, but they were not very effective until they became subsumed in the national Artisans' Association after World War I. Thereafter, the association and not the guilds became the most effective vehicle of artisanal interests. The Retailers' Association, formed by local merchants from two previous organizations in 1896, was a product of the general mobilization of occupational interests in this period. But this *Verein*, which promoted "common interests of trade and commerce," also established a separate department for *Geselligkeit* that soon became "a club in its own right." The Retailers' Association remained "purely social" until well into the Republic. Finally, after World War I the local Property Owners' and Landlords' Association was to become an important political and economic vehicle of the elite and middling bourgeoisie. But the association had just seventeen members at its 1900 founding and seventy-nine in 1914. This was small by the association's standards during the Republic, when it had about six hundred members.[30]

In an age when organized sectional interests changed the face of German politics, why did some groups form more successful economic pressure groups than others? Absolute levels of economic suffering fail to explain such differences. Relatively better-off craft workers and not unskilled, impoverished factory laborers formed the first unions in Marburg. Only businessmen whose establishments were listed in the local Trade Register could be members of the Retailers' Association until the 1920s.[31] Contrasting levels of social differentiation in each group may have played a part in determining their relative success, but such differences were not as highly developed in Marburg as they were in more industrial cities, such as Bochum.[32] More important than these factors was the position of each group in local and national polities.

For some groups, economic interest associations were a rational response to the situation of being outsiders. Workers, peasants, and white-collar employees possessed little collective power in local politics because of restrictive electoral systems for both the city parliament and Prussian state house. Additionally, workers faced the threat of state repression and became increasingly isolated from the economic, social, and political organizations of nonmanual groups after midcentury. They relied on their own social networks—in the workplace, in family life, and in neighborhoods—to form independent trade unions with support from a nationally organized party. For peasants, who possessed few precedents for formal national associations, an occupational organization was a defensive response to state encroachment, capitalist penetration in the countryside, and urban disinterest in the politics of country people. White-collar employees, relatively new products of the city's expanding service sector, were without traditions of associational activity until well after midcentury. They resorted to pressure groups to strengthen and make sense of their ambiguous economic position in the Wilhelmine social terrain. All three groups looked beyond the local or regional political scene for support of their perceived interests.

The advantages of national special interest organizations were less substantial for others. There were exceptions, to be sure, and the motivations behind the formation of such associations were complex. Growing state regulation of health services necessitated occupational *Verbände* among physicians.[33] Elite women who formed "Women's Work, Women's Study" were moved in part by lack of equality for women not only in elite bourgeois circles but in the wider society as well. But generally, the focus of power for town elites was the local and regional polity: voluntary clubs and associations, schools, savings banks, chambers of trade and crafts, local and county government, the city parliament and Prussian state house, the university, or churches. Less prestigious Marburgers also found a secure place in the local polity by deferring to elite townsmen and those who worked in their behalf in these institutions. The defense of these local structures was therefore much more important to the majority of the town bourgeoisie than was the introduction of economic associations linked to national pressure groups. The hard realities of power politics lay behind the militant localism of the bourgeoisie.

Thus when bourgeois occupational associations like that of local retailers were founded, they immediately settled into traditional patterns of local social life. They were less central to the specific economic needs of their memberships than trade unions were to

Social Democratic workers. Economic associations were similar to nationally organized political parties for the town *Bürgertum*: both were gray strands in a complex fabric of more richly colored and salient patterns. Yet economic associations became nested in a changing social milieu. The most important change was that the rise of organized interests challenged the right of town elites to represent the perceived public good, to act as guardians over notional general interests, in short, to hegemonize the local population. This challenge was obvious in the case of social democracy and trade unions, though we must not overlook the formal adaptation of socialist workers to bourgeois models in singing clubs and other social groups.[34] But the rise of organized sectional interests also disrupted the internal coherence of the bourgeoisie. Indeed, in a city that continued to have a below-average working-class population and a relatively small Social Democratic movement, tensions within local bourgeois networks were potentially more disruptive than were challenges from without. The Marburg bourgeoisie had become more economically differentiated, more politically divided, and more fragmented into associations and clubs of varying size and strength than ever before. How did the Marburg elite, moral and material backbone of bourgeois voluntary organizations, address such tensions? Did the elite fragment or withdraw from local organizational life, or did it provide a center of gravity for an increasingly bewildering spectrum of club activities? Did it continue to play its hegemonic role in local social interactions?

It is useful to begin with a specific illustration. Martin Wenck was national secretary of the National Social party from 1897 to 1901; he became editor of the Marburg-based *Hessische Landeszeitung*, a liberal daily, in 1901. In a city elite dominated by conservatives and National Liberals, he was truly an outsider. He complained that "class spirit and party narrowness" dominated social relationships in the city. When he applied to the elite Museum club for membership, he experienced difficulties because of his affiliation with the *Landeszeitung*, the political opposite of the local conservative daily, the *Oberhessische Zeitung*. But when Wenck reminded the Museum that he was university educated and had once been a pastor, he gained entrance to the club, its social contacts, and its rich collection of books and periodicals. In this case respect for the badges of bourgeois culture, education and a professional position, overrode party differences. Marburgers could hardly gainsay Wenck for emphasizing political divisiveness, but the newspaper editor failed to see that this corner of local organizational life, though influenced directly by party strife, also buffered political contention.[35]

Social organizations did not, of course, eradicate party divisions; but events such as Wenck's admission to the Museum reinforced ideas of conflict absorption. This form of apoliticism, based on unspoken assumptions and commonsensical approaches to political strife, depended more substantially on everyday social networks than did the apoliticism of party and pressure group representatives. The Gymnastics Club 1860 and Sharpshooting Club, like the Museum club, cushioned political rancor through such "unofficial" patterns and customs, as we will see presently.

Having nourished social ties between university and townspeople, elite clubs like the Museum weakened by the turn of the century in Marburg. This occurred in similar organizations in Freiburg and Tübingen also.[36] But, in contrast perhaps to what happened in larger or more industrial cities—and we need a great deal more research on the subject to make authoritative comparisons—social erosion in Marburg caused some elites to participate in a more diverse assortment of organizations.[37] They joined charity and educational groups, religious associations, nationalist clubs, and sports associations. Between 1880 and 1918 more than half of all members of boards of directors (*Vorstände*) of Marburg social organizations came from elite strata. The most active club officials of elite status were university professors, members of the free professions, and clergymen.[38]

Elites accepted the specialized group life of the turn of the century but still argued that while participating in it, they fused their own interests, social interchange, and the general good of the town. Religious associations provide a good example. The pious Hessian community had an impressive roster of such *Vereine*—the City Missionary Society, Elisabeth Club, Catholic Apprentices' Club, German Evangelical Women's Association, Young Men's Christian Association, and so forth. The membership, goals, devotion to Christian practice, degree of inclusiveness, and form of such clubs varied. But they all gave local elites a chance to widen their influence while working for what was defined as the public good. For instance, the Philipps House was formed for Evangelical charity work. But it also functioned as a central place for other Evangelical organizations and institutions, providing meeting rooms and various support activities. This gave club officials (in 1904 two clergymen, a university professor, a retired master builder, a prosperous apothecary, and a storekeeper) contacts with other church groups and with local Lutheran activity in general.[39] Such contacts promoted "occupational" or even political interests just as easily as they furthered church work and sociability.

Opportunities for social contact between elite and nonelite townspeople may have increased after 1880. This suggests either that Marburg was exceptional or that the argument of increased social isolation of the German elite in the second half of the nineteenth century requires some rethinking, at least at the grass roots level. As with so many issues in the organizational life of local bourgeois groups, this matter has not yet been addressed enough by historians to make sound comparisons possible. For Marburg, we take the example of the Patriotic Women's Association (Vaterländischer Frauenverein). Founded in June 1870, the Marburg VF was the local chapter of the Red Cross. Supported by the crown, the chapter was one of 1,391 local branches in 1908; it had 212 regular members and 82 special members in the summer of 1902. The VF was a service organization founded originally to care for the wounded and disabled in wartime. In peacetime, the group provided medical care "in any area of the fatherland where disasters occurred" and ameliorated "economic and moral emergencies." By performing these specific services for the state, the VF helped to legitimize Wilhelmine power arrangements.[40]

Yet the VF had a local agenda as well. Experience in the VF helped to make local elite women more "capable of organization" (*vereinsfähig*) in a public sphere structured by and for men.[41] Additionally, it was a forum for social contact between elite women (along with several men) and the local lower middle classes—and thus a social location of hegemony. In February 1902 the members of the VF *Vorstand* included the wife of a government councilor, a female vocational school teacher (from a noble family), a clergyman, and a city assessor. A partial list of individuals who joined the organization in 1902–3 includes two female schoolteachers and the wives of ten professors, six independent professionals, six city officials, five military officers, and three storeowners.[42] Of course, we do not know if a Frau Professor conversed with the wife of a modest town shopkeeper or schoolteacher at club social events; but the structure for such contact was at least in place in Marburg. This material structure not only sustained elite influence in charity and welfare work but heightened the moral authority of leading townspeople as well. Though clothed in the style of a new public service association, the VF performed activities that resembled those of older organs of elite sociability. And it performed them in a field of apparently wider social contacts. Not all clubs of the second age of organization facilitated elite contact with ordinary townspeople. But the VF was one of many local associations that formed social bridges within the bourgeoisie, that differentiated constellation of groups extending from nonsocialist craft workers and petty shopowners to university professors and Lutheran pastors.

Economic associations that acted like social *Vereine*, religious societies, community action and welfare groups—these were several avenues of participation in organizational life. Clubs practicing pure sociability widened the picture. The 1913 city address book listed fourteen song clubs, fourteen sports associations, seven veterans' societies, and nineteen social clubs (*Vergnügungs-Vereine*).[43] These organizations wove together strands of material interest, social exchange, and general concerns for the local bourgeoisie. A lack of enthusiasm for strong occupational associations linked to national and regional *Verbände* was not a sign of antimodernism. Rather, it was a practical gesture of local groups whose organizational networks had worked efficiently without fostering big unions or cooperatives.

It would be mistaken to assume that the entire *Bürgertum* was involved in Marburg's clubs and associations. As sociological evidence suggests, organizational life relies on specific groups of activists.[44] Though over one-half of all associational officers were elites, active organizational participation cut across class and strata lines: there were enthusiastic club members from the ranks of elites, students, artisans, civil servants, and blue-collar workers before World War I. The largest occupational groups among club officers in 1880–1918 were self-employed artisans, professors, minor civil servants, clergymen, free professionals, skilled workers, and independent storeowners.[45]

Beyond the circle of club activists was a much larger group of formal voluntary association members. It is impossible to estimate the number of local people belonging to at least one organization. But it is worthwhile to note that one voluntary organization existed for every ninety-nine townspeople in 1913. The size of organizations varied tremendously. The forty-eight clubs and associations listed in the Organization Register before 1918 had as many as 250 members and as few as 7, the legal limit for admission to the Register. The most that can be said is that more than two hundred city organizations created a significant opportunity for involvement in grass roots public life before World War I.[46]

However, there must have been a significant distance between opportunity and practice. Organizations appeared and disappeared. Some clubs listed in the address books or Organization Register existed only on paper. Others were narrow service organizations whose members had little contact with one another. Even in the most inclusive social clubs, many individuals were surely rather passive participants: they were cajoled to attend meetings, pay dues on time, contribute to money collections for special projects, and help attract new members. Organizational life depended on complicated substructures of social contacts, loyalties, and tensions that changed constantly.

A well-organized social club such as the Kurhessian branch of the Kyffhäuser Veterans' Association annually reminded its local officers to keep up with organizational business through the club newsletter, *Parole*. Provincial officers remarked in 1910 that *Parole* deserved "much more attention than it has received up to now."[47] The provincial association also complained that correspondence between local clubs and Kassel was slow and disorganized, causing "frustrating embarrassments and considerable delays in business dealings with the national organization."[48]

Enthusiasm for club activity varied among veterans' locals. The national and provincial associations encouraged members to buy the Kyffhäuser-Verband yearbook/calendar, reputed to bring joy into club members' homes and make "brave citizens" of their children.[49] In 1909 only one-quarter of the nearly 400 members in the largest and most prestigious Marburg veterans' club, the Krieger- und Landwehrverein, bought the yearbook. But nearly half of 269 Krieger-Kameradschaft members bought the publication, while more than one-third of the 53-member Kyffhäuser affiliate Verein ehemaliger Gardisten ordered it. In the city willingness to buy the publication lacked any correlation to group size or prestige. In the outlying county, however, where all veterans' clubs had fewer than seventy members each, more than 80 percent of the membership of local branches purchased the yearbook.[50] In these smaller towns and villages, veterans' clubs played a dominant role in local social life and aroused strong interest in club projects. Such enthusiasm was more difficult to generate in Marburg, where a veterans' club was but one of many competitors in the growing leisure marketplace.

Despite the varied picture of local organizational life presented thus far, many different bourgeois clubs and associations held one sentiment in common: a distrust of nationally organized sectional interests and the parties that spoke to them. This apoliticism was a response to the penetration of the national political marketplace in the city. It was expressed in purely formal ways, as when economic associations, social clubs, and other groups that wanted to be enrolled in the Organization Register wrote into their bylaws that political (and religious) matters were out of bounds. Some organizations dealt with the intrusive political marketplace by not speaking of politics; they buried political events in a dense tangle of social activities and customs. Still other groups used nationalism—the "encouragement, fortifying, and practice of love and dedication for Kaiser and Reich," according to the Prussian Kriegerverein—to seek the social calm that political parties could never deliver.[51] The town bourgeoisie did not ignore national political issues; it simply rejected parties as primary conduits for dealing with such issues and put this rejection into practice in the daily activities of numerous clubs and associations. Though it was a measure of political disorganization in the national sphere, apoliticism was a product of bourgeois social resilience and moral authority at the grass roots. By examining two parts of the organizational landscape in the following sections, we can arrive at a more detailed picture of this local resilience.

Two Sports Clubs

Two of the largest and most important social clubs in Marburg were the Sharpshooting Club (Schützenverein) and the Gymnastics Club 1860 (Turnverein 1860). The former had 125 members in 1912, the latter 300 in 1894. Both organizations were the largest of their kind in the city before the Republic, and both were highly visible elements of local public life. They also encompassed a fairly wide spectrum of local people because each club attracted different age groups.

The Marburg Schützenverein traced its predecessors to the late middle ages, when a "sharpshooting society" of crossbowmen enjoyed the support of Kurhessian autocrats. Local sharpshooters were mobilized to defend the city against the French in 1689, organized in a Schützen-Kompagnie in the absence of Kurhessian troops sent to fight in France in 1815, and used as a city defense force in the early 1830s. Permutations of local sharpshooters' groups were as numerous as the circumstances in which they appeared. By 1848, when a group of townsmen saw "the rebirth of our great German fatherland" as an occasion for forming a new club "partly from the members of the old Kurhessian Sharpshooting Corps," city sharp-shooters could look back on a long history of public activity. Eighty-four townspeople attended the founding of the Sharpshooting Club in 1848. In the spring of that violent year sharpshooters helped Gymnastics Club members and the local Civil Guard (Bürgergarde) patrol city streets. But the authorities dissolved the Sharpshooting Club in November 1850, confiscated all weapons, and transported the club's flag to a Kassel armory. The latter act was a serious gesture, because the flag was virtually a mascot that later accompanied the club to regional shooting matches.[52]

Like local gymnasts, Marburg sharpshooters reformed their organization in the 1860s. They were spurred by the first German gymnastics festival in Coburg in 1860, formation of the German Sharpshooting Association in 1861, and the first German shooting festival in Frankfurt in July 1862, the latter attended by a number of Marburg sharpshooters. Under the leadership of Dr. Julius Wolff, sixty-three Marburgers founded the new Schützenverein in July 1862; fourteen of the sixty-three had been members of the 1848 organization. Whereas the Gymnastics Club appealed to city youth (it required members to participate in regular exercises), the sharpshooters attracted an older membership. Fourteen-year-olds were eligible for membership in the Gymnastics Club, but the youngest person in the Sharpshooting Club in 1862 was twenty-three. The average age of fifty-nine members in the latter club was over forty.[53]

Sharpshooters were fully involved in local public ritual. In 1863 they celebrated the opening of the club's new shooting range by organizing a large festival in which state and city officials, gymnasts, song club members, and sharpshooters from surrounding towns participated. Later that year sharpshooters participated in the fiftieth anniversary celebration of the defeat of Napoleon by Allied armies at Leipzig. The sharpshooters "accompanied the veterans of 1813–15 to the festival site," heard "touching speeches," and assembled around "a great bonfire." In 1871 sharpshooters participated in a citywide torchlight procession observing victory in the Franco-Prussian war, a celebration that occasioned a "salvo of gun-fire" and a "thundering salute to the newly born German Reich." The twentieth, twenty-fifth, and thirtieth anniversaries of the *Verein*, as well as the twentieth anniversary of Sedan, were opportunities for further collective celebrations of sharpshooters and other Marburg clubs and associations. All this represented the public-spirited activity of "free, armed men."[54]

Yet by the turn of the century the club became more solipsistic and less concerned with these patriotic and community activities. Debates over the cost of club equipment, purchase of a shooting gallery, and balancing of the organization's finances occupied the time of *Verein* leaders. In 1902 the club celebrated its fortieth anniversary "as an internal affair [*im Rahmen des Vereins*] with a sharpshooting contest, and a summer festival," a marked departure from earlier, widely attended anniversaries. The world of party politics was conspicuously absent in day-to-day workings of the club. I did not find evidence of club members' party loyalties in the Empire. But if affiliations were nearly as diverse in the Empire as they were in the Republic—when club adherents belonged to liberal, conservative, National Socialist, and splinter parties—then it is clear that this apoliticism defended against the potentially disruptive effects of competing party attachments.[55]

The Sharpshooting Club was more exclusive than other social clubs because shooting required money for guns, clothes, and other equipment. Of course, not all shooting associations were inaccessible to those with limited financial resources.[56] But the Marburg club made joining more difficult by raising fees from six to ten marks for all incoming members in 1896. People who had belonged to the club for more than fifteen years paid nine marks annually and all others paid twelve marks. These fees were comparable with those of more exclusive German sharpshooting clubs and much higher than those of less prestigious ones.[57] The increases undoubtedly limited the size of the club. The Schützenverein had only twenty-six more members in 1912 than it had had in 1863. But the club still attracted new members, having gained 80 of 125 members in 1912 after the introduction of higher dues.[58]

The relative exclusivity of the club was illustrated in the makeup of its membership. Of 125 members on the eve of World War I, 29 (23.4 percent) were town elites. The largest groups were industrialists, building contractors, bankers, and free professionals. The presence of so many elite townsmen was partly due to generational factors: the Schützenverein catered to an older, more established clientele. But there was more to it than this. The other sharpshooting club in the city before the war, the Sharpshooting Society (Schützengesellschaft 1897), based in nearby Marbach, failed to attract local elites. The same may be said of a club that appeared during the Republic, the Schützenklub 1924.[59] Organizations such as the Sharpshooting Club allowed city elites to sustain business and professional relationships. They operated as quasi-occupational associations.

Other tendencies counterbalanced exclusivity. The largest group within the club was the self-employed lower middle class, to which seventy-five members (60.5 percent), including fifty-seven shopkeepers and eighteen craft masters belonged. Among the former were some of the city's more prominent storeowners. Some prosperous members of the old *Mittelstand* served on the club's board of directors along with town elites. But not all of these independent artisans and retailers were prosperous. There were also three white-collar workers, three craft workers, two minor civil servants, and a group of twelve nonelite retirees and other individuals in the club.[60] The Sharpshooting Club was more than an old boys' club for the well-to-do; it was a social network that brought nonelite Marburgers into contact with elite townsmen.

Such contacts provided opportunities for displaying the moral influence of bourgeois elites. Nationalist sentiments provided a good part of the ideological ammunition for doing so. Despite increasing self-absorption, the club said in 1912 that its goal was to provide "the fatherland with young people trained in the use of firearms." It stressed a symbiosis between "old Marburg families" and service to the nation. It reaffirmed sharpshooters' motto: "Sharpen eye and hand for Fatherland."[61] Though vague and indirect, such sentiments hinted at a continued desire for public commitment. Despite ostensible political disinterest, the club nurtured a potential for political activity, a potential that resurfaced in the unsettled Weimar Republic. For the time being, the club's nationalist sentiment represented a refuge from political fragmentation. Patriotic fervor formed a safe zone where devotion to national interests, as they were perceived by sharpshooters, could be divorced from hateful party conflict. Party strife, social exclusivity, and personal antagonisms fragmented local organizational life; but the Sharpshooting Club upheld its claim that unpolitical associations absorbed and muffled party tensions within the town bourgeoisie. All this was crucial for the preservation of elite hegemony. For if social organizations could stifle real political rancor, they could deter people from raising difficult questions about power, justice, and opportunity— the stuff of political life. The daily rhythm of Sharpshooting Club activities accomplished precisely this.

Gymnastics was of more recent vintage than sharpshooting. Originating in the nationalistic gymnastics movement of the early nineteenth century, the Marburg Gymnastics Club was a product of political contention. The first Marburg group, organized by Germania fraternity students in 1819, was suspected by government agents of fostering revolutionary activity and dissolved soon after its formation. Gymnasts regrouped in 1847; split their single club into "republican" and "nationalist" factions in 1848; participated in patriotic sports festivals; sang songs such as "Kick the Aristos out," aimed mainly at Kurhessian autocracy; and encouraged radicalism among young people and the storage of weapons for political revolt. "Overthrowing the tyrants," to use the expression of the Men's League that Turnverein members helped to form, was the goal of this activity. A wave of repression after 1849 erased nearly two-thirds of three hundred gymnastics clubs in Germany. Marburg gymnasts were among the victims of this repression and were left without a Turnverein.[62]

In 1860 another national mobilization of gymnasts spurred Karl Heuser, the son of a well-known Marburg artisan family and a participant in the earlier Gymnastics Club, to form another group. He was joined by a shoemaker and accomplished gymnast, Volpertus Wilhelm Schneider, also from an old Marburg family, who in 1874 would be cofounder of the Marburg Liberal Association. Schneider was also the cousin of Volpertus Heinrich Schneider, one of the first Social Democratic organizers in Marburg. The Turnverein gained the support of the lord mayor, who wrote the Kurhessian police that the club's "main activity, physical education through gymnastics, could in no way endanger public order and security."[63] Nevertheless, the club continued to experience "all sorts of difficulties" from "hard-hearted authorities" in the Kurhessian administration who distrusted an organization devoted to unifying all Germans in a single Reich.[64]

But the new club upheld its pledge to contribute to public order even before national unification by founding a volunteer fire department in 1861. Additionally, it put together a city hall patrol in 1867, while police were temporarily absent during Prussia's annexation of Kurhessen. In 1870–71 sixty club members organized a medical detail.[65] The Turnverein had become a full member of local bourgeois culture.

Once in the vanguard of opposition to Kurhessian autocracy, the club now served the general good through the performance of more mundane activities oriented toward the local community. This shift occurred partly because of the effects of past repression, but mainly because political parties and other organizations tried to assume the political functions once held by the Turnverein. Even so, the club continued to play a broadly political role through public service activities. Club ideology still envisioned a seamless net of the general good, group interest, and social exchange as the basis of organizational life. "Order, morality, loyalty to one's profession, and brotherliness," as 1863 club bylaws declared, were collective goals; but so were the promotion of "physical and moral strengthening and especially love for the Fatherland," as the club further stated in 1884.[66]

But the rise of specialized sports organizations in the second age of organization presented a challenge. In Marburg new associations were formed for soccer, riding, swimming, sharpshooting, tennis, and hockey. There were at least fifteen separate sports clubs in Marburg in 1913. The new organizations not only competed for members but introduced a more specialized brand of sociability as well. Though most of the new organizations proclaimed their patriotism and public-spiritedness, they concentrated most strongly on pursuing the specialized activity for which they were formed. Following the lead of the German Gymnastics Association (Deutsche Turnerschaft), to which it was affiliated, the Marburg Gymnastics Club responded to new competition by establishing separate departments for women and schoolgirls and by adding singing, fencing, and outdoor games to club activities. Additionally, by renovating a gymnasium, the club was "freed . . . from having to use other buildings" for *Verein* functions. This "allowed it to continue an undisturbed expansion of the management of gymnastic activity."[67]

The organization became more departmentalized as members were encouraged to practice specialized activities. This made contact with other sports groups less likely since gymnasts could pursue their interests in the club's own buildings and spaces. Paralleling developments in the Marburg Sharpshooting Club, the Gymnastics Club became more self-involved. The influence of Friedrich Ludwig Jahn, originator of the gymnastics movement, who wanted to make his clients an elite group of patriots in an age of burgeoning German nationalism, remained strong in DT leadership. At the grass roots level such exclusivity was evident in Gymnastics Club bylaws, which in 1860 prohibited club members from belonging to another Turnverein. But DT leaders were so concerned about contamination of their clients by other clubs and so worried about losing power to the growing sports movement that they forbade dual memberships of gymnasts in all other sports associations in the 1920s. They also tried to keep gymnasts' clubs small, resisting the tendency to form mass amalgamated organizations. These policies contributed to widespread segmentation and duplication of functions in organizational life.[68]

Yet Turnverein social composition indicated that the club counterbalanced such exclusivity. The Gymnastics Club claimed to be accessible to "all estates," a ritualistic boast for which there was some basis, at least regarding less elite classes and strata, because the club appeared to have been "petty bourgeois . . . with a proletarian influence."[69] Evidence of the occupations of club members before the Republic is sketchy but suggestive on this point. From 1894 to 1918 there were eight independent craftsmen, six craft workers, five minor city officials, five white-collar workers, and two independent retailers in the organization. Unlike the Sharpshooting Club, the Gymnastics Club was unattractive to town elites.[70] Rooted in the lower middle classes of the city but also including craft workers, club membership spanned growing social divisions within the nonelite, nonmanual bourgeoisie and between nonmanual groups and workers. In contrast, the membership of the Athletic Association (VfB 05), which according to local people attracted "the better society," came mainly from free professionals, better-off shopowners and craft masters, upper-level city officials, and industrialists. The VfB also included university students, who were instrumental in founding a soccer club that later merged with the Association.[71]

Although the history, organization, and social base of the Gymnastics Club were products of broader national development, the Turnverein ultimately made sense only within the local culture. Despite the fact that the DT wished to keep local branches small, the club became one of the largest voluntary associations in the city and the largest of all Marburg sports clubs. By the modest scale of local organizational life, the group was a mass organization in the forefront of new social trends. Though club practices discouraged contacts with other sports organizations, members belonged to other types of voluntary groups.[72] Cutting across a large part of the social structure, the Gymnastics Club was relatively accessible in an age of growing division within and between classes. Such accessibility created a potential for "democratic self-consciousness" in Marburg, just as it did in the very different political atmosphere of Hamburg.[73]

The club remained a very visible element of the local polity. While official DT ideology kept gymnasts aloof from many public activities, the Turnverein's fiftieth anniversary celebration in August 1910 attracted notice from city officials and other clubs. The club was in the forefront of local patriotism, as the strongly nationalistic tone of its 1910 songbook suggested. "German fatherland," one verse read, "we swear to you the higher vow of loyalty! To defend your honor, we take the sword; to defend your freedom, we die as free men!"[74]

These sentiments hardly indicated political immaturity; rather, they expressed an aggressive, nationalistic apoliticism. Club activities virtually shut out the world of parties and parliaments, a world that had split gymnasts into nationalist and republican factions in 1848.[75] Ideally, the everyday machinery of the organization insulated members from a divisive political scene in the Second Empire. But the point of apoliticism was that the general good, the goals of political life in the widest sense of the term, were attainable through structures other than bureaucratized parties tied to mass electorates. The club claimed that it contributed to the public good in an apolitical realm free of party squabbles, that it healed political wounds for the sake of the nation. Paradoxically, however, the claim could be fully tested only in moments of intense political strife. Acclamatory and ritualistic in periods of relative equilibrium, such apoliticism hinted at the possibility of intense and autonomous action if party struggles threatened to disrupt social life. In times of crisis, when political winds made local and national structures shudder, apoliticism and nationalist sentiment could issue into more direct political activity.

Building on previous foundations, the Sharpshooting Club and Gymnastics Club participated in the second age of organization and became leading bourgeois social clubs in Marburg. Though products of political strife, both groups increasingly de-emphasized political matters and broad public involvement, concentrating more on selling leisure to their memberships. But there was no depoliticization of organizational life, no complete abandoning of concern for general issues. Instead, forms of political activity changed as both clubs continued to stress community pride, nationalist sentiment, and concern for what was perceived to be the public good. Nor did the two groups succumb completely to the growing social exclusivity of bourgeois organizational life. Whereas the Gymnastics Club attracted independent and employed lower middle classes and strata along with craft workers, the Sharpshooting Club had the allegiances of the old *Mittelstand* and city elite. In both cases, the nonelite bourgeoisie played a linking role, integrating craft workers in the Gymnastics Club and joining with the town elite in the Sharpshooting Club. Socially and politically, each club helped to maintain bourgeois hegemony and reinforce an image of bourgeois solidarity. Both clubs resisted, modified, and reversed change in an age of widening but segmented public life. Apolitical organizations claimed to counterbalance, contain, and make sense of tensions resulting from rapid population growth, the rise and fall of many different associations, the social differentiation of the town bourgeoisie, and growing political divisiveness. The everyday workings of social clubs made the claim convincing.

Student Associations

Hegemony is by definition malleable; that is, it is capable of being changed and reshaped. Whereas bourgeois social hegemony appeared to be relatively uncontested in the Sharpshooting Club and the Gymnastics Club, the uncertainties of power were more evident in Marburg student associations. These had qualities that set them off from nonstudent clubs. Students had greater freedom to organize than townspeople did, as long as authorities were convinced of the unpolitical character of an organization. That freedom was a product of the neohumanist structure of the university and the privileges many students enjoyed as both potential elites and important local consumers. Unlike most nonstudent organizations —except perhaps youth groups, some sports clubs, or confessional young adults' associations—student associations were generational. Student organizations such as the dueling and color-bearing fraternities were also given to ritualistic practices more exaggerated than those of nonstudent groups. The dueling and color-bearing fraternities in particular were more inclusive than nonstudent clubs, demanding more time and loyalty from members. The "life principle," which theoretically tied students to the fraternity chapter permanently, enhanced such inclusiveness. Finally, partly because of the incubative nature of the university, student organizations experienced more internecine friction than nonstudent clubs. The student clubs extended and exaggerated tendencies present in the wider society.[76]

Attendance at Marburg university more than quadrupled between 1880 and 1914, increasing from 592 to 2,529.[77] This was the general background for an upsurge in student organization in the Second Empire. In 1870 there were at least eight student organizations at the university, the oldest of which was the Corps Teutonia, established in 1825. But the period of most intense organization formation occurred in 1880–89, the start of the second age of organization in the city. In this decade the rate of organization formation was 14 for every thousand students, compared to 8.4 in the previous decade. The rate fell to 4.1 in 1890–99, 1.8 in 1900–1909, and 1.2 in the following decade.[78]

With demographic expansion came greater diversification in organizational form. Before 1870 six fraternities dueled, adopted symbolic colors, or did both. Though they bickered jealously with one another, they shared corporate traditions that made student organizational life relatively uniform. But after the 1880s, new organizations challenged fraternity form. Mirroring the metamorphosis of the university into a mass service institution, students formed specialized clubs for pharmacists, theologians, historians, and mathematicians. Youth groups, stenography clubs, women's associations, religious groups, and political associations gradually added to the changing social mosaic. Additionally, by 1905 Marburg students had organized a Freistudentenschaft, an amorphous organization growing out of a national antifraternity movement that had begun in Leipzig in 1896. Generating offshoots that became formal student associations such as the Akademische Freischar, the Freistudentenschaft itself had no fixed membership and its officers argued that it was not a *Verein* but a spontaneous mobilization of unaffiliated students. A conservative estimate suggests that by 1914 nearly half of all Marburg students were organized in some forty clubs.[79]

From the mid-1870s until the late 1880s, the pure fraternities, organizations that dueled and wore symbolic colors, experienced serious membership losses.[80] But they maintained themselves. Immediately before World War I 16.4 percent of Marburg students belonged to pure fraternities. This included 416 active and inactive students in eleven organizations ranging in size from twenty-one to fifty-eight members. The smallest pure fraternities were the Corps, a generic term used mainly for student associations that belonged to the national Kösener Association (Kösener Senioren-Convents Verband). There were three Kösener Corps in Marburg in 1913, including the already mentioned Corps Teutonia; they had a total of eighty-nine actives. Much larger were the organizations of the Deutsche Burschenschaft, of which there were four in Marburg in 1913. Three of the four Burschenschaften had more than fifty actives, while the other had thirty-one. Additionally, there were always larger numbers of inactive students and alumni living in Marburg who widened the influence of fraternity culture beyond the formal, active membership. Whether we measure active or inactive members, there is little doubt, however, that the influence of these clubs was stronger in Marburg than it was in most other German universities.[81]

Enveloped in ritual and social prestige, the pure fraternity model was seductive, and many student clubs adopted the forms and practices of dueling, color-bearing associations. This process was discontinuous and variable. Some organizations simply became pure fraternities. By the early 1870s the pharmacy students' club assumed the character of a "closed fraternity" by adopting colors and dueling. Founded in 1880, the Student Gymnastics Association (Akademischer Turnverein) adopted dueling and colors the following year, becoming the Turnerschaft Philippina. Students close to Professor Edmund Stengel, without whom beery social functions such as the *Kneipe* "would have been unthinkable," formed the Association for Students of Modern Philology in 1880. After a number of permutations in the Second Empire, this association merged with the Philological-Historical Association Hercynia in 1920 to become the Burschenschaft Rheinfranken, a club that practiced dueling and wore colors.[82]

Other clubs were less unanimous in their enthusiasm for the traditions of pure fraternities. About 30 percent of all enrolled students in 1913 were active or inactive members of modified fraternities, organizations that selectively adopted pure fraternity practices. For instance, the anti-Semitic Association of German Students (Verein Deutscher Studenten), founded in Marburg in 1886, adopted colors but did not wear them. However, its members were allowed to duel. The same was true of Sängerverbindung Fridericiana, which appeared first in 1889 as a student singing club. One of the oldest student clubs in the city was the Christian association Marburger Wingolf, which was a quasi-professional vehicle of theology students. Enjoying amicable relations with pure fraternities immediately before World War I, its members adopted colors in 1848 and wore them, but did not duel. Likewise, Rhenania and Palatia, both Catholic fraternities founded before World War I, wore colors but forbade the duel.[83]

Both pure and modified fraternities benefited from a "structure of protection and connection" provided by influential Wilhelmine alumni associations, the Old Boys. Alumni clubs aided the fraternities by giving financial support, recruiting members, building houses after the turn of the century, and generally supporting traditions of local chapters. Initially voluntary, money gifts to the fraternities were eventually written into the bylaws of alumni clubs. Older groups like the Corps, increasingly exclusive and much smaller than other pure fraternities, were often kept afloat by alumni clubs that had been founded earlier and hence had more members than other Old Boy organizations.[84] There were twenty alumni associations in the Marburg Organization Register before 1914. The first to be registered was the Association of Former Teutons, the alumni of Corps Teutonia. In 1901 its board of directors consisted of four medical doctors, a university professor, and a retired lieutenant colonel. These alumni officials could stay in close contact with their younger brothers: three of the six directors lived in Marburg, and another lived in nearby Giessen.[85]

The power of pure and modified fraternities was enhanced by their "tight organization, impressive external appearance . . . and quasi-official status as representatives of the student body."[86] Dueling evoked most dramatically the influence and conventions of these organizations.[87] Ritualized in countless bloody encounters resulting in highly valued scars across participants' faces, the duel between students, or *Mensur*, was part of an ideology emphasizing elitism and "general culture" in an age of specialized university study. Fraternities administered to the "whole personality," it was claimed, rather than to narrow professional and sectional interests. Dueling, drinking in ritualized binges, wearing colored hats and sashes, and appearing in full uniform with sword at university ceremonies were the externals of this educative role. Ideas supporting the fraternities' view of their educative function were appropriate for claiming that fraternities represented a general student interest, a claim reinforced by university officials and town notables, who treated pure and modified fraternities as "the" student body in public ceremonies. Though rooted in the specific conditions of German university study, the role of fraternities in educating their adherents was part of a broader tendency of bourgeois organizational life to represent itself as the guardian of general interests.[88]

Pure and modified fraternities exaggerated the exclusivist qualities of German organizational life. Dueling was important in this regard because it divided the population into people who were capable of satisfying gentlemanly honor in resolving disputes, those who were *satisfaktionsfähig*, and people who were not. Not only the majority of the population but the greater part of the student body as well lacked this capability. Though the duel became more sport than deadly encounter, it reinforced an exclusivity twice removed: first from the majority of the population, and then from the majority of university students.[89]

Except for Turnerschaften, which attracted many sports club members, pure fraternities were generally more elite and upper-middle-class than other student organizations. Since only a handful of nobles attended Marburg university, most pure fraternity members came from families of better-off government officials, well-to-do merchants, and wealthy but nonnoble rural landowners. In contrast to these students, who were largely from small-town settings and had been educated in high schools that emphasized the classics, members of modified fraternities and other student associations were more urban, more often from the upper and lower middle classes, and more often educated in less prestigious nonclassical high schools. Unaffiliated students or those belonging to the Freistudentenschaft were positioned socially somewhere between these two groups.[90]

Though collectively prominent, individual fraternities grew more isolated from one another and from the rest of the student body. Traditions of exclusivity, heightened by the transformation of organizational life in the late nineteenth century, now became rigid. Like nonstudent bourgeois clubs, fraternities became more preoccupied with internal matters. But this preoccupation was more extreme in student societies than it was in voluntary organizations outside the university. Max Weber spoke of the "intellectual inbreeding" of fraternities, a product of the insular quality of social and cultural relations among fraternity members and between alumni and actives. Increasingly concerned with the rituals of daily group life, the fraternities developed a strong collective interest in preserving hierarchy and authority—whether it was the authority "of the 'actives' over the 'pledges', the alumni over both, or the abstraction of the fraternity ideal over all of them."[91]

The fraternities' drawback from wider social relationships was enhanced by their building of chapter houses, the construction of which was aided by alumni club support. Corps Teutonia again led the way, transforming a garden house into a chapter pub in 1862, expanding it into a larger structure with a tower in 1887, and finally erecting an imposing house on the site in 1905. Other fraternities followed suit, especially after the turn of the century. The often sumptuous houses gave members regular meeting places for drinking, noontime meals, and other fraternity functions. But they also gave fraternity students fewer reasons or opportunities for being involved with other students and townsmen. This was reflected in complaints voiced in 1905 by retired vice-mayor Siebert, who was critical of flagging student interest in the elite Museum club, once the provider of social interchange between town and gown. According to Siebert, student fraternities had "become more exclusive after building their own social facilities."[92] Ironically, the strengthening of fraternity life, a bastion of local tradition, contributed to the breakdown of structures that had traditionally ensured student contacts with local elite.

The self-isolation of individual fraternities was part of a general fragmentation of the Marburg student body, a more extreme version of what happened in town. Pure and modified fraternities experienced among themselves "frictions of every sort," including nightly disturbances, duels, and fistfights.[93] Students were aware that internal splintering at times reached absurd proportions. Writing in 1916 about fraternity life right before the war, one Marburger Wingolf student remarked that the "legitimate inclusiveness" of his group bordered on "eccentricity." He and others worried that fraternity students thought "nothing was necessary beyond the boundaries [of the organization]. . . . One has his fraternity friends," the *Wingolfist* stated, "and avoids contact with others."[94]

Nonfraternity students criticized fraternity exclusivity and inattention to general student interests. Chief among the critics was the Freistudentenschaft, whose members the fraternities called "finches" (*Finken*). The Marburg Freistudentenschaft appeared in autumn 1905, but it was suspended by the university two years later for holding an unauthorized assembly and committing other offenses. Reorganized after two semesters, the Freistudentenschaft had a presidium that was elected at the end of each semester in a general assembly of unincorporated students. In addition, depending on student demand, the Freistudentenschaft organized specialized departments for political discussion and field trips to factories, for lectures and discussions on liberal arts and the natural sciences, for French conversation, and for sports. The Freistudentenschaft demanded "equal rights with the fraternity students" in student governance, more social services, and reading rooms and cooperative structures at the university. After much contention with what the "finches" called "selfish" fraternities, the Freistudentenschaft in 1908 gained one representative for every forty votes its candidates received in elections to student government, the Studentenausschuß.[95]

Yet evidence suggests that the fragmentation of fraternity life, isolation of the fraternities from nonfraternity organizations, and dissociation of fraternities from the town after the turn of the century were not as dysfunctional as they appeared. In the two decades before World War I pure and modified fraternities maintained a preeminent position in student life despite their minority status and the challenge of new organizations and tendencies. This was one dimension of a broader reshaping of bourgeois social life in the city.

Take the issue of the fraternities' capacity for cooperation with one another. Even before 1900, student solidarity in the Empire developed mainly in periods of crisis. A notable instance occurred on 21 July 1893 when Corps Hasso-Nassovia, a pure fraternity, mobilized a large number of students against an instructor who aroused antagonism with his overbearing discipline and critical remarks about students.[96] But after the turn of the century a paradoxical development occurred. Georg Heer noted that the "isolation of individual fraternities," though serious, also "contributed not a little to lessening the sources of irritation between them," and this "facilitated a decent understanding and unanimous will to stick together in student and patriotic matters."[97]

Pure fraternity solidarity was evident in a number of ways in the last years before World War I. Building on fraternity initiative and the negotiating skill of university librarian and professor Wilhelm Fabricius, Marburg pure fraternities concluded the so-called Marburg Agreement in December 1911. This agreement regulated conditions for dueling between fraternity members and between fraternity and nonfraternity students. After numerous disagreements, eleven Marburg pure fraternities, each belonging to one of the four major national dueling fraternity alliances (Kösener Corps, Deutsche Burschenschaft, Turnerschaft im Vertreter-Convent, and Landsmannschaft), organized a Local Cartel to implement certain provisions of the pact. The Local Cartel displayed its solidarity in 1912 when it demanded that student government expel the modified fraternity Burschenschaft Sigambria, which had "disturbed the peace" in some unspecified way. But the eleven pure fraternities accounted for only one-third of Studentenausschuß representatives and were thus unable to wield majority influence. When they could not get the support of student government, they seceded and formed their own council. Negotiations for a new universitywide student government began after the breakup thanks to the initiative of the chancellor and modified fraternities such as Marburger Wingolf. Though the war cut negotiations short, the pure fraternities had made their collective statement: they could act together.[98]

Pure and modified fraternities also absorbed the challenges of the Freistudentenschaft. The fraternities derived advantages from the amorphousness of the Freistudentenschaft and the suspicion of university officials toward nonfraternity students. The *Finken* would see many of their economic and social programs endorsed by postwar student governments.[99] But before World War I the pure and modified fraternities possessed enough resources to limit the effectiveness of nonfraternity student initiatives and skew them in particular directions.

Similarly, the fraternities created solidarity by resisting Jewish student organization. Expanding student enrollments and narrowing job opportunities created antipathy toward "foreign" elements at German universities.[100] Only 2.3 percent of the Marburg student population consisted of Jews. But Marburg was dubbed "*the* university of anti-Semitism." One reason for the strength of anti-Semitism was the extraordinary confessional homogeneity of Marburg students, who were more than 80 percent Protestant at a time when less than 65 percent of all Prussian students adhered to the Protestant faith. Confessional uniformity enabled Marburg students to "target" Jewish students and their organizations. But more important was the 1882 decision of the prestigious Corps Teutonia to prohibit Jews from membership. No records of events that led to this action were available for the present study. But this respected organization undoubtedly influenced other fraternities to follow its lead. Additionally, new clubs such as the Association of German Students, formed in 1886, introduced active and ideological anti-Semitism into student life. Finally, anti-Semitism was furthered by student participation in the Böckel movement. In a logical culmination of these developments, the fraternities contested the right of Jewish *Vereine* to participate in student government. Fraternity members were involved in "repeated scuffles" with students of a Jewish fraternity in 1911, and the university suspended the latter after conflict threatened to escalate into pistol duels.[101]

Anti-Semitism was part of a general reshaping of interfraternity relations that stressed ideas uniting rather than dividing fraternities. Increased interest in politics and heightened nationalism performed a similar function. The Association of German Students, the Bismarck League, and other nationalist associations promoted radical nationalism in both university and town. Though nationalist *Verbände* were very small at Marburg university, nationalist sentiments could mobilize an extraordinary number of students. In 1906 the *Oberhessische* reported that "one thousand students and alumni of *alma mater Philippina*" attended an assembly that "enthusiastically expressed its support for the rapid buildup of our naval fleet" and "paid homage reverentially and with true German conviction to his Majesty, the most zealous and conscientious advocate of German seapower."[102]

Despite the influence of these nationalist associations and tendencies, increased fraternity concern about political questions in the decade before World War I did not generally lead to direct political activity—electioneering, agitating on behalf of a nationalist *Verband*, or joining a national political party. Students were advised to avoid partisanship at the university.[103] Those students who did join or work for political associations were exceptional. Radical nationalism and anti-Semitism were sources of potentially wide political mobilization, but this potential would not be fully realized until the Republic.

Rather than promoting nationalist fervor, prewar fraternity life more often dampened political enthusiasm and conflict. The fraternities channeled and repressed extreme tension over student and political matters. Thus in this regard the fraternities operated much like local sharpshooting, gymnastics, religious, and veterans' associations. Moderation, repression, and grass roots order were their goals, not emotional outpourings of nationalist sentiment or political involvement. This, in combination with skillful negotiation between professors and the Prussian Ministry of Education, explains why such potentially divisive issues as the national debate over allowing Catholic fraternities to organize in 1904/05 were resolved with comparative ease in Marburg. The channeling and repressing effect of fraternity activities produced a "reason and willingness to compromise" in Marburg student conflicts.[104] Such repression was functional: if serious tensions could be avoided, then the most difficult questions of power, authority, and legitimacy—of who possessed the material and moral right to lead—might be shunted aside.

Looking back on organizational life before the collapse of the student council in 1912, a fraternity reporter captured the texture of student relations: "People were polite and correct with one another, but cool and stiff, proper—there were relatively few scuffles—but nobody did anything. In those days the Studentenausschuß was therefore more interested in preservation of order than in creative work. The committee organized beer parties and torchlight processions; that was the essence of one's work. The relationship between that situation and true student unity might be likened to that of the police state to the educative state: public order, little activity."[105] The observer despaired over student government impotence, just as Max Weber lamented the lack of political initiative among elites and the middle classes. Yet there was something quite useful about this impotence: student fraternities, like their counterparts in bourgeois organizational life, had made it their goal to channel, deflate, and defeat conflict and thereby maintain their tense position in the social hierarchy. Moreover, they saw in this a patriotic goal and an extension of their traditional task of educating the whole personality—in short, they believed that they were serving the general, and therefore higher, political interests of the nation.

The difference between fraternities and the two social clubs discussed before was that the moral authority of the former had been seriously challenged. It was no longer possible to speak of fraternity hegemony on the eve of World War I. Thus, the material support of alumni clubs was essential to fraternity survival. Similarly, fraternity life required and received the backing of university professors.

University instructors who came of age in the Second Empire were part of an expanding, divisive, and fragmented educational institution. Not only were there more students and departments; there were also increasing variations in the subjects instructors taught, the pay they received, and the influence they possessed. The Marburg university faculty before World War I was a mixed collection of academics, extending from a tiny group of mandarins to a larger body of upwardly mobile *Privatdozenten* who used the university as a stepping stone to advance professionally. Devotion to social peace, virtually regardless of the issues at hand, was the only thing uniting this differentiated group. Moreover, social peace might limit Prussian state intervention at the university, where a state-appointed commissioner (*Kurator*) represented government interests. Defusing conflict and preserving harmony thus became crucial functions of the university chancellor (*Rektor*), who was elected annually by professors.[106]

No foolproof method existed for encouraging student harmony. Even nationalist enthusiasm—ostensibly the easiest device for producing student solidarity—failed to yield uniform results. On 13 June 1913 liberal political scientist and chancellor Walter Troeltsch informed the city magistrate that fraternities could not reach agreement about their involvement in a big torchlight parade honoring Bismarck because of what appeared to be purely internecine disputes. The chancellor expressed "deepest regret" that local dueling fraternities were paralyzed by jealousies and disagreements. Instead of participating in the main event, dueling and other fraternities decided to hold a separate beer party and torchlight procession. Though Troeltsch counseled against prohibiting these actions, he also informed the magistrate that he, former chancellors, and members of the university senate would not attend these separate celebrations.[107]

Most instructors were patrons of the fraternity system in spite of the fact that they disagreed with many fraternity actions. Though a majority of professors supported nationalist ideology, the real bond between faculty and fraternities was a perceived need to maintain harmony. Preservation of the existing distribution of resources, through which fraternities maintained their tense preeminence, therefore became part of the professors' agenda for the university. It is true that many professors resisted the mobilization of the Freistudentenschaft for thorny legal reasons. But an overriding desire to avoid conflict was their central motive. One cannot help but note Chancellor von Sybel's testy preoccupation with maintaining calm as he complained of the lengthy position papers and general debate generated by nonfraternity student activities in 1907. "It is not right," wrote von Sybel about the Freistudentenschaft on 20 March, "that students, who are prone to spend too much time on questions of organization in the first place, are unnecessarily held in a state of tension and excitement over such issues. . . ."[108] Fraternity power interacted with the concern of Marburg professors to stabilize their position in university and polity.

Supported by alumni clubs, allied to teachers, and determined to suppress serious conflict, the fraternities escaped from the Empire with a considerable store of organizational and ideological resources. This was a special case of bourgeois adaptation to changes in organizational life. But the activities to which adaptation gave rise—drinking, dueling, ostentatiously wearing colored caps and sashes—rigidified in a ritualized code increasingly antagonistic to many students and townspeople. Fraternities were less capable than town clubs of retaining both moral and material leadership over their followers. Nationalism and ideological anti-Semitism offered vehicles for strengthening fraternity influence and exploiting longings for student solidarity. The ultimate goal was to muffle and channel such longings, to blunt serious conflict and stop the erosion of fraternity power. This strategy worked when conflict was relatively tame, as it was in the Empire. But it was impossible to predict if student social associations could absorb conflict in times of more intense political divisiveness.

The rise of mass politics and organized sectional interests prompted an uneven but discernible response from the city bourgeoisie. Whereas blue-collar workers, peasants, and white-collar workers organized relatively powerful occupational associations, the town *Bürgertum* was less willing to adopt such organizational forms. Nonetheless, town elites led and joined social organizations and institutions that pursued special interests. They maintained contacts with nonelite *Bürger* and were able to preserve their moral authority over local club life. Yet the price of this resisting, modifying, and reversing was the suppression rather than the resolution of tensions within the local bourgeoisie. Even though they hardened lines between socialist and nonsocialist communities of sentiment, bourgeois social organizations said that they cushioned conflict and thereby served an apolitical, national interest. The process of adaptation to new realities was relatively successful in the Marburg Sharpshooting Club and Gymnastics Club 1860 but less so for pure and modified fraternities, whose members needed powerful elite allies. Taking account of the unevenness and variability of this adaptation, what would happen to bourgeois social organizations when unprecedented social conflict and political turmoil erupted after 1914?

four

Binding Together
the Folk Community:
Social Organizations,
1914–1930

The second age of organization spanned the years from roughly 1880 to 1930. But the post-1914 period witnessed more than a simple continuation of prewar tendencies and patterns. There were changes in the number, types, leadership, and membership of Marburg social organizations. Additionally, the nature and intensity of social organizations' political involvement changed. Spurred by growing political tensions, social organizations helped to lead an unprecedented surge of apoliticism that escaped the control of bourgeois elites in the middle and late 1920s. While older forms of apoliticism persisted, many spokesmen for Weimar apoliticism argued that social organizations would do more than cushion political strife—they would bind together a moralistic, antisocialist "folk community" of disparate classes and strata. Independent of party control, efforts to form a folk community eventually provided a rich environment for Nazi agitation. The era of the war and Republic—and the middle and late 1920s in particular—thus saw not only an acceleration of tensions that had originated in the Empire but also an unprecedented rupture between the social and the political authority of the local bourgeoisie. The present chapter discusses the unfolding of these changes in post-1914 social organizations.

Changing Structural Patterns

Voluntary associations were part of a developing leisure market-place. Who entered this marketplace through voluntary associations? Who possessed resources for dominating the marketplace? By examining trends in association leadership, we can provide partial answers to these questions. Table 4-1 contains evidence for a shifting group of club officials, individuals who moved in and out of organizations, forming and reforming boards of officers in a tangle of social relationships specific to particular associations at particular times. We must be satisfied with viewing general, shared changes that mask some of the singular twists and curves in patterns of social leadership over five decades.

A very important development between the Empire and Republic was a change in the makeup of officials of Marburg social organizations.[1] The biggest shift involved the local elite, which comprised university professors, individuals in the free professions, clergy, bankers, prosperous building contractors, factory owners, high government officials like the lord mayor and various department heads, military officers, well-off retirees, high school teachers with doctorates, better-off landowners living in the city, and the spouses of these individuals. Though the share of leadership positions held by elites no doubt decreased even before 1880, we can hardly overlook a large dropoff that occurred in the Weimar Republic. Having occupied more than one-half of all leadership posts in the Second Empire, local elites saw their share drop to 37.7 percent in the Republic. During the Third Reich, elites' share of board of directors (*Vorstand*) seats increased again, but did not approach the level of the Second Empire. Yet elites were still the largest group of all organizational leaders in Marburg in the postwar period. During the Republic, elites were three times more likely to be officials than to be ordinary members in social organizations. Organizational life reproduced fundamental hierarchical relationships of the local class and status structure.[2]

The most important change within elites was an overall decline of university professors in leadership positions. Professors lost ground with regard to the proportion of such positions they held among all officials and among all elites (the latter having dropped from 36.4 to 15.8 percent between the Empire and Republic). Both proportions rose slightly in the Third Reich, but they never attained the level of the Second Empire. Obviously, this was a relative decline. University professors still gained election to the city

Table 4-1 *Percentage Distribution of Occupations of Social Organization Officials in Marburg, 1880–1936*

Stratum	Subgroup	1880–1918	1919–32	1933–36
Elite				
	Professors	19.4	6.0	6.5
	Free professionals	11.3	7.1	6.6
	Clergy	5.7	2.7	1.9
	Entrepreneurs	3.2	4.9	3.6
	Civil servants	2.8	4.9	5.7
	Women without professions	2.4	4.3	6.1
	Military officers (including retired)	2.4	1.5	1.0
	Pensioners	2.4	3.6	3.3
	High school teachers	2.0	1.3	1.9
	Others	1.6	1.4	1.7
	Subtotals	53.2	37.7	38.3
Nonelite independents				
	Trade registrants	12.9	6.4	3.6
	Craftsmen	5.7	11.4	7.6
	Retailers, innkeepers	4.8	7.0	10.5
	Farmers	0.4	0.3	0.0
	Subtotals	23.8	25.1	21.7

parliament, served in political parties as leaders and spokespersons, and joined nonpolitical clubs and associations. Marburg's best-known public figures were still university professors. They included Martin Rade, whose national newsletter, *Die christliche Welt*, and left liberal political activity kept democratic sentiment alive during the Republic, and Viktor Bredt, who helped organize the Economic party, one of the first major splinter groups of the Republic, and served briefly as justice minister under Brüning. Moreover, even though the share of leadership positions held by these individuals declined, professors were still overrepresented among club officers.[3]

The decline was due in part to increasing professional obligations and generational differences that affected the public-spiritedness of

Table 4-1 continued

Stratum	Subgroup	1880–1918	1919–32	1933–36
Nonelite employees				
	White-collar	3.2	7.3	13.7
	Civil servants	8.1	12.0	9.0
	Teachers	3.6	4.6	4.6
	Others	0.0	0.1	0.2
	Subtotals	14.9	24.0	27.5
Workers				
	Craft, skilled	5.7	7.8	7.3
	Unskilled	0.0	2.0	3.1
	Subtotals	5.7	9.8	10.4
Nonelite Berufslosen				
	Retired	1.6	2.1	1.3
	No occupation	0.8	1.3	0.8
	Subtotals	2.4	3.4	2.1
Total		100.0	100.0	100.0
Total numbers		248	940	524
Percent women		4.4	7.9	9.5

SOURCES AND METHODOLOGY: See n. 1, this chapter.

university instructors, and much of the decline may have taken place by the turn of the century.[4] But a more general change was also underway in Marburg. This becomes clearer if we focus on the other large groups of elite club officials. The share of club leadership roles for free professionals, clergy, military officers, and non-university teachers with doctorates declined after 1880. Free professionals were the largest group among all organizational leaders and among all elite leaders after World War I, but their overall share of both categories was dropping.

The relative nature of the decline must once again be stressed. There were still many club officials from the free professions and clergy. They included such townspeople as the physician Heinrich Corell, chair of the well-heeled Athletic Association in 1921 and a DDP candidate for city parliament in 1919; the lawyer Hermann Bork, a candidate for city parliament on the DNVP-DVP ticket in 1919 and official of the Burschenschaft Alemannia alumni association and the Association of Former *Gymnasium* Students; the pastor Dr. Karl-Bernhard Ritter, a board member of the Marburger Wingolf alumni club, a participant in the Wingolf fraternity's evening discussion sessions, and a member of the County Veterans' Association; and the pastor Wilhlem Plannet, who between 1919 and 1924 could be found as a board member in the "St. Jacob" Charity Association, the Hostel Association "Herberge zur Heimat," and the Philipps House.[5] In the Republic clergymen such as Ritter and Plannet were active "blessing, legitimizing, propping up or running along behind, most of the organizations and events in the culture," to use Stephen Yeo's words about Reading clergymen.[6] Lawyers, doctors, clergymen—all these bourgeois elites remained active as directors and organizers of local club life.

But with the exception of military officers, the groups that were losing ground collectively made up a large part of the *Bildungsbürgertum*, the vanguard of the first age of voluntary association formation. They were being replaced during the Republic and Third Reich by other elite groups. These included factory owners, high administrative officials, leading women, and well-to-do pensioners. Whereas these groups collectively accounted for less than one-quarter of all leadership posts held by elites in the Empire, they held more than 40 percent in the Republic.

The chief cause of this shift was a continuing expansion of Marburg organizational life, a process that began in the late nineteenth century and continued in the 1920s. In 1913 there was one voluntary organization for nearly every one hundred Marburgers; by 1920 the number was less than ninety, and by 1925 it dipped to seventy-three. In January 1930 there was one club or association for every sixty-three townspeople.[7] The organizational net had become broader than ever before, and consequently Marburg club officialdom was even more shifting, open, and complex in the Republic than it had been in the Empire.

These social changes failed to produce immediate ideological cleavages; both old and new elites subscribed to established traditions of public activity through voluntary associations. To use the word of one contemporary observer, an "automatic" club elite persisted, absorbed change, retained a coherent social identity, and transformed itself in the Republic. Like club officials of the early nineteenth century, this elite was generally Protestant, patriotic, and more well-to-do than most Marburgers.[8] Its members shared a sense of obligation to the community that was colored by immediate economic interests but rooted in traditions of public-spiritedness and loyalty to the town.

A brief look at the Schaefer family illustrates this continuity. Johann Conrad Schaefer (1848–1928) founded a wallpaper factory in Marburg in 1879. He built his establishment from "the smallest beginnings" and created what one colleague said was a firm "renowned throughout the world."[9] If that assessment is a bit hyperbolic, it is nevertheless true that the Schaefer factory was an important economic resource in a city with so little industry. The scion of an old Marburg family, Johann Conrad considered participation in public life a duty that status and influence prescribed. Schaefer cofounded the Retailers' Association in 1896 and participated in the Conservative Association, the Chamber of Trade, the Preservation Society, the Association for the Advancement of Local Tourism, and a veterans' club.[10] Service to the community, patriotism, and Christianity were the touchstones of Schaefer's existence when he was not making money. Committed to public activity, he occupied a place in Marburg life similar to that of early nineteenth-century industrialists.[11] Later generations of German industrialists were less likely to recognize community obligations. But Marburg manufacturers remained committed to public activity in spite of "specialization and management ideology."[12] Partly because of a lack of industrial development, Marburg manufacturers were not "set apart from the rest of the community," as was the tiny group of nonnative industrialists in Bochum.[13]

Schaefer allowed his son Bertram to take over the factory after his eldest offspring, Viktor, died in the war in 1916. In 1922 Bertram took full control and improved the incorporated factory until it stood "in first place in the German wallpaper industry in terms of its capacity." Most importantly, Bertram ran the establishment "in the spirit of his father." Bertram was dedicated to "sociopolitical tasks in the factory and cultivated general interests."[14] Besides establishing a number of social facilities for workers at his plant, Bertram belonged to numerous local groups, including the Hessian Flying Club, the Marburg Rowing Club, the Athletic Association, the Employers' Association for Clerical Workers, and the nationalist association Flottenverein. He was an honorary member of the town's biggest veterans' association, the Krieger- und Landwehrverein. He was also a member of the DNVP-DVP ticket for city parliament in 1919 and the Chamber of Industry and Trade during the Republic.[15] Like his father, Bertram held to elite traditions of involvement in local organizations, despite his being confronted with a more complex and polycentric public sphere.

Notwithstanding the example of Bertram Schaefer's inheritance of a leadership role, organizational leadership in the city was now open to a wider group of nonelite *Bürger*. From 1880 to 1935 a more differentiated group of the town bourgeoisie took control over an expanding number of leadership posts. Having obtained command of less than 40 percent of these posts in local clubs before 1918, the independent and employed lower middle classes gained almost half of them in Weimar and the Third Reich. The economic well-being of select lower-middle-class businessmen and officials, heightened "consumption" of leisure, increasing numbers of white-collar and manual workers in the labor force, and, above all, general increases in the organization of the population explain this growing quantitative presence of ordinary *Bürger* in club officialdom.[16]

The share of independent shopowners and craftsmen who were organization officials fluctuated but remained high. It increased from 23.8 to 25.1 percent between the Empire and Republic, only to fall to 21.8 percent under Nazi rule. Though its share in the work force was declining, the self-employed lower middle class was a surprisingly stable leadership group in local voluntary organizations. Independent artisans such as Friedrich Kuhn accepted such organizational activity as a community obligation in the same way elites did. Kuhn was an official of the Marburg Zither Circle (Zitherkranz) in 1911–12, and a board member of the Gymnastics Association 1885 (Turngemeinde 1885) in 1921. Additionally, he served as a city magistrate in 1925, joined the Tailors' Guild in the 1920s, and later ran as a candidate for city parliament under the banner of a special interest slate. An example of a retailer who filled a leadership role was the incorporated storeowner Rudolf Schimpff, an official of the Civic Association and a regimental veterans' association in 1930, and a member of the Krieger- und Landwehrverein and DVP in the middle 1920s.[17] Organizational activity by independents like Kuhn and Schimpff facilitated political involvement. Moreover, because association leadership presupposed relative economic health, the continued presence of lower-middle-class independents among club officials reflected substantial well-being in the face of Weimar's economic crises.[18]

"Unregistered" independents gained more leadership posts after 1918. These were townspeople who were listed as independent entrepreneurs (*Gewerbetreibende*) in city address books but who were not in the Trade Register for "open" trading companies. The local

Retailers' Association admitted only trade registrants until July 1928, and it is defensible to assume that, on the whole, unregistered individuals were less prestigious than their registered counterparts. An example of the former was Adam Krapf, a self-employed tailor in 1930, though not a master or Trade Register entrant. He was an official of the Athletic/Sports Association in 1913, and in 1925 he was elected to the *Vorstand* of the Sharpshooting Club 1897.[19] From being less than one-half of all self-employed club leaders before 1918, unregistered independents increased their share of leadership positions to almost three-quarters in the Republic and more than four-fifths after 1933. Craftsmen accounted for the biggest share of unregistered independents in the Republic, but retailers took the lead in the Third Reich. This was related in part to divergent economic experiences. Whereas the town artisanry's importance to economic life decreased, nonelite retailers rebounded from business hardships in the early Republic and continued to play a big role in local commerce. But not until the Third Reich did these economic changes make their mark on club life.[20]

The share of club leadership posts held by the independent lower middle class as a whole remained relatively stable, but that held by the employed lower middle class tended to fluctuate. This was a result of employees' expansion not only in the town work force but in the membership of the NSDAP after Hitler took power as well.[21] Consisting of middle and lower-level government administrators, office and shop clerks, and lower and middle school teachers, these classes and strata increased their collective share of leadership positions from 14.9 percent of the total in the Empire to 24 in the Republic and 27.5 in the Third Reich. They thus overtook the independent *Mittelstand* in club leadership. But it is worthwhile to note that the employed *Bürger* surged ahead of local independents as organizational leaders well after the city became a university and administrative center. The social holding power of self-employed shopkeepers and artisans delayed the advance of local administrative strata in voluntary organization leadership.

A shift toward club leadership by less prestigious groups also occurred within the new *Mittelstand*, though the timing here was different from that in the independent stratum. Because of the relative security and prestige offered by government employment, minor civil servants were the elites of employees. In both Empire and Republic they held larger shares of club leadership posts than white-collar workers. Georg Fülling, a judiciary clerk, sat on the board of directors of the Cavalry Association in 1925 and the Social

Club "Hessen" in 1927. Also active was the postal official Heinrich Merle, who besides being a candidate of the Interest Alliance in 1929, served as an officer of the Hiking Club 1907, a regimental veterans' association, and the local branch of the Club "Gabelsberger," which became the German Stenographers' Association during the Nazi dictatorship.[22]

But white-collar employees were gaining ground on government officials. The ratio of civil servants to white-collar workers holding leadership posts declined from 2.5 to 1 in the Empire to 1.6 to 1 in the Republic; in the Third Reich, white-collar employees overtook civil servants as club and association officers. Whereas white-collar employees made up only 3.2 percent of all organizational leaders in the Second Empire, they accounted for 7.3 percent in the Republic and 13.7 percent in the Third Reich, the latter share exceeding that of government officials, nonelite teachers, and unregistered shopkeepers and craftsmen. One such white-collar employee was Emil Wißner, a salesman, who was president of the German National Commercial Employees' Association in the early 1920s, a member of the Gymnastics Club 1860 since before World War I, and later a prominent National Socialist. Another white-collar worker, Konrad Gils, an office clerk, was secretary of the Evening School Association (Fortbildungsverein) in 1911 and a member of the State party in 1930.[23]

Lower and middle school teachers were the most stable of new *Mittelstand* strata, in that they held between 3.6 and 4.6 percent of all leadership positions during the fifty-five years covered by this study. Moreover, by 1933–36 the share of official posts held by high school teachers had returned to a level attained in the Empire. Teachers continued to serve as resident experts in organizational life, taking up leadership roles in singing clubs, choirs, dog breeding societies, religious associations, fraternity alumni clubs, and many other organizations. Typical was Gustav Fischer, who listed his occupation as *Lehrer*. He was an official of the Marburg Men's Song Club in 1913 and the Elisabeth Club in 1919 and 1930.[24]

In addition to members of the preceding groups, working-class individuals helped to widen organizational leadership. Their share of *Vorstand* posts increased from only 5.6 percent in the Second Empire to 9.8 percent in the Republic and 10.3 percent in the Nazi dictatorship. Though the share of working-class people who were club officials was well below this group's proportion of the city labor force (29.6 percent in 1925), the overall trend was toward more working-class involvement in organizational leadership.

A wider range of workers gained access to official posts in voluntary associations. Craft and skilled laborers organized Marburg's first trade unions and Social Democratic party. They dominated and shaped working-class organizational life in the Second Empire, when none of the working-class leaders accounted for in table 4-1 were unskilled laborers. Moreover, craft and skilled workers provided the largest share of working-class club officials in the next two periods, with 79.3 percent in the Republic and 70.4 percent under Nazi rule. Typical of these individuals was the printer Hubert Weber, who was an official of the Printers' Association in 1930 and an SPD city parliament representative in 1919, 1925, and 1929. But unskilled laborers became more visible in local clubs. In the Republic and Third Reich it was increasingly common to see people such as factory worker (*Fabrikarbeiter*) Johannes Emmerich take up leadership posts in local voluntary organizations. Emmerich was an official of the Factory Workers' Association in 1930 and Gymnastics Association 1885 from 1927 to 1934.[25]

There was also a gradual shift in the gender composition of voluntary organization leadership. In the Second Empire less than 5 percent of club officials were women. But this share increased to almost 8 percent in Weimar and nearly 10 percent in the Third Reich. In all three eras, elite women without professions were in the forefront, making up more than half of all women officials from the Empire to the Republic and nearly two-thirds in the Third Reich. They included individuals like the dentist's wife Maria Corell, who was a *Vorstand* member of the Association for Former Members and Friends of the Elisabeth School. Another example of an elite female club official was Frau Professor Joseph, who founded the Housewives' Association in 1915 and acted as its leader until 1919, served as an official of the German Evangelical Women's Association at the start of the Republic, and became a member of the People's Church Association in 1919. In 1919 Joseph was also a candidate for a city parliament seat on the DNVP-DVP ticket. But these elite *Berufslosen* were by no means the only women who were directors of organizations. An example of a nonelite female club official is Elisabeth Hast, who gave her occupation as "teacher" (*Lehrerin*). She was a *Vorstand* member of the Teachers' Association in 1930 and an official of the Housewives' Association in the same year. An active politician, she also ran for city parliament for the DVP in 1924 and 1929.[26]

The leisure marketplace—or, more accurately, that part of the marketplace structured by voluntary associations—underwent considerable change from 1880 to 1935. Nonelite groups gained more club leadership posts during the Republic, a process the Third Reich turned back slightly. But during the Republic and the Nazi dictatorship less prestigious groups within nonelite strata came to have increasing control over leadership positions. In this administrative and service center the overwhelming number of club leaders came from the town bourgeoisie. Thus more and more nonelite *Bürger* possessed the skills, contacts, responsibility, and social prestige that associational activity brought. Still, elites certainly had not been pushed aside; they continued to take seriously their traditional commitments to the local public sphere. The widening of organizational leadership occurred while local elites retained considerable influence in the board meetings, membership assemblies, and social activities of Marburg's many voluntary associations.

If the underlying cause of changes in organizational leadership was an expansion of club networks, what were the contours of this expansion? The Weimar Republic was a period of intense organization formation. Marburgers formed 2.09 clubs for every thousand townspeople in 1910–19. But of forty-eight organizations for which founding dates could be determined in this decade, twenty-seven appeared in 1919 alone. In that year townsfolk started sixteen occupational and other special interest associations, four political parties, three community action organizations, two veterans' clubs, one religious organization, and one student *Verein*. Organization formation reached 3 associations for every thousand inhabitants in 1920–29 and 5.9 in the overall period from 1918 to 1935. These figures are higher than those for the two most important decades of organization formation before World War I, 1880–89 and 1890–99, in which 1.92 and 2.79 associations per thousand Marburgers were formed. It is little wonder that local newspapers commented on the vigor with which townspeople threw themselves into organizational activity in the Republic.[27]

The number of voluntary organizations for every thousand townspeople—what I refer to as organization density—rose steadily in the Weimar Republic. From 10 in 1913, organization density rose to 11.3 in 1920, 13.7 in 1925, and 15.9 in 1930. This evidence suggests that greater organization of the population was both a cause and effect of increased tensions between and within classes in the Weimar Republic and of the general political mobilization of those years. It also demonstrates that the rising tide of apoliticism in Marburg in the 1920s was accompanied by increased opportunities for organization.[28] Besides political tensions, social differentiation due to population growth was a spur of increasing organization density. So was the university, a traditional motor of local club life. Student associations formed the second largest group of voluntary organizations in the city until the middle 1920s, though this share fell between 1914 and 1934, and fraternity alumni associations formed the single largest group in the Marburg Organization Register from 1900 to 1945. Clubs such as the University Association and the Association of Blind Students added to the roster of organizations generated by the university. Additionally, the church continued to play a prominent role in propping up *Verein* culture. Religious clubs, church choirs, Catholic and Lutheran youth groups, bible study organizations, and missionary societies peppered the landscape of local associations.[29]

But the major stimulant of voluntary organizations was the continued strength of the local bourgeoisie. In cities where large-scale trade unions and big capital dominated social and political life, or where the critical mass of people available for organization was greater, voluntary organizations centralized and consolidated their resources.[30] This occurred in a limited fashion in Marburg also. But in the Hessian university city, bourgeois groups exerted more influence on organizational culture, and maintained some of the traditional forms and workings of *Vereine*. Instead of favoring big, well-organized associations that pooled the resources of many small groups, town elites persisted in their taste for small, jealous, and often castelike clubs. This persistence—the source of that "club mentality" (*Vereinsmeierei*) so hated by social critics on both the left and the right—made possible a textured, dense organizational life that resisted "rationalization" into large, citywide *Verbände*.

Bourgeois organizational strength is best illustrated by comparison with socialist trade unions. The trade unions provided sociability as well as economic defense; they therefore reflected broader trends in working-class social life. Marburg trade union membership was on a downward slide in the Republic (see table 4-2). Only tobacco workers and white-collar workers, who in 1919 belonged to the two smallest unions in the list, gained members in the period covered by the data, whereas five others had significant drops in membership. There were fluctuations in membership between 1914 and 1927. For instance, railway workers' trade union membership was on the upswing in 1927 after recovering from the inflation, when membership sank from 150 in 1919 to 15 in 1924. But the trade unions eventually lost their gains of the early Republic, entering the difficult years of mass joblessness in the Depression seriously weakened by membership declines.[31] To make matters worse, working-class social *Vereine* complained of apathy and passivity among their adherents.[32] Faltering trade union organization, bad economic conditions, and weakened ties of sociability combined to depress working-class organizational life and reduce capacities to act politically.

Precisely the opposite occurred for bourgeois social organizations. One organization listed in table 4-2, the Property Owners' and Landlords' Association, more than doubled its membership between 1919 and 1930, registering the biggest gains in the early Republic when membership jumped from 255 in 1918 to 467 in 1921 (an increase of 83 percent). In this respect the association's experience paralleled that of trade unions in the early Republic, as townspeople rushed to pursue their group interests. Other evidence for 1922–23 indicates that the hyperinflation cut into the activities of the Property Owners' and Landlords' Association, affecting everything from publication of a newsletter to social activities. But the *Verband* recovered from the inflation and became one of the city's most active organizations. Its leaders worked with the Economic party in the early Republic and played an influential role in organizing special interest slates for municipal parliament elections. Other bourgeois organizations made less impressive but clearcut membership gains. One group, the hiking club, lost two members between 1929 and 1932, but these were difficult years of unemployment and declining per capita income in Marburg, and such modest losses were hardly serious. More importantly, the group reported increases in the average size of club hikes and other activities. Similarly, the Volunteer Medical Corps, whose membership gain was the smallest for the groups listed in table 4-2, reported that the proportion of active members in total club membership increased from 17.6 percent in 1927 to 23.4 percent in 1930.[33] During these years of difficult economic conditions and political turmoil, holding membership levels steady or increasing participation in club functions were signs of stability and resilience. Membership gains such as those recorded by the other associations in the list indicate the relative vigor of bourgeois organizational life in the Republic.

Membership in Marburg student associations reflects a comparable pattern (see table 4-3). Considerable fluctuations took place in the pure fraternities' membership after World War I, and in the late 1920s there were declines in the absolute number of pure fraternity students, the proportion of active fraternity members among

Table 4-2 *Membership Changes in Fourteen Marburg Voluntary Organizations, 1914–1933*

Group	Year	Members	Year	Members	Percent Change
Socialist trade unions					
Bookbinders	1925	43	1927	11	−74.4
Textile workers	1919	100	1927	32	−68.0
Woodworkers	1914	149	1926	58	−61.1
Metalworkers	1922	200	1927	80	−60.0
Railway workers	1919	150	1927	72	−52.0
Communal, state workers	1919	400	1927	390	−2.5
Tobacco workers	1919	19	1927	38	+100.0
White-collar	1919	25	1927	120	+380.0
Bourgeois social organizations					
Upper Hessian Hiking Club	1929	456	1932	454	−0.4
Volunteer Medical Corps	1927	153	1932	158	+3.2
Fishing Club	1923	120	1932	150	+25.0
County Veterans' Association	1919	1,600	1927	2,980	+86.3
Housewives' Association	1927	620	1933	1,200	+93.5
Property Owners' and Landlords' Association	1919	275	1930	600	+118.2

SOURCES: See nn. 31 and 33, this chapter.

all fraternity students, and the share of active and inactive pure fraternity students among enrolled students. In contrast, other types of organizations—Christian associations, student political *Bünde*, modified fraternities—steadily gained members. But leaving aside these important differences between student groups, evidence suggests that the long-term trend of associational membership from 1914 to 1930 was upward. At the outset of the Republic, the Marburg student body was less organized than it had been before the war. More than one-third of all students belonged to an organization in Marburg in the summer of 1919, whereas nearly one-half had been organized in 1914. Though the share of all organized students fluctuated, there was a steady increase in the early 1920s. In 1924–29, a crucial time in the political history of the city, the share was higher than the prewar proportion, averaging 49.7 percent for the six summer semesters of this period. The proportion of organized students declined in summer 1930, but the share of organized students averaged a good deal more than one-half in 1931–33. Although the percentage increase in the absolute number of organized students between 1927 and 1931 (33.5 percent) is a little less than that of enrollments (37.4 percent), the picture leaves an impression of relative stability and uneven increases in the overall organization of students. If formal organization is one measure of the capacity of students to act collectively, the Marburg student body as a whole was either holding steady or gaining in this regard.[34]

Were we able to find the more luxuriant detail of student organizational life for nonstudent associations, the trend might be similar, though fluctuations would undoubtedly be milder because of townspeople's greater economic and residential stability. Most importantly, we would find stability or slow increases in the proportion of townsfolk affiliated with voluntary organizations, especially after economic recovery in 1924.

Quantitative evidence outlines organizational developments in the Republic. The nonelite bourgeoisie acquired more leadership posts in a widening net of local associations. The *Bürgertum* benefited from a flourishing organizational scene more than did the working class. Bourgeois organizational life prospered after 1918 while working-class organizational life declined after a surge in the early Republic. For the town bourgeoisie there was increased organizational activity from below at a time when liberal and conservative parties were weakening from above. The Marburg bourgeoisie was socially strengthened at a moment when the disarray of nonsocialist and non-Catholic parties exceeded all previous boundaries. Did these developments enhance the "blunting" function of social organizations, which had worked relatively effectively in the Second Empire? Did they make it easier to soften tensions between and within local classes and strata, away from the daily conflict of party politics? Or was all this the opening for greater political divisiveness in social organizations and for direct political action by these organizations? By deepening the picture of post-1914 developments suggested by quantitative material, the remainder of this chapter addresses such issues.

Table 4-3 *Membership in Marburg Student Organizations, Summer Semesters, 1914–1933*

Year	Total Organized Students	Organized Students per 1,000 Enrolled
1914	1,201	474.9
1919	1,388	353.7
1920	1,352	427.6
1921	1,168	469.5
1922	1,093	456.6
1923	979	415.7
1924	952	442.2
1925	1,040	521.3
1926	1,153	506.8
1927	1,424	514.6
1928	1,627	494.1
1929	1,908	502.5
1930	1,821	464.8
1931	1,901	500.0
1932	1,777	518.1
1933	1,767	555.7

SOURCES: HSAM 305a, Acc. 1954/16, 1–78; *DHS* 4 (1930): viii, 10 (1932/33): 11, and 12 (1933/34): 20.

When Solidarity and Numbers Mean Everything

World War I touched off a current of activity in bourgeois organizational life that was to continue, with a significant interruption, into the middle and late years of the Republic. In 1914–18 social organizations were called on to perform duties that government was unable to shoulder. Illustrative of this was the claim made in a 1915 circular of the Committee for the Care of War-Disabled Veterans. "The Reich, state, and the communities will not be able to accommodate fairly all the demands for care that severely wounded, crippled and incapacitated soldiers place on them," the circular read. Government would have to rely on "the willingness of the private sphere to help." In the case of the war-disabled, leaders of a variety of clubs were asked to recruit members who were "willing to collect donations for the cause."[35]

Women's clubs were particularly distinguished in public-spirited activity in the war. A local army colonel's wife took charge of the National Women's Service branch in the city and organized the making of clothing for troops and civilians. The Red Cross and Patriotic Women's Association took charge of a refreshment stand for troops who stopped at the train depot. Other groups followed the example of Marburg women. The County Agricultural Association, which negotiated with the city over the production and delivery of foodstuffs, and the Bakers' Guild, which agreed to regulate the price of baked goods, were among the examples. Trade unions and local employers in the building trades organized a wartime commission in 1915 to forestall unemployment. The city transformed a number of local fraternities into hospitals and first-aid stations. In 1917 Reich authorities mobilized county administrative officers to appoint local notables who would "enlighten" the population about war goals, encourage people to persevere, and urge consumers to follow rationing guidelines. Among the latter were leading women, university professors, city officials, factory owners, pastors, and well-to-do shopowners—all of whom used their considerable influence to propagandize local *Vereine*.[36] Though of varying effectiveness, these activities touched many organizations and created numerous opportunities for cooperation between social life and government. More importantly, such efforts were concrete reminders to townspeople that the local bourgeoisie served national interests.

With the involvement of so many associations in these public activities came increased sensitivity to sectional interests. Most obviously, war generated the self-organization of veterans. By winter 1915/16 a Marburg branch of the Berlin-based Academic Aid Association offered "war-disabled academics more individualized advice and attention" than that provided by "general wartime agencies." In April 1918 Marburgers formed the Association of War Disabled Veterans. Its first public assembly was held on 7 July 1918.[37] The net of associations for the war-disabled would expand in the Republic.

Wartime economics sharpened awareness of other material interests. Remarking on public opinion of city administration in the war, the businessman and city economic commissioner Stumpf noted the "impertinent tone dominating offices and businesses" because of shortages and rationing. Present since the beginning of the war, disaffection prompted the formation of new economic organizations and the activation of old ones. For housewives, wartime stringencies created growing problems for household economies. This led to formation of the city's first economic interest association solely for women. Established in 1915 by Frau Joseph, the wife of a university professor, the Housewives' Association became one of the largest and most active occupational organizations in Marburg during the Republic.[38]

At the opposite end of the spectrum was resistance to forming new economic interest organizations, a resistance that originated in a similarly heightened sense of material interests. In August 1914 Reich and Land authorities made efforts to ease the credit difficulties of artisans and retailers by encouraging cooperatives. The city magistrate wanted to strengthen Marburg's "weakly developed system of cooperatives," but local guild leaders, officials of the Business Association and Merchants' Association, and the director of a merchants' cooperative opposed such attempts. They argued that a new credit cooperative was "purposeless" because, as a member of a larger system of cooperatives beyond the control of local merchants and artisans, it would have to underwrite the debts of other organizations.[39] The formation of the Housewives' Association and the resistance of small business to new economic *Verbände* were two different results of the same development, namely, a heightened awareness of occupational interests. Though authorities strove to call forth patriotism and self-sacrifice, the war furthered the rise of organized sectional interests that had begun prior to 1914.

Herbert Freudenthal has argued that *Verein* sociability increased during World War I in Hamburg.[40] There is compatible evidence for Marburg. Military control, the draft, membership losses, and financial difficulties created severe problems for most local voluntary organizations. But *Bürger* who remained in Marburg, those to whom the task of upholding town social life had fallen, strengthened organizational infrastructures. In many areas of social life, World War I increased bourgeois control over organizational resources, a process that strengthened social interchange in numerous associations.

Student fraternities provide some of the richest evidence. Deprived of so many members by the needs of the state, fraternities nevertheless maintained networks of sociability. This was done partly through fraternity correspondence. There is in this correspondence the poignancy of a Verdun-bound Marburg Alemannen (a member of the Burschenschaft Alemannia fraternity) who wrote of his good luck at "not yet being wounded or sick," and who mentioned sadly not having seen any fraternity brothers in the field. But there is also business as usual. Members wrote to one another

about admission of new students, the future of fraternities at German universities, dues payments, and merry "student and sexual
life" in Berlin, where one member of Marburg Alemannia spent
part of the war. Though there was disagreement over the propriety
of dueling during wartime, Marburg fraternity members fought the
Mensur as early as December 1916. In February 1917 university
chancellor Leonhard was compelled to send a memorandum to "all
student *Vereine*" reminding them that wartime ordinances established an ll p.m. curfew for all restaurants, taverns, and clubs. "It is
doubtful," wrote Leonhard, "if the continuation of social activities
after eleven o'clock in the rooms of fraternity houses . . . is permis-
sible." Such practices constituted a "bypass around the ordinance"
that, Leonhard said, must not be allowed. When in January 1918
one Marburg fraternity correspondent warned his colleagues not to
"booze it up too much" for the Kaiser's birthday celebration, he
knew that this annual drinking bout would take place in the midst
of war just as it had before 1914.[41]

Correspondence, dueling, and drinking mixed with service to the
national good, as some fraternity students perceived it. Public-spiritedness on the homefront was reflected in debates over an old
problem among students, unification in a single national student
organization. Different concepts for achieving this goal circulated
among Marburg students at the university and the front.

One plan came from modified fraternities. One representative
each from the Association of German Students, Student Gymnastics Association, and Academic Association tried to gain support
for a local branch of a Student Lodge in 1917. The lodge stressed its
"omnibus character," political and confessional neutrality, and coherent philosophical outlook. It was not an interest group (*Zweck-
verband*) or a "combat organization" (*Kampforganisation*). Instead,
supporters of the lodge argued that they were organizing "a community based on shared experiences and common work." Whereas
lodge members said they did not want "to impugn the spirit of
legitimate forms and traditions of the student body," they pledged
to "unite members of old and new organizations on the basis of
shared experiences as true students in academic life." The lodge set
up a coordinating committee, sent letters to students at the front,
and started discussion groups dealing with "persistent conflicts"
between student organizations. Although it excluded women, the
lodge supported goals that members of early student professsional
clubs and the Freistudentenschaft had championed and that Weimar student governments would adopt.[42]

The pure fraternities countered with their own suggestions for unifying students. Warning that the lodge tried to organize students on a "Russian or English model," one member of Alemannia in August 1917 stressed that there was only one reliable way of achieving "eventual unification of students," namely, devotion to "collective tasks and further sacrifice for King and Fatherland. If all student organizations declare themselves *for this work* after the war," the student said, "then there won't be time for all the strife." Stressing that German student unity was "born in the difficult days of the outbreak of war," pure fraternities used the conflict to outline schemes for organizing students in peacetime.[43] The underlying assumption of such plans was that pure fraternities would represent students and lead the omnibus organization that everyone anticipated.

Many nonstudent associations were resilient in the face of wartime hardships. The city's largest veterans' organization, the Krieger- und Landwehrverein, reported that its 1917 annual assembly was "well attended" even though 181 of 389 members were in the field, that the club had collected more than 1,500 marks for support of widows and orphans, and that "the economic situation of the club was satisfactory." The Evening School Association reported in early 1917 that in spite of dropping an annual Christmas celebration, it would continue the regular winter lecture series with "the usual number" of speakers. Later in 1917 the association reported that it reopened its library, which still had "an enthusiastic clientele, even in wartime." Sports organizations such as Soccer Club Germania 08 maintained social ties by holding matches during the war.[44]

Notions of "community" and *Volk* increasingly became the ideological currency of bourgeois social interaction. This was recast language adapted to wartime but related to the cross-class imagery of bourgeois liberalism, nationalism, and anti-Semitism. The Kaiser's *Burgfrieden*, a civil harmony imposed from above, should not be treated lightly in this regard. For within the local bourgeoisie there was not only a willingness to listen to language of the general good; there were also concrete instances of supporting perceived national interests in welfare work, lecture series, soccer, and debates over student solidarity. This activity was far more influential at the grass roots than were mass festivals, anti-Semitic tracts, and other manifestations of nationalist traditions present before World War I. It is hardly surprising that in Marburg the Fatherland party would find support with imagery of the "German people's will" (*Volks-*

willen) and plans for "unification of all patriotic forces without regard for their party political stance." But not only political parties employed such language. The student associations already cited strengthened these sentiments in the field and at home. Nonstudent clubs such as the Hesse Association (Hessenbund), formed in August 1918, did likewise. The Hessenbund was formed by people with diverse political views, from the bookstore owner Gottlieb Braun, who supported the Fatherland party and later the DNVP and NSDAP, to Professor Edmund Stengel, later a DDP member until 1928. Its specific concern was Hessian folklore and art. But it stressed that "in the situation that most likely will face us after the war we can achieve something salutary and lasting when *all forces work together.*"[45]

Such language was an ideological toggle switch fostering popular enthusiasm for national solidarity. Subsequently exploited and reshaped by the Nazi party, the notion of an all-embracing national community resonated in local bourgeois organizations. Despite wartime stringencies, declines in nutritional standards due to food shortages, and tremendous human losses—in short, despite factors that gave Germans good reason for feeling that they faced economic and social ruin in the bitter last days of war—a commitment to the elusive public good heightened. Above all, the local bourgeoisie upheld the networks of organizational life, structures that facilitated public commitment. This was the most important heritage of the war for the Marburg *Bürgertum*, which claimed that it represented the general good better than any other group.

Wartime mobilization of voluntary organizations carried over into the early Republic.[46] The *Hessische Landeszeitung* spoke approvingly in its "Retrospective Look at the Past Week" on 25 November 1918 of activity by "all estates, associations and guilds" that "encouraged members to discuss their legitimate interests." The paper marveled that "despite the cares, people have not lost their vigor."[47] Marburg *Bürger* believed that traditional practices of social life would return the community and nation to normalcy. This was a national pattern, and "as if from second nature, [Germans] again settled into" accepted club routines, whether the site was Marburg or Hamburg, Göttingen or Frankfurt/Main.[48]

The Republic continued and extended bourgeois concerns about representing group interests. Of 164 organizations formed in Marburg in 1918–32, more than 56 percent were occupational and other special interest associations, a proportion nearly double that of the pre-1917 years. Marburgers were aware of the trend. All groups in the city—from newly unionized socialist white-collar workers, who were reminded that "power lies only in organization," to fraternity members such as the writer who exhorted Kösener Corps members to "organize before it's too late!"—expressed their conviction that pursuing sectional interests was an unavoidable condition of contemporary life.[49]

One of the best examples of this pursuit of sectional interests can be seen in the activity of local religious organizations. It was rare to see religious organizations step into the light of political conflict. The church more normally melted into the culture of the town, as religious values permeated both religious and ostensibly nonreligious associations. But the Social Democrats had displaced a Reich government supported by the Protestant church. The new regime declared worship to be a private matter and recommended that public financial support for churches be stopped. Reminded of the example of the Third Republic in France, Protestant church leaders feared that a separation of church and state would be damaging to Protestantism.[50] Although such misgivings proved to be unfounded, and the church emerged from the war stronger in some respects than before, the potential danger of new religious policies sparked a surge of activity in grass roots religious organizations.

In Marburg on 9 December 1918 six speakers "from the various strata and interested parties of the Evangelical community" addressed a huge audience of church members to promote debate on church policy toward the new regime. The discussion leaders included Martin Rade, a university theologian and soon member of the DDP, and the bookdealer August Sonnenschein, later chair of the DNVP. Thus conservative as well as liberal wings of the bourgeois political spectrum were represented at the meeting. The university professor Stephan told the audience that such discussions were intended to remind voters in upcoming National Assembly elections that Protestantism was not "a meaningless, fragmented anachronism, but a united power to be reckoned with." By early 1919 Marburg religious groups formed a People's Church Association (Volkskirchliche Vereinigung). The association warned against attacks on the church from government circles; exhorted church members to guard Protestant interests; and counseled caution toward the new regime's church policies even after National Assembly elections made a separation of church and state inimicable to the Evangelical population less likely.[51]

The actions of religious organizations were one sign of a deeper change in bourgeois attitudes toward large, specialized associations competing for power in the national polity. Although the Marburg bourgeoisie continued to look upon such groups with chagrin, there was a resigned acceptance of the situation and a resolve to adapt to the dominant direction of change. An example from the Kösener Corps fraternity newsletter suggests the ambiguities of this acceptance. Representing the most exclusive of student associations, a Corps alumnus observed that "the call to organize is a sign of the times."[52] Noting the full hegemony of special interest associations in the present "democratic-socialist regime," the writer reminded his brothers that the state no longer dealt "with single individuals, or with small clubs, but rather with large-scale associations." "Numbers," he observed, "now mean everything."[53] The lesson was as obvious as it was regrettable, as the Corps writer noted sarcastically: "So we see trade union organizations of . . . all occupational groups including the unemployed, and all we need now is a special interest organization for felons. Because of this mania," he continued, "Corps students will also have to reflect on how they can achieve a broad special interest association with those who share similar principles."[54]

In addition to greater organization, increased awareness of sectional interests, and calls for national solidarity, here was another central theme of the war and Republic for local bourgeoisie: mass organization, which both big labor and big capital had already achieved, meant everything. Marburg *Bürger* may have reached this conclusion more slowly than their counterparts in larger or more industrialized cities. Still, by the middle 1920s, they were more willing than ever before to support large-scale, national pressure groups. This was a significant adaptive moment in the campaign to maintain bourgeois moral leadership and material power in the city.

In spite of adaptation, older patterns of *Verein* culture persisted. A song club official told members to "be true to your *Verein*," a sentiment echoed by other organization leaders.[55] Such appeals seemed to place club loyalty above other concerns and strengthen bourgeois narrowness. Additionally, self-absorption reinforced the exclusivity of club members in the wider society and of club activists in particular organizations. Within singing clubs, to continue with this type of association, active participation in singing practice and club programs was confined to specific organization members. The share of such members ranged from 50 percent in the Liederkranz and 43 percent in the Liedertafel, both bourgeois clubs, to just over 33 percent of the Social Democratic song club Eintracht, which had 105 members.[56] The main activity of the club, singing, was closed to large groups of members in all three organizations. Singing demanded time and some talent, and not all townspeople possessed these resources. But the examples suggest a general picture of narrowing opportunities for active involvement and greater membership passivity in increasingly exclusive social clubs. Both tendencies widened the distance between social clubs and public life in general.[57]

Pure and modified fraternities remained exclusive clubs absorbed in their rituals and practices. The university chancellor noted continued "closure [*Abgeschlossenheit*] of the fraternities toward one another" in 1920. Disputes between pure and modified fraternities over assigned positions in the Reich Founding Celebration of 20 January 1926 led to the breakup of the Corporation Committee, an interfraternity council, and caused the fraternity chronicler Georg Heer to lament "that students are still far away from . . . real unity of thought and practice." The encapsulation of some fraternities led to implosion. Seeking to avoid rather vaguely described internal differences in 1928–29, Marburger Wingolf divided its membership into three departments with officers at the head of each.[58] Narrowminded practices of club life once again shaped the social experiences of students and *Bürger* in the Republic.

But wartime enthusiasm for new forms of solidarity and increased interest in large, well-organized *Verbände* combined to make club officials more aware of the need to fight such narrowness. The Retailers' Association, which in Wilhelmine Marburg had been a social organization of better-off shopowners, opened its doors in July 1928 to businessmen who were not enrolled in the Trade Register. Women's groups, primary targets for critics of bourgeois exclusivity, formed a City Association in the 1920s that included the Housewives' Association, German Evangelical Women's Association, Teachers' Association, Society for Germandom Abroad, Jewish Women's Association, and the Catholic Mothers' Club. Rheinfranken fraternity officials said they wanted improved ties with town notables, especially military officers, through various social functions. Marburger Wingolf asked if fraternities were "still contemporary" (*noch aktuell*) in view of their devotion to narrow corporate principles. Local religious associations supported a drive to consolidate Lutheran and Reformed churches in the 1920s. Despite their self-isolation, voluntary organizations were involved in *Verein* anniversary ceremonies, patriotic festivals such as the Reich Founding Celebration, and other activities.[59] Much of this failed to overstep narrow organizational boundaries. Nevertheless such activity reflected a desire to renew traditional images of openness and accessibility in bourgeois social life.

Yet it was more than an image. *Bürger* spokesmen never abandoned traditions stressing a full interweaving of the general interest, special interests, and shared social interchange. Solipsism and specialized associations were products of the time; but might they not encourage a rethinking of the relationship between specific interests and the elusive public good? The answer of most Marburg bourgeois groups would have been affirmative. The experiences of townfolk in World War I played an important role in shaping this response. Notions of a folk community existed before 1914, but bourgeois Marburgers thought they saw a concrete example of such solidarity in the war. When veterans' association leaders or fraternity spokesmen invoked the "front experience" (*Fronterlebnis*) at local festivals and club meetings, they reinforced a collective memory of wartime solidarity. It hardly mattered if the *Volksgemeinschaft* never really materialized in the war; more crucial was the feeling, the belief, that it had existed. Expanding, mobilizing voluntary associations were among the sluiceways that channeled this sentiment for the local bourgeoisie. National solidarity and the numbers required to achieve it now meant everything. These sentiments reinforced the appeal of the intense apoliticism of Weimar, a forceful antidote to rancorous party struggles.

Heightened Apoliticism

Increased organization, intensified concern for group interests, and widened commitment to a vaguely defined public good—these were increments of change accumulating before and throughout an era of heightened apoliticism in the Republic. State intervention in social organizations created conditions for this change after 1918, just as it had touched off voluntary association activities in wartime. The Weimar Constitution intentionally lowered the costs of organization as Social Democratic leaders announced on 12 November 1918 that "the rights of organization and assembly admit to no restrictions." But more important than legal changes was the regime's need to rely on organizational life for political stability. Unable to gain a monopoly over the means of repression, the Majority Social Democrats called upon paramilitary squads, civil defense units, and other organizations to create conditions for a parliamentary democracy.[60]

Marburg bourgeois organizations quickly exploited Social Democratic reliance on social life. No better example of bourgeois social power at the start of the Republic can be found than the history of the local Workers' and Soldiers' Council, led by Social Democrat Bruno Poersch. Formed on 11 November 1918 "to create order," the council argued that it was the "controlling instance of the Revolution." But it was never more than a demobilization committee. The real job of controlling the course of revolution in Marburg went to routine bourgeois organizations and institutions—social clubs, fraternities, economic associations, the city government, the university.[61] Only ten days after the council appeared, the *Hessische Landeszeitung* lamented poor attendance at an assembly of the Civic Association (Bürgerverein) called to discuss council business. Competing assemblies of the Hansa Association and a white-collar workers' organization may have contributed to low attendance, but the *Hessische* commented that the "lord mayor and assistant mayor apparently did not send representatives to this public meeting at all." This was noteworthy, the *Hessische* continued, "because at earlier assemblies, which other groups sponsored, they rarely missed attending."[62]

In mid-December the council grudgingly admitted that bourgeois *Vereine* had seen to it that "the breakdown of the old powers did not result in Bolshevist chaos."[63] Bolshevist chaos had never been a threat; but bourgeois social organizations had smoothed the transition from war to Republic. This had enabled the conservative *Oberhessische* to speak admiringly of Marburg's calm in early December.[64] Insofar as social organizations muffled conflict, they acted within prewar traditions. But there was something artificial about such efforts to downplay disagreement; the violent Republic was, after all, not the Empire. Voluntary associations could now be drawn into more direct political activity, and this created new problems and opportunities for the *Bürgertum*.

Events following the abortive right-wing Kapp Putsch on 13 March 1920 increased political involvement of social organizations in Marburg. The university once again led the way in linking national events with local life. In 1919 government and military officials had tried to engage students for paramilitary activity in service to the Republic. Building on such attempts and unable to stop fighting between insurgent Communist and Republican forces after the coup, authorities asked university students nationwide to join temporary volunteer military units that would restore order in 1920. Officials not only exploited student patriotism but spoke to specific professional interests as well. A 19 March 1920 advertisement in Marburg newspapers called for students to "put aside . . . personal interests and strive for common goals." Authorities offered to postpone classes and give special consideration in scheduling exams for students who joined military units, street patrols, and emergency work service (Technische Nothilfe).[65]

The appeal was successful. Within twenty-four hours of the 19 March call to arms, more than eight hundred students turned out to join the Student Corps (Studentenkorps, or Stuko), the collective appellation of student volunteers attached to the Eleventh Army Brigade.[66] The components of the corps had been present since 1919, when Kassel Reichswehr officials mobilized small numbers of students from universities and technical colleges in volunteer units. But in March 1920 Marburg students entered a new stage of active paramilitary service. They were to be engaged in Thuringia, where anti-Kapp mobilization and Communist and Independent Social Democratic agitation alarmed the authorities. The volunteers amounted to more than one-fifth of the total student enrollment in Marburg, a population artificially swollen by demobilized soldiers. The response to Stuko contrasted sharply with earlier student distrust of voluntary units designed to defend Weimar.[67]

The Student Corps consisted of two batallions, with six companies in the first and four in the second. Pure fraternity members made up the vast majority of volunteers in the first four companies of the first batallion, which contained Corps, Burschenschaft, Landsmannschaft, and Turnerschaft students. Additional companies included Marburger Wingolf students and members of the Catholic fraternities. The second battalion consisted of four more companies, one of them (the Ninth) the so-called People's Company, which contained approximately one hundred students and townsmen who supported the Republic. It was led by DDP member and theology professor Heinrich Hermelink and Marburg law student Ernst Lemmer, also a Democrat. Accompanied by fraternity flags and cheering crowds, Stuko volunteers marched to the train depot before departing for Thuringia.[68]

Most Stuko members said that they were apolitical and were interested solely in reestablishing "peace and order." This might entail shooting "Spartacists," according to company commander Heinrich Bogislav von Selchow, a forty-three-year-old naval officer and Marburg history student.[69] This stance mirrored fraternity members' perceptions of an apolitical—but potentially violent—realm of antidemocratic, antisocialist, and anti-Semitic thought free of party political interest. Conversely, because the People's Company supported the Republic, Stuko said this unit had "party political" interests that made it "militarily unuseable." The presence of the student Ernst Lemmer, an outspoken public critic of nationalist students in 1919 and now a member of the "politicized" People's Company, reinforced fraternity antipathy towards the latter.[70]

Unlike the Tübingen volunteer Student Batallion, which saw no military action, sixty men of the Studentenkorps received orders from von Selchow to seize "Spartacists" who had been denounced in the village of Bad Thal. Twenty Stuko members were responsible for escorting fifteen prisoners to Gotha along the Eisenach-Gotha highway at 5:30 a.m. on 25 March. Within three hours all fifteen prisoners were dead. The evidence suggested an execution. But the fraternities defended fourteen students who were indicted for manslaughter, arguing that the prisoners had attempted to escape.[71] In two trials, one before a military court in June and another before an assize court in December, the students were found not guilty.

But there were other ramifications. The main political effect of the killings was to sharpen conflict between workers and fraternity students. Before the coup, supporters of the Republic in Marburg publicly criticized fraternity students for their "doubtful" allegiance to Weimar, a suspicion fueled in part by General Ludendorff's appeal to students to join the forces defending the coup. On 16 March Marburg workers, white-collar employees, and civil servants joined nonlocal groups in a demonstration and protest strike against the *Putsch*. This event drew between three hundred and four hundred participants and ended with demands for the confiscation of weapons given the fraternities by the Reichswehr in 1919. Though protest quieted when Stuko departed for Thuringia, news of the shootings once again escalated conflict.[72] Now the trade unions accused fraternities of preparing for counterrevolution by hiding weapons, agitating for the coup in university classes, and drawing up lists of pro-Republic politicians who were to be rounded up after the coup. Among the most vocal critics of students was Lemmer, who along with Professor Walther Schücking was the first to report the Thuringian shootings to military authorities. Protest was heightened by criticism of Stuko from Social Democratic Reichstag representatives and Prussian Minister of Education Konrad Haenisch, who called the students "rogues" and accused them of "cowardly assassination." Later in 1920 antagonism between fraternity students and their critics would escalate into violence.[73] No longer the quiet city of local conservative imagination, no longer stolid in the face of postwar political struggle, Marburg was split by open class conflict.

Against the backdrop of Reich politics, however, Marburg was relatively calm. This was due mainly to the activity of Marburg notables, especially university professors, who helped to contain the effects of the shootings. They did so by smothering antipathies toward students and deflecting criticism of the fraternities. There was no conspiracy. But by allaying tension within their own ranks, professors reasserted the primacy of social harmony at the university in order to defend students more effectively.

Such harmonizing efforts took a variety of forms. Though Chancellor Wilhelm Busch admitted not having full details of the shootings, he expressed unequivocal support for the Student Corps in a 31 March letter to the university commissioner. Writing that the Student Corps "never pushed politics," the chancellor emphasized that "these young men were willing once again, not only to interrupt their studies, but to lay their lives on the line for the domestic peace of the fatherland." The chancellor and university deputation wrote Haenisch on 17 July 1920, asking him to retract his statements about "Marburg rogues"—which Haenisch did later in the year.[74] When professors Hermelink and Rade, both supporters of the Republic, aroused students' ire by criticizing them and calling for conciliation with workers, Chancellor Franz Bruno Hofmann stepped in. He and a colleague helped to "soothe" (*beschwichtigen*) students' antagonism toward Hermelink. When the assize court ruled in favor of the fraternity students in December, university authorities expressed pride in their students. "Though the present regime has up until now withheld its gratitude from students," the declaration pointedly read, "we, the academic authorities, at least want to express ours."[75] Other factors—faltering electoral support for the Weimar coalition, splits between SPD and USPD, increasing economic hardships—helped to blunt protest against Stuko. But by vigorously defending the fraternities, university professors did most to smother Republican attacks.

Yet the unique quality of students' foray into political conflict was hardly obfuscated by the wall of support thrown up by the university. Social organizations had stepped over the boundary between relatively passive absorption of conflict or cooperative alliance with the government, on one side, and direct, violent political activity, on the other. For students and the local bourgeoisie generally, the idea of conflict absorption—of "indirect" political activity—remained influential. But the underlying political system had changed. The moment of Student Corps violence was the local manifestation of this wider political reality. Apoliticism now encompassed more direct and potentially violent political mobilization. Not the war but the turmoil of the postwar period introduced a new element in the repertoire of social organizations.

Two processes hampered sustained political activity by Marburg social organizations until the middle 1920s. First, the Reich government gained partial control over nonparty groups in the political sphere. Thanks to pressure by trade unions and the Allies, the student volunteer military units were dissolved; what was left of the Student Corps went underground to practice "military sport" (*Wehrsport*). Government agents monitored burgeoning networks of paramilitary leagues and radical nationalist groups such as the German-Völkisch Defense and Combat League (Deutschvölkischer Schutz- und Trutzbund). Legislation gave police agents authority to observe veterans' associations and small-caliber sharpshooting clubs, but such authority was used haphazardly and unevenly. Throughout the Republic, police powers were used sparingly against nationalists and more stringently against Marxists. Marburg police officials' decision not to repress right-wing university students' political activity was the most glaring example of selective use of this legislation locally. Extraparliamentary organizations were still too powerful to make parliamentary sovereignty possible. Nevertheless, after plowing through the first contentious years of the Republic, the Weimar state succeeded in repressing temporarily the most violent opponents of parliamentary government.[76]

Second, the hyperinflation of 1922–23 dampened the activity of most local organizations. Despite the unevenness of economic hardship in Marburg, material conditions generally reduced *Verein* sociability in 1922 and 1923.[77] The hyperinflation may have been a spur to political activity by a small number of radical groups. But if one looks at organizational life in the broadest sense of the term, it is clear that the inflationary storm chipped away at the quotidian group relationships that gave townspeople a sense of continuity and social interchange.[78]

Individual examples of the inflation's effects abound. A highly organized local *Stammtisch* substituted coffee for beer during the hyperinflation. Though seemingly mundane, this action merited mention in the club's 1927 commemorative publication. A women's adult education club gave up its annual lecture series in late

1923, citing the risks of such undertakings in the economic crisis. A number of organizations reported membership losses, lagging attendance at meetings, and serious cutbacks in club facilities. The VfB, a prosperous sports organization compared to the more plebeian Gymnastics Club 1860 (which became the Gymnastics and Sports Club 1860 in 1920), noted significant membership losses during the hyperinflation; only the strong soccer and track departments "kept themselves up somewhat."[79] Routine business of organizational life, from collecting membership dues to renting halls, became uncertain. The inflation made it difficult to look beyond daily concerns of making a living. It made little difference whether Marburgers seethed about the Versailles Treaty, hated the weaknesses of the Weimar state, or deplored politicized city government. They could do little about such resentments, because in 1922–23 public discourse was too weak. Communications networks thinned in the hyperinflation, and they would have to be rebuilt before local organizational life recovered.

The return of relative economic stability after 1923–24 encouraged "consumerist" apoliticism—a withdrawal from political life in favor of leisure. Individuals had more discretionary income with which to attend movies, watch soccer games, buy clothes, and pay membership dues in different clubs. Local newspapers reflected this change, as advertisements for leisure-time pursuits increased after 1923. The small amount of literature presently available on consumption patterns in the Republic suggests that white-collar workers, civil servants, skilled workers, petty professionals, artisans, and retailers swelled the number of new consumers. To the extent that such consumption patterns touched voluntary associations, traditions of sociability in bourgeois organizational life now entered the marketplace more fully than ever before. This occurred in a variety of settings, from major cities such as Frankfurt/Main to smaller towns such as Weinheim an der Bergstraße.[80] By devoting social energy to the "consumption" of *Verein* activities, the local bourgeoisie potentially shut out the contradictions of Weimar party conflict.

But heightened apoliticism in the middle 1920s was more than a reflection of changing consumption patterns. For one thing, it was a sign of more aggressive grass roots opposition to the national party system. In city parliament, nonparty alliances spurred resistance to political parties per se. Alliance leaders were often former bourgeois party members who by their example encouraged townspeople to reject political parties in municipal life. Stronger antiparty sentiment gained real momentum in 1924, when more than half of the voters in city elections cast ballots for nonparty slates. This success continued in 1929, when the slates gained more than 40 percent of the vote in municipal parliament elections.[81]

These election results were surface manifestations of a deeper apoliticism throughout bourgeois organizational life. The candidates of the special interest slates were members of other associations, and their social activities were not confined to the parliamentary arena. In 1924 the leading candidate of the probusiness Working Alliance of Economic Associations (Arbeitsgemeinschaft der wirtschaftlichen Verbände), Wilhelm Münscher, was a member of the Marburg Sharpshooting Club, the Property Owners' and Landlords' Association, and the Technical Engineers' Club between 1919 and 1933. In 1930 Heinrich Ilk, also a member of the Working Alliance, belonged to the same sharpshooting club as Münscher. In addition, he had been an officer of the County Artisans' Association from 1921 to 1930 and a member of the Shoemakers' Guild. In 1925 he was listed as a member of the Reichsbanner, the Republican paramilitary league. The self-employed retailer Johannes Stumpf, leading candidate of the Bourgeois Working Alliance (Bürgerliche Arbeitsgemeinschaft) in 1929, had been a DDP politician in 1919. He was also a member of the Credit Reform Association and Association for Aid of Blind Students after 1916. One of Münscher's fellow candidates in the Working Alliance of Economic Associations was the independent carpenter Hermann Wildhack, who had belonged to the County Artisans' Association since 1921 and was a member of the Men's Singing Club "1842" in January 1930.[82] If a leading edge of apoliticism was the attack on political parties by interest group coalitions, the roots of that movement reached deeply into other Marburg voluntary organizations. It is impossible to know if coalition members tried to mobilize their clubs against the party system. Nonetheless, by virtue of the networks these individuals belonged to, the structures for antiparty mobilization existed in the middle and late 1920s.

Bourgeois social organizations also intensified their efforts to muffle political debate. The elite Stammtisch Käsebrod, a club in its own right with more than one hundred members, reported a decline in political discussion in the organization in comparison with earlier times. During the Empire, according to the published report of the club in 1927, Käsebrod acted like a "shadow" city government. In the war, Käsebrod became a "meeting place" where notables discussed "the events of the day . . . and high politics and strategy." But Weimar was different. Though the mayor and university commissioner remained Stammtisch members, the club allowed "no politics or political gossip," according to a chronicler; instead, Käsebrod stressed "a relaxed social tone."[83] It is doubtful that the group eliminated all political discussion. The chronicler's portrayal of club practice was undoubtedly more an injunction than a description—a reflection of the desire to insulate this social circle from the contentiousness of Weimar party and class strife.

Veterans' associations harbored the same desire. Karl Wilser, a minor postal official and officer of the Marburg Krieger-Kameradschaft in the 1920s, recalled that club members "were all comrades. We marched together, sang together, politics played no role." When asked if political interests in the club had been stronger in the middle and late 1920s than at other times, he said "No. Never."[84] One must handle such recollections with caution; they are inevitably colored by the passage of time. But Wilser's view is compatible with expressions of apoliticism by other Weimar organizational leaders. For Wilser as well as other townspeople, disdain for "politics" reflected a desire for—but not neccesarily the practice of—removing bourgeois clubs from the world of party political struggle.

Social clubs and veterans' associations, to say nothing of many other local groups, contained members of the liberal, conservative, Nazi, and splinter parties.[85] In a time of heightened conflict, what better strategy existed for overcoming tensions produced by competing party affiliations than that of limiting political discussion, of continuing traditional practices whereby social organizations repressed and absorbed party conflict? But such efforts were becoming less successful. The boundary that social associations had drawn between political clashes and sociability became more permeable, as the experiences of many organizations suggested.

Though language and symbolism varied, many student associations, including the socialist student club, clamored for political education without partisanship. This was an intensification of prewar trends.[86] Traditional educative goals would now include political schooling but not involvement in political parties. Yet the distinction between education and activity, between political discussion and political passion, became more difficult to maintain. Stronger internecine disputes characterized Marburger Wingolf's history from the early years of the Republic. In 1919 the fraternity reported that "animated" discussions over the reform of student organizational life took place. In 1920 a Marburger Wingolf reporter noted that fraternity actives had experienced difficulties "winning over pledges for the corporate ideal, because some of them had been weakened [*angekränkelt*] by the modern democratic spirit." During the 1920s the fraternity's discussion evenings featured debate over trade unions (1920), nationalism (1925), liberalism and conservatism (1925), the social question (1926), medical, racial, and ethical dimensions of Wingolf's concept of morality (1927), student government (1927), the relationship of corporatism and Christianity (1928), and the necessity of "national-political education" without partisanship (1928). For Marburger Wingolf, political education ultimately did produce partisanship: thirteen fraternity members joined the Nazi Student League before January 1933, more than joined from any other student association in the city before Hitler achieved power.[87]

Other student groups experienced similar problems. The Catholic fraternity Rhenania reported "petty squabbles over the intensity and worth of particular political approaches" in 1924. When the Deutsche Burschenschaft ruled in 1925 that Burschenschaft and Reichsbanner membership were incompatible, a Marburg Burschenschaft Germania alumnus reported that internal debate over the decision caused some *Burschenschafter* to use "the general press to attack their own organization." Aside from this specific issue, "factions and parties" within Marburg Burschenschaften became more distinct. Burschenschaft Arminia belonged to the "Red Line," which promoted "citizenship training" and "participation in student politics," while Alemannia belonged to the "White Circle" and Germania the "Black Association," each expressing opposition to or variations on these views. Each viewpoint and faction became more cohesive, and by 1927 the Red Line had its own newsletter. It is hardly surprising that students and university officials reported a strong political interest at the university by the turn of the decade, before the Nazi electoral triumph of September 1930 and before the worst part of the Depression.[88]

University officials were less able than ever to limit the effects of political divisiveness. University officials saw the consequences of student political activity in the Republic during the Studentenkorps incident. They supported the reorganization of student government in Marburg in 1927 against the wishes of the Prussian state because they felt this was important "from the standpoint of the university." They failed to prevent students from making vociferous anti-Republic statements dealing with "war guilt lies" in 1929, when Chancellor Felix Genzmer attended summer solstice celebrations of the fraternity-dominated student government. Attending in order to "keep the demonstration in check," the chancellor made it clear that he, like other German university officials, valued harmony with the student body above everything.[89] But tactics that worked in the Imperial period failed in the contentious Republic, when a significant minority of Marburg students joined the Nazi movement.

Similarly, nonstudent clubs became more ineffective in controlling the tensions of political debate and competing party political loyalties within their memberships. An example is provided by what happened in the Housewives' Association, the largest women's occupational association in the city. Disputes in the national association with which it was affiliated led to the formation in 1921 of a breakaway club, the Reich Association of German Housewives. The Marburg *Verband* debated the causes and potential consequences of the split from at least February 1927 until mid-1930. Then, after a contested election for a new board of directors in the Housewives' Association, former members of that group and others organized a Marburg branch of the new Reich Association. Although personal differences played some part in the conflict, debate and division in the Housewives' Association were fueled primarily by escalating party political competition within the organization in the 1920s. The renegades had wanted housewives to take a more active role in politics by adopting "strict Christian-national" principles and accused Housewives' Association leaders of discrimination against members who favored party political activity. In a rare public venting of personal and political tensions in the Housewives' Association, a representative of the group wrote in a local newspaper that association bylaws dealt "only with economic questions, whereas religious and political questions have never been considered or debated."[90] But this was an admission of the deep scars that political contention had left on the group.

What could be done now that social organizations were less able to absorb political tensions? Subscribing to relatively static notions of apoliticism and nationalism had been the solution of the prewar Gymnastics Club, the Marburg Sharpshooting Club, pure and modified fraternities, and many other organizations. But, to restate the essential point, Weimar was not the Empire. Nor were conditions in the middle Republic similar to those of 1918–19. Postwar conflict in general and the violent example of the Student Corps in particular had added new activism to the repertoire of social organizations. Additional processes—economic stabilization after 1923–24, growing dissolution of both national and local parties starting in

1924, increasing organization of the population, widening of leadership skills to ever-larger segments of the *Bürgertum*, membership growth in bourgeois organizations—created a potentially more volatile political atmosphere.

Reacting to the new situation, some bourgeois spokespeople reinterpreted traditions of apoliticism, arguing that defensive or static apoliticism kept *Vereine* from playing a fruitful role in local and national polities. The postal official Wilhelm Langenberg, director of the Marburg-based *Oberhessen* branch of the large Central German Song Club and a member of the Concert Association, suggested this in his statement during Reich Health Week in April 1926. "Right along with the sports movement," the *Oberhessische* reported him to have said, "the German singing movement should not be forgotten. Its great goal is to contribute to the health of the German people by cleansing the German soul. Particularly today, in a time of the German people's need, a time of both internal and external antagonisms, it is the German song that binds together members of the folk [Volksgenossen] and above all links Germans outside the national boundaries to the fatherland."[91] In contrast to gymnastics and sharpshooting associations, bourgeois song clubs participated routinely in all kinds of political festivals and were not uniformly opposed to the Republic, despite being nationalistic.[92] But Langenberg expressed a notion shared by individuals in many diverse associations. This view posited the world of social organizations as an alternative to political parties. Singing—or exercising, praying, marching, sharpshooting, and playing the zither—would bind together the folk community if divisive politicking would not. Because such views emphasized harmony between sociability and the general interest, they were firmly in the tradition of social clubs in the first age of organization. However, because Langenberg's perspective implied intense action rather than mere "sentiment" (*Gesinnung*), it possessed a dynamic element that had been less pronounced in earlier forms of apolitical nationalism.

One important vehicle of expression for such sentiments was the patriotic festival, where social organizations could create an apolitical alternative to party conflict. In the case of the Reich Founding Celebration, held annually in January, the university and veterans' associations took the lead. The university's part of the event usually began with a "festive parade consisting of teachers as well as fraternity officers." It brought together town notables, professors, and students in sweeping displays of harmony. The same emphasis on unity was important to the County Veterans' Association, which joined singing clubs, gymnastics associations, and veterans' club youth groups in the yearly festival. Both parts of the ceremonies received extensive coverage in the *Oberhessische*.[93]

Bourgeois clubs defended their hegemony over patriotic festivals against opponents, gaining city authorities' assistance in the process. The Social Democratic party protested in 1919 to the mayor that continued celebration of Bismarck's birthday by students and townspeople was a "provocation" that kept up memories of "the good old conquered regime." Despite the protests, Marburg organizations—including the DNVP, but above all singing clubs and social organizations allied in the citywide United Patriotic Association—continued to celebrate the day.[94] Representing social liberal thought in Marburg during the Republic, the *Hessisches Tageblatt* clashed with the nationalists when it tried to widen involvement in Memorial Sunday. The *Tageblatt* charged that by 1929 Memorial Sunday, instituted to honor the dead of World War I, had become an affair of nationalist organizations that excluded Marburg's "republican population" from participation. Unlike other cities, where less nationalistic organizations assumed control over the ceremony or where the festival failed to galvanize townspeople, in Marburg veterans' associations and the Young German Order dominated Memorial Sunday. In November 1929 the *Tageblatt* charged that one nationalist *Verband* had used that year's ceremonies to agitate for new members. Both the city magistrate and police chief defended the 1929 festival, saying that the ceremonies had been of a completely "unpolitical character." Oberbürgermeister Johannes Müller told the Prussian district president that the *Tageblatt* had taken an overly "subjective" stance, prompted by the somewhat too partisan activity of the Young German Order—a "derailment" that Müller said was addressed in private conversations between county Kriegerverein chair Friedrich Immanuel and the offending speaker.[95]

Patriotic ceremonies assumed added significance as forums for displaying material strength, moral leadership, and apolitical commitment to the general good—all notionally vivid counterexamples to the contentious world of party politics. The moral element of such collective displays was all-important. A leading figure of the County Veterans' Association was the retired colonel Immanuel, an active and popular local joiner. In the 1928 Reich Founding Celebration Immanuel urged the audience to overcome "party political viewpoints" and work instead for "the victory of morality over the crass materialism of the present, the cultivation of German virtues, family life, Christian faith, individual personality, national honor

. . . and the unity of the German people."[96] Here was the bundle of moral issues contained in bourgeois apoliticism.

But Immanuel and other notables did not confine their ideological message to such large, well-attended ceremonies. Immanuel emphasized such themes in countless settings, from routine meetings of the Young German Order, of which he had been a member since 1924, to those of the German Officers' League, church associations, and youth groups of the County Veterans' Association. Similarly, moral themes permeated the supposedly narrow aims of economic interest associations. In 1926 the Property Owners' and Landlords' Association made use of propaganda stressing that "the *Mittelstand* doesn't fight for reasons of naked egoism, but rather for culture and morality." A Civil Servants' Association speaker noted in 1928 that "civil servants have an enemy in today's materialistic spirit, which recognizes no ethical element in the economic system." "Hearty applause" followed the remarks.[97] In all such cases, opinion leaders contrasted the perceived moral qualities of the apolitical *Bürgertum* with the divisive and demoralizing influence of materialism and party strife.

Aggressive, moralistic apoliticism faced two sets of limits, one tenuously maintained by supporters of the Republic. Bourgeois Marburg had pushed socialist organizations and their allies to the margins of the local polity, a political project in which the *Oberhessische Zeitung* played a significant role. The *Oberhessische*, which was the most widely circulated daily newspaper in Marburg, rarely covered working-class festivals such as May Day, preferring instead to report on the May festival of Corps Hasso-Nassovia in 1923 or of "the corporations" in 1925.[98] Nevertheless, if the Republic's defenders gained outside support, they could make a collective show of strength in Marburg, as they did in the early Republic when they opposed the Student Corps and protested the murder of Walther Rathenau.[99] In September 1929 Hessian locals of the district Reichsbanner demonstrated in Marburg against the anti–Young Plan referendum drive. Aiming for a "front of the Republic's supporters that will be upheld without regard to party affiliation," a large crowd of Reichsbanner members assembled at the train depot to greet the arrival of the national chair, Otto Hörsing. Hörsing could not attend the demonstration, but the size and noisiness of the crowd prompted the *Tageblatt* to write that "one had finally to admit . . . Marburgers also live in a Republic."[100]

The other limit of newly mobilized and strident apoliticism was self-imposed. Apoliticism postulated that party politics was morally indefensible and injurious to national solidarity. Consequently there was no central organization—no party—to transform the moral power of apoliticism into concrete action. Traditions of sociopolitical asymmetry, of treating political parties as ancillary organizations in a wider social-political universe, returned to haunt apoliticism in the Republic. This was reflected in the national campaign for a referendum against the Young Plan, which was led by bourgeois party activists and supported by a number of social organizations. Though ostensibly concerned with foreign policy, the referendum was also important as a test of bourgeois solidarity. Led by the DNVP head, Alfred Hugenberg, in summer 1929, the referendum drive sparked a broad mobilization, bringing out "referendum advocates of every breed," according to the *Tageblatt*.[101] The university again provided the conduit between national political conflict and local events. Hugenberg used a speaking engagement sponsored by the Marburg AMSt to initiate his campaign. The Nazi Student League also brought a number of prominent speakers to the city to push for the referendum. The DNVP announced formation of a local committee for the referendum at a party meeting in Marburg on 26 September.[102] Leaders of social organizations—veterans' associations, the Blacksmiths' Guild, the County Artisans' Association, the Hessian Peasants' Association—participated in the committee. The committee knew what it was about, announcing on 16 October that the referendum drive was "the last possible method whereby all political and economic groups can be brought together in united effort that clearly and decisively rejects the present disastrous foreign policy. . . ."[103]

This was a "last possible method" not because bourgeois mobilization was spent but because it was the last opportunity for traditional political groups to exploit heightened apoliticism. They failed. The national committee against the Young Plan had organized a petition drive, gained the signatures of the required 10 percent of the electorate, and brought Hugenberg's so-called "freedom law" before the Reichstag on 30 November 1929. The proposed law went down to defeat, as the anti–Young Plan groups had expected, and thus became the object of a plebiscite on 22 December. Here was the chance, Hugenberg and his allies thought, to exploit the German people's dissatisfaction with their government's domestic and foreign policies. But the referendum was a great disappointment to nationalist groups, which saw their efforts gain less than one third of the required votes needed to turn the proposal into law. Meanwhile, just 15.7 percent of eligible voters in the city and 32.7

percent in the county voted for the measure. Though both counts exceeded the national average of 13.8 percent, local advocates of the referendum movement had to admit defeat.[104]

Changes and tensions originating in the previous four decades culminated in the 1920s. War, the hyperinflation, and the Depression of 1929 exposed the fiscal weaknesses of the industry-poor university and service city and opened municipal affairs to unprecedented political contention. Party political disunity, an established feature of Marburg life since the 1880s, reached new heights in the 1920s, as bourgeois parties in the national and local polity gave way to splinter parties, municipal special interest alliances, and, in 1929, an unsuccessful mobilization of opponents of the Young Plan. Before the Depression, therefore, the Marburg bourgeois party universe had dissolved. The sources of this dissolution can be found decades before in the conditions under which local liberal and conservative parties responded to the challenge of mass politics. Yet the age of most decisive bourgeois party disarray came in the 1920s in general, and between 1924 and 1930 in particular.

Throughout all this, organized social life remained the reservoir of an apoliticism that claimed to bury political conflict in the machinery of club routine and everyday sociability. Yet the social sphere did not remain unchanged. Increasing numbers and types of voluntary organizations, widening circles of club leadership and membership, acknowledgment of the centrality of group interests, strengthened enthusiasm for an elusive national good—all this altered the networks of organizational life. Above all, as political strife widened in the Republic, conventional methods of conflict absorption in social life seemed increasingly inadequate. Bourgeois club leaders responded with a heightened and more strident apoliticism, a heated disavowal of the importance of party political divisions in social life. In the process of using older arguments more aggressively, however, adherents of conflict absorption discovered a new role for social organizations. Bourgeois spokesmen were inspired by traditional notions of the folk community, which had gained impetus in World War I, and emboldened by the successes of the immediate postwar years, when social organizations, including violent student fraternities, actively suppressed political conflict in the early Republic. Armed with these experiences, leaders of social organizations claimed they would do more than cushion political rancor—they would counterbalance conflict by preparing the way for a national, apolitical harmony. Such ideas had been present before the 1920s; but they had never before received such forceful representation in the meeting halls, soccer fields, shooting ranges, churches, and homes in which Marburg organizational life operated.

This created a situation rich in paradox. Heightened apoliticism —from older notions of conflict absorption to newer ideas of using social clubs as building blocks of a new, antisocialist, moralistic folk community—disengaged social life from party political affiliations more substantially than ever before. By 1929, well before the Depression caused its most serious hardships, the Marburg *Bürgertum* was more homeless politically than at any previous time. The rupture between social and political life had never been greater, the divisions in social organizations never more pronounced. But social organizations registered stability or gains in membership, dominated the shape and content of local patriotic festivals, filled the public sphere with moral condemnations of the Republic in particular and party politics in general, and remained more powerful than local working-class associations, which lost both members and morale in the 1920s after initial gains in the early Republic. If social life were to harness the energies released by mobilization and internal divisiveness, it needed, more than ever before, a political anchor. Apoliticism needed an organized political representative. But what organization or movement would provide such a representative? With the benefit of hindsight, we know that national socialism would be the exploiter of this situation. In 1929–30 this movement had begun to gain collective control over the time and loyalty of individuals in bourgeois organizational life, over the resources contained in the networks of social interchange. We turn to the process of Nazi mobilization in Part II.

Two contrasting views of Marburg: (top) the idyllic Hessian university town, 1925; (bottom) the gray Am Grün neighborhood as seen from a point looking northwest from across the Lahn River, 1920. (both Bildarchiv Foto Marburg)

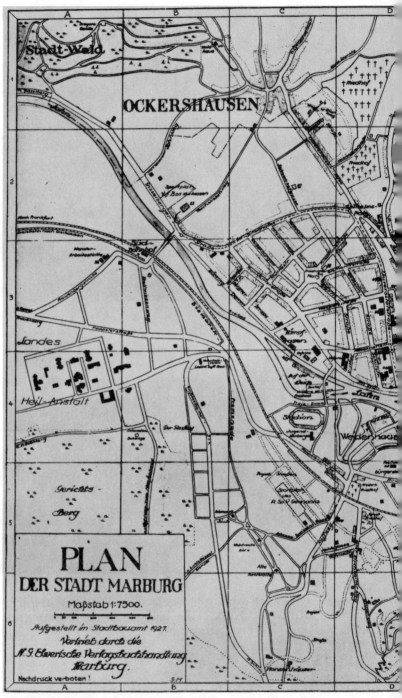

Map of Marburg in 1927. The *Oberstadt*, congested upper city just south of the castle (*Schloß*), was the medieval core of Marburg. The older outlying neighborhood of Ketzerbach was situated north of

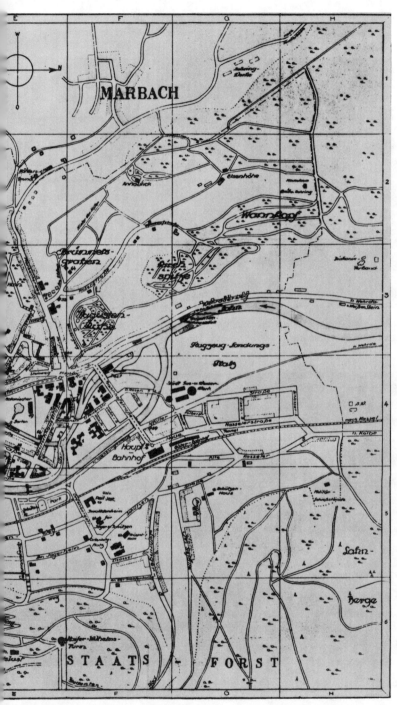

the castle in quadrants E-3 and E-4 and that of Weidenhausen in quadrant D-4 southeast of the castle (see chapter 6). (Verlag Elwert)

The Ketzerbach Neighborhood Association, 1912.
(Bildarchiv Foto Marburg)

The Song Club Liederkranz, 1920. Seventy-fifth anniversary
celebration of one of Marburg's largest men's glee clubs,
on market square. (Friedrich Unkel)

The Marburg Volunteer Fire Department, 1934. (Friedrich Unkel)

Marburg's oldest student dueling fraternity, the Corps Teutonia, 1925.
(Bildarchiv Foto Marburg)

Fraternity ritual. Dueling fraternity students' parade in the 1927 celebration of the four-hundredth anniversary of the university, in the Bahnhofstraße. (Bildarchiv Foto Marburg)

Fraternity sociability. Fraternity students in a festive parade marking the four-hundredth anniversary of the university, 1927. (Bildarchiv Foto Marburg)

Town and gown. Faculty, fraternity students, and townspeople at the 1927 celebration of the four-hundredth anniversary of the university, at the monument for fallen soldiers of World War I. (Bildarchiv Foto Marburg)

A Marburg dueling fraternity, Burschenschaft Arminia, 1935. (Bildarchiv Foto Marburg)

Heſſiſche Bauern!

Wißt Ihr, daß an erſter Stelle der Liſte der **Deutſchen Volkspartei**

der Jude Rießer

ſteht. Stellt damit nicht die Deutſche Volkspartei ebenſo wie die Deutſche demokratiſche Partei, die Ihr alle mit Recht bekämpft, J u d e n an maßgebende Stelle? Liegen Eure Intereſſen da, wo die der Großinduſtrie und des Großkapitals liegen, oder werden ſie vertreten durch eine Partei, die ſich früher und jetzt ſtets der Landwirtſchaft warm angenommen hat, nämlich der **Deutſchnationalen Volkspartei?** Die Namen

Heinrich Lind, Landwirt, Niederiſſigheim, **Georg Chriſtian,** Landwirt, Unterlieberbach **Alwin Möhn,** Landwirt, Dauborn,

die auf der Liſte der Deutſchnationalen Volkspartei kandidieren, geben Euch Antwort hierauf! Denkt daran, daß Tauſende von Demokraten zur Deutſchen Volkspartei übergetreten ſind und viele davon bereits nach kurzer Zeit in leitenden Stellen der Deutſchen Volkspartei ſitzen. Ihrem Einfluß wird es bald gelingen, die „Ideale" der Demokraten in der Deutſchen Volkspartei zu verwirklichen.
Wählt alſo die Partei, die als einzige Partei ſich gegen das Judentum wendet,

die Deutſchnationale Volkspartei!
Wählt Liſte Helfferich!

Marburg anti-Semitism. Campaign advertisement of the conservative DNVP for the 1920 Reichstag elections, in the local newspaper, the *Oberhessische*. The top lines read: "Hessian farmers! Do you know that the German People's party ticket is headed by the Jew Rießer?" (*Oberhessische Zeitung*)

Nazi ritual. National Socialist celebration of the return of the Saar basin to Germany, Marburg city hall, 1 March 1935. (Friedrich Unkel)

Wahlaufruf

des

⌐⌐ Völkisch-Sozialen Blocks ⌐⌐

Volksgenossen!

In letzter Stunde rufen wir Euch mahnend zu: Tut am 4. Mai Eure Schuldig=
keit, wählt **völkisch**!

Haltet Abrechnung mit den internationalen Linksparteien unter jüdischer
Führung (Demokratie, Sozialdemokratie, Kommunisten). Sie haben uns durch
den fluchwürdigen 9. November 1918 und durch ihre seit dieser Zeit unumschränkte
Herrschaft (Erfüllungspolitik) in unser heutiges Elend geführt. Alle ihre Ver=
sprechungen sind eitel Lug und Trug gewesen, und so ist es auch mit dem, was
sie uns heute wieder versprechen, (Sachverständigen=Gutachten).

Nutznießer ihrer Politik ist einzig und allein das internatiale Judentum
(Börsenmacht), das deutsche Volk und unser Vaterland gehen dabei zu Grunde.

Haltet Abrechnung mit der Deutschen Volkspartei!

„Von roten Ketten macht Euch frei allein die Deutsche Volkspartei," lautete
die Parole 1920. Und wie sah die Wirklichkeit aus? (Eine Leimrute!) Unter
der Führung Stresemanns mit der jüdischen Frau (geb. Kleefeldt) wurden diese
Ketten fester den je geschlungen. Daß in Preußen noch immer Herr Severing
gegen das Deutschtum regiert, verdanken wir ganz allein dieser sog. **Deutschen
Volkspartei**. Auch sie ist eine Partei mit bestimmendem jüdischem Einfluß (Frau
Stresemann, Otto Wolff, Rießer u. a. m.) und ist vor allem eine Partei des Groß=
kapitals. Für die Not des Volkes hat ihre Führung weder Herz noch Verständ=
nis, die Dividenden und Tantiemen sind ihnen wichtiger.

Haltet auch Ihr deutschen Katholiken Abrechnung mit dem Zentrum, das sich
offen mit dem Marxismus verbündet hat.

Wählt darum **völkisch und sozial**!

Wir wollen Deutschland dem Deutschen wiedergeben.

Wir wollen die Befreiung

der Arbeit von der Ausbeutung durch Zins und Dividende, Tantiemen und
Spekulation,

der Wirtschaft, des Handwerks und der Bauernschaft aus ihrer Abhängigkeit
von Juden=Banken und =Börsen,

der Regierung, der Parlamente, Parteien und Gewerkschaften von jüdischer
Führung und Verführung, des deutschen Geisteslebens,

von fremdrassiger, jüdischer Leitung und Bevormundung.

An unserer Spitze marschiert der **deutsche Arbeiter Hitler** und mit ihm
der von jüdischem Hasse verfolgte Volksgenosse **General Ludendorff**,
beide aus der Erkenntnis heraus, daß die Erlösung nur durch das schaffende
Volk kommen kann.

Folgen wir ihnen! Auf zur befreienden Tat!

Wählt die Listen des **Völkisch-Sozialen Blocks**

das sind:

1. für den Reichstag:

Nr. 9 **Blume, Freisler, Nürnberger,** Landwirt **Müller.**

2. für die Stadtverordnetenwahlen:

Liste **Hinneburg, Zetl, Wienecke.**

Wahlleitung des Kreisverbandes Marburg des Völkisch-Sozialen Blocks.

The swastika appears. First appearance of the Nazi swastika in Marburg's
largest daily, the *Oberhessische*, in a campaign advertisement of the VSB,
a Nazi-conservative coalition, for the May 1924 Reichstag elections.
(*Oberhessische Zeitung*)

Goering in Marburg. Four scenes of the Nazi official Hermann Goering's visit to Marburg, 8 June 1933: (top left) Goering in the flag-bedecked upper city; (top right) An enthusiastic crowd lines the route of Goering's procession; (bottom left) An SA formation accompanies Goering; (bottom right) The crowd moves into the street at the conclusion of Goering's appearance. (Friedrich Unkel)

part two

Networks of Nazism

ƒiʋe

From *Stammtisch* to Party: Nazism to 1933

olitical observers may have been puzzled to see that nazism was a relatively weak force in Marburg in 1929. Since the Second Empire the city had been a springboard of new political organizations. The Thuringian shootings put Marburg fraternities in the forefront of nationalist violence. Social Democratic politicians labelled Marburg the city "with unlimited possibilities for reaction" and others referred to the town's "Fascist university."[1] More importantly, the city became a center of bourgeois apoliticism, ostensibly compatible with Nazi visions of being "beyond parties." In May 1924 Reichstag elections the Marburg Völkisch-Sozialer Block, in which the NSDAP played an important but not dominant role, gained 17.7 percent of the vote, a share well above that which it gained in the Reich and towns of comparable size. But by 1929, the National Socialist party and its student arm were only loud, activist organizations on the margins of party politics. They established a presence, but nothing more. Imaginative observers might have characterized the Marburg NSDAP as a politicized *Stammtisch*, an inclusive social club consisting of agitators but few followers. How could the NSDAP make the transition from *Stammtisch* to political party? How could it combine Marburg's political resources to produce a workable strategy for electoral gain? How could the NSDAP become a mass party not in the sense that it mobilized deracinated or undifferentiated groups but that it gained a wider social following than had any previous nonsocialist or non-Catholic party? These were the central questions that occupied Marburg Nazi agitators from the founding of the party until Hitler's seizure of power.

The Tensions of Early Nazism

The Marburg NSDAP was built on fragments of local organizational life. According to National Socialist sources, the first twelve individuals who joined the party in May 1923 were also members of the Young German Order. Other early members belonged to temporary volunteer military units, the anti-Semitic Deutsch-Völkischer Schutz- und Trutzbund, and a melange of similar organizations. Party chroniclers disagreed as to whether native Marburgers or exiles from the French-occupied Rhineland founded the organization. Nazi writers often glorified party founders, and it would be unsurprising if they favored stories of brave, exiled Rhinelanders playing a big role in organizing the first Marburg NSDAP local. Regardless of the story employed, chroniclers attributed early party activity to prior nationalist and *völkisch* groups.[2]

The NSDAP fused conventions of prewar, wartime, and postwar organizational life. Party members grasped the symbols of German militarism, partly because many of them had fought in World War I and partly because they joined temporary volunteer military units in the first contentious years of the Republic.[3] NSDAP members were on the borderline between military experience and civilian life, but they were hardly unable to adjust to the conventions of bourgeois society, as some contemporaries and later historians theorized.[4] Civilian life was suffused with militarism and political violence for five years after the global conflict, and party members responded to war and warlike civilian life by emphasizing military style. Each member was enrolled in the SA (Sturmabteilung, or storm troops), where marching and military paraphernalia set the tone. Nazi chroniclers' most detailed recollections of these years concentrated on the style of party uniforms and armbands and the thrill of marching in the 1923 Nuremberg rally. A revolt into military style, purposely opposed to "bloodless" bourgeois parties and parliamentary custom, nazism was an early outgrowth of more assertive apoliticism in the Republic.[5]

Nazi apoliticism surfaced in a number of other ways. The party valued *putschist* action rather than precise political goals. Participating with the Young German Order in a German Day celebration in Butzbach in June 1923, the Marburg NSDAP burned a red flag that had been draped ostentatiously from a tree in the city square, an action that prompted "frenzied" shouting from the city's "red populace," according to a Nazi writer. On 8–9 November 1923, when the Marburg Reichswehr was called away to fight Communist groups in Thuringia, the Marburg SA, which numbered about twenty-five people, volunteered for temporary military service. In the absence of army troops they took control of the city barracks, no doubt boldly imagining themselves as violent masters of the situation. Throughout such actions, the party had no concrete political goal other than activism.[6] Yet the NSDAP was hardly departing from accepted political conventions; throughout Germany in the first six years of the Republic, agitators took politics beyond the voting booths and into the streets.

Even more important to early party history than paramilitary activity was shared social life. The paramilitary bravado of the early NSDAP took second place to a rather traditional taste for *Gemütlichkeit*. The party *Festschrift* recalled the 1923 Christmas celebration, which "brought together loyal party comrades and their families in a warm . . . celebration in Lahnlust pub," as any club social event might have.[7] Party members attended regular meetings as well as marking special occasions in the Lahnlust and Schützenpfuhl taverns. Later, Nazi students frequented the well-known Weidenhausen pub Hannes, where Käsebrod notables also met. Though "discussion evenings" dealt with ideological issues, they were more important for the sociability they offered Nazi cliques of young men.[8] Expressed partly as a complete aversion to bourgeois political models in favor of paramilitary practice, Nazi apoliticism also manifested itself in social interchange that reduced party politics to ancillary status.

The early NSDAP was a mix of paramilitary league and *Stammtisch* rather than a political party; this feature held Nazi adherents together socially but also kept them from gaining wider political influence. Three other factors combined to isolate the NSDAP on the margin of local politics. First, in terms of opportunities for gaining members and influence locally, the Marburg NSDAP appeared too late. After the hectic first years of the Republic, the fraternities retreated into their houses as the idealistic postwar generation left the university. Moreover, by making routine activities all but impossible, the hyperinflation diminished the capacity of bourgeois associations to respond to political events.[9] Marburg Nazis organized on the downward side of postwar mobilization; events superseded them. Second, local party organization was inappropriate for mobilizing a wide following. The Nazi party failed to meet the requirements of political action—bureaucratized organization, party discipline, participation in elections—necessary for appealing to groups other than militaristic cliques. Third, the strength of sociopolitical asymmetry in Marburg hindered Nazi mobilization. By quickly stabilizing the local polity, notables and bourgeois social organizations—with the help of fraternity violence—made Nazi activism unnecessary.[10] Only when the underlying conditions of this asymmetry were altered could the party expect to play a more prominent role locally. Until then, the NSDAP would be "on emergency standby," as it described its inauspicious role while awaiting word of Hitler's wrongheaded coup attempt in Munich in November 1923.[11]

The Völkisch-Sozialer Block, a national electoral coalition in 1924 between Nazi party leaders and members of the Ludendorff-led German-Völkisch Liberation party (Deutschvölkische Freiheitspartei), enabled Marburg nazism to widen its influence temporarily.[12] Part of the importance of the Völkisch-Sozialer Block was to familiarize Nazi party members with Hessian political anti-Semitism. Like agitators of the Böckel movement, VSB speakers, including a number of university students, appealed to the rural and small-town population. Nazi members of the VSB found their "initial resonance" in the countryside; they tried to "latch onto" the anti-Semitic traditions of Hessian towns and villages.[13] Observers noted that VSB assemblies in the villages Caldern and Michelbach were the best-attended actions of the Reichstag campaign in those communities.[14] Imploring people to vote "racist [*völkisch*] and social," and aiming their propaganda at rural Hessian workers, shopkeepers, artisans, and peasants, VSB agitators combined direct economic appeals with racial prejudice. "We want the liberation," their *Oberhessische* advertisement of 3 May read, "of work from the exploitation of interests and dividends, of royalties and speculation; of the economy, the artisanry and the peasantry from their dependence on Jew-banks and Jew-markets; of the regime, parliaments, parties and trade unions from Jewish leadership and seduction; of German cultural life from racially alien Jewish leadership and tutelage."[15] Accustomed to the political anti-Semitism of an earlier period, Hessian country and small-town people found such ideological themes familiar.

Like the Böckel movement, the VSB was also an urban and small-town phenomenon. Formed initially in Kassel in March 1924, VSB locals soon appeared in Marburg, Wetzlar, Weilburg, Herborn, and Kirchhain. The Marburg local, "especially busy" in the May Reichstag campaign, held its first electoral assembly in the City Meeting Hall. University students played a prominent role in this agitation. Additionally, the VSB put up candidates for city council elections held on the same day as Reichstag elections. At the head of the slate for municipal parliament was Ludwig Hinneburg, oldest of the first twelve members of the local NSDAP and party leader in 1923. He was joined by Adolf Zetl, a printer, and Friedrich Wienecke, a master builder.[16] The VSB praised "the German worker Hitler" and the "folk comrade Ludendorff, the persecuted victim of Jewish hate." Ludendorff, who despite his commitment to modernizing the army could be identified in the public mind with the traditions of the Prussian Officer Corps, personified the anti-Semitism of German elite circles. With the aggressive anti-Semitic tone of the 1920 Reichstag elections still reverberating in the local polity, Ludendorff's racism seemed consistent with local traditions. By calling for the liberation of "German cultural life from racially alien Jewish leadership and tutelage," moreover, the VSB aimed its propaganda at "academic Marburg."[17]

Receiving 17.7 percent of all votes, the Marburg VSB made a more impressive showing than its Bavarian counterpart, which gained 17.1 percent. There was now a Nazi party representative in city parliament, a candidate of the Greater German Folk Community (Großdeutsche Volksgemeinschaft), the railway porter Arthur Alt.[18] Disaffection resulting from the hyperinflation undoubtedly played a role in the elections, and the spring of 1924 witnessed a protest vote that would reappear and broaden in the dangerous autumn of 1930. But another factor, more a product of local power struggles than of national issues, explains VSB success more convincingly.

The Marburg VSB enjoyed temporary electoral gains because the coalition embodied an important tension in local party politics. The VSB furthered traditions of popular politics introduced locally by Böckel, the Agrarian League, Hellmut von Gerlach, and others. The goal was a broad "moral" coalition of notables, the *Bildungsbürgertum*, university students, artisans, retailers, officials, white-collar workers, peasants, and manual laborers. VSB propaganda, which featured swastikas in local newspapers for the first time in Marburg's history, stressed the need for a party that was "racist *and* social."[19] Conversely, traditions of "notables' politics" also shaped the VSB. The coalition was closely identified locally with Ludendorff, the supposed military hero. Representing an elitist, *völkisch* variant of bourgeois apoliticism, Ludendorff's racist thought reverberated with moralistic disdain for mass politics. Yet this apoliticism was hardly conducive to building a big antiparty constituency because Ludendorff's aversion to parliamentary politics led him to explore primitive notions of Germanic religiosity that isolated him from political affairs and from potential supporters. Suspended between contrasting political styles, speaking out of both sides of its collective mouth, the VSB was a volatile coalition. It was capable of flarelike success at the polls as well as sudden defeat, which it experienced in the November 1924 Reichstag elections, when only 6.2 percent of all votes went to *völkisch* candidates locally.[20]

Representing local National Socialists who rejected the VSB, the GVG was perhaps even more illustrative of the contradictions of Nazi activity in 1924. In April 1924 the Marburg GVG founded a youth club whose leaders were dedicated to the "spirit of Adolf Hitler and Ludendorff" and "the coming struggle." The GVG struck a militant pose. Yet like the youth group Wandervogel of the Empire, the club favored hiking and decried "alcohol, nicotine . . . and smut."[21] The bourgeois Wandervogel had considered themselves radical, but their rejection of parliamentary activity had also led to political passivity. Tied to a weak party and wary of parliamentary intrigues, GVG youth could easily slide into a similar passivity by stressing changes in life-style rather than political agitation. What was the NSDAP: revolutionary cultural *Bund*, traditional anti-Semitic people's party, elitist opponent of the Republic, paramilitary league, or mass party? The Marburg GVG certainly had few answers for these difficult questions.

After the May 1924 elections, an unidentified *Hessischer Beobachter* writer decried the provincial leadership of the Hesse-Nassau VSB, the "party clique" allegedly responsible for splitting the *völkisch* movement into two lists in Marburg city parliament elections. Quoting the anti-Semitic politician Theodor Fritsch, who attacked "party egoism," and Hellmuth Gerloff, who declared that "organization is the deadly enemy of almost every movement," the writer expressed a deep apoliticism shared by many GVG and VSB supporters. Yet, not wanting to overlook *völkisch* electoral success, the writer proudly noted that a GVG member was elected to the Marburg city parliament and that *völkisch* candidates had attained the second largest share of votes locally in the May Reichstag elections.[22] The writer failed to point out that such victories usually resulted from party organization and discipline. Similar ambiguities would characterize Nazi activities for much of the time before Hitler came to power, though electoral successes in the early 1930s would disarm critics who felt uneasy about organization and electoral clout.

Although Hitler wanted to build a popular following after 1924, financial resources for this difficult task were unavailable locally. The Marburg party relied on private donations to support travel to the Nuremberg party assemblies, important sources of inspiration for local cadres. After 1924 subscriptions for the party newspaper failed to generate substantial income, and the party was financed from sales of booklets, postcards, and magazines published by the national organization. The street vendors who sold this material, often university students reputed to be fanatics, were driven less by passionate zeal than by the pecuniary needs of an organization that in June 1927 reported rather pathetically that it possessed salable literature worth sixty marks.[23]

Organizational problems added to these financial difficulties. Leadership changed hands constantly. One local group leader, the tailor Georg Pfau, was usually absent from party activities "for professional reasons." Party membership lists in 1924 contained over one hundred names, but at least one-half of these individuals "were no longer in Marburg or no longer considered themselves to be participants" in the movement.[24] One party member, Wilhelm Emrich, said that he left the NSDAP in 1928 because the party had virtually dissolved.[25] The local party claimed it attracted 131 new members between 1925 and 1928, but 102 people left the organization in the same interval. This reflected a fluctuating, volatile membership, a characteristic of the party not only in this period of marginality but in the era of real growth in 1930–33 as well. It is understandable that the NSDAP attracted no attention from the conservative *Oberhessische Zeitung* until summer 1930.[26]

Factionalism, lack of direction, significant fluctuations in the party's electoral successes—these characteristics of bourgeois party organization were exaggerated in the Nazi party in the mid-1920s. The NSDAP appeared to be a drastic caricature of the fragmented local polity that produced it.

The party exaggerated bourgeois tendencies in another respect. Like bourgeois party adherents, local Nazis were involved in numerous clubs and associations, as subsequent quantitative data will demonstrate. The decision by party leaders to allow dual memberships for participants in some organizations was thus a concession to continuing practice.[27] It is crucial to emphasize that in many cases Nazi party members were not burrowing their way into local associations, passionately carrying Hitler's message to townspeople. Instead, numerous party members had been involved in local clubs before they carried NSDAP cards, and Nazi party involvement was part of ongoing social intercourse. Despite all this, after

1924 there were no significant electoral successes until 1930. Collectively the NSDAP labored on the margins of the polity, while individually party members were integrated in bourgeois organizational life. It was a sociopolitical asymmetry more radical than anything the established parties had experienced.

We can concretize the relationship of the NSDAP to local organizational life by focusing on a single party member. Fritz Schwalm joined the Marburg Nazi Student League in the summer of 1929.[28] Schwalm's involvement in the Nazi party was not the result of generational revolt: his father, who was a craft master living in the Ketzerbach district and a supporter of *völkisch* political parties before 1914, encouraged Schwalm to join the NSDAP.[29] Born in 1910, Schwalm was part of the generation of young men who "missed" World War I and flooded the ranks of the NSDAP in the late 1920s and early 1930s. He became a member of the right-wing youth group Adler und Falken in 1924, serving as local group leader from 1927 to 1929. Planning to be a high school teacher, Schwalm enrolled at the university and joined the Hochschulgilde Saxnot, one of a number of nationalist student associations that appeared in Marburg during the Republic, in summer semester 1929, the same semester he joined the NSDStB.

For Schwalm the NSDAP represented better than other parties "the ideas of the youth movement." These ideas included, above all, an egalitarianism that bourgeois organizational life no longer offered. Though the student guild was obviously confined to university students, Adler und Falken and Saxnot were theoretically accessible to "every German, regardless of estate or occupation." The NSDAP seemed to be the party that realized the folk community of Wandervogel ideology; it was the "national, suprapolitical [*überparteiliche*] grouping" so many other parties had tried to be.

It would oversimplify matters to argue that Schwalm's experience in youth and student groups prepared him for nazism. In one sense, of course, this is true, and it goes to the heart of the present study. Prior organizational memberships equipped Scwhalm with leadership skills, an attachment to certain ideological traditions, and personal contacts. Schwalm transferred these resources to the NSDAP after 1929. But he acted independently; he was not a conspirator engaged from above by party leaders looking for more and more contacts in local social life. Moreover, Schwalm's experiences with nazism heightened his distaste for "politics." Some of Schwalm's fellow club members, who joined him in the NSDAP, considered themselves "better, clearer thinking National Socialists" than the majority of Nazi party adherents. This was an unsurprising attitude for individuals socialized in isolated national-*völkisch* or exclusive bourgeois youth group traditions. Using the party as an outlet for leadership aspirations, many of these individuals gained high-level positions in the NSDAP.[30] But Schwalm, who by his own account became in 1932 a training leader (*Schulungsleiter*) in the SS (Schutzstaffel, or elite guard), recalled that he and other members could never attain "certain top positions" that party "apparatchiki" from the circle of "old fighters" guarded closely. Moreover, Schwalm expressed dismay that by late 1932 "particular democratic rules" were abandoned in the NSDAP.[31]

Schwalm and his comrades discovered that the NSDAP was no longer a "movement . . . but a party." It had become "too narrow," and many former members of *völkisch* groups concluded they were "too good" to strive for leadership in the organization. They shrank from organizational rigidity, "radicalism," and "concentration of all power . . . in the person of Hitler." Warned by his father in 1929 that in politics "two heads are better than one," Schwalm lost his enthusiasm for nazism by late 1932. He retained his party membership but realized that he belonged to a political machine that lacked tolerance for the comfortable indiscipline of bourgeois associations and parties. His apoliticism, sharpened by his resentment of Nazi old fighters, consisted of the familiar distrust among some sections of the German lower middle classes of bureaucratic and centralized mechanisms of mass politics.

The example of Schwalm highlights a major question of Nazi survival in the years of political marginality: how was the party to utilize its organizational contacts? The solution was to build the political machine that Schwalm later decried. But building this machine took time; Nazi membership fluctuated wildly; and Nazi party adherents who possessed affiliations to other clubs and associations varied in their commitments not only to the Nazi cause but to the goals of non-Nazi organizations as well. The National Socialist movement would be built on the shifting social foundations of party membership and organizational ties. Hence, between the moment when a systematic mobilizing strategy took hold and the juncture at which it became more fully consolidated, the party attracted individuals who valued "democratic rules," accessibility, and (compared with what would come) relative political indiscipline. To many Marburg *Bürger* the NSDAP was not a mass party but an apolitical people's movement. Meanwhile, to the generation of party activists slowly gaining power in the late 1920s it was apparent that nazism could exploit this identification with apoliticism only by adopting up-to-date political tactics and rigid discipline. We turn now to the efforts of these men.

Political Activists

Nazi ideologues praised Böckel's contribution to the anti-Semitic cause, but they noted that "the time was not ripe" for Böckelian ideas. More importantly, Böckel allegedly lacked "the personality of a leader," and consequently, the "anti-Semitic movement broke down into numerous groups and factions that fought one another." In Marburg after 1924, both political conditions and the organization of the anti-Semitic movement changed, and a new group of party activists did much to bring about the new circumstances. These activists were men who, by learning to exploit Marburg's heritage of political volatility, constructed the foundations of the National Socialist mass movement locally.[32]

A central figure was Hans Krawielitzki. After joining the party in 1927, Krawielitzki became the National Socialist city group leader (*Ortsgruppenleiter*) in late 1927 and district (*Bezirk*) party leader in 1928. The son of a Lutheran pastor who moved his family to Marburg in 1908, Krawielitzki was hardly an imposing or charismatic figure. He studied law in Marburg and Berlin but failed his doctoral examination. Though he came from the town elite, Krawielitzki lacked the distinction of belonging to an established Marburg family. Moreover, his life experiences differed significantly from those of anti-Semitic politicians who reached maturity before the Republic. Too young for military service during most of World War I, Krawielitzki became a soldier in the summer of 1918. After a short time in military service, he joined a paramilitary Free Corps in 1919, the Marburg Student Corps in early 1920, and the Young German Order later in 1920. These were organizations with no true equivalents in the Wilhelmine age. Krawielitzki was thus schooled in a more violent and activist brand of politics than prewar anti-Semitic agitators had been. Additionally, "out of pure practical experience," he would later say, he learned that in politics "propaganda . . . is the decisive thing."[33] More a bookkeeper than a demagogue, Krawielitzki saw that a stable and bureaucratic structure produced consistent propaganda. Devotion to paramilitary violence, belief in the primacy of propaganda, and talent for bureaucratic organization made Krawielitzki an unprecedented political figure in Marburg politics.

Marburg university students readily endorsed this heady activist approach to politics. They were the most effective Nazi agitators locally. They thus continued the tradition of using the university as a motor of political mobilization. Kuno von Eltz-Rübenach, an agricultural science student in Marburg in 1928, was simultaneously head of the SA and the NSDStB. Born in 1904, he resembled Krawielitzki in that he missed military service in World War I. He gained his understanding of political matters first through membership in a number of "nationalistic school groups" at the *Gymnasium* and later in various racist groups such as the Greater German Youth League. His militaristic approach to politics found expression in a close identification between his SA and Student League work. It had been "in good taste" for Marburg NSDStB members to belong to the SA, but von Eltz emphasized this connection even more, just as Student League members in other universities did.[34] In addition, like the national Student League leader Baldur von Schirach, von Eltz encouraged contact with fraternity students, many of whom supported the Marburg NSDStB well before it became a powerful force in student government. Finally, von Eltz organized mass assemblies designed to enhance the visibility of nazism in political life.[35]

The most effective speaker in the NSDAP in the late 1920s was also a university student. Nicknamed the "drummer of Oberhessen," Wolfgang Bergemann distinguished himself by speaking at nearly seventy of one hundred NSDAP assemblies in the four-county Marburg Reichstag district before the 1928 elections. Were they not adorned with anti-Semitic and antisocialist remarks, his recollections in the party *Festschrift* would remind one more of stories recounted at college reunions than of descriptions of Nazi agitation. Bergemann bicycled into the countryside, made vitriolic anti-Semitic speeches before small crowds in village pubs, and then returned to the Hessian city, ready for the same routine the following evening. Government officials noted that when Bergemann left Marburg for Jena in late 1928, the number of party assemblies dropped significantly.[36] In the context of a great deal of literature emphasizing the wide support that nazism enjoyed in German society, it is always useful to remember that just a few committed and well-connected individuals could lay the foundations of Hitler's success in a town like Marburg.

Krawielitzki, von Eltz-Rübenach, and Bergemann gained leadership positions in the party after the seizure of power.[37] They employed the most advanced ideas of political agitation, but they also possessed academic backgrounds. These traditional paths of social influence were important to local Nazi leaders. In early 1933 four top NSDAP officials in Marburg possessed doctorates.[38] Krawielitzki was without this distinction, but he had studied at two universities and was the son of a local pastor. These were qualifications of which any local bourgeois party could approve. Nazi activists in Marburg could not do without the political advantages of university study.

Influenced by the unprecedented conditions of postwar Germany but rooted in traditional social hierarchies, Nazi party activists developed a syncretic political style that matched their variegated background. They advocated direct appeals to specific group interests. Yet they insisted that special interests take second place to the general interest—that group activity entailed a moral obligation to the nation. This obligation, it was claimed, was lacking in the one-sided materialism of the socialists. But, like Social Democrats and prewar political anti-Semites, and unlike bourgeois party leaders, Nazi activists recognized that this moralistic conception presupposed mass mobilization in a central political party. Their syncretic strategy placed grass roots national socialism somewhere between the traditional left and right. Rather than being radical in any precise sense of the term, local Nazi agitators fused seemingly opposed traditions.

Yet a radical potential was contained in National Socialist syncretism. By creating a disciplined political movement, the Nazis tried to break through the bourgeois asymmetry between strong social organizations and weak political parties. An end to asymmetry suggested a more balanced relationship between social activities and political power. But this would lead to an attempted fusion of social and political life in the Third Reich, a swallowing of social organizations by a political machine legitimized through state power. Only when party agitators tried to erase distinctions between "power" and "society" did national socialism lose its intermediate character for the town bourgeoisie. Until then, the radical potential of nazism was suggested but never developed fully. Nazi activists first developed this syncretic strategy while appealing to peasants and the *Bildungsbürgertum*.

The Hessian countryside remained the political no-man's-land of Hellmut von Gerlach's day. Fluctuating electoral support for bourgeois parties, sustained SPD strength, tension between the county and provincial leadership of the Hessian Peasants' Association (Hessischer Bauernverein), and competition between the county branch of the Peasants' Association and the County Agricultural Association (Landwirtschaftlicher Kreisverein) made the countryside an appropriate target for Nazi agitation.[39] Fanning out into the countryside and small towns of the district, party organizers claimed they received a sympathetic response from communities where memories of the Böckel movement remained alive. Like Böckelian speakers, Nazi agitators stressed the social and economic dimensions of anti-Semitism, a notionally practical prejudice aimed at Jews who held commanding positions in economic life but who, in the words of a local farmer, "had never worked an honest day."[40]

Again like Böckel agitators, the Nazis spoke to the resentment and suspicion that country and small-town people had of their "betters"—*die da oben*. Usually, appeals to this suspicion appeared in a mosaic of criticism directed against the Weimar parties, conditions of economic life, and current social customs. For instance, in a Nazi assembly of sixty to seventy people, only eight or ten of whom were party members, held in the Warzenbach village tavern in February 1929, Bergemann wove together a number of themes: he spoke against Gustav Stresemann's links to "Jewish finance capital," the "shockingly low-necked gowns" that were worn by women attending a press ball in Berlin where the Prussian minister of police was seen, and the questionable financial policies of the Hessian Peasants' Association's leadership.[41]

Yet there were important differences between nazism and prewar Hessian anti-Semitism. Böckel and his supporters had railed against parliamentary politics, to be sure, but they had also agitated for wider suffrage and fewer restrictions on voluntary associations. They supported policies that potentially widened access to political life. Böckel's eventual disillusionment with parliamentarism should not obscure the considerable democratic potential of Hessian populism. In contrast, Nazi spokesmen, building on postwar antipathy toward the Republic in the countryside, wedded their critique of party politics to plans for dictatorship. At a 25 March 1928 meeting of the county Peasants' Association at which all party representatives presented their views for the upcoming Reichstag elections, the Nazi speaker Georg Pfau trumped all other speakers by condoning a statement by Bauernverein members that they opposed "parliamentarism in its present form." Pfau said that this opposition "pointed toward a dictatorship" in which "the common good goes before individual interest." Whereas the other speakers could only warn against further splintering of the party scene, the Nazis advocated doing away with it entirely.[42] One element of Böckel's attack on German politics, a rhetorically violent aversion to parties and parliamentary procedures, had now issued into a single-minded advocacy of dictatorship in the Nazi response to country people's interests. But since parliamentarism was identified with narrow class interests—the materialism of socialists and liberals—and since allegedly immoral bourgeois notables were turned into objects of scorn, Nazi dictatorship appeared to be a middle course between two failed extremes.

The party's first target group in the city was "academic" Marburg, consisting of university students, professors, and other members of the *Bildungsbürgertum*. The Nazi Student League assumed much of the responsibility for addressing this group, and its influence quickly overtook its size, which was relatively small until the last eighteen months of the Weimar Republic.[43] By early 1929, outside of regular party discussion evenings, most of the big public lectures and assemblies in the city were either solely or jointly sponsored by the NSDStB.[44] "Swastika students" were the main representatives of nazism in the city.

The league first came into contact with academic Marburg through the fraternities. League statutes, submitted to the university chancellor on 21 May 1926, indicated that the NSDStB limited itself to concerns "of a political character" and left social matters, especially those pertaining to fraternity life, to the discretion of individual members.[45] This conceded a broad area of activity to the fraternities. In practice, however, Student League members could hardly delimit their interests so easily. In the autumn of 1929 Heinrich Link, who succeeded von Eltz as league leader, complained that von Eltz had ignored the "intellectual absorption" of members in favor of marching and SA membership. Instead of this "superficial" approach, Link offered more rigorous political and intellectual schooling, a politicized challenge to the fraternities' program of educating the whole personality.[46] League attacks on fraternities most often concentrated on fraternity politics in the AMSt, that "spineless, useless abscess," but the NSDStB rarely missed a chance to criticize all "philistinized" dueling fraternities.[47] Nevertheless, by targeting university students, the NSDStB had to bow to fraternity influence until the establishment of the dictatorship, when the party gained dominance not only in student politics but in organizational life as well.

The Student League also appealed to the nonstudent *Bildungs-bürgertum*. The first assembly to attract these Marburgers in significant numbers occurred in January 1929, when the Thuringian Nazi official Dr. H. S. Ziegler spoke before about two hundred people including university students, high school teachers, women, medical doctors, civil servants, and "elderly privy councillors."[48] Delivering a speech entitled "The Bolshevization of German Culture," Ziegler, who with his doctorate and his "objective and convincing" manner spoke the language of the town elite, took traditional tastes beyond their nineteenth-century boundaries. The speech transformed the apoliticism of the *Bildungsbürgertum*, which viewed party politics largely in cultural terms, into the more violent and militaristic language of the Nazi movement. Ziegler "outlined . . . the fronts of the ever-continuing cultural struggle [*Kulturkampf*] against foreign infiltration," according to the *Ober-hessische*, "and drew a picture of the conscientious German as a contemporary soldier in the fight against inferior peoples."[49] Though racism was part of the ideological heritage of the *Bildungsbürger-tum*, National Socialist language transformed the custodians of culture into trench soldiers in a larger racial struggle. Attempting to be socially acceptable to academic Marburg, the Nazis also transformed the key concepts of local ideology. The result was political imagery linking postwar racism and militaristic terminology with elite cultural traditions. Though the imagery appeared startling and drastic to contemporaries, the NSDAP used it to fuse several (not entirely compatible) ideological themes.

Their frequency more than any other factor distinguished National Socialist assemblies from those of Hessian populism and bourgeois politics before 1930. Of course, mass rallies already played a part in the Nazi repertoire. One of the first big rallies to attract country people occurred in April 1928, when the party held National Socialist Hesse Day in Marburg. It featured SA parades and speeches by national party leaders Ernst von Reventlow and Robert Ley. But these events were notable exceptions before 1930. More common were rather traditional political assemblies. Agitating for upcoming Reichstag elections in spring 1928, the party staged over one hundred rallies in the countryside. It held 159 assemblies in the Reichstag district that year, and in early 1929 the NSDAP held 18 assemblies in the county alone.[50] In most assemblies a chair called the meeting to order, made a number of introductory comments, introduced the main speakers, and, depending on the potential for heated debate or violence, directed questions and discussion after the presentation. By the turn of the decade the party began to include other forms of entertainment such as theater evenings featuring "Andreas Hofer" and "Swastika and Soviet Star," performed by the National Socialist Traveling Theater Group. But it was not until major electoral success in autumn 1930 that these features were added on a routine basis.[51] In the late 1920s, frequency and intensity more than form set NSDAP assemblies apart from those of other political contenders.

If Nazi activists grasped for new agitational forms, their success depended more on the political ecology of the region than on tactical brilliance. In particular, the level of repression created a favorable environment for Nazi activity. "Repression" means raising the cost of a group's pursuit of some shared goal, and a number of factors significantly lessened repression of national socialism in the city and county in the late 1920s and early 1930s.[52]

A major factor was the nature of Socialist responses to nazism. Besides certain government officials and antiracist organizations, the Social Democrats had been the potentially most consistent opponents of anti-Semitic parties in the north Hessian countryside. In the Republic, the SPD and Reichsbanner continued this tradition. The Social Democrats were the largest vote-getter in the county until 1930. In the city the party maintained itself electorally even as the local KPD gained increased support in the second Reichstag elections of 1932 (7.9 percent). A socialist student group, formed in 1919, had twenty-two members in summer 1929, only six less than the Nazi student organization.[53] It is therefore too simple to argue that the Social Democrats in particular or democratic groups in general lacked the human resources to resist nazism. Though nationalist forces virtually eliminated Social Democrats, Marxists, and outspoken republicans from local political life, resources were still available for attacking the NSDAP, particularly when the latter was politically marginal.

Three processes hindered application of these resources in Marburg after 1924. First, unemployment weakened the trade unions and the Social Democratic party.[54] Second, socialist students possessed neither a structured link with the Social Democratic party nor the ideology to conduct political agitation. Instead of being a student arm of the SPD, the socialist student group stressed "dissemination and deepening of socialist ideas without specifying a particular method of implementing them."[55] Third, Marburg Social Democrats were the best local target for symbolizing Nazi opposition to the Republic. Any provocation of the SPD by the Nazis, even one that ended in defeat for the latter, could serve the important propaganda task of identifying the "enemy."[56] It was therefore not a pathological need for violence that compelled Nazi agitators to hold assemblies in Reichsbanner strongholds, but a reasoned tactic designed to portray the NSDAP as the most decisive opponent of the Republic.[57] The Nazis reversed the relationship between populist anti-Semitism and Social Democracy. In the Empire, Social Democrats followed anti-Semites from village to village in hopes of a confrontation. In the Republic, the Social Democrats were victims of this provocative strategy. Not the lack of resources but limits on their use in the specific conditions of the late 1920s shaped the SPD response to nazism in Marburg.

Even if defenders of the Republic had been more powerful, they could have resisted nazism successfully only with support from government and university officials. But Social Democrats and republicans failed to get that support. Provincial authorities considered Marburg a haven of right-wing groups. In the summer of 1930 Prussian Interior Minister Carl Severing wrote that Hesse-Nassau was "far behind" other regions in reporting on the "right radical movement."[58] Alluding to the political ferment of the 1920s, District President Friedrich Friedensburg told his county administrative officers and police commissioners that as of early 1929 the Marburg region had "been the object of state authorities' attention for a number of years." At lower administrative levels, there appears to have been little coordination on strategy against the Nazi movement between city and county officials. When Friedensburg met with officials of his district in Kassel in the spring of 1930, the Marburg *Landrat* Ernst Schwebel stressed KPD weakness and growing NSDAP strength in his county. But Marburg Lord Mayor Johannes Müller implied that the Nazi threat was not as substantial as Schwebel thought; he cautioned against making "unnecessary martyrs" of National Socialists.[59]

Müller's response typified the view of someone who dealt with political issues in the unpolitical terms of German city administration. But the statement also reflected a clearcut policy of city and police officials, who protected university students from local police as well as outside authorities. Relations between city officials and police, many of whom belonged to the SPD, were strained. One critic charged that police chief Lange angrily encouraged his Social

Democratic officers to "go over to the Communists . . . they would like to help you."[60] Marburg police officers could hardly count on unequivocal support from police and city officials in cases involving student drunkenness or collective violence in which students took part.[61] Viewing such tensions among city authorities, Hessian and Prussian officials grew uneasy about the chances of repressing nazism in Marburg city and county.

University officials did little to assuage this uneasiness. There was no attempt to keep the Nazi Student League from organizing in Marburg in 1926, as there had been at the Technical College in Darmstadt, where the University Senate barred the NSDStB in the same year.[62] Attempting to keep the university free of political contention, Marburg professors indirectly facilitated Nazi mobilization by defending university students against outside intervention. Internal harmony had become even more difficult in the Republic than it had been in the Empire because of disagreements between professors over Weimar's legitimacy. The university's attempt to police its own affairs transformed the institution into a haven of student political activity against the Republic.[63]

Leading SPD politicians cited convincing evidence of the collusion of Marburg police officials in protecting students from harsh fines or court sentences after confrontations with patrolmen. Marburg, it was said, was the city "with unlimited possibilities for reaction" because of leniency toward students.[64] In early 1929, members of a watchdog organization that supported the Republic complained of Nazi student activity at the university. But the chancellor, bristling at outside intervention, demanded that the group name local informants before further action be taken. This would hardly have ensured the security of those informants.[65] In early 1930 Nazi, Saxnot, and other students made "insulting catcalls" during an official visit of Prussian Education Minister Carl Heinrich Becker. Though this was "behavior unworthy of a student," in the words of the chancellor, university officials prosecuted no one, arguing that they were unable to determine who shouted the insults.[66] From the point of view of leftist critics, such actions were to be expected from the "Fascist university" and its "uniformed swastika professors."[67] These were heated exaggerations, to be sure, but the failure of university officials to repress dangerous student political activity eventually helped the Nazi cause.

The status of university students in Marburg also favored the Nazi movement. One requirement of National Socialist activism was time, and students possessed this resource. Being a student offered time to think about politics and agitate for a political cause. Additionally, Marburg students enjoyed a favored position as economic resources and future elites. More than other local groups, students could expect a degree of tolerance from town dwellers. When one NSDStB member donned a cardboard tube plastered with vicious anti-Semitic slogans and strolled Marburg streets as the "wandering kiosk,"[68] his deadly serious mission most certainly drew knowing glances from *Bürger* who expected such behavior from students and who saw the activity as a mix of college-boy pranksterism and political sloganeering that was occasionally tasteless but not really harmful. Indeed, oppressive measures would have created the martyrs that the mayor, conservative university professors, and other notables—all with a vested interest in keeping Marburg quiet—wanted to avoid. Nazi political activism flourished partly because key groups and individuals chose not to repress it.

Toward the Mass Party

The Marburg NSDAP reached a turning point in mid-1930. No longer a paramilitaristic *Stammtisch*, the party still awaited significant electoral victories. With 5.5 percent of the vote in the city and 9.4 percent in the county in 1928 Reichstag elections, the party failed to achieve VSB totals of May 1924. Moreover, other splinter parties, the Economic party in the city and the Christian National Peasants' and Rural People's party in the county, topped the Nazis in 1928. In city parliament the lone NSDAP representative was completely ineffectual. The Nazi vote in council elections declined from 6.4 percent in 1924 to 5.3 percent in 1929. In the county parliament the party held just two of nineteen seats. Organizationally, the party gained visible but limited success. Though party assemblies attracted large audiences, there were still only sixteen locals in the four-county Marburg district in autumn 1930. In the city the NSDAP had no more than one hundred members. Participation with the German Nationals and other nationalist nonparty organizations in the 1929 referendum drive helped the NSDAP, but without further electoral successes, the advantages gained in the campaign could never be fully exploited.[69] At the university, the Student League had gained attention with its assemblies and placed members on the AMSt newspaper, the *Marburger Hochschulzeitung*. But in summer 1929 the NSDStB had only twenty-nine members, and the Stahlhelm student group, with forty members in the same semester, was still the largest student political organization in the city. Moreover, with party slates banned from AMSt elections until 1931, the league could hardly expect to translate its resources into electoral power.[70] Finally, by mid-1930 the party had begun to secure a place in the organizational infrastructure of the town bourgeoisie, but the political potential of these social resources remained unexploited.[71]

Electoral victories in 1930–31 helped the Marburg NSDAP move beyond these barriers. Nazi success in the city (28.8 percent of the vote) and county (33.2 percent) in September 1930 was accompanied by massive shifts of voters away from the bourgeois parties (see table 2-3). The city DDP, DVP, and DNVP lost 3,188 votes between them, whereas the NSDAP gained 2,866 votes over its 1928 total and two new splinter parties added 1,317 votes to their showing in previous Reichstag elections. Electoral participation rose from 69 percent in 1928 to 73 percent in 1930, but four of five previous Reichstag elections had attracted wider voting. The increase in voting participation in Marburg between 1928 and 1930 was not as substantial as that in the Reich during the same interval. While popular apoliticism may have induced some townspeople to vote for the NSDAP or a splinter party, it may have encouraged others to abstain from Reichstag voting altogether. The abstainers probably returned to the polls in July 1932, when 88 percent of Marburg's eligible voters cast ballots. Excepting the unlikely possibility that the 1930 electorate consisted mainly of previous nonvoters, it appears that new voters accounted for some share of Nazi increases in 1930 but that defections of previous voters from other parties were responsible for the largest part of Nazi gains. At the same time, nazism probably did not gain all the defectors' votes; good showings by the CSV and KVP in 1930 indicate that some bourgeois and Center defectors may have voted for these parties instead of the NSDAP. In the county all bourgeois parties lost support, while the Christian Nationals dropped from 23.5 percent in 1928 to 10.5 percent in 1930. Here new voters may have played a more substantial role in Nazi success because voting participation jumped from 62 to 74 percent between 1928 and 1930. But the Nazi electoral share jumped nearly twenty-four percentage points between the two elections. Because it is unlikely that all new voters supported Hitler, the backing of defectors from other parties could account for the largest part of Nazi increases in the county also.[72]

The Nazi Student League was unable to exploit the September 1930 success immediately because student government statutes prohibited party slates for elections. Consequently, the influence of the NSDStB was considerably less in Marburg than at the Technical University in Berlin or Brunswick, where Nazi students had gained footholds in student government.[73] An unexpected controversy over the appointment of an SA student to the AMSt vice-president's office in summer 1930 gave the Marburg League an opportunity to do away with this electoral obstacle. The Finkengruppe, representing the Freistudentenschaft in the AMSt and advised by the theology professor Hans von Soden, protested the SA student's appointment, claiming the post for itself. It backed this protest by walking out of the student assembly and refusing further dealings with student government. AMSt leaders feared the controversy would damage relations with conservative university professors, who supported student government as a bulwark of apolitical harmony. AMSt leaders therefore called for a round of debate and testimony, a process that failed to forestall negotiations between the Finkengruppe and the NSDStB in which the former received the contested office and the latter a pledge to support free elections in the AMSt. "With that," NSDStB leader Fritz Weibezahn wrote some years later, "we achieved our main goal."[74]

Held in July 1931, the elections gave the NSDStB 1,525 votes, or 49.6 percent of the total and twenty-one of forty-two AMSt seats. Voting participation (71.9 percent) was lower than in 1927 (77 percent), when students decided on the fate of a new Prussian student ordinance.[75] But the results made so-called swastika students the most cohesive force in Marburg student government just ten months after the NSDAP electoral breakthrough in the city.

How can these initial successes be explained? We should first discuss what seems to be the most obvious factor, namely, the Depression of 1929. The Depression was not a direct factor in either electoral victory, but it created a broad backdrop for other more important processes. Unemployment, the main tracer of the deteriorating economic situation, was still too low in the city in September 1930 to influence Reichstag elections. What is more, not sudden and drastic unemployment but chronic joblessness and underemployment were the most severe problems in the city and county.[76] In 1930 there was heightened concern in occupational associations about economic hardships, but most economic demands, such as those supporting independent trade and artisanry, had been on the agenda of local organizations since the beginning of the Republic. In the countryside the economic situation had been deteriorating since well before September 1930, and the Depression was not a sudden shock.[77] Among university students, debates before the AMSt elections indicated that economic issues were either secondary or only one of a number of concerns. The NSDStB treated economic issues perfunctorily before the 1931 elections.[78] Clearly, after Hitler benefited from the 1930 protest vote, the worsening Depression caused Nazi party electoral and membership increases to be far greater than they would have been otherwise, and the NSDAP could never have been the mass movement it became without the hardships of the economic crisis. But in the Hessian town the economic disaster was less important to the rise of nazism in 1930 and the first half of 1931 than were other considerations.

More crucial were two sociopolitical factors. The first had to do with the interplay of organizational life and the Nazi party. The town bourgeoisie became more organized in the Weimar Republic, as the previously presented evidence on organization formation and density suggested. More nonelite *Bürger* were gaining organizational skills and social contacts. Additionally, bourgeois social organizations gained members or remained stubbornly resilient while working-class organizational life faltered. There was also a general mobilization away from the bourgeois parties, a trajectory vividly demonstrated in the appearance of economic interest coalitions in city politics in 1924–29. But other organizations contributed to this process even more. Social clubs adopted a number of mechanisms —from older practices of muffling political tension to aggressive domination of nationalist festivals—to encourage popular apoliticism. At the university the Stahlhelm, NSDStB, Hochschulring, and other organizations became more lively; students took a greater interest in politics by late 1929, although they advocated nonpartisanship. These trends coalesced in a moralistic and nationalist consensus driven primarily by bourgeois nonparty organizations.[79] Before September 1930 the NSDAP was politically marginal compared with the bourgeois parties, more dependent than the bourgeois parties on social ties, and willing to present itself as the culmination of efforts to build an apolitical and antisocialist community of sentiment. The NSDAP had an opportunity to be the political head of this mobilized tangle of social organizations.

The second factor was Nazi dynamism. Though bourgeois elites began the apolitical mobilization of the 1920s, numerous weaknesses—a failed referendum against the Young Plan and ineffectiveness of the AMSt and Hochschulring among them—exposed the limits of their mobilization efforts. Bourgeois elites lost control over popular apoliticism, bourgeois parties fumbled away still more support, and Nazi party activists successfully grasped for the resources that were now available, showing more dynamism than liberal or conservative competitors. But Nazi dynamism was necessary in an underfinanced and marginal organization seeking a path out of political impotence. Political activism was a matter of survival, not a result of extraordinary brilliance or perspicacity. In a very real sense Nazi agitators exploited the advantage of political "backwardness."

But advantages over the bourgeois parties were only temporary. Against a historical backdrop of fragmented party politics, the rise of the NSDAP appeared to be little more than another phase of fluctuating electoral sympathies. How could Marburgers not expect the NSDAP to flag just as the Böckel movement, the National Socials, right-wing bourgeois party alliances, the Fatherland party, the Weimar coalition, and the VSB had? In light of its volatile party membership and individual party members' shifting affiliations with local voluntary associations, how could the NSDAP hope to maintain and control its suddenly large following? How could a Nazi regional leader (*Gauleiter*) Karl Weinrich, who cautioned that "the child of September 14 won't live long," not fear the impermanence of the victory?[80]

Despite such fears, Weinrich and others may have realized that there was something different about the NSDAP compared with previous political contenders. Well before the 1930 elections the local NSDAP conveyed to the town bourgeoisie an image of unprecedented social breadth. In July 1930, for instance, the *Oberhessische* reported that the NSDAP held one of the largest assemblies in city history, exceeded only by Hugenberg's gathering a year earlier. The audience consisted of "numerous women, citizens of the city, very many farmers and students." The assembly featured four speakers. They included Elsbeth Zander of the German Women's Association in Berlin, who talked about parents' responsibility to children in making Germany safe for nationalism and business. Professor Werner of Giessen, a member of the political anti-Semitic movement of the Second Empire, followed Zander with comments on Prussian government repression of nazism. The third speaker, Herr Engel, was a skilled worker and member of the Berlin city parliament who castigated the wastefulness of city government and said that the NSDAP supported "all those who must work to make a living." Finally, Wolfgang Bergemann, who now resided in Kassel, delivered a rousing speech that ended with the proclamation,

"Where a Nazi stands, there is Germany." The audience rose to sing "Deutschland über Alles" and shout "Sieg Heil."[81] By stressing such themes, the party integrated a broad range of group demands in a movement committed to national interests.

The 1930–31 electoral victories were more lasting than expected, because the NSDAP was gaining control over a field of social organizations wider than that supporting bourgeois parties. Beginning before September 1930, this process—fueled more strongly than before by mounting economic difficulties—gained momentum after the first Reichstag successes. It was partly a result of Nazi infiltration of voluntary organizations. By the summer of 1928, von Eltz claimed that the NSDStB had "respresentatives" in at least five major Marburg student organizations.[82] Later, the Nazi Student League attended regular discussion evenings of fraternity and nonfraternity student groups. In late 1931 the national NSDStB leader von Schirach ordered all local leagues to establish "contact organizations" consisting of trustworthy members in the fraternities. The goal was to monitor fraternity actions, stir up conflict, and "disarm" fraternity leaders. The process worked well in the Christian-conservative fraternity Marburger Wingolf, an organization with thirty-eight active members in summer 1930. By 1933 thirteen *Wingolfisten* had joined the Nazi movement. Additionally, members of the Association of German Students, Turnerschaft Philippina, Studentenverbindung Chattia, Burschenschaft Germania, the Students' Gymnastics Club of Kurhessen, Corps Teutonia, and many other student groups joined the NSDAP. Parallel processes of cross-affiliation occurred for town organizations. Nazi nonstudent party members could be found in bourgeois occupational associations, sports clubs, municipal nonparty coalitions, and many other groups.[83] Through infiltration, the NSDAP gained moral authority over organizations in which it also established a material base. It was becoming the political hub, the focus of legitimacy and material power, that bourgeois constituencies had lacked.

But it would be wrong to see infiltration as something planned in great detail by party tacticians. Nazi occupation of bourgeois networks also occurred through parallel and independent actions that escaped full party control. Some party members, such as DHV chair (since the early 1920s) and Gymnastics Club member (since before World War I) Emil Wißner, achieved positions of power in local organizational life before entering the NSDAP (as Wißner did in 1929). Wißner used his influence in both organizations, but especially in the DHV, to recruit members for the Nazi cause. His authority also extended to neighborhood life, as Wißner got DHV members who lived in his apartment building to join the NSDAP. Other party members also employed their affiliations with the NSDAP to achieve influence in non-Nazi organizations. The baker and member of the local County Artisans' Association Ludwig Schweinsberger, who joined an independent nonparty slate in the 1929 city elections to protest association policies, joined the Nazi party in June 1931. The following October he gained a seat on the board of directors of the County Artisans' Association. In this case, Schweinsberger joined the Nazi party to force the Artisans' Association to defend artisanal interests more effectively. Kurt Hübner, a member of Corps Teutonia in 1925–28 and 1930–31, joined the NSDAP in late 1930 and then gained the AMSt presidency.[84] In these and other cases, the NSDAP conceded much power to party members, partly because it could not monitor everything, and partly because their actions necessarily furthered Nazi occupation of social networks. Indeed, because social penetration was often the result of independent activity by party joiners, the NSDAP's capacity to hegemonize the population increased; Nazi joiners' ostensible distance from centralized party control enhanced the legitimacy of their message. Unpredictable and chaotic, such unauthorized grass roots activity promoted Nazi social conquests just as effectively as did approved, stamped, and standardized party propaganda.

This had paradoxical results. Though the NSDAP was a vociferous critic of bourgeois exclusivity, Nazi mobilization after 1930–31 produced stronger ties between the party and the organizations it attacked. Simultaneously, local bourgeois organizational life persisted, as routine social activities went on in Weimar's twilight.[85] Fraternity beer drinking, dueling, soccer playing, and rowing continued despite the growing influence of the NSDStB and a 23 percent drop in the total number of active pure fraternity students in 1930–32. Declining numbers and growing political divisiveness appear to have made the fraternities more determined than ever to pull together in the social sphere. Moreover, the suspension of some activities, caused by growing economic difficulties in the Depression, gave a special quality to those parties, hikes, and sporting events that escaped the cost-cutting ax. The same was true of modified fraternities. Contributing the largest single group of students to the NSDStB before the seizure of power, Marburger Wingolf organized fewer and more modest cultural and social activities in winter 1931/32. But discussion evenings, informal parties, and sporting activities were well attended, and the semester reporter noted that economic stringencies had produced "a spirit of great togetherness" in the group.[86] Former NSDStB chair Hans Glauning argued in 1931 that fraternities remained important for "cultivating individual character," a task for which the Nazi Student League was still unprepared.[87] This observation was seconded by pure and modified fraternities through social practices. The daily business of voluntary organizations continued as the Nazis occupied—partly intentionally and partly as a function of routine social processes—a growing number of clubs and associations in university and town.

Deepening social roots established the NSDAP at the center of an evolving *völkisch* polity. The success of Hitler's visit to Marburg in April 1932, which attracted 20,000 people from the city and countryside, was only partly due to the charisma of the *Führer*. It was also a direct outgrowth of the party's stance as a vehicle of popular involvement in local public life. Hitler was an attraction because the party was; the party was attractive in part because of its positive image in conversations in the marketplace, local stores, university classrooms, fraternity houses, meeting halls, soccer fields, and homes. Hitler's seemingly mysterious mass appeal could hardly have been so extensive without the unplanned propaganda of daily social life.[88]

Local interests and traditions came to be incorporated in party organization as a result of this social process. The party bowed to specific group interests by forming a National Socialist Schoolteachers' League, a Factory Cell Organization, a Civil Servants' League, a Hitler Youth Group, and a Women's Club. The NSDStB placed increased emphasis on social programs such as counseling services for women students, housing referral agencies, financial aid, and factory tours. The Student League protested against increases in student fees and supported the establishment of a volunteer labor camp. Groups also demanded sociability, and the NSDAP found that it had to take a businesslike approach to leisure time, just as the Gymnastics Club 1860 had decades before. Party collective action became more "folksy" (*volkstümlich*) as films, music, and military exercises supplemented the political content of many assemblies.[89]

The NSDAP attached the independent social trajectories of many local organizations to a mass party. It was a moral-political coalition integrating sociability, special interests, and general concerns for all nonsocialist, non-Communist classes and strata. Hitler may have thought of the people as gullible dupes of party propaganda, but local National Socialists were deadly serious about reconnecting the frayed threads of local social and political life on a truly popular basis.

In 1932 the party confirmed its unprecedented standing in the city by gaining 53.3 percent of the vote in the year's first Reichstag election and a smaller but still impressive 49.2 percent in the second election. In the AMSt, the NSDStB received 63.2 percent of the vote and twenty-four of thirty-eight seats, giving it a commanding majority that distinguished the Marburg group from its Tübingen counterpart, which received a decisive but less impressive 53 percent in July 1932.[90] Later that year the party organized neighborhood cells and blocks consisting of fifty and ten members respectively. Between June 1931 and August 1932, the NSDAP held more than one-third (35.2 percent) of all political assemblies in the city.[91] Neither fanaticism nor Hitler's charisma compelled the party to maintain such levels of organization and activity. Rather, the moral importance of the party, its unique standing as an accumulator of traditions of bourgeois apoliticism, obligated the NSDAP to undertake such actions.

The Limits to Mobilization

Nazi occupation of social networks hardly seemed permanent. A decline at the polls in Reichstag elections from 53.3 percent in July 1932 to 49.2 percent in November 1932 verified the suspicions of Nazi leaders and observers that NSDAP electoral strength had reached a peak. The NSDStB had become the dominant student group in the AMSt, but a drop in voting participation from 71.9 percent in 1931 to 62.7 percent in 1932—still high by the standards of most student elections—reflected waning enthusiasm in student politics. In the theology department, students supported by Professor von Soden had already resisted League attempts in summer 1931 to take control of the department's student council, as the NSDStB received only 18 of 268 votes.[92] These were electoral manifestations of a deeper social reality that limited Nazi mobilization under the conditions prevailing before the party seized power.

The limits of nazism were created partly by the same apolitical conventions that facilitated the sudden expansion of the party. Apoliticism cut in at least two directions. It accommodated Nazi ideology because both opposed parliamentarism and democratic mass parties. However, apoliticism also defined the boundaries of

Nazi mobilization of voluntary organizations. Having promoted apoliticism, and having seen many of their followers embrace the Nazi cause, bourgeois organizational leaders now wanted to prevent a fusion of social life with the Nazi movement. Declarations of political neutrality by *Verein* leaders in Marburg therefore increased after 1930–31 as the Nazis transformed social support into political gains.[93] The question of how to resolve the relationship between organizational and political life would take on real significance after Hitler achieved power, but the matter need not occupy us more in the present context. More serious for the NSDAP in the last years of Weimar were direct acts of resistance.

Marburg working-class parties placed significant limits on Nazi mobilization. The Communist party received 7.9 percent of the vote in November 1932, making it the fourth largest vote-getter in the city. The KPD distributed more handbills and posters in the city from June 1931 to August 1932 than did the NSDAP. In that period, the KPD held 101 assemblies in the county, accounting for 16.3 percent of all political gatherings. The Communist party in Marburg was more active in this period than the SPD in holding assemblies and distributing political literature, though the reverse was true in the county. Local police officials identified the KPD with the unemployed, whose cry, "We're hungry, give us jobs and food!" echoed in a number of large demonstrations in the Marburg market square in 1930–33. The Social Democrats occupied a larger and more stable social space than the Communists, but the SPD was no longer the largest party in the county after the Nazi electoral showing of 1930. Nevertheless, from June 1931 to August 1932 Social Democrats held 14 assemblies in the city and 168 in the county.[94]

Socialists and Communists were involved in a major incident of collective violence with the Nazi party in February 1931. The incident took place in Ockershausen, a predominantly working-class neighborhood consolidated with the city in 1931. Describing the neighborhood as a "totally red nest" that the party wanted to subjugate, NSDAP agitators announced a party assembly and public lecture in the Ruppersberg tavern of Ockershausen. As they marched into Ockershausen, they were greeted by neighborhood residents who shouted, "Today you're not in Marburg. . . . Now you're going to get it . . . You Nazi swine." An hour before the assembly Social Democrats and Communists gathered in the Wilhelmsplatz to march to Ockershausen, where they quickly disrupted the Nazi assembly with catcalls and insults. When the leader of the assembly, an NSDStB member, began to yell back, Reichsbanner members shouted, "Social Democrats to the fore!" and charged. As fighting began, the police official Diederich immediately dissolved the assembly and had his men use rubber truncheons to restore order. Police then detained Nazi party members in the hall and escorted them out of town while Ockershausen residents shouted, threw rocks, and finally prompted police to pull their guns. A number of minor injuries were sustained by police officers hit with flying debris, by four Nazi university students, and by three Communist party members. Not surprisingly, Nazi spokesmen later praised the "correct behavior" of local police in escorting them from Ockershausen.[95] But the Nazis were doing more than admiring modern techniques of crowd control. They not only escaped serious physical injury but also discovered that they had reached a limit in their drive to become a mass party. The police, directly protecting the NSDAP, and hoping to avoid more extensive violence, saved the party from expending more resources in this embarrassing discovery.

Competition for readers between the liberal *Hessisches Tageblatt* and the conservative *Oberhessische Zeitung* also placed limits on Nazi mobilization. Though the *Oberhessische* won the commercial battle, the small *Tageblatt*, formed in 1926, introduced a note of disagreement and antagonism in public life. Whereas the *Oberhessische* accommodated itself to the rise of nazism and its editor, Dr. Ernst Scheller, later became a Nazi official, *Tageblatt* publisher Hermann Bauer criticized the NSDAP at every chance.[96] The liberal daily referred sarcastically to Nazi proclamations of the coming "Third Reich" and placed blame for the "bloody brawl" in Ockershausen on the NSDAP. The *Tageblatt* told its readers that the NSDAP motto was "With Terror and Poison against Political Enemies."[97] The feisty daily saw to it that some town dwellers would never raise their hands willingly in the Nazi salute.

Wavering electoral success, bourgeois apoliticism, direct working-class resistance, and lack of complete unanimity in public opinion on nazism—these factors suggested the inability of the NSDAP to exploit fully its temporary moral authority over the town bourgeoisie. Membership growth and electoral success added to tensions in the Nazis' organization. Rising membership raised the issue of how people were to be absorbed into the party. In 1930 Heinrich Link had criticized von Eltz for ignoring this question in the Student League and SA, organizations Link said were nothing more than *putschist* squads without a comprehensive ideology. Though the party had changed since von Eltz's departure, it did not achieve success in the "intellectual absorption" of members after 1930–31. The National Socialist folk community was a useful myth, certainly, but it was hardly the integrative moral force that party leaders proclaimed.[98]

Increased use of popular entertainment at party assemblies suggested that the NSDAP was selling an entertainment package to its members just as social *Vereine* had done since the late nineteenth century.[99] This fell far short of educating adherents in a deep or lasting manner, and it undoubtedly failed to create a genuine sense of community. Beneath the symbolism of the folk community was party leaders' fear that the Nazi movement could disintegrate quickly. By organizing cell and block attendants in late 1932, the party demonstrated its concern over the possibility that the distance between "the leader and movement" was widening.[100]

Tensions within the National Socialist organization also arose because some party members discovered the "real" NSDAP. We have already noted Fritz Schwalm's experiences in this connection. Schooled in the apoliticism of bourgeois youth groups and student guilds, Schwalm was left with a distate for politics that was greater than ever after his activity in the Nazi party in 1932. Disciplined organization and the concentration of power in the hands of the NSDAP leadership seemed to sever the ties between Nazi folk community and bourgeois apoliticism, ties that Schwalm and others valued.[101]

Schwalm's reaction exemplified the contradictory relationship between the Nazi party and local organizational life. Some Marburg party members realized that the NSDAP was a frighteningly unprecedented political organization. More than a special interest organization, certainly more than an apolitical club, the NSDAP alarmed many *Bürger* because of its increasingly centralized, disciplined, and bureaucratic structure. There was good cause for alarm. After January 1933 the party aimed for a radical transformation of the social bases of politics. Instead of "merely" recasting social and political life on a popular basis, the party tried to destroy distinctions between the two. Because Nazi occupation of bourgeois organizations was simultaneously crucial to Nazi success and threatening to full Nazi hegemony, we turn to the social background of party members in the next chapter before discussing the NSDAP after Hitler gained entry to the inner circles of political power.

six

A Relief Map of Nazi Party Membership

azi spokesmen said they wanted a society in which "the system of individuals and their material interests means nothing [and] the *Volk* means everything."[1] This vision stressed loyalties to race and nation and attacked the "chaos of interests" caused by German political parties. If the NSDAP wanted this message to be convincing, one of its tasks, aside from the very important project of appealing to a wide range of voters, was to attract a more diverse party following than bourgeois, class, and confessional parties. Most local Nazi party members gained a feeling for the social composition of the Hitler movement not by reading membership rolls but by encountering other party members in assemblies, discussion evenings, and social outings. Face-to-face contact at the local level was the most immediate source of individuals' knowledge about the organization they had joined. The problem in this chapter is therefore the following: what assemblage of individuals in the Marburg NSDAP allowed party ideologues to argue persuasively that they represented the national will instead of a single class or social group? The result will be something like a topographical map in which I identify what a geographer would refer to as high relief areas—regions of the local organizational, residential, and occupational structure in which there was above-average recruitment into the Nazi party. Unlike the geographer's precise map, however, this map can reveal only an approximation of volatile social relationships. The topography of a region changes, but social networks change more rapidly.

Organizations

Did Marburg Nazis participate in the parties, clubs, and associations that have occupied our attention in preceding chapters? Table 6-1 demonstrates that between the founding of the local branch and the end of 1935, 428 Marburg NSDAP members were affiliated with at least one non-Nazi organization in addition to belonging to the party. Membership fluctuations, the vagaries of National Socialist recordkeeping, and incomplete data on all local organizations hinder exact statements about the number of Nazis who had cross-affiliations. One must recognize the imprecision that results from discussing the interplay of two shifting social constellations, the Nazi party and organizational life; inevitably, the data err on the conservative side. But it is reasonable to estimate that more than a quarter of all Marburg party members were affiliated to non-Nazi groups at some time between 1923 and 1935. A minority of Nazi party members possessed ties to non-Nazi associations, just as a minority of townsfolk joined local clubs. However, like many joiners in the wider population, those in the party were often important people—organizers, opinion makers, movers and shakers. They were the Nazi joiners.

Nazi joiners were arguably the most important party adherents locally because they brought indispensable skills and social contacts to national socialism. Unlike party voters, whose support for nazism was often limited to an individual act of marking a ballot, Nazi party members who belonged to other associations came into direct contact with potential voters, sympathizers, and members. They may have been respected or disliked by their peers; they may have been more or less zealous, openly endorsing Hitler's message, quietly wearing an NSDAP or NSDStB lapel pin that attracted the interest of curious club members, or saying nothing at all about their party affiliation. Ultimately, how an individual used his or her Nazi affiliation in grass roots *Vereine* depended on specific circumstances that can be evoked most accurately in memoirs or fictional accounts. Except for those association members who kept their party ties secret, however, NSDAP members with cross-affiliations at least had the opportunity to "blend" nazism into local social life and legitimize National Socialist ideas.[2] In these regards, Nazi joiners were members of a distinct, crucial, and relatively well-connected subgroup within a larger, shifting population of party sympathizers, voters, members, and leaders.

The evidence raises formidable doubts about "mass society" in-

Table 6-1 *Marburg NSDAP Members' Cross-Affiliations, Compared to Sample Joiners'*

	National Socialists		Sample
Individuals with cross-affiliations			
students	156	(36.4%)	
nonstudents	272	(63.6%)	103
total	428	(100%)	103
Total affiliations[a]			
students	315	(29.7%)	
nonstudents	747	(70.3%)	284
total	1,062	(100%)	284
Total organizations			
student	31	(15.7%)	
nonstudent	167	(84.3%)	57
total	198	(100%)	57
Affiliations/individuals			
students		2.02	
nonstudents		2.75	2.76
total		2.48	2.76

a. Includes Nazi party affiliations
SOURCES AND METHODOLOGY: see appendix.

terpretations that see in nazism a movement of deracinated individuals.[3] Of course, Nazi joiners might have been isolated *within* organizations. Yet if we define a "cluster" as two or more members of the same voluntary organization who were in the NSDAP, nearly 84 percent of all cross-affiliations before 1933 were clustered in fifty organizations. This accounts for 48 percent of all associations in which pre-1933 NSDAP joiners were found.[4] Though the Marburg Nazi party did attract single individuals in local organizations, it more often mobilized groups of joiners from a diverse spectrum of local clubs—forty Gymnastics Club 1860 members, thirteen Marburger Wingolf students, thirteen members of the local German Civil Servants' Association, and so forth.

Nazi party members distinguished themselves from the majority of the population, which did not belong to voluntary organizations at all. Despite Germany's reputation as a country of passionate joiners, only a large minority of citizens was involved in clubs and associations, and an even smaller part of the adult population was made up of active social leaders. The 428 Nazi joiners constitute a group of involved public figures because they belonged to at least two organizations.[5] The ratio of affiliations to individuals for these party members was 2.48. This is lower than the same ratio for individuals in a systematic sample of nonstudent townspeople who also possessed at least two organizational affiliations. I refer to the latter as ordinary or sample joiners. However, if we eliminate Nazi students, who routinely possessed just one cross-affiliation, the number of memberships for each individual increases to 2.75, almost identical to the ratio for ordinary joiners. Regarding this measure of involvement in local associations, Nazi joiners were much like the 103 sample joiners.[6] This reinforces the point made earlier that Nazi penetration in local organizational life was in part a product of routine social process, and it suggests that Nazi joiners reproduced the more general patterns of joining that can be seen in the town population.

Before September 1930 the ratio of organizational memberships to individuals was 2.59 for 46 people with cross-affiliations. In 1930–33 the ratio dropped to 2.31 for 154 individuals, and after 1933 it increased to 2.57 for 228 individuals.[7] The data suggest three points about the intensity, contours, and meaning of Nazi social diffusion.

First, a small group of comparatively intense joiners belonged to the NSDAP before Hitler's 1930 electoral breakthrough.[8] Through the cross-affiliations of these people, the Nazi party established itself in an active, comparatively well-connected segment of the local population. However, Nazi joiners often acted independently and without central direction in this early period, and much of Nazi social diffusion depended on the interests and personal circumstances of individual party adherents. Second, in 1930–33 Nazi joiners were more likely to belong to only one organization other than the party. The proportion of NSDAP members with just one cross-affiliation reached its peak (nearly 82 percent) in these years, and the ratio of affiliations per person dropped accordingly as the increasingly popular NSDAP began to recruit less intense joiners. Evolution into a mass party in 1930–33 gave the NSDAP a wider range of organizational contacts, though party joiners in these years possessed fewer cross-affiliations than pre-1930 or post-1933 groups. Nazi social diffusion in this period was thus more dependent on less involved joiners than on the very active joiners who brought the Nazi message into local associations in 1923–30.

Third, after Hitler took power, the ratio of affiliations to individuals equalled that of the pre-1930 period. This occurred in part because the party attracted more elites, individuals who possessed more organizational contacts than the 1930–33 joiners.[9] But in these years the environment of joining also changed as the dictatorship remade local organizational life. Nazi diffusion depended less on routine social patterns than on flagrant political compulsion, not-so-subtle intimidation, and infiltration of organizations by party activists. In short, the meaning and motive of cross-affiliation changed for NSDAP adherents after Hitler assumed power. It is crucial to stress this qualitative difference between the pre-1933 and post-1933 quantitative evidence.

Significantly, a large proportion of organizational affiliations of Nazi party members were formed prior to party membership. This is demonstrated by evidence for student associations, the only local organizations for which precise measurement on timing is possible. Line B of table 6-2 demonstrates that most Nazi students were affiliated with other organizations before joining the Nazi Student League and continued their cross-affiliation for at least the semester they entered the party. Typical is the student who was an active member of the fraternity Chattia from summer semester 1929 to winter semester 1930/31, and who joined the NSDStB in winter semester 1929/30.[10] Line A, which includes only affiliations prior to Nazi membership, and line B together account for more than 63 percent of the student cross-affiliations. But this proportion of prior joiners may have been even larger. Line C indicates that nearly one-fifth of all Nazi student joiners became affiliated with non-Nazi organizations in the same semester they joined the party; unfortunately it is impossible to determine which of these non-Nazi affiliations occurred before the individual's entry into the party during that semester and which occurred afterward. Finally, many of the cross-affiliations in line D resulted from infiltration of student organizations by NSDStB members.

The general trend is clear: students who became involved in nazism possessed prior social contacts and experience in the everyday machinery of organizational life. Numerous individual examples, some discussed in the previous chapter, suggest that this applies to most nonstudent Nazi joiners as well. Nazism's success depended first on exploiting the prepolitical resources of German social life and then on conquering the party political sphere. Nonetheless, one must avoid leaving the impression that these resources were stable or ripe for Nazi picking. Organizational affiliations changed, loyal-

Table 6-2 *Timing of Nazi Students' Affiliations with Non-Nazi Voluntary Organizations, 1926–1934*

Timing of Affiliation	N	%
A. Prior affiliations only	17	22.4
B. Both prior and concurrent affiliations	31	40.8
C. Simultaneous starting affiliations	15	19.7
D. Subsequent starting affiliations	13	17.1
Totals	76	100.0

Explanation of categories:

A. Refers to affiliations with non-Nazi organizations in the semester before becoming an NSDStB or NSDAP member.

B. Refers to affiliations with non-Nazi organizations in the semester before joining the NSDStB or NSDAP and concurrent affiliation in a Nazi and non-Nazi organization for at least one semester.

C. Refers to beginning affiliations in both NSDStB or NSDAP and a non-Nazi organization in the same semester.

D. Refers to beginning affiliation with a non-Nazi organization in a semester after becoming a member of NSDStB or NSDAP.

SOURCES: HSAM 305a, Acc. 1954/16, 1–78; HSAM 327/1, 5488.

ties shifted, and people moved in and out of the Nazi party, just as they entered and left other voluntary associations. The evidence momentarily captures moving aggregations of social relationships and political resources.

What kinds of organizations did Marburg National Socialists belong to? Leaving aside for the moment the more specialized problem of students, the evidence suggests that nonstudent NSDAP members were involved in much the same sorts of organizations as sample townspeople.[11] Significantly, the percentage distributions of the first three categories of organizations in table 6-3—political, occupational, and sports associations—follow in the same order for Nazi and sample joiners except in 1933–35, when sports affiliations are more numerous than occupational affiliations for National Socialists. Moreover, the three categories take up similarly large shares of total cross-affiliations, comprising 82.3 percent of all Nazi joiners' affiliations and 77.1 percent of all affiliations for the sample group. The conventional nature of Nazi joiners, their gen-

Table 6-3 *Percentage Distribution of NSDAP Nonstudents' Cross-Affiliations, by Type of Affiliation, Compared to Sample Joiners', 1923–1935*

| Type of Organization | Percent of Total Affiliations | | | |
| | National Socialists | | | Sample |
	1923–33	1933–35	Total	Total
Political[a]	43.6	52.3	48.7	38.7
Occupational	20.7	15.1	17.4	25.7
Sports	14.7	17.2	16.2	12.7
Veterans'	5.9	3.4	4.4	5.3
Nationalist	4.9	1.8	3.1	1.0
Other special interest	2.3	3.6	3.1	6.0
Charity/community action	4.3	2.0	3.0	6.0
Cultural	1.0	3.9	2.6	3.2
All others	2.6	0.7	1.5	1.4
Total	100.0	100.0	100.0	100.0
Total affiliations	305	442	747	284

a. Includes NSDAP affiliations.
SOURCES: Refer to the appendix.

eral similarity to a sample of ordinary members of local associations, is once again striking.

There were differences in organizational background between the two groups. Political ties took up a larger share of affiliations for Nazi joiners than they did for ordinary organization members, particularly for the 1933–35 National Socialists. This is unsurprising since Nazi party affiliations must be counted among Nazi joiners' affiliations to make Nazi and sample joiners comparable. The largest share of political affiliations of Nazi joiners, nearly two-thirds of the total of 364 political affiliations, included links to the NSDAP.

Nonetheless, similarities between the two groups of political affiliations are interesting. The remaining ninety-two political affiliations of NSDAP joiners consisted of fifty-two (56.5 percent) ties to local nonparty coalitions of interest group representatives, twenty-four (26.1 percent) to the major bourgeois parties (DNVP, DVP, and

DDP/Staatspartei), and sixteen (17.4 percent) to a miscellaneous group of parties, including three to the Christian Social People's Service, one to the Center party, and one to the KPD. Municipal special interest slates gained extensive electoral support in Marburg by appealing to businessmen, homeowners, renters, Lutheran women, and many other groups. They were much more important to the political experiences of Nazi party members than the major political parties were. This is particularly true for individuals who joined the party after the seizure of power; such individuals held seventy-five of the ninety-two non-Nazi political cross-affiliations, most of them dating from the pre-1933 era. Opposing the influence of major parties in municipal life, nonparty slates in the Hessian town strengthened apoliticism and prepared the ground for National Socialist attacks on the Weimar party system.[12]

The political background of ordinary joiners was broadly similar. Forty-five (40.9 percent) of the 110 political affiliations of the sample group were Nazi party ties, a fact reflecting the deep imprint of the NSDAP on the active, organized part of the local population. But aside from these affiliations, ordinary joiners most often belonged to nonparty special interest coalitions, which accounted for thirty-two of the remaining sixty-five political ties. The three bourgeois parties accounted for another eighteen of the remaining political cross-affiliations, and a miscellaneous group of parties—Center (four), Fatherland party (three), SPD (three), Christian Social People's Service (three), Independent Social Democrats (one), KPD (one)—made up the rest.

Nationalist associations were political groups despite their claims of representing a purer national interest independent of party rivalries. Having witnessed a flowering of such associations as the Pan-German League and Colonial Society in the late nineteenth century, Marburg was home to an even more militant group of nationalist clubs in the Weimar Republic. But these organizations were important only for the 1923–33 Nazi joiners, who had five cross-affiliations with the proto-Nazi Greater German Youth League, two with Stahlhelm, and eight more with a variety of groups including the Young German Order. Leaders of nationalist associations conceded that their organizations failed to reach deeply into the social life of local communities.[13] If we assume that Nazi cross-affiliations encompassed organizations that were important to nationalist constituencies, the relative weakness of the Marburg patriotic societies in the general anti-Weimar mobilization of the 1920s and 1930s is evident. Obviously, Nazi party members and other nationalists belonged to patriotic associations; but other organizations were more significantly engaged in the grass roots attack on the Republic and in Nazi mobilization.

Cross-affiliations with occupational associations were less important for Nazis than for ordinary joiners, especially after the seizure of power, when the NSDAP absorbed many of these associations. This may reflect a peculiarity of the Hessian university city, where a relatively small trade union movement had minimal impact on organizational structures. In contrast, in larger or more industrial cities, big trade unions and more powerful Social Democratic parties forced bourgeois groups to build strong economic pressure groups that could compete in local power struggles. Nevertheless, occupational associations form the second largest group of cross-affiliations for the NSDAP overall. Before the Nazi seizure of power, the largest accumulations of these cross-affiliations came from the Tailors' Guild and Locksmiths' Guild, each contributing eight members to the NSDAP. But the local German Civil Servants' Association had the largest total number of Nazi cross-affiliations in this category, with 8.7 percent of all occupational group ties (two before the seizure of power and eleven after). Then came the Retailers' Association (6.3 percent), the DHV (4.7 percent), and eighteen additional groups with two or more affiliations each. Nazi party members affiliated with local occupational associations came overwhelmingly from bourgeois Marburg. This was an extremely differentiated group ranging from comparatively well-off members in the Retailers' Association to white-collar workers of the local DHV and craft guild members affiliated with the County Artisans' Association. A proliferation of occupational associations within the town bourgeoisie is evident in this fragmented organizational mosaic of NSDAP joiners.

Significantly, I found only two affiliations with the free trade unions of the Social Democratic movement, one with the Printers' Union and one with the Construction Workers' Union, both held by Marburgers who joined the NSDAP after Hitler's gaining of power. There were no such affiliations among NSDAP joiners in the Republic, when the regional Trade Union Cartel representing Marburg and four other counties numbered about 1,400 members.[14] Similarly low Nazi cross-affiliation with the Social Democratic and Communist parties was noted previously. Only one former Communist party adherent, who also joined the Nazi movement after January 1933, appeared in the ranks of NSDAP joiners. The data may exaggerate nonparticipation of former members of free trade unions and the Social Democratic and Communist political parties in the NSDAP because of greater availability of data from bourgeois organizations. But the evidence still reflects an important reality: free trade union, Social Democratic, and Communist cross-affiliations were rare within the Marburg NSDAP. Exacerbated by the Thuringian killings and the surge of popular apoliticism in the middle years of the Republic, class divisions in Marburg apparently made National Socialist membership an unlikely alternative for the organized working class of the SPD and KPD. These conditions did not exist in other communities less torn by open class antagonism or in larger cities, where SA branches induced some former Communists and Social Democrats to join the National Socialists.[15]

The evidence on occupational affiliations raises two other points. First, NSDAP members possessed ties to organizations with limited economic and political goals that contrasted sharply with the ideological aims of Nazi propagandists. The National Socialist party gained some support precisely because the goals of many organizations seemed too limited and selfish to rank and file members. But these individuals never abdicated their material interests once they joined the NSDAP. Much intraparty conflict after January 1933 stemmed from this feature of the organizational background of party members.[16] Second, party members gained political expertise from these occupational affiliations. Organizational experience of any kind is political education, partly because of the importance of parliamentary procedure in voluntary associations. But economic interest associations played a more direct and ultimately disruptive role in German political life since the Second Empire because they were politicized in both nation and province. Thus data on occupational group cross-affiliations reinforce the point that Nazi joiners possessed significant political experience.

Sample joiners belonged to a similarly wide range of economic organizations. The largest cluster of ordinary joiners' affiliations with occupational groups originated in the craft guilds, which account for 15.1 percent of all affiliations. The Civil Servants' Association had the next largest accumulation, with 12.3 percent of the total. But remaining affiliations reflect membership in an even broader array of occupational associations than was the case for Nazi joiners: there were twenty-one additional occupational associations, each with four affiliations or less. The organizational ties of both ordinary and Nazi joiners mirrored the extreme economic fragmentation of townsfolk.

Sports clubs figured more prominently in the organizational

background of Marburg National Socialists than in that of the sample of ordinary townspeople, especially in 1933–35. Still, such cross-affiliations were important to both groups. The largest group of Nazi sports club members came from the Gymnastics and Sports Club 1860, which had been the largest sports association in the city since the late nineteenth century. One-third of sports club affiliations were grouped in this organization, fourteen of them belonging to individuals who joined the party before the seizure of power and twenty-six to those who joined afterward. The *Oberhessische* noted the importance of such joiners in its report of a May 1933 assembly of the Gymnastics and Sports Club in which "a considerable number of gymnasts . . . in the brown dress uniform of the National Socialist movement" participated.[17] A prominent and respected community organization, this club was a crucial conduit for the social diffusion of local nazism. Having widened its following in the late nineteenth century, the club galvanized its members for public commitment without providing a political outlet for this commitment. Instead, the Gymnastics and Sports Club absorbed political tensions through sociability, community service, and ritualistic nationalism.[18] Nazism exploited the popular following of the club, used it to advance the party's social respectability, and swept numerous Gymnastics and Sports Club members into a social movement bent on direct rather than indirect political and nationalist activity.

The next largest group of sports club affiliates came from the Athletic Association (VfB 05), which accounted for 17.4 percent of all sports cross-affiliations. This group included eight individuals who joined the party before January 1933 and thirteen who joined during the Nazi dictatorship. This is significant because many *Bürger* regarded the VfB 05 as an elite organization, compared to the Gymnastics and Sports Club 1860.[19] Additionally, 12.4 percent of sports cross-affiliations were with local sharpshooting associations, which often attracted better-off retailers, craftsmen, civil servants, and others. If we add another seven affiliations (5.8 percent) from the Hessian Flying Club and two (1.7 percent) from the Equestrian Club, both elite organizations, the importance of prominent upper-middle-class townspeople among Nazi joiners becomes more evident. We return to this issue below.

One expects to find NSDAP members in local sports clubs because of the relative youth of the party. But there are better ways of explaining why Nazi joiners were more attracted to these associations than were ordinary joiners.[20] National socialism fused prewar military traditions, memories of World War I, the ideology of postwar paramilitary activity, and radical militaristic opposition to the pedestrian Republic. This mix, a syncretic "revolt into military style,"[21] drew heavily upon the dominant culture, where sports associations and militarism were important to the local club scene. But the revolt into military style actively embraced an alternative culture that compensated for experiences most postwar youth had missed: the camaraderie of the trenches, sacrifice, and discipline. This applies particularly well to Marburg NSDAP activists such as Krawielitzki, von Eltz-Rübenach, and others, who were too young for extended service in the Great War. For them military sport (*Wehrsport*), riding, sharpshooting, gymnastics, and general athletic activity filled this perceived void. The evidence for sports clubs traces this sentiment partially, but it is also manifested in evidence regarding student groups, youth clubs, and nationalist associations. It is impossible to state precisely what affiliations represented the new military style of Weimar Germany. We can only suggest that the revolt shaped a significant part of the experiences of ordinary Germans and an even larger part of the social background of NSDAP members. Initially, popular militarism was an alternative to political fragmentation; but such militarism could also intervene in the political sphere, as the history of Nazi mobilization suggests.

Despite contributing to a new military style, sports associations joined other local clubs in maintaining older traditions of *Verein* sociability, a crucial feature of the Nazi joiners' background. Constituting a larger share of cross-affiliations for pre-1933 Nazis than for 1933–35 Nazis or for sample joiners, veterans' clubs promoted such grass roots social interchange. With eleven cross-affiliations for Nazis and six for ordinary joiners, singing societies had the largest affiliation cluster among the miscellaneous special interest clubs. They also promoted local *Geselligkeit*.[22] Founded mainly before World War I, these clubs facilitated community loyalty and nationalism through social activities. Additionally, local bourgeois parties and occupational associations were often more important as outlets for talking, drinking, and socializing than for pursuing other goals. Sociability was a foundation of organizational life and Nazi mobilization.

Yet this raises the problem of compatibility between nazism and local organizations even more provocatively than before. Nazi ideology presupposed the fusion of local communities in a national, racist, and classless society. The Nazi vision of community was counterposed to the club life of the self-absorbed local bourgeoisie. Had they found the leftist Kurt Tucholsky politically acceptable, Nazi agitators would have gained inspiration from his satirical 1927 poem "The Member," in which a solipsistic club activist proclaimed, "Here I live. / And here one day they'll bury me / in my *Verein*."[23] Many bourgeois social clubs had drawn back from national party involvement in the late nineteenth century. In World War I and the Republic bourgeois social organizations tried to foment nationalism while rejecting political parties and "high politics." The Nazi movement stressed suprapolitical organization to bridge the contradiction between political activism and *Verein* narrowness, but this hardly resolved the issue in the Third Reich, as we will see.[24]

Student clubs are the source of one-fourth of all cross-affiliations.[25] As table 6-4 demonstrates, the diversity of Nazi students' organizational backgrounds is striking, particularly in view of the internecine fights of student life. The Nazi party could argue with some justification that it appealed to pure fraternities, modified fraternities such as Marburger Wingolf, and a varied group of postwar student guilds, Christian student associations, and university sports *Verbände*. The NSDStB was also attractive to students without cross-affiliations, who may have made up nearly 70 percent of Student League members.[26] Thus, the resolution of past tensions and the fusing of many different students into one nationalist movement appeared likely on the basis of the Student League's social backing.

Pure and modified fraternities were the most important organizations for Nazi student joiners. These fraternities accounted for nearly 80 percent of all cross-affiliations before the seizure of power and nearly 90 percent in 1933–35. Before 1933 pure and modified fraternities played a major role in facilitating the spread of nazism among local students. In the first two years of the Third Reich the advantages of belonging to the pure fraternities were still strong enough to attract a diminishing number of Nazi students who could find time to join organizations outside the Student League, SA, or NSDAP. The same could not be said for the modified fraternities or nonfraternity student clubs. These organizations were usually dissolved before the pure fraternities. Moreover, in 1933–34 antagonism between pure fraternities and the NSDStB was not so developed as to deter all League members from participating in such organizations.

Throughout Nazi activities at the university, traditions of frater-

Table 6-4 *Percentage Distribution of Nazi Students' Affiliations, by Type of Student Organization, 1926–1935*

Type of Organization[b]	Percent of Total Affiliations[a]	
	1926–33	1933–35
Pure fraternities	47.7	80.8
Modified fraternities	30.2	6.9
Political groups	8.1	4.1
Others	14.0	8.2
Totals	100.0	100.0
Total affiliations	86	73
Total students	84	72
Total organizations	29	19

a. For individual affiliations, see the appendix.
b. For explanation of categories, see chap. 3, n. 80.
SOURCES: HSAM 305a, Acc. 1954/16, 1–78; HSAM 327/1, 5488.

nity sociability persisted. Victims of declining material resources in the face of National Socialist challenges, the pure and modified fraternities maintained something of their cultural authority in student life. Paralleling the role of bourgeois sociability in the history of nonstudent Nazis, fraternity social practices intertwined with Nazi politics. This was an advantage for the NSDStB before the seizure of power, when the Student League sought social respectability; the league exploited fraternity customs to become lodged within student life. But it was also a disadvantage in the Third Reich, when sustained fraternity influence hindered full coordination of the student body. Cross-affiliations created tensions and contradictory loyalties for Nazi student joiners, just as they did for nonstudents.

Like the evidence on affiliations, data for the occupational makeup of Nazi joiners cannot stop a volatile and shifting set of social networks in its tracks. But the evidence suggests both social diversity and the commanding presence of the town bourgeoisie among Nazi party members with cross-affiliations (see table 6-5). A most interesting feature is the proportion of pre-1933 workers. They account for more than 18 percent of the Nazi group, well above their share for the ordinary joiners. Though this proportion fell as the party became more socially respectable in the dictatorship, overall it remained higher for Nazis than for the sample. Nineteen of the twenty working-class pre-1933 Nazi joiners were skilled laborers, whereas eleven of the twelve working-class joiners who joined the party after Hitler came to power were skilled. These workers could be found mingling with independent artisans, storeowners, and civil servants in a variety of clubs. Instead of having belonged to Social Democratic or Communist organizations, they had been members of guilds and nonsocialist clubs. One such individual was Jakob Müller, a tailor not listed in the city address book as an independent entrepreneur, who was a member of the Gymnastics Association 1885 since at least 1921, the Tailors' Guild in the 1920s, and the NSDAP since the second half of 1932.[27]

Bürgerlich workers were overrepresented in the Marburg NSDAP relative to their representation in the group of sample joiners. This parallels findings of recent sociographical literature, which show that laborers who were not committed to the organized working-class movement and toiled in handicrafts and small-scale manufacturing voted for and joined the Nazi party more commonly than traditional arguments assumed, but that workers in industrial sectors were underrepresented in the ranks of NSDAP voters and members relative to their proportion of the labor force.[28] The image of social breadth propagated by National Socialist activists could be very compelling in the light of this working-class presence among Nazi joiners in the city. Moreover, the data reaffirm earlier evidence suggesting that active joiners came from all points in the local class and status hierarchy. Whereas nazism attracted disaffected groups throughout society, its success was based ultimately on attracting these contact persons, opinion makers, and mobilizers from grass roots infrastructures. These individuals may have been angry, but the crucial difference between them and other party members and voters is that they possessed the resources needed to transform anger directly into action.

Despite working-class involvement, the upper and lower middle classes still predominated among Nazi joiners, just as they did among ordinary joiners. Taking the upper middle class first, local elites were underrepresented in the pre-1933 Nazi joiners. Only free professionals, consisting mainly of doctors and lawyers, were significantly overrepresented compared with the sample. This profile once again contrasts with that of the Nazi party's national electorate before 1933, in which elites and the upper middle classes may have been overrepresented.[29] But in view of the tremendous num-

Table 6-5 *Percentage Distribution of Nonstudent NSDAP Joiners, by Social Strata and Occupational Subgroups, Compared to Sample Joiners, 1923–1935*

		National Socialists			Sample
Stratum	Occupation	1923–33	1933–35	Total	Total
Elite					
	Professors	0.0	4.9	2.7	2.0
	Free professionals	7.3	5.6	6.3	3.0
	Clergy	0.0	0.0	0.0	2.0
	Entrepreneurs	2.7	4.9	3.9	5.9
	Civil servants	0.9	2.1	1.6	0.0
	Women without professions	0.9	1.4	1.2	3.9
	Military officers (including retired)	0.0	2.1	1.2	1.0
	Pensioners	0.0	2.8	1.6	0.0
	High school teachers	1.8	2.8	2.4	1.0
	Subtotal	13.6	26.6	20.9	18.8
Nonelite independents					
	Craftsmen	20.9	16.1	18.2	13.9
	Retailers	18.2	16.7	17.4	16.8
	Subtotal	39.1	32.8	35.6	30.7

ber of connections these individuals possessed, mobilization of a comparatively small group of elite joiners was a valuable resource for any party, especially one on the margin of the local polity for most of the Republic. Nazi elite joiners were particularly well connected: their average number of affiliations was 3.67 before the seizure of power, higher than that for sample joiners (3.31).[30] The qualitative significance of this group's presence outweighs its numerical importance before January 1933.

Elite joiners' involvement in the NSDAP increased significantly in 1933–35. The power and influence of the party may have lessened the reluctance of local elites to join it. In this period, there was above-average enrollment in the Nazi party of Marburg professors, free professionals, officials, military officers, elite pensioners, and teachers. Though underrepresented when compared with sam-

Table 6-5 *continued*

Stratum	Occupation	National Socialists			Sample
		1923–33	1933–35	Total	Total
Nonelite employees					
	White-collar	14.6	14.7	14.6	18.8
	Civil servants	10.0	14.7	12.7	17.8
	Teachers	0.9	2.1	1.6	4.0
	Subtotal	25.5	31.5	28.9	40.6
Workers					
	Craft, skilled	17.3	7.7	11.8	7.9
	Unskilled	0.9	0.7	0.8	1.0
	Subtotal	18.2	8.4	12.6	8.9
Nonelite *Berufslosen*					
	Retired	0.9	0.0	0.4	1.0
	No occupation	2.7	0.7	1.6	0.0
	Subtotal	3.6	0.7	2.0	1.0
Total		100.0	100.0	100.0	100.0
Total numbers		110	143	253	101
Percent women		5.5	1.4	3.2	7.9

SOURCES: See the appendix.

ple joiners, entrepreneurs equaled professors as the second largest elite subgroup. The composition of elite joiners suggests that after 1933 the NSDAP offered a political home for both new and old elites, from well-to-do entrepreneurs and free professionals to traditional mandarins of the *Bildungsbürgertum*. But both before and after 1933 Marburg nazism attracted elite joiners—individuals who were more organized, more equipped to lead, more capable of spreading the Nazi message among influential townspeople, and more absorbed in the local organizational culture than individuals from any other class or strata. This was a crucial factor allowing the party to translate apoliticism into political power.

A good example of a member of the local upper middle class who joined the NSDAP before the seizure of power was the building contractor Albert Münscher. Münscher was chair of the Old Boys Association of the prestigious sports club VfB in 1920 and an official of the Employers' Association for the Construction Trades in 1925. He joined the Nazi party in late 1931 or early 1932. An example of an elite Marburger who joined the party after Hitler's rise to the chancellorship was the businessman Gottlieb Braun, one of the most avid local joiners. The owner of a large bookstore and a well-known supporter of nationalist causes, Braun had been a member of the Fatherland party during the war; he joined the DNVP in 1919 and the Young German Order in the early 1920s. He was also a member of the city magistracy. Additionally, he belonged to an array of economic, community action, and social and cultural clubs, including the Concert Association, Association for the Support of the Jäger und Schützen War Invalids' Home, Upper Hessian Hiking Club, Tourism Association, County Association for Retail Trade, and Literary Society, which Braun himself founded. He received NSDAP membership number 2,828,221.[31]

The largest group of Nazi joiners came from nonelite independents. Self-employed artisans and shopkeepers make up 51.1 and 49.9 percent of this group respectively. Compared with sample joiners, both groups are overrepresented among Nazi joiners in the pre-1933 period, while craftsmen are overrepresented in the Third Reich. Nonelite independents reflect the Nazi presence in local guilds and the Artisans' Association as well as social, sports, and political organizations in which retailers were involved. Elites and the independent artisanry and business class—the core of the traditional local bourgeoisie—made up well over one-half of all Nazi joiners. They give NSDAP joiners a more pronounced *bürgerlich* character than the party membership as a whole possessed, as subsequent discussion will indicate.

By attracting craftsmen and storekeepers, the Nazi party mobilized groups with the richest traditions of *Verein* culture among nonelite Marburgers. Despite its gradually sliding presence in the work force, the town artisanry enlarged the proportion of club leadership posts that it controlled between the Empire and Republic. Moreover, retailers who were not enrolled in the local Trade Register increased their leadership role in local clubs throughout the second age of organization. Because of their widespread involvement in the organizational landscape, nonelite independents were linking elements within the town bourgeoisie, upholding contact between elites and members of nonmanual, nonelite strata, in one direction, and between the latter and workers, in the other.[32] Georg Werner Schnaut, a self-employed master housepainter, was typical. He had been a member at large of the board of directors of the Youth Hostel

Association "Herberge zur Heimat" from 1911 until the dissolution of the organization in 1927. In this association Schnaut met members of the local elite, including a university professor, a city building official, a retired Lutheran pastor, and the owner of a local furniture factory. Additionally, Schnaut had belonged to the Painters', Decorators', and Plasterers' Guild since 1914. In 1929 he ran as a city parliament candidate of a Marburg special interest alliance, "Artisans and Businessmen." This was his only political activity before entering the Nazi party sometime after January 1933.[33]

Nonelite service employees were underrepresented among Nazi joiners compared with ordinary joiners. This finding contrasts with subsequent occupational data showing that nonelite employees were overrepresented in the NSDAP. Individuals from service strata were apparently more likely to have been recruited as simple members than as contact and resource persons—as joiners. The largest group of service sector personnel consisted of white-collar employees, whose share among NSDAP joiners exceeded that of minor civil servants before the Third Reich and equaled it in 1933–35. In terms of income, many white-collar employees were hardly different from blue-collar laborers. Moreover, a small proportion of the white-collar work force belonged to a local socialist employees' association. But Nazi white-collar joiners were bourgeois by virtue of prior associational contacts. Six white-collar workers among Nazi joiners belonged to the DHV and three to the Trade Union of White-Collar Workers (Gewerkschaftsbund der Angestellten). There were no joiners who had been members of the left-wing Central Association of White-Collar Workers in Marburg. The previously mentioned salesman, DHV official, and long-time Gymnastics and Sports Club member Emil Wißner was one of the most visible white-collar employees in this nonelite service group of party joiners.[34]

Minor civil servants were also underrepresented among Nazi joiners. This is unsurprising, because in June 1930 the Prussian government prohibited membership of public employees in the Nazi and Communist parties. This worked to hinder any highly vocal advocacy of nazism among Prussian officials and discourage—though not effectively preclude—open membership in the NSDAP. Prussian employees who were also members of local associations were even more vulnerable to government scrutiny than were employees without affiliations, because the former were active in the local public sphere. On the other hand, Prussian repression made some Nazi civil servants adhere all the more strongly to their party, and they no doubt agitated surreptitiously among local officials.[35] As was the case for elites, however, quantitative data for these individuals are less significant than other kinds of evidence. Respected as representatives of government institutions and more securely employed than white-collar commercial workers (but also hard-pressed by cutbacks in public employment), a small number of officials could generate moral support for the NSDAP in key areas of organizational life. An example of a lower-level official among Nazi joiners is the railway secretary Karl Weitzel, a chair of the Railway Secretaries' and Assistants' Association in the German Civil Servants' Association before joining the NSDAP in late 1931. Equipped with skills that were transferable from job to leisure-time pursuits, civil servants were as important as elites and the old *Mittelstand* in the Nazi occupation of local organizations.[36]

Significantly, there was a lower proportion of women among Nazi joiners than among ordinary joiners. This contrasts with the overall gender makeup of the Marburg NSDAP, in which the proportion of women was equal to or somewhat higher than it was in other local political organizations. It also distinguishes the social profile of local joiners from that of nazism's national electorate, in which women outnumbered men in Protestant districts by 1932.[37] Pre-1933 nonstudent female joiners were members of the Red Cross, Seamstresses' Guild, DNVP, Housewives' Association, and the local branch of the Reich Association of German Housewives. The only female student joiner before 1933 was Lucie Scholtz, who belonged to the German Academic Women's Association from winter semester 1928/29 to summer 1931 and who joined the NSDStB in winter semester 1929/30.[38]

Resigning women to traditional public and private roles, Nazi ideology hindered wider participation by female joiners in the NSDAP. The party had little to say about such activist joiners as Luia Wadehn, who joined the NSDAP before 1933 and became an official of the Reich Association of German Housewives in Marburg in June 1933. Instead, the party's warmest praise was for women who played maternal roles. The ideal female Nazi was "the untiring Frau Weintraut, who had mountains of bread for her 'youngsters'" during the electoral campaigns of National Socialist agitators in the 1920s.[39] Women found a mainly ancillary niche within the Marburg NSDAP; activist and independent women in possession of the power that organizational contacts could offer were a small minority.

Nazi joiners were the most important individuals in the grass roots party. They eased nazism's entry in milieus of *Stammtisch* and *Verein* and softened inherent tensions between activist politics and the closed sociability of local clubs and associations. But joiners were a minority in the changing social makeup of the party, just as ordinary joiners were a minority in the town population. Underlying this group of Nazi joiners was a larger, shifting population of party members who may have found in the NSDAP their only organized social and political activity. In order to understand who some of these people were, we turn to the residential and occupational backgrounds of Marburg National Socialists in the remainder of this chapter.

Neighborhoods

Place of residence is an important topographical feature of the local polity.[40] Knowing where the actors of public life resided sharpens one's view of neighborhoods, streets, taverns, meeting halls, and other public buildings—factors that influenced participation in voluntary organizations, politics, and nazism. Moreover, it places Nazis in a broader historical sweep shaped by the transformation of the city from a "university village," as historian Leopold von Ranke once called the Hessian community, into a small university city. Fueled largely by Prussian support for the university, urban growth spurred renovations of Marburg's medieval urban core and spatial expansion in three general areas: along the Lahn valley floor in a northern trajectory determined by the location of the medieval castle, university medical clinics, and the main train depot; along the valley floor south in a path marked by the south train station and the small military garrison; and finally up the valley walls, first to the west on the *Schloßberg* below the castle and then, in the 1920s, toward the northern and eastern hills and forests on the east bank of the Lahn River. All this produced new buildings, altered vistas, varied architectural styles, and distinct neighborhoods.[41] How did townspeople who became NSDAP members fit into this changing mosaic?

I address the question by discussing the pattern of residence by electoral precinct (*Wahlbezirk*) for 366 Nazi party members for whom I verified addresses. The density of party members (number of Nazis per thousand heads of household in 1930 in each precinct) was above the city average (54.5) in seven of twelve electoral precincts. In order to discover whether there was something distinctive about the social makeup of the Nazi party members and general population of the precincts in which the Nazis recruited most successfully, I compare nonstudent Nazi recruits and a sample group of nonstudent householders in two categories, one consisting of the three precincts with highest NSDAP density and the other of the three precincts with lowest density. The base for calculating density is the total number of heads of household in the precincts (see table 6-6).[42]

Taking NSDAP recruits initially, the most obvious difference between precincts was the number of university students the party recruited in each of them. I have eliminated these individuals from the main body of table 6-6 in order to make the comparison with householders. But it is important to note that in high-recruitment precincts there were 36.2 Nazi students for every 1,000 householders whereas in low-recruitment districts the number was 21.6. Though students made up more than half of all party recruits in both kinds of precincts (57.4 percent in high-recruitment precincts and 51.4 percent in low-recruitment precincts), higher densities of students in the party occurred in precincts where NSDAP recruitment was most successful overall. More than likely these were neighborhoods with shifting groups of students who rented accommodations, moved, resettled, and rented again. It appears that where nazism garnered more support among local students, it also recruited more effectively in the nonstudent population. Students played a crucial role in carrying the Nazi message to townsfolk; where students were available for party work, there were increased chances for Nazi agitation. The presence of students, therefore, is a principal cause of Nazi success in the high-recruitment precincts.

As for other Nazi recruits, it is important to discuss nonelite service employees in precincts with both high and low levels of recruitment. In both types of precincts, the largest nonstudent group consisted of lower-middle-class employees, with independents, blue-collar workers, elites, and nonelite *Berufslosen* following. The largest group within the employees was white-collar workers, who accounted for nine of the fourteen individuals in the category in the high-recruitment precincts and all of them in the low-recruitment precincts. Whereas nonelite independents were the largest group of Nazi joiners, employees figured more prominently in Nazi recruitment of the general population. These individuals may or may not have been affiliated with organizations.

We know from previous evidence that white-collar workers were gaining a stronger foothold in the leadership of local voluntary associations in 1918–33, though they were not as involved as the city's elites, nonelite independents, and minor civil servants.[43] Yet except for certain groups such as DHV members, associational affiliations may have been less important for white-collar employees than for artisans, retailers, or town elites. This suggests one previously ignored reason for white-collar workers' very unstable voting support for nazism.[44] White-collar workers of smaller, less industrial towns possessed organizational traditions less deeply nested in the local culture than those of artisans or elites. Nazi white-collar workers thus had fewer chances to build daily social contacts and convince colleagues of the rightness of the Nazi cause; comparatively thinner organization may have reduced chances of Nazi mobilization. Only further research on white-collar constituencies can explore the validity of this suggestion.

Other groups merit attention once we compare the social makeup of the precincts. Sample householders are roughly similar with regard to proportions of elites, nonelite independents, and employees in both high- and low-recruitment precincts. The largest differences are between the working classes and nonelite *Berufslosen* of the two types of precinct. Low-recruitment precincts have a more pronounced working-class character than do high-recruitment precincts. This is due largely to the predominance of skilled laborers and dependent craftsmen, who outnumbered unskilled workers by more than fourteen to one in the precincts with low recruitment but by less than two to one in those with high recruitment. Considering the success of the Social Democratic party among craft and skilled workers, it seems that these workers may have stalled Nazi activity in the low-recruitment precincts.[45]

Lower recruitment in precincts with larger working-class populations suggests that the Marburg Nazi party was less successful than the national party in attracting working-class Germans. However, the occupational makeup of the party will demonstrate that when compared to other Marburg nonsocialist parties, the NSDAP did very well in recruiting the working class. And the social composition of Nazi joiners demonstrated that a significant minority of workers previously attached to bourgeois associations was attracted to nazism.[46]

The proportion of nonelite *Berufslosen*, consisting of pensioners and people without professions, was also lower in precincts with lowest Nazi recruitment. This is due partly to the presence of more women in high-recruitment than in low-recruitment precincts. Many women had lost their husbands in the war, and they took in

Table 6-6 *NSDAP and Sample Householders per Thousand Householders, by Strata and Occupational Subgroups, in Precincts with Highest and Lowest Nazi Recruitment, 1923–1933*

Stratum	Occupation	National Socialists Precincts		Sample Precincts	
		High	Low	High	Low
Elite					
	Professors	0.0	0.0	1.8	3.0
	Free professionals	0.6	1.2	2.9	3.6
	Clergy	0.0	0.0	0.0	0.0
	Entrepreneurs	0.6	0.6	1.8	1.2
	Civil servants	1.2	0.0	1.8	0.6
	Women without professions	1.2	0.6	2.3	2.4
	Military officers (including retired)	0.0	0.0	1.1	0.6
	Pensioners	0.6	0.6	1.8	1.8
	High school teachers	0.6	0.0	0.5	0.0
	Subtotals	4.8	3.0	14.0	13.2
Nonelite independents					
	Craftsmen	4.1	1.2	8.7	6.6
	Retailers	1.7	3.6	5.8	6.0
	Subtotals	5.8	4.8	14.5	12.6
Nonelite employees					
	White-collar	5.2	5.4	14.6	14.4
	Civil servants	2.9	0.0	10.5	11.4
	Teachers	0.0	1.2	6.4	3.6
	Subtotals	8.1	6.6	31.5	29.4

boarders to keep up their incomes. Student boarders were especially popular, and it is to be expected that larger numbers of nonelite female *Berufslosen* would be accompanied by higher proportions of students. Some Nazi students may have influenced their landladies to join the NSDAP. This is supported by subsequent evidence demonstrating that before 1933 the NSDAP attracted a bigger share of nonstudent women than did other Marburg political parties. It is

Table 6-6 *continued*

Stratum	Occupation	National Socialists Precincts		Sample Precincts	
		High	Low	High	Low
Workers					
	Craft, skilled	4.6	2.4	7.6	17.4
	Unskilled	0.6	1.2	4.1	1.2
	Subtotals	5.2	3.6	11.7	18.6
Nonelite *Berufslosen*					
	Retired	1.2	0.0	14.6	17.4
	Without occupations	1.7	2.4	9.9	3.0
	Subtotals	2.9	2.4	24.5	20.4
Total nonstudent Nazis/1,000		26.8	20.4	—	—
Total numbers		108	70	165	157
Total Nazi students/1,000		36.2	21.6	—	—
Total Nazis/1,000		63.0	42.0	—	—
Total women/1,000		4.1	3.0	31.5	16.2

SOURCES: See n. 42, this chapter.

also worth noting that women who were lower-middle-class pensioners (*Rentnermittelstand*) enthusiastically voted for the NSDAP in July 1932 elections.[47]

How might one characterize the neighborhoods of the precincts? Instead of cutting up neighborhoods in the way that city officials determined electoral precincts, it is more useful to construct a thumbnail typology consisting of four main types of neighborhoods, three of which characterize some part of the high-recruitment precincts.

The first type is made up of upper city (*Oberstadt*) neighborhoods. Largely a product of pre-Wilhelmine Marburg, these neighborhoods were shaped by the winding streets and tightly packed shops and residences that cascaded down in a southeastern direction below the castle (*Schloß*), 287 meters above sea level; by the central market square, which fronted the municipal Rathaus; and by the Barfüßerstraße, one of the main residential and commercial streets cutting through the medieval urban core south of the castle. Modernized and, in the eyes of many townspeople, unduly homogenized during feverish building and renovation in the late nineteenth and early twentieth centuries, these areas still bore traces of an older Marburg, one which had prompted eighteenth-century travelers to call the city the "ugliest Gothic hole."[48] While many university students rented accommodations here, the largest groups among heads of household in the old city neighborhoods were lower-middle-class artisans, shopkeepers—many of them descendants of families who had owned lodgings in the central urban core for centuries—and pensioners.

Similarly rooted in Marburg's pre-Wilhelmine past were old outlying areas that made up the second type of neighborhood. These included the Weidenhausen–Am Grün neighborhoods (see photograph, page 167) straddling the Lahn River southeast of the *Oberstadt*, and the Ketzerbach area north of the castle. Built outside the medieval urban core, these neighborhoods possessed coherent identities well into the 1920s. The Weidenhausen–Am Grün areas had once been a center of the local leather trade, and they remained densely populated commercial and residential neighborhoods in which students, white-collar workers, lower-middle-class professionals, craft workers, craft masters, and shopkeepers lived.[49]

The most colorful of older outlying areas was the Ketzerbach neighborhood. Built into an elevated notch in the valley wall, Ketzerbach took its name from a brook where the ashes of executed religious heretics were supposedly strewn in the thirteenth century. Like Am Grün, it had been a handicrafts section, where in 1850 there were still twenty-nine pottery workshops in addition to other artisanal establishments. Every four or five years Ketzerbachers celebrated a festival that commemorated the community's 1859 effort to fill in the constantly overflowing brook (Bach) and plant a row of trees. The *Bachfest*, accompanied by often tipsy calls of "der Ketzerbach ein Hujaja!" strengthened neighborhood identity. University students were also integrated into neighborhood culture. Besides renting rooms in Ketzerbach and other old outlying neighborhoods, they used the ritual call of the *Bachfest* to celebrate success in passing university examinations.[50]

Like older outlying neighborhoods, the third type of neighborhood lay outside the medieval urban core. But in contrast to Am Grün, Weidenhausen, and Ketzerbach, these neighborhoods gained shape and character from a pre–World War I spurt of urbanization in Marburg. The Biegen quarter east and northeast of the central city, for example, once the site of workshops of dyers, clothmakers, and ropemakers, became a modern suburb of apartment buildings, offices, and wide streets in the late nineteenth and early twentieth centuries. The Lahn River, Bahnhofstraße, and Deutschhausstraße formed a triangle northeast of the castle that was similarly Wilhelmine. But it was peppered by university clinics throughout the neighborhood. The other main component of this third type of neighborhood was residential; it consisted of the area around the Frankfurterstraße southwest of the *Oberstadt*, a section developed chiefly during southward expansion of the city in the late nineteenth century.

Not surprisingly, the architecture and more uniform street layout of Wilhelmine quarters bore a modern stamp that contrasted with the meandering streets and choppy skyline of shops and residences in the urban core and older outlying neighborhoods. Though students, craft masters, and workers did live in these newer neighborhoods, there were also large groups of lower-middle-class salaried employees, civil servants, and widows in them. Moreover, major streets like Frankfurterstraße or the less populated Gisselbergerstraße in the extreme south of the city attracted more well-to-do Marburgers; seventeen of twenty-four elite townspeople among sample householders in districts of high Nazi recruitment came from these and other avenues of precinct 5 on the southwestern tip of the town.[51] Perhaps because of the more pronounced residential flavor of the third type of neighborhood, Wilhelmine quarters possessed less coherent community traditions than the first two types of neighborhood. But because all or part of Wilhelmine neighborhoods were built on the valley floor, they were still close to the urban core and the intense public life it generated.

The fourth type of neighborhood was marked by urban expansion southward toward the south train depot (*Südbahnhof*) and up the valley hills to the west, north, and east of the urban core. Like Wilhelmine areas, these districts originated in the late nineteenth and early twentieth centuries. But large groups of better-off individuals and their families settled in these neighborhoods. Universitätsstraße south of the central city was especially attractive to university professors, and tree-lined Bismarckstraße in the same area drew doctors, lawyers, better-off widows and pensioners, and city officials.[52]

Small parts of precincts 3 and 10 in the extreme west end of Marburg, two of the three precincts in which Nazi recruitment was lowest, attracted well-to-do Marburgers. The western neighborhoods also contained numerous fraternity houses, products of the Wilhelmine age, but the majority of fraternity students lived elsewhere in the city. Moreover, precincts 3 and 10 contributed ten and fifteen workers respectively to the thirty-one workers among sample householders in precincts with lowest Nazi recruitment. They lived on streets relatively isolated from the upper city proper. One such street was Marbacherweg, which issued from Ketzerbach in a southwestern direction, where four workers from the sample group —a housepainter, a carpenter, a mechanic, and a blacksmith—lived. Finally, the northernmost parts of the fourth type of neighborhood were split between newer residential sections built in the 1920s, small factories and workshops, railway facilities (northeast of the castle), and forested hills.[53] In comparison with the first three types of neighborhood, the fourth type contained newer and more prosperous residential areas that were decentralized and relatively uninvolved in the public life of the urban core.

There was no archetypal Nazi neighborhood, but there were discernible residential patterns for NSDAP members. The three precincts in which Nazi recruitment was most successful straddled the *Oberstadt*, old outlying neighborhoods, and Wilhelmine quarters. The *Oberstadt* and older suburbs preserved neighborhood traditions, and the Wilhelmine quarters enjoyed close relationships with core neighborhoods. Nazi high-recruitment neighborhoods had higher proportions of elites, the lower middle classes, students, nonelite *Berufslosen*, and women among heads of household than did low-recruitment neighborhoods. Low-recruitment precincts had considerably bigger working-class and smaller *Berufslosen* populations than did high-recruitment districts. As for the social composition of Nazi recruits discussed in this section, the most notable difference between high- and low-recruitment precincts was that Nazi students were more concentrated in the former than in the latter.

At the neighborhood level, the concrete connection between social life and Nazi mobilization is exemplified in the recollection of an NSDAP member about a local tavern:

> If one wants to reminisce about the unforgettable years of struggle in Marburg, it is impossible to do so without respectfully remembering the Hannes, that old student pub in Weidenhausen where the now-deceased proprietor Father Reith— we also called him "Uncle Schorch"—held sway with great skill and fatherly sternness. It was there where we fortified ourselves after tiring party work. It was there where we spent many agitated hours debating. It was there where a

"guerrilla war" of words broke out with the elite Stammtisch Käsebrod.[54]

The Hannes lay outside the three precincts of highest Nazi recruitment, but it was situated in one of seven districts with above-average recruitment in 1930. Operating both as a forum for the Nazi party and an elite *Stammtisch,* such pubs helped the Nazi party to become a part of everyday networks of neighborhood sociability. Instead of being a product of dissolution, nazism was an outgrowth of such intact social bonds.

Occupations

Unless they had access to party records, most Marburg Nazis assessed their group's social composition largely on the basis of face-to-face contact in social gatherings, meetings, assemblies, and demonstrations. Individual members at these collective actions must have come into contact with a wide variety of local people, because Marburg NSDAP membership shifted from year to year. In the first half of 1926 the party registered twenty-four new members but lost twenty-nine; in 1927 nineteen people joined the party but sixteen departed; in 1928 the loss of sixteen members balanced a gain of sixteen. The fluctuations must have been even greater after 1930, when the local party made substantial gains and began to speak solely in terms of net increases in party membership, a device that masked entries and departures. But these experiences did little to contradict an impression of social diversity fostered by imagery of *Volk* community; indeed, they probably enhanced such notions because more and more Marburgers were touched by the growing Nazi universe. Evidence on occupations of Marburg National Socialists reveals that there was a greater diversity of groups in the Marburg NSDAP than in other political parties locally, though some groups joined the NSDAP in greater numbers than others.[55]

Table 6-7 contains the relevant information on nonstudent entrants in the Marburg NSDAP. First, the data suggest that city elites participated extensively in the Nazi party, though they entered the party in greater numbers after January 1933 than before. Prior to the seizure of power, eleven free professionals, four elite women without stated professions, four high school teachers, three entrepreneurs, two military officers, one high-level city official, one well-to-do retiree, and one landowner gained party cards. In 1933–35,

Table 6-7 *Percentage Distribution of Occupations of Nonstudent NSDAP and Other Political Party Members in Marburg, 1919–1935*

		National Socialists					
Stratum	Subgroup	pre-1933	1933–35	Total	Bourgeois	Worker	SI
Elite							
	Professors	0.0	2.2	1.4	11.6	1.4	0.9
	Free professionals	4.5	5.3	5.0	7.1	0.0	4.9
	Clergy	0.0	0.0	0.0	0.0	0.0	0.0
	Entrepreneurs	1.3	1.4	1.4	5.8	0.0	2.7
	Civil servants	0.4	2.6	1.8	1.9	0.0	1.3
	Women without professions	1.6	2.5	2.1	4.5	0.0	4.9
	Military officers (including retired)	0.8	0.7	0.7	2.6	0.0	0.9
	Pensioners	0.4	1.0	0.7	0.6	0.0	2.2
	High school teachers	1.6	1.4	1.5	7.1	0.0	0.0
	Others	0.4	0.0	0.2	0.0	0.0	0.0
	Subtotal	11.0	17.1	14.8	41.2	1.4	17.8
Nonelite independents							
	Craftsmen	12.6	8.2	9.8	21.9	4.3	27.1
	Retailers	9.3	9.9	9.7	12.9	0.0	14.2
	Subtotal	21.9	18.1	19.5	34.8	4.3	41.3
Nonelite employees							
	White-collar	22.4	21.9	22.1	5.8	20.0	10.7
	Civil servants	11.0	15.2	13.6	6.5	7.2	15.1
	Teachers	2.0	2.4	2.3	6.5	1.4	3.1
	Subtotal	35.4	39.5	38.0	18.8	28.6	28.9

seventy-one elite Marburgers joined the party, including fourteen notable women.

Despite these totals, overall elite involvement with the NSDAP was not as substantial as one might expect judging from the importance of these individuals as Nazi joiners. Whereas almost 21 percent of Nazi joiners came from elite strata, only 14.8 percent of the less select party membership was from these groups. Moreover, elite involvement with the party was not as extensive as it was in

Table 6-7 *continued*

Stratum	Subgroup	pre-1933	1933–35	Total	Bourgeois	Worker	SI
		National Socialists					
Workers							
	Craft, skilled	14.7	11.6	12.7	2.6	45.7	6.2
	Unskilled	1.6	4.1	3.2	0.0	17.1	0.4
	Subtotal	16.3	15.7	15.9	2.6	62.8	6.6
Nonelite *Berufslosen*							
	Retired	2.4	2.4	2.4	1.3	2.9	3.6
	No occupation	13.0	7.2	9.4	1.3	0.0	1.8
	Subtotal	15.4	9.6	11.8	2.6	2.9	5.4
Total		100.0	100.0	100.0	100.0	100.0	100.0
Total numbers		246	415	661	155	70	225
Percent women		17.9	9.2	12.4	16.1	7.1	11.1

KEY:
Bourgeois = DNVP, DVP, DDP, Staatspartei
Worker = SPD, USPD, KPD
SI = seven special interest coalitions in city parliament elections, 1919, 1924, 1929, and 1933.

SOURCES: NSDAP *Verzeichnis*, in HSAM 327/1, 5488; *MEB*, 1913, 1920, 1925, 1930, and 1934/35; *OZ* 25 and 28 February, 2 and 3 March 1919, 26 March 1924, 9 November 1929, 2 March 1933; lists of *Wahlvorstände*, in HSAM 330, Mbg C, 2676–2678.

the DNVP, DVP, and DDP. Elites made up almost half of all DVP members and more than one-third of DDP members.[56] Additionally, only after the seizure of power was the share of elite entrants in the NSDAP almost equal to that in nonparty special interest coalitions. Marburg elites aided Nazi occupation of organizational life substantially, but in general they failed to support Hitler's party as strongly as they did bourgeois parties or municipal election coalitions.

A similar point can be made for independent retailers and craft masters. The NSDAP was certainly successful in attracting these individuals, enrolling at least thirty-one self-employed artisans and twenty-three shopkeepers before the seizure of power. But the self-employed lower middle class was proportionately much more important in the ranks of the Nazi joiners, amounting to nearly 40 percent of all party joiners before Hitler came to power. As for self-employed artisans and retailers in other parties, they were more prominent in bourgeois parties and special interest coalitions than they were in the NSDAP. The coalitions were especially attractive to craft masters, who outnumbered retailers in these nonparty groups by nearly two to one. The ratio of crafts to retail in the DDP was more than two to one, but this was for a comparatively small group of nineteen independents compared to ninety-three in the coalitions. From more than one-quarter to over one-third of the main bourgeois party members came from the self-employed lower middle class.[57] The Marburg Nazi party relied heavily on the self-employed lower middle class to bring the Nazi message to local organizations, but in general it provided a less attractive political home for this group than did other nonsocialist parties in the city.

Just the opposite was true for white-collar workers, lower and middle school teachers, and minor civil servants. Evidence for these groups reflects a gradually rising curve of participation in the NSDAP as we move from joiners, to residents, and finally to party members in general. Nonelite service employees were not as prominent as independents among Nazi joiners, but the proportion of service employees in NSDAP membership increases when we consider residential patterns; and in party membership overall, nonelite bourgeois employees emerge as the biggest nonstudent group in the NSDAP.

The most important contrast between Nazi service employees and those in other parties is that the former possessed a stronger white-collar character. Before the seizure of power, the Nazi party attracted fifty-five white-collar workers, twenty-seven minor civil servants, and five schoolteachers; after Hitler's advance to the chancellorship, these numbers increased to ninety-one, sixty-three, and ten. Thus 63.2 percent of nonelite service employees were white-collar workers before January 1933 and 55.5 percent after. In the SPD ten of sixteen employees were white-collar workers, whereas all four employees were white-collar workers in the KPD. But civil servants outnumbered white-collar workers thirty-four to twenty-four in special interest alliances, and five to two in the DVP. In the DNVP there were four white-collar workers compared with three officials. Marburg's white-collar workers, a growing part of the local labor force since the 1880s, outnumbered civil service employees more substantially in the NSDAP than in any other Marburg nonsocialist party. By the end of the Republic nonelite employees made up more than 35 percent of the local work force.

Moreover, white-collar employees outnumbered officials by almost two to one. By giving white-collar workers a prominent place in its social following, the NSDAP mirrored these features of the local work force more accurately than its political competitors.[58]

Like elites and independents, National Socialist workers made up a larger share of party joiners than of party members in 1923–33. This changed after the seizure of power, when working-class Nazis declined to 8.4 percent of all joiners and 15.7 percent of all party adherents. However, after Hitler became chancellor, the working-class share in party membership fell by .6 percentage points compared with that share in the Republic. Working-class involvement in the Marburg NSDAP actually decreased after January 1933 and was lower for the next three years than it had been in the Republic.

Yet comparison with other parties again reveals the distinctiveness of the NSDAP. Marburg National Socialists attracted larger groups of local workers than other bourgeois parties or nonparty alliances, although the share of workers in the party remained below the percentage of workers in the work force (29.6). More than 16 percent of Nazi party members came from the working class before 1933 and more than 15 percent afterward, while less than 3 percent of bourgeois party membership and less than 7 percent of nonparty slate membership was working-class. In this important comparative regard, the Marburg NSDAP was more attractive as a political home for the local working class than other nonsocialist parties were. Moreover, the NSDAP after 1933 broke the barriers of its earlier constituency of skilled workers by attracting unskilled laborers, who numbered seventeen of sixty-five (26.2 percent) workers in the party after Hitler took power, compared with just four of thirty-six (11.1 percent) before. Continuing its tradition as a vehicle of skilled workers, the Marburg SPD featured twenty-four craft workers among the twenty-seven workers included in the data for table 6-7. Only the KPD, in which I found eight skilled and nine unskilled workers, reversed this trend. The Marburg NSDAP was not only a viable nonsocialist alternative for the local working class; it was also an organization that unskilled workers joined more enthusiastically than they did the SPD, the oldest party in the city.

Finally, there were higher proportions of nonelite *Berfuslosen* in the Marburg NSDAP than in other parties listed here, particularly before the seizure of power. One way of clarifying this is to refer to the proportion of women in Marburg parties. The NSDAP attracted a higher proportion of women before 1933 than any of the other parties, though bourgeois parties were close behind. But more than one-quarter of *Berufslosen* in bourgeois parties appear in the elite stratum of women without professions. The wives and widows of prominent Marburgers, these women were actively involved in party political work. But in the NSDAP the share of elite women without professions amounted to only 1.6 percent, leaving a much higher number of nonelite women. Almost 63 percent of these appeared in the nonelite *Berufslosen*. Here Nazi party membership in the city parallels a national trend in the Nazi electorate. Reacting to cuts in pensions and other state benefits made by the Brüning and Papen governments, Protestant women of the *Rentnermittelstand* became staunch supporters of the Nazi party at the polls by 1932.[59] Like many townspeople who saw in nazism an accessible social movement capable of addressing their economic grievances and, above all, giving political voice to their distrust of Weimar parties and parliament, a significant minority of nonelite Marburg women rallied to the Nazi cause.

But there are always Marburg's eccentricities. The most distinctive feature of the local NSDAP is the extraordinarily high share of students in each of the three stages of party history. In my data students accounted for 68 percent of all party members before September 1930, 48.5 percent in 1930–33, and 43.2 percent from January 1933 to the end of 1935.[60] This raises a number of comparative issues. First, we need to gain some perspective on the success of Marburg nazism among university students. The Nazi party attracted student support through three organizations at the university, the largest and most influential being the NSDStB. By winter 1931/32, the local NSDStB had sixty-nine members, making it the largest nonfraternity organization at the university.[61] Nevertheless, other Nazi student leagues, in places allegedly less Fascist than Marburg was reputed to be, mobilized more successfully. Certainly more powerful than the Nazi Student League in Tübingen, Marburg's structural (but not political) analogue, the Marburg NSDStB was less powerful than the Halle and Würzburg leagues.[62]

Second, student data point up a strong urban element in the Marburg NSDAP. Exactly 35 percent of 140 students who joined the Marburg Nazi student organization in 1926–32 listed their homes as being in cities of 100,000 people or more, a percentage higher than that of NSDAP members in the Reich (27.0) and of the German population as a whole (26.8).[63] As among the rest of the Marburg student population, moreover, only a little more than one-fifth of all Marburg NSDStB students came from Hesse-Nassau. Only eight of them came from Marburg.[64] In a town branded by critics as a provincial citadel of reaction, the largest social group within the local Nazi party had a distinctly urban background. Marburg student agitation for the NSDAP had little to do with the notional lack of sophistication of German small-town politics.

Finally, Marburg Nazi students were similar to Student League members elsewhere with respect to the subjects they studied. The most overrepresented majors among Marburg NSDStB members were law and politics, theology, and arts and letters.[65] This is important because it suggests that there was little direct relationship between unfavorable professional expectations and membership in the NSDStB. We have considerable evidence documenting the physical and mental hardships faced by Weimar university students in a capitalist system that provided too few jobs for a growing population of graduates.[66] But majors with the worst job prospects, medicine and natural sciences, were underrepresented among Student League members.[67]

The same indirect relationship between politics and economics characterized nonstudent party members. In 1925 the least well-off of all townspeople, skilled and unskilled workers, formed 15.9 percent of all party members, even though they made up nearly 30 percent of the local work force. Moreover, though independent craftsmen joined the NSDAP just as frequently as did shopkeepers, the economic situation of the latter was worse than that of the former in the Republic. Finally, town *Berufslosen*, most of them elderly female pensioners and many of them victims of serious economic misfortune, were overrepresented in the Marburg NSDAP compared with their representation in bourgeois parties and municipal coalitions and heavily overrepresented in the Nazi electorate nationally by 1932. But in Marburg they were underrepresented as members of the Nazi party relative to their share of the total population, which amounted to almost one-fifth in the year Hitler took power. There are obviously different ways of expressing economic discontent politically; but economic hardship was hardly the only or the best predictor of membership in the Marburg NSDAP. It is doubtful that Marburg, for all its special characteristics, was very peculiar in this regard.

This chapter discussed three features of the social background of Marburg National Socialists: organizational affiliation, residence, and occupation. Nazi support was uneven; some areas of Marburg's political topography showed higher relief than others. Though Nazi party membership shifted and changed, the party recruited most heavily from bourgeois occupational associations, sports clubs,

pure and modified student fraternities, and nonparty special interest alliances. NSDAP recruits most commonly lived in precincts
where there were more elites, nonelite independents and service
employees, students, *Berufslosen*, and women than in precincts
where the party was less successful. As for occupations, the
NSDAP featured higher proportions of nonelite service employees,
workers, nonelite *Berufslosen*, and women than did other nonsocialist parties.

Being the product of a university and service city, this social map
of the local Nazi party is unsurprising. But there is a more general
point that speaks to wider issues in the sociography of nazism. Nazi
imagery of the folk community could not have gained moral authority without containing some truth. Workers did join the Nazi
party along with students; and the self-employed and dependent
lower-middle-classes did rub shoulders—symbolically, if not literally—with representatives of the town elite in the NSDAP. The
mixture of organizational, residential, and occupational patterns
discussed here made the Nazi message of cross-class social harmony a believable idea. It seemed a unified *Volk* had emerged from
the fragmented town bourgeoisie. This impression must have been
much more powerful at the local than at the national level. It was
through dealings with everyday social relationships that Marburgers learned of bourgeois social exclusivity, of the caste spirit of
some local clubs, and of the bitter prejudices that divided socialist
and nonsocialist camps. Nazi solidarity stood in stark contrast to
these small-town class and status divisions. The volatility of the
Nazi constituency reinforced rather than damaged the impression
that the NSDAP was more accessible and open than previous political parties, pressure groups, social clubs, and other voluntary associations; disorganization and the constant entry and exit of townspeople in the party made of the NSDAP a positive alternative to
organized social life.

But there was a danger in this social reshaping by an "apolitical"
movement. NSDAP activists intended to subjugate social milieus
to a mass party; the folk community would have its costs. Conversely, some members of the Nazi rank and file were less than
enthusiastic about seeing social life radically recast. They wanted
to re-create a balance between social and political life on a *völkisch*
rather than bourgeois foundation, but they were reluctant to see
social ties absorbed in a total political community. The consequences of this clash were played out in Marburg in the first three
years after the seizure of power, the period to which we now turn.

Seven

Remaking the Bourgeoisie?: Nazism, 1933–1935

𝔄 battery of individuals with ties to many organizations stood poised under the Nazi party banner as Hitler assumed the German chancellorship. Those individuals soon confronted the contradictions of their support for the NSDAP. Though Nazi activists enjoyed control over a formerly contentious political sphere, they wanted to reshape social organizations to meet the needs of a classless, racist *Volksgemeinschaft*. For Nazi activists this meant that social and political spheres would be collapsed together in a radical extension of an earlier syncretic approach to local politics. Conversely, bourgeois social organizations continued to believe in multiform apoliticism. Though proponents of apoliticism welcomed Nazi desires to place national interests beyond politics, they also presupposed that everyday social life could keep political struggle at arm's length. Adherents of this tradition hoped that local bourgeois culture would be compatible with centralized and notionally suprapolitical Nazi rule. By rapidly taking control of material resources contained in local associations, Nazi activists dashed such expectations, bringing the dictatorship into the song festivals, shooting matches, and soccer games of the town. But Nazi coordination of organizational life was uneven and incomplete. And the material power of the party exceeded its moral authority over the bourgeoisie. The stresses between Nazi party power and incomplete social rule in the first crucial years of coordination are discussed in the following pages.

Nazi Party Hegemony

Nazi political power in 1933–34 was unprecedented in local history. The most obvious resource of the party was its identification with Hitler, the charismatic political dramatist. But at the grass roots level, organizational resources were more important for cementing Nazi rule. Party membership in the city increased from 700 in late 1932 to more than 1,300 in May 1933, when the NSDAP stopped accepting new members. In the county the party had fourteen locals, one "base," and a total of approximately 2,000 members, nearly four times the number it had had in 1931. The NSDStB had grown to 256 members in summer 1934, becoming the largest student organization at the university.[1]

Electoral successes were no less impressive. In the 1933 Reichstag election, ominously described as a "settling of accounts" by former Marburg student and later National Socialist judge Roland Freisler, the NSDAP received 58 percent of the vote in the city and 63 percent in the county. In the county council, the party gained fourteen of twenty-five seats; in the city parliament, twenty of thirty seats. With two-thirds of the municipal parliament seats, the NSDAP brought coherence to a body that had seen twelve separate slates represented since 1929. Here the Nazis appeared to deliver on their promise to abolish special interests in politics. Plebiscites held in 1933 and 1934 also strengthened the party's hold. In 1933, 95 percent of the eligible city electorate gave Hitler and the NSDAP a vote of confidence, and in 1934 the same share of eligible townspeople approved Hitler's consolidation of the chancellorship and presidency.[2]

Other than in the two plebiscites, which occurred after all parties except the NSDAP were banned, Nazi electoral successes were tainted. Indeed, the March 1933 Reichstag elections showed that at least four parties—the KPD, SPD, Center, and DNVP—still enjoyed some support in Marburg. The DNVP's share of the vote decreased from 15 percent in November 1932 to 11.1 in 1933. But compared to DVP and DDP candidates, who combined for only 4.9 percent of the total vote, the DNVP made a respectable showing. Moreover, the SPD increased its proportion of the vote from the last election in 1932 by .2 percentage points, and the Center lost only .3 percentage points. Although its share declined by 3.1 percentage points, the KPD still managed to get 4.8 percent of the vote under conditions of extreme repression. The NSDAP established party political hegemony in the sphere of liberal and conservative parties, but it failed to get complete electoral domination over its enemies by March 1933.[3]

Changes in local government and administration made such electoral limits increasingly irrelevant. The most visible casualty of the old regime among city officials was Oberbürgermeister Johannes Müller. Müller was a victim of Marburg's volatile political scene. Trying to calm political passions, he banned an NSDStB assembly in Marburg in 1931, an action that made him a target of Nazi propaganda. Unlike his Tübingen counterpart Adolf Scheef, who faced a much calmer political environment and retained enough power to stay in office until time for his normal retirement in 1939, Müller lost his job soon after the NSDAP took power. On 28 March Krawielitzki and other Nazi leaders told Müller that they were unable to work with him. The party placed Müller "on leave" for the remainder of the year and then "retired" the former DVP member on 1 January 1934, leaving the post vacant and allowing Vice-mayor Walter Voss to serve as interim chief city administrator.[4]

Dr. Ernst Scheller took over the office of Oberbürgermeister in April 1934. Krawielitzki, the county NSDAP leader until July 1934, became the *Landrat*, the highest administrative officer in the county, in the summer. He and other National Socialist officials displaced democratic structures of government with a state that demanded "responsibility to the *Führer.*" By issuing new ordinances dealing with municipal administration, the Reich increased its power and lessened already diminished municipal influence. Moreover, the mayor and county councillor were now freed from having to deal with contentious parliamentary bodies.[5]

Though its control in government and administration was less than total, the party held enough power to begin its promised task of remaking social life. For the present discussion it is useful to think of three constellations of social networks as targets of the Nazi project. The first consisted of social milieus on the margins of local life, namely those of the Social Democratic and Communist parties. The second comprised networks indirectly tied to bourgeois organizational life but less marginal than the SPD and KPD. These included mainly university professors who had been sympathetic to the Republic or otherwise not a part of the more patriotic and nationalist professoriate; Jews employed in particular institutions and businesses; and nonacademic left liberals such as Hermann Bauer, of the *Hessisches Tageblatt*. The third, the core constellation, encompassed voluntary associations and institutions of the elite and nonelite bourgeoisie. The Nazis could "coordinate" the first two groups relatively easily, though not completely, in 1933, as the present section will demonstrate. However, when dealing with core networks of the local polity, the Nazis proceeded more cautiously and their gains were more ambiguous. The core networks are discussed in the following section.

Starting in early February, police searched the dwellings of at least 123 persons, 65 of whom were Communists. Armed with a stream of emergency decrees issued by the Prussian government, police imprisoned Communist leaders and agitators and annulled the election of a Marburg Communist resulting from the 1933 city elections. The "Decree for Reestablishment of a Professional Bureaucracy" of 7 April, usually associated by townspeople with the removal of "undesirable" university professors, also affected city workers and employees who belonged to or campaigned for the Social Democratic and Communist parties in March 1933.[6]

A decree of 1 February prohibited Communist open air assemblies and virtually made the KPD illegal. But Marburg Communists still demonstrated against fascism on 3 February thanks to Müller's decision that such action was legal because it was planned for a closed room. Moreover, party agitators distributed political literature in the city and university, and kept up contacts with couriers from Frankfurt/Main. Occasionally these networks helped Communists in acts of political vandalism. On the night of 19/20 September 1935, for instance, unidentified individuals painted "Communism is undying!" on the castle, a local church, and various structures in the upper city. But splashed paint was a measure of the narrowing limits of Marburg Communist politics.[7]

Instead of joining the KPD in a campaign for a general strike, the SPD tried to preserve its place in the local polity by concentrating on routine political activity. When Nazi violence against Social Democratic assemblies increased in February, the Marburg SPD called a protest march led by the Reichsbanner and socialist students. Though the SA tried to provoke the more than two hundred participants, the "prudence of the marchers and the excellent behavior of the local police probably avoided the worst," according to the *Hessisches Tageblatt*.[8] Unlike its more radical counterparts in other German cities, the Marburg SPD refused to join the Communists in an anti-Fascist front.[9] It concentrated on mobilizing voters against the NSDAP, an effort that gave the party a slight increase in voting strength in March 1933 over its strength in the last election of the Republic. In city parliament and county council elections, meanwhile, the SPD held four mandates apiece.

Effective in normal times, such activity failed to defend the SPD from Nazi force. Hindered initially from participating in city parliament, the Social Democratic party and allied organizations— Reichsbanner, Friends of Nature, the Socialist Workers' Youth— faced formal dissolution on 22 June. Simultaneously, local trade unions, already weakened by unemployment, tried to defend themselves by preserving their memberships. The contortions to which this defensive posture gave rise were evident on National Labor Day in Marburg on 1 May 1933. The local free trade union commission encouraged members to march in the Nazi-led festivities—but not as trade union representatives. Instead, "in order to preserve the unified image of the celebration," the commission counseled members to march with other clubs or in "voluntary groups." This was a desperate attempt by the local working class to retain a place in social life by sacrificing its own political imagery. But compromises were no longer possible: in the next three weeks the Nazi party dissolved all Marburg trade unions.[10]

What of the second group, the milieus less obviously marginal than those represented by the SPD or KPD but no less dangerous in the eyes of National Socialist activists? The Nazis could capture some of the resources contained in these networks by outlawing all political parties on 22 June. However, the NSDAP knew that groups and individuals in the second constellation were not as dependent on party politics as were Social Democratic or Communist workers. Thus, the party attacked other areas of the local polity such as the liberal *Hessisches Tageblatt*, which the Nazi *Festschrift* called an "evil, democratic stream of poison." The SA occupied the newspaper's offices, prohibited it from reporting on municipal parliament politics, and threatened *Tageblatt* advertisers with boycotts in the spring of 1933. By late April the paper closed.[11]

At the university, the NSDAP used the 7 April "Decree for Reestablishment of a Professional Bureaucracy" to eliminate a number of professors, including the political economist Wilhelm Röpke and the Jewish linguist Hermann Jacobsohn, who later, in a tragic act of desperation, committed suicide by throwing himself before an oncoming train at the Marburg south depot. The Marburg theology department, which would later distinguish itself in the church's resistance to Nazi coordination, lost a number of eminent faculty members, including Martin Rade, Samuel Biaboblocki, Heinrich Hermelink, and Hans von Soden, who was eventually reinstated.[12]

On 1 April the party began a boycott of Jewish shops to protest "horrific propaganda overseas" regarding the treatment of Jews in the Third Reich. The Nazis "advised" townspeople not to frequent stores owned by Jews or seek services from Jewish doctors, lawyers, and other professionals.[13] A 22 April decree established special procedures for the matriculation of university students who, regardless of citizenship, were not of "German descent." This decree was based on the so-called ethnic principle of citizenship (*Volksbürgerprinzip*) for which so many nationalist students fought in the Weimar Republic. The same decree contained guidelines halting academic "overcrowding" by limiting the share of "non-Aryans" to 5 percent of all students and 1.5 percent of all incoming students at each university. In Marburg, this decree had little concrete effect because the proportion of "non-Aryan" students in both categories fell short of the specified ceilings by a wide margin. Student nationalism in Marburg in the Republic had already made the city less attractive than other university towns to Jewish and foreign students.[14]

Yet Nazi coordination of the second complex of networks was hardly complete in the period covered by this study. The publisher Bauer may have been deprived of a mouthpiece for criticizing the regime, but in 1934 he printed and distributed numerous copies of Vice-Chancellor von Papen's speech in Marburg.[15] Though a number of university professors lost their positions, some of them, such as von Soden, were reinstated. Others—for example, the feisty art historian Richard Hamann and the popular lecturer and historian Wilhelm Mommsen, both former supporters of the Republic—retained their positions without endorsing the Third Reich. The theology faculty became a center of resistance by both students and instructors against Nazi attempts to coordinate the Protestant church.[16] The National Socialists worked to eliminate Jews from local public life, but this was limited repression compared to the radical and barbaric solutions to the "Jewish question" that would be conceived and implemented in World War II. In spite of boycotts of Jewish stores and party harassment of individual Jews, racist persecution remained sporadic, haphazard, and without identifiable direction.[17] If full Nazi hegemony was hindered by the second group of networks, what might the party expect from the core constellation, the spectrum of clubs and associations that had made Nazi social conquest possible?

Contours of *Gleichschaltung*

Described by the *Oberhessische* as having been "unforgettable in local history," National Labor Day on 1 May 1933 evoked most clearly the tensions between the Nazi party and core social networks in the first six months of the dictatorship. The festival gained prestige by being compared with its predecessors in the Republic. The NSDAP said it transformed what had been a "Marxist party festival" into a "people's festival" accessible to all townsfolk, not just the Social Democratic or Communist working class.[18] The festival was not only larger but also more hierarchically organized than any previous collective action in the history of the city. Festival organization was "determined" by the local representative of the Reich minister for propaganda and popular enlightenment. Aided by full publication of the schedule of May Day activities in the *Oberhessische*, the party organized marches, speeches, and a torchlight procession that concluded the day.[19]

The torchlight procession was particularly suited for symbolizing Nazi visions of the future. Beginning at the Hermann-Göring Straße, the new name of Kasernenstraße, the procession was led by NSDAP organizations. These included SA marching bands, the Nazi Civil Servants' League, the Factory Cell Organization, and the Combat League for the German *Mittelstand*, under whose banner "the artisanry" of the city now marched. Nazi office holders and other party members came next, followed by the paramilitary Stahlhelm. Other organizations—veterans' associations, "non-Marxist" trade unions and occupational associations such as the DHV and Trade Union of White-Collar Workers, Catholic clubs, Hitler Youth, and student organizations—took assigned spots in the procession. The Gymnastics and Sports Club 1860, later the beneficiary of consolidation of local sports associations in the city, led a group of gymnastics, swimming, soccer, canoeing, sharpshooting, hiking, and bicycling clubs. At the end of the parade marched members of two of the city's oldest service organizations, the Volunteer Fire Department and the Volunteer Medical Corps. Participants marched through city streets until they met at the upper end of the Ketzerbach neighborhood, where they threw their torches into a flaming bonfire that symbolized the fusion of worker, student, and *Bürger* into one *Volk*. The participants then marched away, disbanding in preconceived spots in Pilgrimstein Avenue, Deutschhaustraße, and Elisabethstraße nearby.[20]

On 6 May the *Oberhessische* published a snapshot of one National Labor Day celebration in order to give its readers a "small memento of this noteworthy day."[21] What it had given them was a photographic map of the Nazi polity. It consisted of core social networks stripped of the signs and symbols of Social Democratic, Communist, Catholic, and bourgeois political parties—a triumph of apoliticism. It was without troublesome Marxist trade unions, and it tolerated occupational associations only to the extent they were attached to the party or did not pursue interests opposed to Nazi plans. In addition, social life was hierarchically organized according to the most modern principles of management. Social organizations were ostensibly as businesslike as the military; club leaders would no longer tolerate indiscipline in their attempt to administer all community affairs.

Yet National Labor Day raised questions for which Nazi symbolism had no immediate answers. If the National Socialist regime sought full integration of the people in managed networks of social life, what was to be the nature of popular participation? Was it to be largely passive and acclamatory, going no further than supplying the torches for evening processions, as Gymnastics and Sports Club 1860 leaders had reminded their members to do for the 1 May celebration? Or was the role of an organization to go beyond the "pleasant role of passive participation," to use the Stahlhelm's words, and influence public life "in its own right"?[22] In short, if the Nazis claimed to have integrated all townspeople in one *völkisch* polity and to have reestablished ties of general and special interest, would they also realize the egalitarian potential of this accomplishment?

The party grappled with these questions well before the 1 May festivities. Nazism was no longer satisfied only with party political concerns, as it had been earlier, and no longer willing to concede compensatory political functions to organizational life. The party wanted to galvanize townsfolk for the task of expanding political leadership into social hegemony, and its policy toward bourgeois clubs and associations, the substructures of mobilization in the Republic, was a test for determining how far this process would go.

Scholars supportive of the National Socialist regime typically worked out theoretical models for addressing this issue after Nazi policy had been implemented. Nevertheless, it is worthwhile to mention one concise statement by the legal scholar Wolfgang Meyer that suggests the place of organizational life in the Third Reich. "The new state has the power and strength to be the general guarantor of all public tasks," Meyer wrote in 1935. "Therefore there is no more room for the *Verein* in the form it has assumed until now. It was called to maintain public interests that the absolute state had once been obligated to guarantee; the Leadership State now takes back these tasks. The *Verein* is no longer independent of state power. . . . a stratification and reformation of organizations commences."[23] The passage simplified radically the historical problem of relationships between the state and organizational life, but it suggested that the Nazi party was trying to absorb voluntary organizations into a modern and industrial "absolutist" state. Separate social and political spheres would cease to exist, and only "truly private" organizations, those that claimed no role in the shaping of general interests, would escape National Socialist coordination.

How did Nazi policy toward local organizational life develop in practice? Events from January 1933 to late 1935 can be arranged on a continuum of coordination.[24] On one extreme was outright and immediate dissolution of organizations. This was the fate of both Social Democratic and bourgeois parties and their auxiliaries. However, parts of leftist and bourgeois networks were absorbed into Nazi party and government entities. In these cases, independent, registered voluntary associations became public corporations. This happened to bourgeois occupational associations and trade unions. At the other extreme of the continuum were organizations that had no public role in the opinion of Nazi leaders and were thus of no interest in the regime's plans for coordination. The best examples were small social clubs such as Contentia, Frohsinn, and Amicitia, which remained intact and persisted in their daily rituals of sociability.[25]

Between these two extremes lay a variegated terrain of associations. This middle part of the continuum encompassed a majority of organizations in Marburg in the first year of the dictatorship.[26] Even if some of these organizations were absorbed into party or state corporations, they led a relatively independent existence in comparison with organizations of the local working class. This middle ground best illustrates the scope and eventual failure—apparent by late 1935—of *total* Nazi coordination.

Transforming previously independent voluntary associations into public corporations implied internal changes in each organization. These changes included an end to many democratic practices— election of officers, discussion and debate in membership meetings, and legal protection for *Verein* members under the civil code. In place of internal democracy, the NSDAP instituted the Leadership Principle, which established "authority downward and responsibility upward." Club members now became "the retinue" (*Gefolg-schaft*); the leader rather than the membership assembly now determined activity. A hierarchical structure based on a centralized association at the top, a regional association at the intermediary level, and a local branch at the bottom replaced the alleged chaos of organizational life.[27]

The Nazi party used these general notions as a template to co-ordinate local clubs. The NSDAP attempted first to replace club officials if they were not party members or if they were unsympathetic to nazism. The number and nature of leadership changes usually depended on the political stance of a club before coordination. Within the Artisans' Association, noted for its criticism of Weimar, little alteration was needed. All seven individuals who took places on the governing board of the association on 23 March 1933 had been officials in the organization before January 1933. Five of them had been association officials since autumn 1930, and two others since autumn 1931. Ludwig Schweinsberger, a baker who joined the NSDAP in 1931, was one of the latter. Two other board members joined the party soon after Hitler came to power. In June Dr. Adolf Wagner, a County Artisans' Association officer and chair of the Combat League for the German *Mittelstand*, verified that the association's "board of directors conforms to the guidelines of political coordination in its present makeup, and therefore changes will not be necessary."[28] Similarly, DHV leaders boasted in mid-May that "the coordinations, which in the last weeks have become so common," were unnecessary. Association officials crowed that the DHV was "the only Jew-free trade union" in the city; its members had been in the NSDAP "when it was still dangerous to be a Nazi."[29]

In contrast, the local German Civil Servants' Association, once a mouthpiece of consumer interests against retailers and artisans in city parliament, required more changes. The *Oberhessische* reported on 26 April that all members of "Marxist parties" had left the organization. The remaining majority concluded that a "personal union" between the association and the Nazi civil servants' auxiliary would be "advantageous." In the first week of May Nazi party member Bernhard Buehner took over the local association cartel, and later that month he oversaw elections for a new governing board that suited Nazi wishes.[30] Among working-class organizations that month, meanwhile, there were sixteen "dismissals and coordinations."[31] The Hessian Peasants' Association steered its way between these alternatives by making its former chair honorary president and naming as second president Konrad Elmshäuser, an NSDAP member since 1926 and chair of the party's Agrarian-Political Section (*Agrarpolitisches Apparat*) in the county.[32]

Similar patterns occurred in the city's sports associations. The Gymnastics and Sports Club contained a large number of Nazi party members before 1933. The previous chair, high school teacher Dr. Wilhelm Stier, gained reelection with approval of the local commissar for coordination. Stier, now officially the club's *Führer*, announced in mid-May an "abrogation of democratic principles" in the club and appointed a twenty-five-member Gymnastics Council on which at least six NSDAP members served.[33] Later that month in the Swim Club, the lawyer and NSDAP member Böttcher also gained reelection, appointed a new board of officials, and emphasized that coordination in the Swim Club was unnecessary "because the leadership and activity of the *Verein* since its founding have always been strictly nationalistic."[34] Conversely, the VfB 05, sports club of the upper middle class, formed a completely new board of directors representing National Socialist interests more fully than before. Having selected new officials, the VfB adopted Nazi style as members shouted "Sieg Heil!" in a meeting reported in the *Oberhessische* on 11 May. Of course, none of this obscured the fact that the new club directors were newcomers to the party, having joined after Hitler's seizure of power.[35]

Despite the apparent efficiency of coordination, the NSDAP takeover caused friction between the state, party, and organizations, as an example from the Central German Song Club (Mitteldeutscher Sängerbund), an affiliate of the German Song Club, in late 1933 suggests. The Kassel-based MDSB leader H. R. F. Wilke, who also headed the Kurhessen Nazi Cultural-Political Section, was able to increase the membership of the MDSB threefold by absorbing working-class song clubs and so-called "wild *Vereine*." The "fragmentation" and "dissension" of these organizations had prompted the MDSB to move in, according to Wilke. In Marburg County, meanwhile, the teacher Schütrumpf, a MDSB member and official of the NSDAP Section for Veterans' Benefits, achieved similar gains. Following instructions from Krawielitzki and city MDSB official Dietrich, Schütrumpf increased the number of MDSB *Vereine* in the county from 40 in January 1933 to 111 at the end of the year. All this, MDSB members said, expressed the "spirit of the present" and "National Socialist thinking." But it also created many "misunderstandings within local song clubs" that had come to the attention of the Prussian Ministry of Culture. The ministry reminded local officials that "none of the existing choral societies and clubs had the right to intervene in the affairs of another association"—only state authorities could do this. The ministry urged that song clubs be free to carry on their patriotic work undisturbed by such interventions. Noting that the MDSB overstepped its authority by portraying itself as the only song club recognized by the Nazi party, the ministry nevertheless allowed the changes to stand, partly because talks between club officials had calmed disagreements and partly because state officials wanted to avoid "a new disturbance."[36] Between the realms of government, the NSDAP, and organizational life, individual club leaders used Nazi coordination to gain control over new resources, generating many new disputes throughout the process.

Some bourgeois voluntary associations resisted coordination for a surprisingly long time and prevented full Nazi leadership in club life. Coordination of women's associations was an especially protracted process. Soon after the establishment of the Nazi dictatorship, it appeared that Frau Professor Josephin Strecker, who chaired the large and influential Housewives' Association, would try to heal the rift among women's clubs that had led to the formation of the rival Reich Association of German Housewives in the Republic. Frau Strecker informed club members in May that her association was ready to take its place in the German Women's Front alongside other clubs, including the National Socialist Women's Association (Frauenschaft). But Strecker also stressed the "full independence" of her organization in fighting for the "freedom of the German *Volk*," a qualification the NSDAP did not fail to notice.[37]

In April 1934 the Nazi party unified national women's associations in the Reich Community of German Housewives, bringing Strecker's *Verband* and the rival Reich Association into the same omnibus organization. The following June in Marburg representatives of both associations met to discuss consolidation, as the formation of the Reich Community demanded, and create two committees composed of leaders of each organization. To ease this process, both Frau Strecker and the Reich Association chair Frau Zahn agreed to step down. Frau Strecker asked that the former vice-president of the Housewives' Association, Frau Eva-Maria Jonas, be made chair of the new organization, a request the Reich Association approved. But the district (*Gau*) Deutsches Frauenwerk, the Nazi-led national association for women, refused to allow Jonas her post, and appointed instead Frau Professor Herforth, who had presided over the meeting in which members from both clubs formed the new local branch of the Reich Community. Meanwhile, Frau Professor Strecker continued "to take the stand that the Marburg Housewives' Association still existed and that she was still the chair."[38] The association continued on paper for two more years, though it was impossible for it to play a useful public role. Thus, Frau Strecker drew the unavoidable conclusion. "Since all women's work must be centrally organized and implemented only through the [Nazi] party," she announced in a 3 July 1936 meeting attended by approximately 160 club members, "the Association can . . . no longer function; the organization, still having 1,000 members, should not sink to the level of being a simple coffee klatch. We ask therefore that you approve the proposal of dissolution, though this is most painful."[39] The proposal was passed. Reduced to a "private" club without any pretensions of public service, the Housewives' Association refused to accept its diminished role and informed the County Court of its dissolution.[40] Yet what had been the largest women's association in the city could still bring a relatively big group of members together in mid-1936, despite having been officially dissolved two years previously. Though ultimately dominant, the NSDAP gained neither immediate victory nor moral leadership over the Housewives' Association. If the term "hegemony" is used to describe a relatively active, substantial, and negotiated consent of the ruled to an ultimately coercive leadership, then it is not completely applicable to the situation of these Marburg women at this point in the Nazi dictatorship.

The fraternities faced even less favorable prospects of remaining independent. NSDStB strength and a relatively closed environment at the university made fraternities more vulnerable than nonstudent clubs to Nazi power. Yet even here coordination was a protracted process of tension and negotiation. Like nonstudent organizations, student clubs were to be organized according to the Leadership Principle. The NSDStB tried to fuse itself with student social life, an action that institutionalized long-standing conflicts of jurisdiction among students but never resolved them. This explains the zigzag course of Student League policy toward the fraternities, which in turn attempted to steer an unsteady line between party, NSDStB, and student government officials. Fraternities were represented symbolically in student government through a new corporate chamber. They continued to duel, thanks to a Reich decree decriminalizing the practice. However, as party sections gained more control over the NSDStB in early 1933, the league and the SA began to demand more of fraternity students' time and loyalty.[41]

Nazi coordination broke through a division of labor between the NSDStB and the fraternities, and the league reached into social and cultural practices of fraternity life.

The Nazi party could dispense with student political associations such as the Socialist Student Group or the Political Group of Catholic Students in 1933. These organizations had never been very important to university students.[42] But the more powerful fraternities and associations persisted. Active pure fraternity membership still amounted to 289 students in sixteen groups in summer 1934.[43] No organization in the Nazi camp could hope to have these structures dissolved in 1933–34, the threats of a few zealous SA students notwithstanding. It was not until July 1935 that Hitler and his aides felt strong enough to eliminate the fraternities and build "comradeship houses" under exclusive Nazi control.[44]

Before this the party entangled fraternity students in an alternative net of political, cultural, and social obligations. By winter 1933/34, 70 of 256 Student League members belonged to either pure or modified fraternities.[45] But the Nazi movement took advantage of this foothold in fraternity networks in order to subjugate rather than to mobilize fraternities, using the SA to detach students from their previous loyalties. Writing the director of the dueling fraternities' national association on 5 July 1934, Landsberg lawyer Gunther Kranz said that Marburg dueling fraternities complained of an "unbelievable strain" caused by SA demands on students. The SA expected students to attend three hours of schooling, two hours of shooting practice, regular inspections, and marching drills every week. In addition, students attended a one-week SA camp each semester. During one SA "university camp" in July 1934, an SA leader lined up fraternity students and bluntly told them, "My function is superfluous, the fraternities will soon disappear just like the KPD." When dueling fraternity leaders tried to have the SA man reprimanded, they found that other SA officials agreed with his opinion. The stormtroopers refused to apologize. Using language more suited to an earlier era of fraternity insolence, Kranz wrote that the corporations "did not receive even the slightest satisfaction [*Genugtuung*] for being put on the same level with the KPD."[46]

The fraternities were made more vulnerable by the behavior of university professors and officials. Though university professors enthusiastically celebrated National Labor Day in 1933,[47] they continued to view the university in the light of pre-1933 experiences. They wanted social harmony at all costs, and because the NSDStB had become the largest and most powerful of student organizations, this stance now worked to the advantage of nazism. In early 1934 the University Association (Universitätsbund) emphasized heightened cooperation between teachers and students at the university, wrote approvingly of the social policies of Nazi-led student government, and warmly recalled a protest meeting held in the main university assembly hall in which former Marburg instructor and then chancellor in Breslau Dr. G. A. Walz delivered a "sharply worded speech" against the "Versailles *Diktat.*" "The city has taken on a different tone," the association said "because of SA students, whose uniforms often turn up in university lecture halls." Moreover, "the spirit of comradeship, inextricably connected to national socialism" had not only contributed to the political education of students but decreased "nightly disturbances of the peace" by 90 percent as well.[48]

Nazi student leaders recognized the need to address this concern for order. This recognition lay behind the action of student government chair and Nazi party member Kurt Hübner when, in November 1933, he mollified SA students who had demonstrated against the law professor Manigk for his critical remarks on National Socialist legal theory. After dutifully fielding the chancellor's criticism of the SA demonstration against Manigk, Hübner consulted party officials and asked SA students to refrain from further disturbances.[49] In these and other cases, university officials, by cooperating with the Nazi party to ensure social harmony, reduced the terrain on which fraternities could function. By spring 1936, when most fraternities were all but destroyed, the chancellor prohibited the fraternities from celebrating their traditional May Day festivities outside their houses and ordered members not to wear their colored caps and sashes until further notice. Simultaneously, the chancellor, after discussions with Krawielitzki and the SA official Vielstich, enouraged "educative work in the interest of the movement [and] on the basis of the SA" among students. Sounding the familiar theme, the chancellor reported to the university commissioner that "absolute calm rules, and this will continue."[50] The apoliticism of the university, a product of professors' need to maintain social order, could also accommodate Nazi rule.

Nazi attacks on fraternities began soon after Hitler achieved power, surged forward unevenly in the next two years, and ultimately intensified in 1935.[51] Comradeship houses, intended by party officials to be independent of fraternity control in recruitment and education policies, were to supplant student corporations in

1934–35; they were to be student versions of Nazi "state organizations" directed by the NSDStB. Besides absorbing traditional educative functions of the fraternities, the Nazi Student League became a professional ladder. By late 1935 allegiance to the fraternities had become politically and professionally more disadvantageous than ever. Todenhöfer, former Burschenschaft Arminia member and leader of the NSDStB *Gau* in which Marburg was located, made this explicit in a 1935 speech before townspeople and local Burschenschaften assembled in the market square to "celebrate" the coordination of fraternities. "We are only a small part of the entire people," exclaimed Todenhöfer:

> and we cannot oppose the people's wishes. The German Burschenschaft has put its colors to rest as of 18 October because they are no longer appropriate in the eyes of the *Volk*. The German student's color is the color of the German worker, the brown shirt. Whoever continues to wear the colors of the student fraternity places himself outside the community and is a reactionary. . . . Who doesn't belong to the Student League is its enemy. . . . Whoever doesn't take advantage of this opportunity, has no claim to subsequent leadership because the future leaders of the state and the movement will for the most part be taken from the ranks of the Student League. . . .[52]

The harsh and dictatorial presence of the NSDStB in student life, reflected in Todenhöfer's threatening tone, had become so onerous by late 1935 that students avoided the once-favored "summer university." Regardless of a German student's opinion of nazism, he could find bigger, less *gemütlich*, and more anonymous urban universities that allowed for less political surveillance than did Marburg.[53]

Pure and modified fraternities contributed much to Nazi mobilization and continued to look for ways in which to serve "the National Socialist cause in the first rank."[54] Criticism of the dictatorship did not stem from disagreement with its antisocialist and racist ideology but rather from the self-perception of fraternity leaders, who still thought in the haughty and elitist categories of an era that was quickly dissolving. Thus they, like many townspeople, decried the style and ultimate goal of Nazi coordination. "We emphatically reject," a member of Turnerschaft Saxonia had written in 1933, "any methods toward the fraternities that are usually reserved for the red trade unions."[55] Though Burschenschaft Arminia did not object to comradeship houses in mid-1934, its members insisted that they have the right to reject unwanted students. In addition, three Marburg Burschenschaften called for resignation of their national leader, Otto Schwab, who had tried to change the Burschenschaften and their alumni associations into what fraternity historian Heer referred to as "National Socialist cells."[56] Hardly a direct assault on the Fascist citadel, such criticism and uneasy noncompliance nonetheless introduced a subtle drag not only on Nazis' desires to be feared but on their intention to have full moral authority in social life as well.

By summer 1935, the number of active pure fraternity members had fallen by nearly three-quarters since summer 1930. The share of actives among total pure fraternity students had declined from 58.8 percent in 1932 to 42.9 percent in 1935. But there was still a combined total of 315 active and inactive members of these organizations in the city that summer. In winter 1935/36, after seven new comradeship houses were introduced in Marburg, Arminia had twenty actives, but rejected four others proposed by student government. By spring 1936 only a handful of fraternities remained, but the chancellor and Nazi officials continued to worry about "violent assaults" between NSDStB and fraternity members.[57] Though nazism bested the fraternities, coordination failed to bring unchallenged party control by late 1935 and early 1936.[58]

The contradictions of Nazi rule heightened throughout coordination. Begun in the late Republic, party centralization created distance between the NSDAP and grass roots support, reducing local branches to public relations outlets for the national party and state offices.[59] The county leader Krawielitzki himself commented on the inadequacies of centralized leadership, bureaucratic decision making, careerism, and opportunism.[60] The ultimate goals of the party became less clear to Nazi officials and supporters locally. The Empire and Republic had given townspeople wide latitude for the pursuit and defense of specific material interests but little opportunity to define and shape general concerns; interest politics had stripped the moral element from public life. National Socialist rule, claiming to restore the primacy of general interests by emphasizing a new racial and national order, gave party members even more opportunity to pursue sectional concerns. Meanwhile, notions of *völkisch* harmony languished in stale public relations messages issued from above by party organs. Popular disillusionment after

1933 stemmed partly from the fact that party ideology was more open than ever before to contradictory interpretations, while group interests became more salient under the Nazi banner.

The result was that the idealism of nationalist mobilization dissipated—even when many people in city and hinterland favored Nazi smashing of working-class unions and all political parties, the dismissal of Jewish and non-Jewish university professors, and the persecution of liberal opponents of the regime. In the county, farmers were dissatisfied because the party eliminated Jewish cattle and egg dealers, businessmen who turned out to be more advantageous to local economies than previously thought. Meanwhile, Hitler Youth, according to farmers, literally trampled over country people's interests when they showed disregard for farm property near vacation camps. Shopkeepers were upset over increasing shortages of fresh fruit. Consumers complained about the high price of meat, a well-known Marburg lament. Nazi policies toward the university also caused dissatisfaction and grumbling. Many student rooms were unoccupied in 1933, according to an unsigned party report on the state of university-city relations, and city government faced a mounting "burden . . . caused by assistance to impoverished small creditors" who could no longer find renters.[61]

Opportunism, revenge, and selfish careerism found full expression in the Marburg Nazi party. Fritz Schwalm complained that plebeian old fighters jealously guarded important party leadership posts and hindered upward mobility for truly talented individuals.[62] One long-time party member, the printer Adolf Zetl, once failed to get a publishing contract with the NSDAP for printing the party organ *Hessische Volkswacht*. Pledging to retaliate against the *Volkswacht*, Zetl, who was also an officer of a local veterans' association, had advertisements for the United Veterans' Clubs' celebration of Reich Founding Day in 1934 printed in the *Oberhessische* instead of the party newspaper.[63] In 1936 Harro Jensen, a university instructor and Marburg party member, appealed to his friend Krawielitzki to help forestall his dismissal from the English department at Heidelberg. Jensen alerted the Marburg county leader that the Heidelberg replacement was not an NSDAP party member, and he noted that throughout German universities the NSDStB had lost influence over "professional matters" to "elements of older generations, which were in no way National Socialist." Unconvincingly, Jensen told his friend that the matter "did not in the first place really concern me, but rather national socialism."[64]

"Many people who have recently joined the party are leaders in other organizations whose interests they one-sidedly represent," a May 1934 Gestapo report on Marburg read. "Because of this," the report warned, "the danger is that the fundamental principles of the National Socialist idea will be forced into the background."[65] The implied distinction between idealistic old fighters and selfish late-comers was widespread, but it was more than a product of the sour resentments of party bosses. Because Nazi goals of reestablishing a hegemonic general interest failed, competition over special interests reemerged in the National Socialist party and in social life. Was not this situation conducive to considerable social resilience in the face of Nazi rule, particularly among groups that possessed resources the NSDAP was unable to capture?

Resurgence of Apoliticism

Social Democrats, Communists, and bourgeois enemies of the regime lost political parties, social clubs, trade unions, business associates, and other points of contact. What was left to them were partially intact networks of friends, family members, neighborhood dwellers, coworkers, and churchgoers. Conscience and conviction could inspire anti-Nazi action, but it was the persistence of social networks that ultimately enabled enemies of the regime to undertake limited resistance. Private networks of friends and professional associates made it possible to assist Jewish townspeople in leaving German soil.[66] Vandals who painted anti-Nazi slogans on local buildings relied on similar networks outside parties and formal associations.[67]

Conversely, the majority of the town bourgeoisie, though without political parties after June 1933, was part of the National Socialist polity by virtue of membership in the party or in a coordinated club. Two central institutions of local life, the university and the Protestant church, now figured more prominently than before in this reshaped *völkisch* polity. Partial coordination by nazism undercut many associations fostered by Marburg university and the church, and the organizational field surrounding the two institutions had been narrowed considerably. Thus, when Nazi coordination threatened them, the university and especially the Protestant church, along with voluntary organizations included in their orbits, were forced to step forward. Both institutions played an active role in a new surge of apoliticism in the Third Reich.

Since the early Republic, the University Association was influential as a support organization, but it took on a more definite political importance in the first years of the Third Reich. Having pledged itself to work for the "spirit of national renewal," the association nevertheless tried to shield the university from many party policies.[68] Noting numerous unoccupied professorships at Marburg university in summer 1933—a consequence of the regime's brutal purge—the association urged officials to find as replacements "the best available people, who bring with them not only outstanding intellectual capabilities but also the will to work along actively in the national and social tasks of the university and its students." But the Universitätsbund also expressed fear that what it referred to euphemistically as the National Socialist "cleansing process" (*Reinigungsprozess*) in university faculties would endanger Marburg university as a "center of true German science and national feeling."[69] Unwilling to criticize the regime and insistent on portraying Marburg as a nationalist university, the University Association nevertheless struck a note of uncertainty in its remarks that contradicted both the aggressive style and supposedly clear intent of Nazi leadership. Subsequently, the association's cautious championing of university interests would intersect with a larger political conflict.

The occasion for this intersection was German vice-chancellor Franz von Papen's delivery of a major policy address in Marburg on 17 June 1934. Von Papen selected Marburg specifically because of its conservative University Association, dueling fraternities, and professoriate. Designed not to criticize nazism as such but to attack the more radical elements of the new regime, his speech was perfectly attuned to the efforts of the association and its allies.[70] He spoke in the Auditorium Maximum of the university and addressed issues with which townspeople had direct experience. Striking a pious tone, von Papen declared that "final truth exists only in God."[71] Displaying his nationalist credentials, he praised the "community of the German nation," a welcome contrast to the "fragmentation" and "hopelessness" of the Republic. However, despite the "unity of spirit" of the new Reich, von Papen regretted "that the refining process of such historical import had also produced some slag [*Schlacken*]." In particular, the Nazi regime had closed public life to debate and shrouded "the voice of the German *Volk*" in a "secretive darkness"; it had transformed the "justifiable fight against a certain 'intellectualism' into [a fight] against 'spirit' [*Geist*]"; it had, moreover, carried "politics" too far. Von Papen was explicit on this last point: "The statesman and politician can reform the state, but not life itself. . . . Based on this knowledge, the Leader declared in '*Mein Kampf*' that the task of the movement was not religious reformation but the political reorganization of our *Volk*. . . . Not all life can be organized. . . . The state is organization, but life is growth. Connections and interrelationships certainly exist between life and organization, but they have their limits, which must not be overstepped, lest we endanger life."

Von Papen was thinking of the SA and its alleged agitation for a social revolution. But his comments issued into a general attack against the secularization of "eternal values," the "new class struggle" that threatened to break out, "false romantic notions" of "carriers of the revolutionary principle" within the party, and "150 percent National Socialists" who were ready "to contest the existence of world-famous scientists, because they possessed no party book." In short, von Papen attacked forces that threatened to destroy bourgeois asymmetry between power and society and replace it with a new "total" state in which social and political realms were fused. Von Papen voiced the sentiments of Germans who fought to preserve sociopolitical asymmetry now that a single party ostensibly representing the national interest had achieved political hegemony. Von Papen's claim—that he "had placed himself unreservedly in the service of National Socialism"—was therefore true as long as nazism stopped short of coordinating organizations such as the University Association.

The vice-chancellor, who "flaunted his Christianity" and was (since 1932) the "irresponsible pacemaker of dictatorship," soon would gladly accept a post in Vienna after the bloody purge of the SA and conservative members of the regime.[72] But in Marburg "all oppositional forces gained a strong impetus" from his speech, which was "retyped and duplicated in reactionary circles and widely distributed," according to a 5 July police report.[73] Besides KPD members, the "reactionaries" mentioned in the report included the feisty Hermann Bauer, who sidestepped the Nazi communications blackout by printing and distributing numerous copies of the speech before the NSDAP found him out. Marburg professors and other townspeople voiced approval of the speech, while city and county Nazi officials were dismayed over its effect.[74]

The church's importance to bourgeois social life increased through the actions of the Confessing church (Bekennende Kirche), which for many Marburgers became a point of crystallization in the defense of sociopolitical asymmetry in the first two years of Nazi rule. The immediate spur for the formation of the Confessing church was the effort of the German Christians (Deutsche Christen) to coordinate the churches. Founded before the seizure of power and advertised as the "SA of Jesus Christ," the DC intended to use the party and government to change churches into dependent state organizations much like coordinated voluntary associations. German churches were somewhat like public corporations in the first place, but they possessed certain rights that made them something less than state institutions. DC plans were therefore considered radical. The DC agitated for centralization of church authority under a Reich bishop who would rule according to the Leadership Principle. It wanted abolition of parliamentary bodies in the church, passage of racial laws to "purify" church membership, and removal of the Old Testament from religious instruction.[75]

Armed with Hitler's support, the DC entered church board elections in Evangelical Lutheran and Reformed congregations in July 1933. Facilitated by church regulations that sought to avoid open political contention, the DC helped to assemble "unified lists" of candidates that were dominated by German Christians in most congregations. In Marburg, where the DC leader was Oskar Wolf, a teacher and NSDAP member since mid-1932, two-thirds of the *Einheitsliste* consisted of DC members. This was a significant proportion, to be sure, but it was somewhat less than in communities such as Frankfurt/Main, where 78 percent of the church board lists consisted of DC candidates.[76] The ease of DC victories in such "elections" throughout Germany made Nazi coordination of the Protestant church appear swift and effortless. However, disagreement over selection of the Reich bishop had developed in May, and DC lists failed to gain a majority of the vote in the Berlin–Dahlem and Barmen–Gemarke congregations.[77] The Deutsche Christen were by no means in total control.

National antagonisms interacted with local events. The DC attempted in September 1933 to introduce legislation that barred "politically unreliable" members and baptized Jews from holding positions in the church. The proposed laws were so controversial that even the Kurhessian Synod, dominated by German Christians, asked the Erlangen and Marburg theology faculties to consider whether the so-called "Aryan paragraphs" were compatible with "the teaching of the Holy Scripture, the gospel of Jesus Christ, and the lessons of the Apostles." Led by Professor von Soden, whose students had successfully resisted an NSDStB takeover of the theology department student council in 1931, the Marburg theology faculty issued an opinion on 20 September. It declared that anti-

Semitic clauses in the proposed legislation were "incompatible with the essence of the Christian church." The Erlangen department argued that, in view of the legitimate aims of the "national renewal," the church must keep baptized Jews from holding church offices. But the Marburg faculty had made a decisive criticism that propelled it into the center of the church debate.[78]

There were important limits to participation by Marburg theologians in this church response. Faculty members acted with extreme caution. When von Soden went to his colleagues for support in signing a public letter of protest against the new Reich Bishop Ludwig Müller, he could get only two colleagues, Rudolf Bultmann and Schlier, to cooperate. Moreover, both the Marburg opinion of 20 September and the Berlin pastor Martin Niemöller's later call for a Confessing church based on theological reappraisal and reconciliation dealt only with the issue of baptized Jews in the church. This was hardly a full attack on the National Socialist state or on party terror against Jews, Communists, Social Democrats, and others. In fact, many Protestants shared the strident and thoroughly un-Christian anti-Communism of the Nazis. This was true not only of national Confessing church leaders such as Niemöller but of townspeople who joined the church protest in 1934 as well. Even the city's first female university instructor, fair-minded and humane Luise Berthold, who joined the BK in autumn 1934, overlooked the fact that fanatical anti-Communism was a dangerous aspect of Nazi ideology pointing up the brutal intolerance of the regime for any political alternative.[79]

The Confessing church emerged in the spring of 1934 from the church conflicts of the preceding year. In Marburg the BK reached a total membership of one thousand people, each of them in possession of a red card, the symbol of the movement. Berthold went to von Soden himself to obtain the card.[80] Former associates of the liberal theologian Martin Rade and religious socialists at the university also joined the movement. BK strength in Marburg university faculties made living with the everyday reality of the dictatorship "not so bad," in the words of Berthold.[81] Theology students— once again relying on von Soden—were among the most numerous and consistent participants in the movement, while townspeople "from all classes" also found their way to the BK, according to Berthold.[82]

Not class but the church congregation was the foundation of BK mobilization. All but one of the city's pastors joined the Emergency Pastors' League, a forerunner of the BK, and between 50 and 60 percent of pastors in the county belonged to the group. The county pastors were particularly important to the BK because they were more intimately involved in the daily lives of congregants than were their more urban colleagues.[83] The Confessing church also generated the formation of new clubs like the BK student group. Formed in 1934, it had about one hundred members two years later, when it regularly met in the former Marburger Wingolf fraternity house, a well-known center of conservative Christian ideology in Marburg but also the site of strong support for the NSDStB in the Republic.[84] Serious challenges to the Nazi monopoly of collective action, BK gatherings attracted more than a thousand people.[85] The presence of von Soden, a member of the innermost circles of national BK leadership, did much to strengthen the Marburg BK, and ongoing traditions of religious socialism at the university provided intellectual support. Conservative, at times provincial, and profoundly Protestant, Marburg became a fulcrum of the Confessing church.

Open struggle between the DC and Confessing church was rare. In June 1934 between five hundred and eight hundred DC members demonstrated outside the home of the BK leader Ritter. They shouted, "Get him out here! Pastor Ritter must go to the concentration camp!"[86] But BK methods were not conducive to such street actions. Rather than encouraging outright conflict, the Confessing church acted through the ostensibly unpolitical institutions of local life. Surreptitious activity—holding the red BK card and attending regular Sunday sermons—rather than open conflict in the city's market square, taverns, and university lecture halls was the political style of the Confessing church. The church found in liturgical ritual "its own form of resistance [*Widerstand*], more effective than proclamations, demonstrations and speeches."[87] Hardly active resistance of the kind that underground Communist cells bravely conducted, this was nevertheless concerted defensive activity by Marburgers who were uncomfortable with direct political action. From the point of view of participants, the BK was a significant step in countering an environment of repression and suspicion.

But what kind of step? To answer this question, two dimensions of BK activity need to be mentioned. First, partly through BK action, the Protestant church retained its corporate position. This allowed church pulpits, congregation newsletters, and other routine vehicles of non-Nazi communication to persist in the Third Reich. The Gestapo reported that it could hardly control the distribution of church publications, to say nothing of less routine BK actions.[88]

Whereas bourgeois associations were absorbed into the Nazi party, the church remained a fundament of local life. It was a relatively independent part of the cultural furniture that served as a defense against full National Socialist takeover.

Second, BK success manifested the continued influence of apoliticism. For BK members, Nazi activity against the church was not essentially political. Luise Berthold believed that the root cause of national socialism was "de-Christianization of the world." She saw the "Christian sphere" as the logical terrain for "the most bitter and most lasting resistance [*Widerstand*]" to nazism. For Berthold, the BK was "a question of faith," not a matter of party conflict and power. The "anti-Christian" nature of national socialism, which for Berthold explained the party's anti-Semitism, was the core of the issue for the Confessing church.[89] Instead of increasing her concern for political matters, Berthold said, her allegiance to the BK aroused a previously latent religiosity. "I participated regularly in church services which in Marburg almost always took place in the spirit of the Confessing church," she would later write. "I discovered the church hymnal anew," she recounted, "especially the hymns of the Reformation. I now read the Bible with quite different eyes from before. . . ."[90] More than a symbolic act for this Marburger, reading the Bible directly denied the legitimacy of party politics in the church. The church struggle was an apolitical defense against Nazi attempts to destroy the boundaries between social and political life.

Similar impulses shaped von Soden's response to nazism. After being ousted from and then reinstated at the university in 1934, von Soden portrayed himself as a conscientious Christian and professional theologian rather than as a political resister. "I am convinced that I have utilized and must continue to utilize the obligation and the right of a theology professor to give his opinion, according to his best knowledge and in good conscience, on theological questions," von Soden stated, "and as a member of a church synod to vote and behave on the basis of that opinion."[91] The former DVP member was undoubtedly aware of a need to tread softly in making such public pronouncements. Yet this was more than a ploy: it suggested that von Soden saw himself as the defender of an apolitical realm of Christian conscience, theological inquiry, and church policy.

Von Soden and Berthold voiced the majority opinion of German Protestants—"politics do not belong in the church."[92] Seen through such Evangelical and apolitical eyes, the BK favored a tradition of aloofness from party political domination. For many townspeople the Confessing church was not political "in the strict sense of the word,"[93] and this made it a practical and available response to national socialism. Though motivated by specific concerns and operating in a very different political environment from that of the Republic, the BK assumed a well-known stance, acting as if public life could be lived without the power struggles of twentieth-century party politics. It took up the banner of apoliticism—the banner that many bourgeois associations found impossible to carry.

Not only the BK perpetuated well-established apolitical traditions. By absorbing local clubs, the Nazi party also swallowed popular apoliticism. In 1935 Nazi diffusion in local culture was complete. Party lectures, social gatherings, discussion evenings, and many other party-sponsored functions now dominated the public life of the town, and non-Nazi clubs and associations were wrapped in Nazi ideology. When white-collar workers in insurance and banking attended a 1935 Nazi Labor Front meeting, speakers told them that "the commonweal, the entire *Volk* must benefit from labor, not the individual." Front spokesman Bunse reminded the employees that in the Republic every white-collar organization "lived and worked for itself." He stressed that bank employees no longer "looked down from on high" at other white-collar personnel, and that "we are all workers." Yet behind the rhetoric, no doubt taken seriously by many of the assembled workers, was a texture of everyday sociability. The meeting took place in one of the centers of local *Geselligkeit*, the Cafe Markees, where a "short musical program" preceded the lecture. After the meeting, "colleagues socialized with one another a while longer." This was in part the standard social interchange of local club life. But was it also a reassertion of grass roots apoliticism?[94]

A second example poses the question in a slightly different way. At an April 1935 ceremony 120 former members of the League of Younger German Girls (Bund Deutscher Jungmädel) entered the League of German Girls (Bund Deutscher Mädchen). Gathered before the Bismarck tower, which was surrounded by a half-circle of burning torches, the leaders of the local BDM branch voiced expected affection for Hitler. Encouraged to live in the spirit of national socialism, the inductees pledged their lives to Hitler, the Reich Youth leader, the branch leaders of the BDM, and "service to eternal Germany." Yet the emotion seemed familiar. The use of torchlights, the assembly before the Bismarck tower, the rather mystical ambience of the ceremony—local clubs and associations had employed all these devices before the rise of nazism. The BDM spokespersons told inductees that "youth was belief in the light and readiness to struggle"—a generalization any club might have made to its initiates. Did the inductees take the adoration of Hitler and Nazi ideology to heart, or was it the opportunity of social interchange, itself filled with symbolic impact, that was most meaningful for participants?[95]

Nazi functionaries were afraid that party propaganda had become a stale and ritualistic element in local culture, which experienced another surge of popular apoliticism, this time under the auspices of Nazi party hegemony. The influx of so many new Marburgers into the party subsequent to the seizure of power had reduced the NSDAP's abilities to school its members in National Socialist ideology. Commenting on a lack of attendance at party functions such as neighborhood cell evenings, Nazi leaders reminded agitators that these gatherings "should appeal not only to the heads but to the hearts of the participants as well."[96] Obviously, any movement seeking to sustain its dynamism must address the emotional needs of followers. But the comment revealed much more about what had happened to the Nazi political project. The failure of Nazi propaganda to gain full moral authority was caused by more than apathy, resentment, or disinterest. It was more than a result of changes in party membership after Hitler gained power. National Socialist ideology, though suffused throughout local culture, had not displaced *Verein* apoliticism.

Townspeople continued to find meaning in this social stance toward party politics. In the Second Empire, popular aversion to the political sphere operated as a cushion against contentious national and local politics. In the Republic, an unprecedented outpouring of apoliticism helped to destroy the legitimacy of all parties except the NSDAP. In the Nazi dictatorship, finally, malleable apoliticism supported a brutal reshaping of party politics but hindered complete sociopolitical rule by the NSDAP. Without its former dynamism, increasingly vulnerable to opportunism, and unable to control all local culture, the Marburg NSDAP resorted to accepted forms of popular apoliticism to stabilize its position. But the party's stated goal—to destroy damaged connections between social and political life and bring about a total interweaving of the two in a racist folk community—remained an illusion.

Conclusion

Recent scholarship asserts the importance of social process in German political history. In the case of the Weimar Republic there has been a growing emphasis since the early 1970s on how "the social constitution of the country had not changed together with its political constitution."[1] This perspective necessitates research on the full interplay of social life and power in specific subject areas. Additionally, it calls for work that analyzes relationships between the Imperial and Weimar periods, a subject that most historians of twentieth-century Germany have dealt with in perfunctory fashion. This study has tried to address these issues in two overlapping ways.

First, it has focused on the interpenetration of organizational and political life over a longer time span than that which most historians have addressed. By beginning with the organizational ferment of the 1880s and 1890s in Marburg and ending with the completion of the first stage of Nazi coordination in late 1935, it has been possible to capture a fuller dynamic of change between and within social and political spheres. While the present study stresses numerous discontinuities—the organizational explosion of the late nineteenth century, World War I, the first violent years of the Republic, the allegedly calm years of stabilization, Nazi activity from 1930 to the seizure of power, Nazi coordination in 1933–35—it has also emphasized a broader chronological arc.

Second, this analysis has sought to extend the historical view of social process spatially, not by encompassing more geographical territory, but by broadening the focus within a delimited geographical setting. There were two dimensions of this project, the first of which—the horizontal—concentrated on a wide range of organizations, from political parties and occupational groups to sharpshooting societies, student associations, women's clubs, and municipal election coalitions. The second dimension—the vertical—entailed a consideration of the depth of NSDAP members' involvement in local associations. This departed from much previous sociographical work, which has concentrated almost exclusively on the occupational background of Nazi party members and voters.[2] That background has commanded a good deal of attention in the present study, and research into the occupational makeup of diverse NSDAP constituencies will continue to pay dividends; but overemphasis on occupation has also diverted scholarly attention from Nazi party members' involvement in other areas of social life.

At the end of this experiment in taking a longer and broader view of German social process and the rise of national socialism it is appropriate to raise some evaluative questions. What have been the results of this study? How does a discussion of one intriguing Hessian city "fit" into the larger picture of Germany's troubled modern history? What research problems do the findings presented in the preceding chapters suggest for the future?

In answering such questions, one must always take note of Marburg's peculiarities. Marburg was a university and service city, a *Dienstleistungsstadt*, in which large-scale industrial manufacturing made few inroads. The city's social structure was dominated by officials, white-collar workers, students, small craftsmen and retailers, professionals, and pensioners rather than by industrial laborers and big industrialists. This socioeconomic structure narrowed the local tax base and hindered city officials from raising adequate revenues for support of the chronically unemployed and poor pensioners. But it also gave the city a built-in resource base of consumers and cushioned the town against sweeping industrial crisis. Additionally, the costs and advantages of the city's nonindustrial character were so complex that no generalization suffices when judging the susceptibility of local people to hardship and its alleged political results. This also applies to the local bourgeoisie, a community of apolitical and antisocialist sentiment encompassing classes and strata with varying economic problems. Marburg economic life enabled the bourgeoisie to maintain routine organizational practices despite structural and short-term economic hardship. In this respect Marburg was not unlike the wider society, where, in my opinion, the social survival of the bourgeoisie facilitated grass roots political activity in the Empire, popular support for the war, rising apoliticism in the Republic, and nazism. Despite economic difficulties and social divisions, the bourgeoisie survived especially well in Marburg.

Bürger groups may have thought of themselves as economic losers. But they could express dissatisfaction partly because they possessed communication networks necessary for political activity.

The elite bourgeoisie and self-employed lower middle class were leaders of local organizational life, though civil service and white-collar groups became more important in this regard in the Republic and Nazi dictatorship. Conversely, groups that experienced the worst economic hardship—the poorest and most elderly pensioners, younger commercial employees and newly established shop-owners, unskilled workers and day laborers—were either less strongly organized or less capable of maintaining organizational links than were core groups of the town bourgeoisie. They were consequently less able than other strata to have their grievances heard in public life. Influenced by resource management literature, this study has therefore emphasized opportunity and capacity to mobilize as crucial determinants of bourgeois political activity.[3] Despite Marburg's obvious idiosyncracies, the town's experiences suggest that historians need to study more closely the multiform bases of local political action, the influence of local opinion makers, and the efforts undertaken by the Nazis to exploit political and economic tensions by appealing to local power brokers. In short, we need to know more about the mechanics of local protest in Germany—about what mobilization required—before we can develop a more deeply textured explanation for why mobilization occurred in the first place.

An important peculiarity of the city was its contentious political scene. The late Bismarckian and Wilhelmine periods saw increased disengagement of bourgeois constituencies from liberal and conservative parties in the Reich. Though their absolute numbers increased from 1890 to 1912, liberal and conservative voters were unwilling to think of their parties as sole political representatives of bourgeois interests nationally. Yet in the most important bourgeois party, the National Liberals, disengagement from the national arena was often accompanied by bourgeois hegemony at home—a result of the "autonomy of the provinces" in the party after the turn of the century.[4] Comparable organizational and regional arrangements counterbalanced national electoral decline for left liberal and conservative parties. But Marburg was different. Here bourgeois party politics was fragmented, partly because of the relative weakness of the Social Democratic challenge, which lessened the urgency of searching for new forms of political unity and allowed greater competition (with fewer perceived disadvantages) within the bourgeoisie. But other factors also created political disunity—the social diversity of the town bourgeoisie, the influence of the Böckelian movement, traditions of political experimentation evidenced not only in the Böckel phenomenon but also in the National Social victory of 1903 and right-wing coalitions in 1907 and 1912, and a combination of flourishing bourgeois organizational activity and the influence of the university. No single party achieved hegemony over bourgeois constituencies in the city; no political group could argue convincingly that it was the most consistent guardian of general interests and specific social claims.

The war and Republic furthered the Hessian town's peculiar contentiousness. World War I debates over the Reichstag peace resolution and formation of the Fatherland party intensified conflict locally. Virtually dissolved in the war, reformed bourgeois parties continued prewar patterns of weak internal organization and vociferous internecine criticism in the Republic. The middle and late 1920s extended previous party strife as liberal and conservative parties lost all legitimacy. But the nature of politics had also changed. Popular politics was no longer the seemingly out-of-place challenger of the Empire but part and parcel of the struggle for power. This in combination with other factors, such as the advance of political violence, made of the Weimar Republic a qualitatively different phenomenon from prewar regimes. The eccentricities of Marburg politics once again pointed up more general features of German public life.

Not surprisingly, Marburg politicians always wore recognizably local costumes. Special interest coalitions, distinctive though by no means unique products of popular politics in the Republic, gained significant electoral backing in the city parliament, especially in 1924 and 1929. Though focused on local concerns, these coalitions reflected the new power of sectional interests in politics. Yet they also housed traditional, moralistic prejudices against party politics as such. Thus local forms of modern interest politics paradoxically facilitated increased disdain for that same politics. The rise of the nonparty coalitions demonstrated that the period 1924–29 completed what the Second Empire had started and World War I had intensified: a long-term dissolution of bourgeois parties locally and the creation of social resources for recasting parties in new combinations of influence and authority. Research by David Arns and Zdenek Zofka as well as this study suggest that bourgeois party strength and the form and intensity of challenges to older political forms varied considerably from region to region.[5] Above all, it appears that if the Weimar Republic featured a qualitatively new politics in German history, the last half of the 1920s was the period in which the nascent mass politics of the Empire matured and crystallized at the local level. Future research will have to deal more systematically with how Weimar politics of the 1920s extended but also transformed mounting contradictions between bourgeois parties and their disengaged but mobilized constituencies.

Socioeconomic structure and party conflict enhanced the political importance of bourgeois social organizations in Marburg. But the local polity featured a group of organizations different from and more varied than the national. Whereas patriotic societies and big economic pressure groups mobilized in Reich politics, other organizations—sports clubs, veterans' societies, religious *Vereine*, and economic associations emphasizing sociability more than agitation—were more important to the local arena. In the absence of detailed research on bourgeois organizational life in different urban settings, it is difficult to say whether Marburg possessed a richer array of social clubs than other communities did. My impression is that Marburg's organizational fabric was more finely textured than that of most medium-sized towns, but only further research can verify this.

More important, however, is the general issue of the almost militant localism of such voluntary groups. Hardly passive objects of an antisocialist consensus directed from national centers of power, bourgeois social organizations learned to use the dominant practices of organized interest politics for local purposes. "Instead of looking at man as a member of groups and institutional complexes passively obedient to their norms and pressures," Jeremy Boissevain has written, "it is important to try to see him as an entrepreneur who tries to manipulate norms and relationships for his own social and psychological benefit."[6] This is an important rule of thumb for dealing with the leaders of grass roots organizational life, people who used everyday social forms to make of the local polity a notionally more legitimate focus of political authority and interest representation than the national sphere.

Marburg social organizations tried to manipulate political contradictions. Apoliticism—diverse, multiform, shifting, and malleable—gave meaning to such responses to party conflict. It was one part of a wider bourgeois politics that comprised restricted suffrages in local and regional representative bodies, distrust of full parliamentary sovereignty at all levels, local instead of national power bases, disavowal of procedures and mechanisms closely associated with interest politics, and a championing of state and nation as repositories of a higher political morality than that of mass parties and pressure groups. Nested in this ideological universe, apoliticism assumed the form not only of common sense—a bundle of sentiments and notions rooted in an often unstated, everyday social philosophy—but of ideology itself. Apoliticism generally reduced political parties to ancillary vehicles of moral and material authority; parties were never equal to or hegemonic over seemingly unpolitical organizations and institutions. Apoliticism was certainly compatible with the antisocialist consensus of Reich politics, which often characterized the party system as the ruin of Germany's future, but antiparty ideology was adapted in large part to the specific ideological needs and circumstances of the local bourgeoisie.

In Marburg, bourgeois social organizations claimed that apoliticism cushioned, channeled, repressed, and blunted political tensions. There was something to the claim. Social organizations either buried the world of party politics in a dense tangle of social customs or emphasized suprapolitical interests paradoxically oriented toward local rather than national concerns. But community loyalty was linked to nationalism and patriotism through everyday activities, from the public service functions of women's groups and gymnastics clubs to fraternity rituals, festivals, and *Verein* anniversaries. Obviously, apoliticism was much more than an irresponsible retreat from national political obligations, having been a mechanism used by the town bourgeoisie to promote nationalist loyalties and maintain its local hegemony in a contentious age of mass politics and sectional interests. Throughout Germany, the social foundations, methods, results, and timing of this apolitical project must have varied tremendously. A mapping of bourgeois apoliticism in different geographical settings, class structures, and organizational milieus would be a valuable contribution to our understanding of urban politics in Germany.

While the German state's conduct of World War I increased economic pressures on the population and intensified political contention, it also entangled social organizations in a wider field of public activities. The state demanded sacrifices, and local voluntary groups responded. Marburg social organizations joined in the war effort through welfare work and propaganda, activities that heightened local bourgeois involvement in national political life. But even more than the war, postwar conflict created new opportunities for direct political action by the town *Bürgertum*. After the global conflict, social organizations delimited the influence of the Workers' and Soldiers' Council by quickly asserting control over economic policy and civil defense. Whereas in the war state penetration spurred "private" action, in the first five years of the Republic the state's vulnerability encouraged the mobilization of social groups. Though state weakness enabled the town bourgeoisie to limit unrest in the first fifteen months of the Republic, it had devastating results in the spring of 1920. Brutal political violence was endemic to the public life of the early Republic, and Marburg now felt the effects of this dangerous development.[7] In March 1920 Marburg student fraternities were mobilized by the state in temporary volunteer military units to defend the new democracy. They responded by killing workers in Thuringia. This incident introduced violent political action into the repertoire of Marburg social organizations and poisoned class relations in both the Reich and the notionally calm Hessian university town.

In addition to adding a new level of violence to German public life, Weimar embraced popular mobilization more completely than the Empire had, as suggested earlier, and many local social organizations became full participants in this process. The last half of the 1920s was the key period for the mobilization of social groups, just as it was for the mounting dissolution of bourgeois parties and the decisive appearance of new political forms; indeed, the two processes interpenetrated during this short but contentious time span. In 1924–29 Marburg social groups organized city electoral slates, asserted control over nationalist festivals, filled the local public sphere with grating condemnations of interest politics, and supported extraparliamentary protest such as the anti–Young Plan referendum. Building on experiences of the immediate postwar years, social organizations were drawn into political conflict more directly than ever before. Whereas all this made the traditional blunting effect of apoliticism more appealing for the local bourgeoisie, it also prodded local groups to invent more assertive forms of apoliticism that ended the legitimacy of the political parties. Ongoing structural changes in local organizational life, most of them set in motion before the war, reflected and shaped these important developments: more voluntary groups appeared, more townspeople became organized, and more nonelite *Bürger* gained leading positions in voluntary associations. Revealing its dual character again, the last half of the 1920s thus accelerated tensions hinted at in the Empire and sparked in the immediate postwar era but also transformed them in the new sociopolitical context of Weimar life.

Social organizations played a significant role in Nazi mobilization. Before its first substantial electoral gains in September 1930, the NSDAP reproduced and exaggerated bourgeois asymmetry by gaining a foothold in social life in spite of its political marginality. In the early and middle 1920s the Young German Order, paramilitary groups, small-caliber sharpshooting clubs, and other organizations contributed to the diffusion of Nazi influence. But after the middle of the Republic individuals with ties to a broader field of bourgeois groups—student associations, occupational *Verbände*, sports clubs, economic interest alliances—entered the Nazi party. Diffusion of the Nazi message in organizational life then gained momentum after September 1930. The Depression accelerated a process initiated well before the economic hardships of the early 1930s in Marburg. In this respect the calm era of the Republic was crucial for local nazism, the explosive growth of the party in 1930–33 having been built on a social and organizational fabric first woven in the middle of the Republic.

That fabric was not designed and produced by Nazi activists alone; it was also shaped by local joiners who created their own spheres of authority between the Nazi party and social life, a subject we return to momentarily. This activity helped to build the organizational infrastructure of Nazi mobilization just as much as infiltration, official party propaganda, and rabble-rousing did. Most studies of the Nazi electorate or party membership fail to explore these daily social activities that drew Germans into the National Socialist sphere of influence. Nazi party members were involved in at least three important spheres of social interchange: workplace, home and family, and organized social life. Despite an ever-growing literature on the NSDAP, there is a good deal of research to be done on Nazi adherents in the latter two spheres.

Bürgerlich social organizations accepted Nazi party hegemony, aided coordination, and often exploited Nazi policy in the first three years of dictatorship. Yet the residues of past apoliticism remained. The Nazis had captured material—but not complete moral —authority over bourgeois social organizations. The NSDAP could not claim unchallenged authority in speaking for group interests or in determining what the general good of the community was and how that "good" was to be attained. Nor could the NSDAP claim to have the full and active consent of townspeople in these matters. Thus the university and church, incompletely dominated by the NSDAP and still influential over a range of local voluntary associations, were able to take the lead in a new surge of apoliticism when Nazi rule threatened to fuse social and political life. A traditional disavowal of party politics found expression again, though it was necessarily more surreptitious and less prone to be organized in the streets than it had been before. The Confessing church in particular tried to brake full Nazi coordination; although halting and uncertain, and unwilling to engage nazism in direct political confrontation, it was nevertheless a most important defense of bourgeois social life locally.

Shared by so many participants in bourgeois social organizations, the grand hope of apoliticism was that one could conduct public life without the mechanisms and practices of mass mobilization. This hope proved to be illusory. Political contradictions always limited the maneuverability of social organizations, always hindered them from acting like the self-contained "small republics" that observers of bourgeois organizations such as Hans Staudinger saw.[8] Nonetheless, the Marburg town elite and its allies were socially hegemonic—or in the case of pure and modified fraternities, resolutely influential despite a loss of moral authority among students—for most of the period from Bismarck to Hitler. Only in the middle 1920s were there serious challenges to elite social hegemony or influence. These challenges came from the bourgeois camp, first with more active apoliticism in the 1920s, and then with national socialism. Internal disarray rather than the Marxist challenge upset a precarious asymmetry between bourgeois social and political experience. But bourgeois asymmetry was decisively challenged only when nazism competed with elites in *both* social and political life. Even then Nazi penetration in social and cultural activities confronted certain limits.

Conversely, assaults on bourgeois political hegemony began locally in Reichstag politics in the 1880s and mounted in city and Land politics with the introduction of universal suffrage in the Republic. Significantly, such attacks also came from inside bourgeois constituencies, first from the antisocialist and populist anti-Semite Otto Böckel, and then from left liberal, National Liberal, and conservative challengers. Party fragmentation made bourgeois political unity impossible, and growing disparities between bourgeois social and political life created an environment favorable to more aggressive popular apoliticism and nazism. By the time of the Depression, social organizations were unable to manipulate political conflict in the interests of the town elite and groups that accepted elite authority. In the local polity this was not the outcome of a lack of synchronization between modern and premodern structures or institutions, a leitmotiv of so much previous scholarship on German politics, but the product of a break in a long-standing and, for the local bourgeoisie, acceptable tension between social power and political organization.

Viewing the long run of bourgeois politics from Bismarck to Hitler against the backdrop of local organizational life, and taking into account the stresses that ultimately produced the rise of nazism, this study emphasizes the sociopolitical power of the grass roots bourgeoisie. It agrees with David Blackbourn and Geoff Eley that scholars of modern Germany need to be skeptical of the "pin-pointing of bourgeois failure" so prevalent not only in Weber's thought but in recent historiography as well.[9] There was a recasting of bourgeois Europe in miniature in Marburg, though this process had a form and rhythm shaped by local eccentricities.[10] Seemingly mundane social organizations helped to remake the local bourgeois polity. They eased acceptance of the rise of sectional interests, fostered wider participation of nonelite *Bürger* in associational leadership, increased the role of social clubs in the new consumerism of the 1920s, and filtered tensions of mass politics through local power arrangements. Additionally, relying on social organizations to counterbalance its bewildering division into numerous classes and strata, the town bourgeoisie anticipated the intent (if not the form) of Nazi arguments by thinking of itself as an antisocialist and apolitical community of sentiment morally superior to all political challengers.

All this was ultimately a response to a deeper phenomenon that the present study has necessarily been unable to discuss: the fragmentation of the modern state, a process that produced agonizing violence and contention in Germany. In future research on the late nineteenth and twentieth centuries it may be useful to think of grass roots politics in the context of a paradoxical development of increasing state authority and simultaneous diffusion of the state in a tangle of social organizations and institutions. The state's intrusion in various areas of social and economic life was exemplified in Marburg by Prussianization, the decline of municipal authority vis-à-vis Reich government, the mobilization of social organizations by the state in the war and early Republic, and the straitjacket of the Nazi dictatorship. However, in the words of Michael Geyer, the state also became "a highly dispersed entity whose center and parameters [shifted] continuously in as yet unexplained and poorly understood processes."[11] The Weimar Republic did little to stem this long-term development. In fact, it furthered state diffusion by making of politics a series of complex bargains between pressure groups. This opened the state to the notionally private power of many different competing groups and alienated those who felt disadvantaged by the allegedly immoral dance of interest group negotiation.

Caught between traditions of local autonomy and the reality of subjugation to a central power, the Marburg bourgeoisie felt the full effects of the national state's authority and scattering. After World War I, it was asked to do more to serve the state with regard to social welfare and unemployment, given inadequate resources to perform such services, and yet was able to subvert state power in such areas as the policing of local politics. Moreover, it was forced to organize politically in a parliamentary system in which it placed little confidence. All this strengthened the local bourgeoisie's moralistic disdain for a party politics closely identified with the modern state in general and the ineffectual Republic in particular. Yet it also spurred the formulation of new adaptive mechanisms. Hence it is useful, following Geyer once again, to "consider the interwar years as a period of the unmaking of class identities and class boundaries and the making of new ones just as it is a period of the remaking of the state."[12] The unmaking of old alliances and identities nationally had its corollary in the reshaping of the local polity. These issues—the changing political relationship of local bourgeois voluntary associations to an expanding, fragmenting state since the late nineteenth century and the wave of grass roots organizing in the interwar period—require a great deal more consideration by historians.

By occupying local social infrastructures, Nazi agitators exploited bourgeois disengagement from national party structures and captured resources that were set free in the processes just described. Moreover, the NSDAP gained temporary hegemony—not only material power but the right to speak for large parts of the local bourgeoisie in matters of general concern as well—over mobilizing, contentious clubs and associations. Nazism hardly created a unified town bourgeoisie out of disparate social fragments. It did not destroy some previously coherent universe of sociopolitical relations; that universe had been mobilized, and then dissolved of its own contradictions before nazism entered the political stage. The NSDAP gave political form to a cross-class social movement that underwent numerous transformations in its relationship to the political sphere before 1930–33.

But how and why did nazism achieve this? Why did it become successful when it did? I have suggested that Nazi timing depended

in part on changing relationships between bourgeois social and political experience. But nazism did not simply appear, automatically,
once such relationships were altered or damaged.

This was demonstrated in the spring of 1924. The Nazi-*völkisch*
share of the May 1924 Reichstag vote was nearly three times greater
locally than nationally. This was due in part to disaffection with
hyperinflation and stabilization, continued fluctuation of liberal
and conservative party support, and the attractiveness of fusing
elite and popular anti-Semitic forces in the VSB. Because the gains
registered by *völkisch* candidates in spring 1924 stemmed from a
strong protest vote, they were bound to diminish unless more severe crises intervened, as happened in 1930. But an additional reason for the impermanence of the spring mobilization was that Nazi
party activists possessed too few resources to consolidate their advantage. They had too little experience in political agitation and
too little commitment to the parliamentary "game"; relations between conservative and Nazi coalition members were unstable;
Nazi party organization, membership, and leadership fluctuated.
Additionally, the Marburg NSDAP was not yet rooted in bourgeois
organizational life. Without such roots the party lacked wider social contacts and the leadership skills of local joiners. Electoral success outran the party resource base; Nazi political gains were pre-
mature.

The mechanics of successful Nazi mobilization depended ultimately on the creation of a coalition between activists and joiners.
The peculiarly local Nazi activist of this story was the ex-student-
bureaucrat-agitator Hans Krawielitzki, who lived "between the
classes" of Weimar Germany.[13] He had studied for the doctorate but
failed his exams; he had seen little of the war but served in a
paramilitary league after the conflagration; he was the son of a pastor, a local elite, yet he held no permanent employment; he believed that political success derived from dogged propaganda, but
he did not possess the personal dynamism to become an effective
rabble-rouser. His uncertain life nourished a go-for-broke politics
willing to experiment, risk all, and adapt to conditions of extreme
change and fluctuation. Responding to the fluidity of Weimar politics, Marburg Nazi agitators used Reichstag and student elections
and the Depression to place their party at the head of an unprecedented but unpredictable social movement.

Yet not all groups to whom agitators appealed were "masses" in
the sense that they were deracinated. Concentrating almost exclusively on the occupation of SA members, Mathilde Jamin goes too

far in stressing the uprootedness of most Nazi adherents.[14] Despite its electoral support from seemingly amorphous groups of protest voters, the Nazi movement was built on patterned networks of local social life, from those of the *Stammtisch* and sharpshooting club to the paramilitary league, gymnastics society, municipal coalition, and student fraternity. The NSDAP capitalized on economic, social, and political crises and consolidated its tenuous hold over a wide following only when it attracted numerous joiners—representatives of a significant grass roots minority who commanded the resources that membership in voluntary organizations offered. Much of Nazi mobilization depended on the independent social activity of these opinion makers, string pullers, and culture brokers. Responding individually to their environment and perhaps only marginally familiar with Nazi ideology, these were the unauthorized facilitators of German fascism. They folded Nazi thought and practice into their own pursuit of personal advantage and their feelings of loyalty to local organizations and institutions. Party activists benefited from—but never completely controlled—this process of tying the Nazi movement to everyday social relationships. The uncertainty of the situation of Nazi agitators contrasted with the more settled involvement of numerous Nazi joiners in local organizational life. Neither the activists nor the joiners could have existed without the other; neither could have exploited singlehandedly the economic and political crises of Weimar to make of the Nazi party an unexampled protest movement. This study was designed to add to our knowledge about Nazi joiners' cross-affiliations, but there remains much more to be done in the task of analyzing and evoking the texture of such social relations.

All social movements rely on a blend of activism and social diffusion. In this regard, the "normality" of Nazi party adherents requires continued emphasis.[15] The unprecedented quality of the NSDAP is to be found in another area, namely the ideological sphere, where relatively systematic actions are undertaken to rationalize, define, and make meaning of shared social patterns and relationships. I have stressed that from the point of view of many of their local supporters, Nazi ideologues adjudicated between the extremes of the political spectrum. They spoke against a closure of the political system favored by elites and simultaneously attacked Social Democratic and liberal materialism that allegedly reduced politics to the competition of mass parties and pressure groups. Yet Nazi agitators also crowed about the coming folk community, a national polity that claimed to eliminate class divisions and party politics but also swallowed up distinctions between social and political life. The notion of the folk community extended a long tradition of bourgeois moral disdain for mass politics and gave it an unprecedentedly totalistic quality. Whereas nazism appeared to be syncretic but not necessarily radical to most grass roots supporters in the Republic, it displayed its most original and radical qualities in the first years of the dictatorship, when Nazi cadres and their allies tried to collapse social and political experience into a new community of ideological purity and racial solidarity. The Nazi regime aimed to destroy bourgeois asymmetry between everyday life and power by bringing the Nazi party into all corners of local social experience; politics could no longer be held at arm's length. Moreover, nazism destroyed the Weimar system, replacing it with what was claimed to be a morally superior state in which sectional interests were subjugated to the greater national good.

Many Marburgers—disillusioned Nazis, party members who valued traditions of apoliticism, Lutheran pastors and their congregants, conservative supporters of the university—balked at National Socialist totality and were able to brake Nazi momentum. They were able to act in this way partly because they possessed the resources to do so. Not only in the Empire and Republic but in the Nazi dictatorship as well, capacity and opportunity were important determinants of bourgeois political activity. Additionally, because the Nazi party absorbed so many local social networks, it also incorporated an ingrained distrust of party politics. The nature of the Nazi constituency and the formal success of coordination created internal limits on NSDAP plans to fuse social and political experience. But all of this amounted to little direct resistance to nazism. Bourgeois cautiousness and continued partial agreement with Nazi policies reduced the scope of actions by local churches and university representatives. Apoliticism was hardly an effective tool of subversion, having stumbled on the paradox that it could be effective only when it was organized politically. And brutality—another mark of the Nazi regime's unfortunately surprising originality—disarmed or destroyed other bourgeois, Social Democratic, and Communist opponents.

Was, then, Marburg history shaped by Weber's bourgeois philistines—dangerously brutal when organized in the Nazi party and simply ineffectual and solipsistic elsewhere? The Weberian argument has been enormously influential, as I suggested earlier. It has been an inspiration for scholars who have seen in German history a lockstep progression toward antidemocratic state control and an immature subject mentality. There is plenty of ammunition for such arguments. German voluntary organizations did not enlist the local bourgeoisie for parliamentary democracy. But the *Bürger* was also more than a simple philistine. At the local level bourgeois groups saw in nazism a practical vehicle for engaging organizational life in a moral recasting of the political system. Distorted and twisted though this effort may have been, it was suffused with political passion and a sincere desire to rise above one's personal and corporate interest. Marburg's bourgeoisie was capable of rethinking its internal organization and its relationships to the wider social formation and the state. The most disturbing feature of bourgeois efforts to reshape politics was that many disparate, local recastings eventually issued into technological mass killing controlled by a few groups in the fragmented Nazi state. No one in Marburg foresaw this—and for good reason. It was impossible to imagine assembly line barbarism from the point of view of a tangle of local clubs and associations.

Appendix

Evidence for affiliations of Nazi party members to other organizations was built around an undated NSDAP membership list in HSAM 327/1, 5488. The list contained 1,521 names and included individuals who belonged to the Marburg NSDAP (both city and county) through membership number 3,589,239. It is impossible to determine the precise date of the list, but the membership numbers suggest the party drew up the roster sometime after May 1933, when membership number 3,262,698 was issued. Besides containing membership numbers, the list included names, street addresses, and village name (for non-Marburgers). I supplemented the list with names from BDC, Akten des Obersten Parteigerichtes and Akten des Rasse- und Siedlungsamtes. I also took names from the Marburg NSDAP *Festschrift* cited throughout the study. The latter was valuable for finding NSDAP members in the first five years of the local group (*Ortsgruppe*).

I built on the material from these sources by compiling data on the occupations and cross-affiliations of party members in the city. Occupations for Nazi party members (and for Nazi residents, Nazi joiners, sample residents, and sample joiners) were derived from city address books for 1913, 1920, 1925, 1930, and 1934/35. In order to make a party member eligible for a search of his/her non-Nazi affiliations, I verified the presence of the individual in Marburg city limits between 1918 and 1935, either through occupations and/or street addresses from MEB, or through police reports, party correspondence, and other sources. I found 428 individuals with cross-affiliations, a significant number considering the incompleteness of evidence on local voluntary organizations and the shifting nature of both party membership and voluntary group structures. Additionally, I found 366 pre-1933 Nazi residents and 661 nonstudent party members with occupations.

The method used for determining cross-affiliations was a simple yet time-consuming one. I compiled a card index dividing party members according to whether their membership numbers were issued before or after January 30, 1933 and arranged names alphabetically within each division. I then entered information on affiliations as I discovered it. I took a conservative approach during the compilation stage, entering information only when I could identify a specific organization (rather than "a *völkischer* club," or some other general reference), a date of membership, or additional information indicating that the person was involved in an organization between 1918 and 1935. In assembling data such as the affiliation/member ratio (see table 6-1), I counted cross-affiliations only when they occurred during the same period as an individual party member's involvement with the NSDAP. In other words, if an individual joined the NSDAP before January 1933 but became a member of a non-Nazi social organization after that date, the non-Nazi affiliation was not counted for the pre-1933 affiliations. Other than for evidence that demonstrates directly the timing of cross-affiliations (see table 6-2), this method ensured that most cross-affiliations included in the data either preceded or occurred simultaneously with Nazi party membership. When similar names or initials made it difficult to tell whether I had discoverd a cross-affiliation, and when no additional information was available, I discarded the affiliation. I found that I could analyze my findings without translating the information into machine-readable form, and that my more artisanal approach to the data gave me a good sense of the texture of social networks.

I defined a voluntary organization as any group of persons that possessed a formal name, that had a membership theoretically not determined by birth or class, that shared a sense of identification derived from social interchange and/or group goals expressed in by-laws or some other statement of intent, and that was more or less independent of state authority. Because of their close identification with German government, churches have not been considered to be voluntary associations. But church influence appears throughout the scatter of Marburg clubs, partly through the cultural hegemony of Lutheranism, and partly through churches' direct promotion, support, and approval of different organizations.

I have counted as voluntary organizations the municipal non-party coalitions of 1919, 1924, 1929, and 1933. There are two reasons for this. First, participation in the coalitions usually meant that each individual candidate was a member of another organization. For instance, the Interest Alliance included members of the local Renters' Association, and the small business slates were often coalitions of retailers', homeowners', and artisans' associations.

Thus, the coalitions are proxies for other organizational memberships, though I have always counted only the coalition membership and not the presumed occupational association tie, unless this information was verifiable from an additional source. Second, the nonparty slates were more cohesive than might be assumed at first glance. Though they were organized for contesting municipal elections, their candidates often referred to them as separate, ongoing entities. When artisans organized the United Independents' slate in 1929, for instance, they referred to it as "Liste 11" and advocated that "the two artisans' organizations—the Artisans' Association and Liste 11—be united" (see "Für Einigkeit im Handwerkerstande," *OZ* 11 November 1930). Moreover, the coalitions represented continuous threads in local party politics. The civil servants' list included representatives of the local German Civil Servants' Association and ran candidates in every city election of the Republic. Other lists formed and reformed around similar constellations of interests in 1924, 1929, and 1933.

As for other organizations, I have generally relied on local practices when my own definition of a voluntary organization created ambiguities. When local people referred to a group as a *Vereinigung, Verbindung, Klub, Bruderschaft, Bund, Verein, Verband,* or *Gesellschaft,* I usually counted it as a voluntary organization. When the "Marburger Vereine" section of the local address book or *Vereinsregister* carried the name of a particular organization, I accepted this usage. Any other method would, in my opinion, have resulted in an overly narrow definition limiting my view of social networks.

The sources used for finding and verifying non-Nazi affiliations were numerous. The local *Vereinsregister,* housed in the Marburg *Amtsgericht,* was one of the most valuable sources. All voluntary organizations not based on a business enterprise were eligible for registration in the *Vereinsregister* as long as they possessed at least seven members. The Reich Organization Law of 1908 defined a voluntary organization as an association of individuals who agree with one another to pursue self-defined but general goals on a continuous basis. Until 1919 any organizations pursuing "religious, political, and sociopolitical" aims were ineligible for registration. But even after this provision was dropped, the chief county administrators (*Landräte*), who exercised final authority over the register, had wide latitude in determining the legal qualifications of individual organizations. Moreover, practices varied throughout Germany as to the stringency with which the provisions of the Reich Organization Law were applied. The register required organizations to submit the names of club officers, bylaws, and changes in either of these areas. I used information from 148 organizations in the Marburg *Vereinsregister*. Besides the composition of *Verein* boards of officers (some of which contained occupations and city of residence) and bylaws, the register contained scattered correspondence, minutes of membership meetings, excerpts from newspaper articles, membership lists (usually without occupations), founding and dissolution dates of the organization, and the like. A useful discussion of the legal characteristics of the Organization Register is E. Loening and O. Loening, "Vereins- und Versammlungsfreiheit," *Handwörterbuch der Staatswissenschaften*, vol. 8 (Jena, 1913), pp. 542–61.

In addition to the *Vereinsregister*, I used city address books, newspaper articles, interviews, questionnaires, *Verein* publications such as newsletters and anniversary *Festschriften*, police reports, and other archival materials for membership in various organizations. Readers should refer to the notes and bibliography for particular sources. Marburg is particularly good for research on students because student associations were required to submit membership lists each semester to the chancellor. With the exception of student associations, however, there is no single, centralized, and continuous source for determining Nazi party members' organizational past.

Obviously, such data are never without problems. As I noted in chapter 6, the "meaning" of cross-affiliations changed after Hitler's seizure of power, and NSDAP adherents who remained or became members of non-Nazi voluntary associations during the dictatorship were operating under very different conditions from those that had prevailed in the Empire or Republic. This study has discusssed these changing sociopolitical circumstances in an effort to elucidate differences in the nature of cross-affiliations before and after January 1933. Another problem was that data compilation depended on the availability of many scattered sources, and I cannot claim to have produced a complete organizational genealogy of Marburg NSDAP members. Yet with information on almost 200 organizations to which party members belonged, and comparative data for sample joiners (see chap. 6, n. 5), the evidence rather strongly evokes the participation of Nazi party members in the city's organizational fabric. For other issues and complexities of the evidence, refer to the text and notes.

A complete list of NSDAP members' affiliations follows in table A-1. I have listed all organizations except those for which I found only one affiliation for both the pre-1933 and post-1933 periods. These organizations are simply identified as "others." Data for the numbers, types, formation, and density of voluntary organizations (see table A-2) were derived from the *Vereinsregister,* the MEB volumes already mentioned, and newspapers and secondary sources. Marburg address books include between two-thirds and four-fifths of the city's organizations at a particular moment. The evidence listed in table A-2 takes the number of city organizations for 15 January of each year, except for 1934, which uses 15 February. For an idea of which organizations are included in each category, refer to table A-1. The totals exclude Ockershausen, the "industrial" village of 1,500 people which was consolidated with Marburg in 1930 (effective 1 January 1931).

I have mentioned Marburg's organization density at a number of points in the text. Organization density conveys no information about the average size of organizations or about the nature of participation in them. But the measure is useful as a general vehicle for discussing the structure of social life in a community. Not much evidence exists on organization density in the period we are studying, though we do have a sketchy picture of the situation in smaller German towns. Max Weber estimated that the density measure for German cities of about 30,000 inhabitants was 10. As Marburg approached this population total in the 1930s, however, it already had a higher organization density. With regard to the few empirical studies that have addressed the question, Marburg appears to rank somewhere in the middle on the density measure. Table A-3 indicates organization density for six small towns—three German, two American, and one English—between the 1920s and 1950. The measurements are not truly comparable because they use different population totals as the base: all townspeople twenty years of age and over for Boulder, fifteen years and older for Middletown, and the total population for Marburg, Weinheim, and Northeim. The organizational density of the non-German towns would be comparatively lower were their population bases increased. In addition, the Boulder data include organizations beyond the boundaries of the city. Perhaps most importantly, the data on which the measurements are based originate in very different historical and cultural contexts. Nevertheless, the measurements illustrate broader comparative densities.

Having consulted much of the current literature on the social foundations of German politics (see the introduction, n. 29, for sources on the social background of nazism), I resorted to a classifi-

Table A-1 *Marburg NSDAP Members' Cross-Affiliations, 1923–1935*

	Before 30 January 1933	30 January 1933 to 31 December 1935	Total
		Time of NSDAP Member's Affiliation	
Student associations			
Landsmannschaft Hasso-Guestphalia	2	13	15
Corps Teutonia	4	10	14
Marburger Wingolf	12	1	13
Corps Hasso-Nassovia	3	9	12
Turnerschaft Philippina	7	3	10
Association of German Students	9	0	9
Landsmannschaft Hasso-Borussia	1	7	8
Burschenschaft Alemannia	1	6	7
Studentenverbindung Chattia	6	1	7
Burschenschaft Germania	7	0	7
Small-Caliber Sharpshooting Club in the Greater German Youth League	5	2	7
Student Gymnastics Association of Kurhessen (Akademischer Turnverein Kurhessen)	5	1	6
Burschenschaft Rheinfranken	1	5	6
Student Sailing Club "Hansa"	0	5	5
Sängerverbindung Fridericiania	2	2	4
Sängerschaft Hohenstaufen	2	1	3
Landsmannschaft Nibelungia	1	2	3
Freie Burschenschaft Normannia	2	1	3
Hochschulgilde Saxnot	3	0	3
Burschenschaft Askano-Silesia	1	1	2

Table A-1 *continued*

| | Time of NSDAP Member's Affiliation | | |
	Before 30 January 1933	30 January 1933 to 31 December 1935	Total
Clausthaler Wingolf			
(in Marburg)	0	2	2
Ernst Wurche Gilde	2	0	2
Turnerschaft Schaumburgia	2	0	2
Großdeutsche Hochschul-			
gilde Volker von Alzey	1	1	2
Others	7	0	7
Subtotal	86	73	159
Occupational/economic			
interest associations			
German Civil Servants'			
Association	2	11	13
Retailers' Association	5	5	10
Tailors' Guild	8	1	9
German National Commercial			
Employees' Association	3	5	8
Locksmiths' Guild	8	0	8
Property Owners' and			
Landlords' Association	3	3	6
Shoemakers' Guild	3	3	6
Cabinet Makers' Guild	3	2	5
County Association for			
Retail Trade	0	5	5
County Artisans' Association	1	3	4
Gardeners' Associaton	1	3	4
Hoteliers' Association	3	1	4
Housewives' Association	1	2	3
Painters', Decorators', and			
Plasterers' Guild	3	0	3
Plumbers' Guild	1	2	3

Table A-1 *continued*

	Time of NSDAP Member's Affiliation		
	Before 30 January 1933	30 January 1933 to 31 December 1935	Total
Trade Union of White-Collar Employees	0	3	3
Butchers' Apprentices Brotherhood	0	2	2
Carpenters' Guild	2	0	2
Electricians' Guild	2	0	2
Blacksmiths' Guild	1	1	2
Building Contractors' Association	1	1	2
Renters' Association	1	2	3
Others	11	12	23
Subtotal	63	67	130
Sports clubs			
Gymnastics' Club 1860	14	26	40
Athletic Association (VfB)	8	13	21
Sharpshooting Club	4	11	15
Soccer Club Germania 08	5	3	8
Hessian Flying Club	2	5	7
Upper Hessian Hiking Club	2	2	4
Bicycling Club 1885	1	2	3
Kurhessian Sports Club	1	2	3
Canoe Club	2	0	2
Equestrian Club	0	2	2
German-Austrian Alps Club	0	2	2
Small-Caliber Sharpshooting Club "Waidmannsheil"	1	1	2
Swim Club	1	1	2
Others	4	6	10
Subtotal	45	76	121

Table A-1 *continued*

	Time of NSDAP Member's Affiliation		
	Before 30 January 1933	30 January 1933 to 31 December 1935	Total
Political parties and municipal coalitions			
Working Alliance	3	15	18
DNVP	3	9	12
Interest Alliance	0	10	10
Artisans and Businessmen	1	7	8
DVP	3	5	8
VSB-GVG	4	3	7
Civil Servants	1	4	5
United Independents	2	3	5
DDP-Staatspartei	0	4	4
Fatherland party	0	3	3
United Businessmen and Farmers	0	3	3
CSV	0	2	2
Evangelical List	0	2	2
Others	0	5	5
Subtotal	17	75	92
Veterans' associations			
Veterans' and Reservists' Club (Krieger- und Landwehrverein)	8	1	9
Cavalry Association	2	3	5
Veterans' Comradeship Club (Krieger-Kameradschaft)	1	3	4
County Veterans' Association	1	2	3
Infantry Veterans' Club	1	2	3
Others	5	4	9
Subtotal	18	15	33

Table A-1 *continued*

	Time of NSDAP Member's Affiliation		
	Before 30 January 1933	30 January 1933 to 31 December 1935	Total
Nationalist associations			
Greater German Youth League	5	0	5
Steel Helmet (Stahlhelm)	2	2	4
Young German Order (Jungdeutscher Orden)	1	2	3
Others	7	4	11
Subtotal	15	8	23
Other special interest associations			
Police and Guard Dog Club	1	2	3
Association of Former Prisoners of War	0	2	2
Poultry Farming Club	1	1	2
Others	5	11	16
Subtotal	7	16	23
Community action organizations			
Student Home	3	0	3
Volunteer Fire Department	1	2	3
Association for the Home for Disabled Veterans	1	1	2
Association for the Home for the Aged	2	0	2
Civic Association (Bürgerverein)	2	0	2
Others	4	6	10
Subtotal	13	9	22
Cultural associations			
Concert Association	0	5	5
Song Club	3	1	4
Central German Song Club	0	2	2
Dance Club	0	2	2

Table A-1 *continued*

	Time of NSDAP Member's Affiliation		
	Before 30 January 1933	30 January 1933 to 31 December 1935	Total
Lutheran Choir Club	0	2	2
Others	0	5	5
Subtotal	3	17	20
All others	8	3	11
Total cross-affiliations	275	359	634
Total organizations	—	—	198

cation of the composition of the Marburg nonstudent *Bürgertum* that seemed to fit local realities. My schema ranked townspeople simultaneously according to a twofold and a fivefold division, each with occupational subgroupings. The first is a very broad classification by social status, that between elite and nonelite townsfolk. Obviously, I could have resorted to a more complex, multilayered arrangement, but I thought this was the fundamental division of the local status landscape. The second classification is by occupation, with the elite divided into ten categories and nonelites into four categories consisting of a total of ten subgroups. This division reflected as adequately as any other classification the general interplay of status perceptions and economic functions.

Relying on local address books, I dealt with a number of ambiguities and problems in classifying townspeople on the basis of status and occupation. It was fairly easy to classify individuals who possessed academic degrees as members of the local elite. Besides university professors and clergy, this encompassed medical doctors and academically trained teachers. Army officers with the rank of colonel or above and lawyers were also easily classifiable in this category. Though terms such as *Fabrikanten* often bedevil scholars working in the national sphere, in Marburg, where only a small number of local people could claim such a designation, individuals

Table A-2 *An Estimate of the Percentage Distribution of Voluntary Organizations in Marburg, 1914–1934*

Category	1914	1920	1925	1930	1934
Student	19.3	21.0	16.9	12.8	10.7
Occupational	19.7	22.6	24.1	23.6	27.1
Sports	11.2	5.9	6.6	8.8	10.1
Parties, city slates	2.7	3.1	3.8	3.2	0.3
Veterans'	3.1	3.5	4.5	6.1	8.1
Nationalist	5.4	3.5	3.4	3.4	2.3
Other special interest	14.3	16.3	16.3	15.7	13.4
Community action	9.9	10.5	12.6	14.0	16.1
Cultural	4.1	8.6	7.3	6.9	7.2
All others	10.3	5.0	4.5	5.5	4.7
Totals	100.0	100.0	100.0	100.0	100.0
Total organizations	223	257	319	407	347
Persons per organization	99.6	88.5	73.0	63.0	79.8
Density (organizations per 1,000 inhabitants)	10.0	11.3	13.7	15.9	12.5

who were described in this way fit fairly effortlessly into the subgroup of entrepreneurs. Moreover, when I had information on the small number of Marburg storeowners who were economically successful, I ranked them with the entrepreneurs also. Generally, in an administrative center with a population of between 20,000 and 30,000 people, it is possible after a long period of research to know who was a capitalist entrepreneur and who was not.

As for high-level civil servants, elite women without professions, elite pensioners, and others, however, classification became more subjective. Because the highest civil service positions (save that of *Landrat*) were generally absent in Marburg, I ranked what might be referred to in the national society as intermediate-level officials in the local elite. Besides the *Oberbürgermeister*, this included *Amtsgerichtsrat, Justizrat, Postdirektor, Oberbaurat, Eisenbahnobersekretär*, and comparable classifications. For pensioners and elite women without professions, I relied on additional information to determine if a person belonged to the city's upper middle class. A *"Frau Prof. Dr."* or *"Fabrikanten-Witwe"* was fairly obvious, especially when I knew the name of the husband. In some cases, however, I was tempted to take individuals with "von" in front of their

Table A-3 *Organization Density in Six Cities*

City	Organization Density	Population
Boulder, Col. (1945)	22.4	11,985
Northeim (1930)	16.0	10,000
Marburg (1930)	15.9	25,634
Middletown, Conn. (1920s)	13.4	27,042
Weinheim (1932)	10.9	18,631
Squirebridge, Eng. (1950)	8.9	15,000

SOURCES (for towns other than Marburg): For Northeim, see Allen, *Nazi Seizure of Power*, p. 16; for Squirebridge and Boulder, Thomas Bottomore, "Social Stratification in Voluntary Organizations," in *Social Mobility in Britain*, ed. D. Glass (Glencoe, Ill., 1954), p. 355; for Middletown, Robert S. Lynd and Helen Merrell Lynd, *Middletown: A Study in Modern American Culture* (New York, 1956), p. 527; for Weinheim, Heinz Schmitt, *Vereinsleben der Stadt Weinheim*, p. 32.

names as elites. Knowing the growing ambiguities of such titles in the period covered here, I generally discarded the names of titled individuals rather than guess their social status. But this occurred in only a handful of cases. "Other" elites usually referred to the small number of prosperous farmers (*Landwirte*) living in the city, though in one case (see table 2-2), a university student was included in the category. Because of the possibility of knowing a great deal about the social status of townspeople in a city of Marburg's size, I am reasonably satisfied that my classification of the local elite reflects a group of people who really came from "better" society.

The same assessment applies to the other classifications. For nonelite independents I took all individuals who were listed in city address books as *Gewerbetreibende*. These individuals could be divided more finely by referring to the artisans and retailers who were listed as having formed "open trading companies" in the *Handelsregister*. Whenever I knew from additional information that some artisans or retailers were particularly well-to-do or enjoyed considerable social status, I placed them in the category of elite entrepreneurs. Additionally, there were a few individuals like gardeners and peasants (*Bauern*) living in the city who were placed in the self-employed nonelite group.

The white-collar nonelite category included sales clerks (many of whom were *Kaufmänner* for whom I could not find evidence of being self-employed), *Angestellten, Bankbeamten,* and the like. For minor civil servants I relied on categories such as *Postsekretär, Oberbahnassistent, Bahnhofsverwalter, Steuerinspektor,* and the like. The teachers include individuals whose occupations were listed as *Lehrer* or *Lehrerin.*

Skilled (*Facharbeiter*) and craft workers (*Dachdecker, Schneiderinnen,* and so forth) were difficult to separate with certainty, and I therefore combined them. I included craftsmen and craft masters when I found no evidence of these individuals being self-employed. Additionally, I included domestic servants in this category. Unskilled workers were all individuals who were listed as *Arbeiter, Tagelöhner,* and so forth.

Finally, nonelite individuals without professions (usually listed as the spouses of nonelite townsmen) and pensioners (*Rentner*) and retirees (those with "a.D." or comparable designations following their names) fell fairly easily into the nonstudent, nonelite *Berufslosen* categories.

Notes

Abbreviations

In addition to the abbreviations used in the text, the following abbreviations are used in the notes.

AKMVR   Amtsgericht Kreis Marburg, Vereinsregister
ASM   Akten der Stadtverwaltung Marburg
AUWAR   Archiv der Universitätsbibliothek Würzburg. Archiv der ehemaligen Reichsstudentenführung und des NSDStB
BAK   Bundesarchiv Koblenz
BB   *Burschenschaftliche Blätter*
BDC   Berlin Document Center
BGLA   Badisches Generallandesarchiv
DCZ   *Deutsche Corpszeitung*
DHS   *Deutsche Hochschulstatistik*
DSt   Deutsche Studentenschaft (central organization of all local student governments)
HB   *Hessischer Beobachter*
HbSw   *Handwörterbuch der Staatswissenschaften*
HJ   Hitlerjugend (Nazi youth group)
HLZ   *Hessische Landeszeitung*
HSAM   Hessisches Staatsarchiv Marburg
HT   *Hessisches Tageblatt*
HV   *Hessische Volkswacht*
HZKW   *Handwerkszeitung für Kurhessen und Waldeck*
KLZ   *Kurhessische Landeszeitung*
LA   Landratsämter (chief county administrative offices)
LR   Landrat (chief county administrator)
MAMSt   *Mitteilungen der Allgemeinen Marburger Studentenschaft*
MEB   *Marburger Einwohnerbuch*
MHZ   *Marburger Hochschulzeitung*
NA   National Archives
NSLB   *Nationalsozialistischer Lehrerbund* (Nazi Schoolteachers' League)
OB   Oberbürgermeister (lord mayor)
OBZ   *Oberhessische Bauernzeitung*

OZ   *Oberhessische Zeitung*
RPK   Regierungspräsident Kassel (president of Prussian state regional administration for Kassel district)
SDR   *Statistik des Deutschen Reiches*
SJDG   *Statistisches Jahrbuch Deutscher Gemeinde*
SJDS   *Statistisches Jahrbuch Deutscher Städte*
Stapo   Staatspolizei (state police)
UAT   Universitätsarchiv Tübingen
UBM   Universitäts-Bibliothek Marburg
VB   *Völkischer Beobachter*
VDSt   Verein Deutscher Studenten (Association of German Students)
VfL   Verein für Leibesübungen 1860 (Association for Sports and Gymnastics 1860)
WB   *Wingolfs-Blätter*
WBe   *Waldecker Beobachter*

Introduction

1. Weber, "Nationalstaat und Volkswirtschaft," pp. 20–21.
2. Quoted in Struve, *Elites Against Democracy*, p. 127.
3. Weber, "Die Erbschaft Bismarcks," p. 319.
4. Weber, "Geschäftsbericht und Diskussionsreden," pp. 443, 440–47.
5. Ibid., p. 442.
6. Ibid., pp. 442, 445. When referring broadly to *Vereinswesen*, I use the term "organizational" rather than "associational" life because the former implies a broader range of groupings encompassing not only political parties and occupational associations but also sports clubs, veterans' societies, and the like.
7. Weber, "Parlament und Regierung," pp. 354–55.
8. Weber, "Geschäftsbericht und Diskussionsreden," pp. 443, 445–46.
9. I take the term from Antonio Gramsci, "The Modern Prince," *Prison Notebooks*, p. 147. For Gramsci apoliticism comprised ideological features—" 'The act for the act's sake', struggle for the sake of struggle, etc., and especially mean, petty individualism . . ."—that were antipathetic to "party spirit" in social movements. Gramsci's understanding of the term was necessarily undeveloped, and I have not tried to "apply" the Italian theorist's notion. But antiparty sentiment, expressed in different forms depending on the social movements and political cultures one is observing, is the basic linking element between my concept and the Gramscian term. The word "apoliticism" seems especially useful when discussing the political views of local bourgeois groups in Germany because it expresses a strong aversion to mass politics rather than a more neutral disinterest in public concerns or an "unpolitical" outlook. There is, finally, an even more practical reason for adopting the term: it is less cumbersome, in my opinion, than "unpolitical politics," a term I used in earlier writing.

10. For concise statements on the alleged political naiveté of Germans, see Craig, *The Germans*, pp. 67, 174–75, 293–94. Less recent but still influential is Stern, "Die politischen Folgen des unpolitischen Deutschen."

11. Yeo, *Religion and Voluntary Organizations*, p. 1.

12. Wehler, *Das Deutsche Kaiserreich*, p. 17; Gillis, "Germany," pp. 316, 332.

13. Sheehan, *German Liberalism*, pp. 239–57. For a discussion of the chronology of liberalism's dissolution, see Wolfgang Mommsen, "Der deutsche Liberalismus," pp. 77–90.

14. Winkler, "From Social Protectionism to National Socialism," p. 1.

15. The quote pertains to urban artisans, as discussed by Volkov, *Rise of Popular Antimodernism*, p. 349.

16. Kocka, *Angestellte zwischen Faschismus und Demokratie*, p. 336. See also Hamel, *Völkischer Verband und nationale Gewerkschaft*.

17. Stern, "Die politischen Folgen des unpolitischen Deutschen," pp. 178–79.

18. Groh, *Negative Integration und revolutionäre Attentismus*; Roth, *Social Democrats*. Weber thought the Social Democrats were as philistinized as Germany's Junkers, bourgeoisie, and lower middle classes. See Struve, *Elites Against Democracy*, p. 127.

19. Dahrendorf, *Society and Democracy*, chap. 7.

20. Blackbourn and Eley, *Peculiarities of German History*; Blackbourn, *Class, Religion, and Local Politics*, pp. 1–22; Chickering, *We Men Who Feel Most German*, pp. 12–15; Crew, *Town in the Ruhr*, pp. 1–10; Eley, *Reshaping the German Right*, pp. 1–16; Evans, *Society and Politics*; Nipperdey, "Organisierter Kapitalismus," and "Wehler's 'Kaiserreich'"; Zmarzlik, "Kaiserreich in neuer Sicht?," and "Kaiserreich als Einbahnstraße?"

21. See the probing and important Blackbourn and Eley, *Peculiarities of German History*, and Crew, *Town in the Ruhr*, pp. 1–10.

22. Blackbourn, *Class, Religion, and Local Politics*, pp. 7–18; Eley, *Reshaping the German Right*, pp. 8–14.

23. Chickering stresses the importance of studying German organizational life at the grass roots. See *We Men Who Feel Most German*, pp. 14–15. On the notion of the public sphere, see Habermas, *Strukturwandel der Öffentlichkeit*. The only historical study of the wider organizational fabric of a single German community over a substantial period of time is Freudenthal, *Vereine in Hamburg*. But this interesting anthropological work does not adequately discuss the political dimension of local *Vereinsleben*. The same may be said for Heinz Schmitt, *Vereinsleben der Stadt Weinheim an der Bergstraße*. The historiography of the late nineteenth and early twentieth centuries would benefit tremendously from a study equivalent to Walker's imaginative *German Home Towns*. Encouraging beginnings for the study of grass roots sociopolitical life by West German scholars are Tenfelde, *Proletarische Provinz*, and Zang, *Provinzialisierung einer Region*.

24. Gillis, "Germany," pp. 317–18.

25. Evans, *Society and Politics*.

26. Schoenbaum, *Hitler's Social Revolution*.

27. Although he provides little information about everyday social networks, Grill stresses the independence of grass roots nazism from central controls in *The Nazi Movement in Baden*.

28. The importance of local social organizations is implied—but never explicated—in the discussion of the "group bases" approach to nazism in Hamilton, *Who Voted for Hitler?*, pp. 437–53.

29. Besides the studies of Schoenbaum and Hamilton, recent works on the social ecology of nazism include Bessel, *Political Violence*; Broszat, "Zur Struktur der NS-Massenbewegung"; Childers, *The Nazi Voter*; Falter, "Wer verhalf der NSDAP?"; Conan Fischer, *Stormtroopers*; Jamin, *Zwischen den Klassen*; Kater, *The Nazi Party*; Larsen, Hagtvet, and Myklebust, *Who Were the Fascists*; Linz, "Notes toward a Comparative Study of Fascism"; Madden, "Early Nazi Party Members"; Reinhard Mann, *Die Nationalsozialisten*; Merkl, *Political Violence under the Swastika*, and *Making of a Stormtrooper*; Schieder, *Faschismus als soziale Bewegung*; and Stokes, "Social Composition of the Nazi Party." I was unable to consult Giles, *Students and National Socialism*.

30. Studies that offer information on previous group affiliations of NSDAP members include Conan Fischer, *Stormtroopers*, pp. 55, 151–53; Merkl, *Political Violence under the Swastika*, pp. 110–13, 146–47, 207–47, 344–63; and Stachura, *Nazi Youth*, pp. 207–58. For a good discussion of mass society literature, see Hagtvet, "Theory of Mass Society."

31. Allen, *Nazi Seizure of Power*. But recent empirical work has also treated mass society theory more kindly. See the favorable remarks on Arendt in Jamin, *Zwischen den Klassen*, pp. 380–81.

32. Heberle, *From Democracy to Nazism*; Kershaw, *Popular Opinion and Political Dissent*; Noakes, *Nazi Party in Lower Saxony*; Pridham, *Hitler's Rise to Power*; Rietzler, *Kampf in der Nordmark*; Stokes, *Kleinstadt und Nationalsozialismus*; Zofka, *Ausbreitung des Nationalsozialismus*. For discussions of local and regional studies in the history of nazism, see Hennig, "Regionale Unterschiede"; Koshar, "Away from the Center"; and Steinbach, "Regionale Parteigeschichte," pp. 223–30.

33. Linz, "Notes toward a Comparative Study of Fascism," p. 42.

34. Hans Mommsen, "National Socialism," pp. 185–86.

35. Among studies containing information on Nazi infiltration of voluntary organizations are Allen, *Nazi Seizure of Power*, pp. 209–26; Faust, *Der Nationalsozialistische Deutsche Studentenbund*, 2:13-35; Gessner, *Agrarverbände*, pp. 234–58; Giles, "Rise of the National Socialist Students' Association"; Gies, "NSDAP und landwirtschaftliche Organisationen"; Hamel, *Völkischer Verband und nationale Gewerkschaft*, pp. 238–57; Krebs, *The Infancy of Nazism*, pp. 3–37; Noakes, *Nazi Party in Lower Saxony*; Steinberg, *Sabers and Brownshirts*; Winkler, *Mittelstand, Demo-*

kratie, und Nationalsozialismus, pp. 157–82; and Wulf, *Die politische Haltung des schleswig-holsteinischen Handwerks.*

36. Zofka, *Ausbreitung des Nationalsozialismus*, p. 37; in the same work see also pp. 81, 92, 103, 139–40.

37. For results, methodology, and sources, see chap. 6 and the appendix. On defining voluntary associations, besides the discussion in the appendix, see Nipperdey, "Verein als soziale Struktur," and Sills, "Voluntary Associations."

38. Maier, *Recasting Bourgeois Europe*, pp. 36–37. On the *Bürgertum*, see Hansjoachim Henning, *Sozialgeschichtliche Entwicklungen in Deutschland*, pp. 97–197, and *Das westdeutsche Bürgertum.*

39. Hopwood, "Paladins of the *Bürgertum*," pp. 214–15.

40. Note that throughout this study I refer to middle "*classes*" and "strata." The singular term "middle class" is misleading because it connotes an economic, social, and ideological coherence that did not exist. For a discussion that—despite its title—emphasizes the complexity of the middle classes, see Stearns, "The Middle Class: Toward a Precise Definition."

41. Laclau, *Politics and Ideology*, p. 114; on the problem of class formation, see Jessop, "Political Indeterminacy," pp. 63–68, and Poulantzas, *Classes in Contemporary Capitalism*, pp. 13–35.

42. For a relevant contrast, which demonstrates the internal splintering and lack of complete amalgamation of elites in an industrializing city, see Gutman, "Class, Status, and Community Power."

43. On small-town elites generally, see Hopwood, "Paladins of the *Bürgertum*," pp. 214–15, and "Bavarian *Kommerzienräte*"; on Marburg's automatic elite, interview with Hermann Bauer, former publisher of the city's *Hessisches Tageblatt*, 1 April 1977.

44. For precise delineations of the self-employed lower middle classes, see Blackbourn, "The *Mittelstand*," and Berger, "Regime and Interest Representation." More generally, see Crossick and Haupt, *Shopkeepers and Master Artisans.*

45. Kürschner, *Geschichte der Stadt Marburg*, p. 279.

46. Lederer, *Privatangestellten in der modernen Wirtschaftsentwicklung*, and *Angestellten vor dem Nationalsozialismus*; Lederer and Marschak, *The New Middle Class.*

47. On workers, see Hansjoachim Henning, *Das westdeutsche Bürgertum*, p. 174; for Marburg nonstudent *Berufslosen*, see below, chap. 1.

48. The discussion of resource management theory of most relevance to historians is found in Tilly, *From Mobilization to Revolution.*

49. Ibid., pp. 69–81.

50. For the notion of assembling and investing resources, see Oberschall, *Social Conflict and Social Movements*, p. 28; for the qualitative implications of resource management theory, see Fireman and Gamson, "Utilitarian Logic."

51. On the essential similarity of mobilizers, see Gamson, *Strategy of Social Protest*, pp. 130–44.

52. For a philosophical argument justifying a bridge between utilitarian arguments and public interests that are nonderivative of private values, see Wolff, *Poverty of Liberalism*, pp. 162–95.

53. I have relied primarily on Gramsci, *Prison Notebooks*, pp. 206–76. For useful interpretive analyses of Gramsci's fragmentary but undeniably important theoretical work, see Adamson, *Hegemony and Revolution*; Anderson, "Antinomies of Gramsci"; Hall, Lumley, and McLennan, "Politics and Ideology: Gramsci"; Lears, "The Concept of Cultural Hegemony"; and Williams, *Marxism and Literature*, pp. 108–14.

54. Gramsci, *Prison Notebooks*, pp. 55–102.

55. See Adamson, *Hegemony and Revolution*, pp. 215–21.

56. On the connectedness of social relations and political conflict, see Jessop, "Political Indeterminacy," pp. 59–63.

57. Koshar, "Two 'Nazisms.' "

58. For secondary literature on Marburg, see Dettmering and Grenz, *Marburger Geschichte*.

Chapter 1

1. For the conservative opinion of Marburg's rural beauty, see *OZ* 29 July 1927 Jubiläumsausgabe; for socialist attacks on the "Fascist university," see *Volksstimme* (Frankfurt/Main), 25 October 1929, in HSAM 305a, Acc. 1950/9, 584; for the "citadel of reaction," see *HV* 4/5 July 1931 in HSAM 165, Kassel I, 6978; on the philistinized city, see *VB* 9 July 1931 and *HV* 11 August 1931; on "radicalization" and socioeconomic structure, see vom Brocke, "Marburg im Kaiserreich," p. 429; Seier, "Marburg in der Weimarer Republik," pp. 560–66 (despite the general thrust of his argument, Seier correctly notes on p. 561 that Marburg's support for nazism was "more differentiated" than has previously been assumed); and Willertz, "National Socialism in a German City and County."

2. Eriksen, "Klima und Witterung," pp. 84–85. On the castle and St. Elisabeth Church, see Keyser, *Hessisches Städtebuch*, pp. 324–26. For the university, see Hermelink and Kaehler, *Die Philipps-Universität*.

3. On the linen industry, see Möker, *Nordhessen im Zeichen der industriellen Revolution*, pp. 86–88; for the quote on pottery, Weber-Kellerman and Stolle, *Volksleben in Hessen*, p. 5; more generally on economic and social background, Kürschner, *Geschichte der Stadt Marburg*, pp. 27–47, and vom Brocke, "Marburg im Kaiserreich," pp. 428–50, which is very detailed and useful.

4. On Kurhessian absolutism in the nineteenth century, see Knobel, *Die Hessische Rechtspartei*, pp. 4–15; for changes in particular artisanal trades in Marburg, vom Brocke, "Marburg im Kaiserreich," pp. 429–35. Using

1849 as the base year, the percentage of the population that emigrated in 1852–64 was 10.1 for Marburg city, 8.0 for the city and county, and 7.1 for North Hesse. See Möker, *Nordhessen im Zeichen der industriellen Revolution,* pp. 30–31, for emigration data, and pp. 83–88, for the linen trades and agriculture in the region.

5. Levy, *Downfall of Anti-Semitic Political Parties,* pp. 48–49.

6. *OZ* 29 July 1927.

7. On student enrollments, see Ehlers and Leib, "Marburg—Stadt und Universität," p. 109; on Marburg's "phlegmatic" students, the quote from Prof. Zeller in Kürschner, *Geschichte der Stadt Marburg,* p. 262; on the importance of the university as a springboard for upwardly mobile young professors, vom Brocke, "Marburg im Kaiserreich," pp. 518–19; on economic links between the university and city, Leister, "Marburg," p. 58.

8. For attitudes toward Prussia in Marburg, see Leppla, "Marburg wird preussisch," pp. 33–37, and Kürschner, *Geschichte der Stadt Marburg,* pp. 264–65.

9. For Marburg's factories, see vom Brocke, "Marburg im Kaiserreich," pp. 429–30; for the comparison with Göttingen, Leister, "Marburg," p. 33. The Holzhauer factory in Marburg, founded in 1762, manufactured chemical instruments. Although it employed ninety workers in the 1890s, the factory hardly made Marburg comparable to Göttingen, where production of specialized scientific instruments was more developed.

10. On the Behring-Werke, see vom Brocke, "Marburg im Kaiserreich," pp. 427–28; for officials' and notables' support of the city's nonindustrial status and Schüler's objection to the auto factory, ibid., pp. 429–30, 522–23; for a darker side of the Behring factory's activity in the Third Reich, Vereinigung der Verfolgten des Naziregimes—Bund der Antifaschisten, *Marburg–Behring–Buchenwald.*

11. *OZ* 29 July 1927.

12. For data on artisanal branches in Marburg from 1776 to 1914, see vom Brocke, "Marburg im Kaiserreich," pp. 433–34; for industry and crafts in the Republic, see tables 1-1 and 1-2.

13. There were 19.6 independent retailers per 1,000 inhabitants in Marburg in 1867–68. The numbers are based on my calculations from the approximate data cited by vom Brocke (see the preceding note).

14. For the tertiary sector, see tables 1-1 and 1-2; on the changed relationship between production and consumption in the modern era, Leister, "Marburg," p. 34.

15. On urban and regional history, see Lee, "Urbanization and Economic Development," p. 285; on regional and intraregional differences produced by modernization, Tipton, *Regional Variations in Economic Development,* p. 143; on north Hessian agriculture, Möker, *Nordhessen im Zeichen der industriellen Revolution,* pp. 55, 70–82.

16. For *Oberhessen* and Kassel district, see Demandt, *Geschichte des Landes Hessen,* p. 586; for Württemberg, Loreth, *Wachstum der württembergischen Wirtschaft,* p. 16.

17. For the relationship of countryside and city, see Leister, "Marburg," pp. 18, 60.

18. Leister, "Marburg," pp. 14–16; Braun, *Das andere Tübingen*, pp. 33–82.

19. LR to RPK, 14 April 1924; Magistrat to Kurator der Universität, 13 May 1924, both in HSAM 310, Acc. 1975/42, 486.

20. Vom Brocke, "Marburg im Kaiserreich," pp. 429–47.

21. For more detailed discussion of local elite politics, see chap. 2.

22. In Konstanz a particular bourgeois political coalition exacerbated economic underdevelopment by resisting industry; in Marburg the same kind of resistance occurred, but, for reasons discussed below, Marburg was fully integrated in the political struggles of the nation and was anything but provincial in the sense that Gerd Zang used the word—that "stagnation, a lack of controversy, calmness in politics as well as in society" prevailed. See Zang, *Provinzialisierung einer Region*, p. 22.

23. RPK to district *Landräte*, 25 August 1914, HSAM 180, LA Mbg, 892.

24. For construction trades, see Kreisarbeitsgemeinschaft für das Baugewerbe, Marburg a.L. to LR, 24 February 1915, and "Eingabe zur Verhinderung der Arbeitslosigkeit durch Belebung der Bautätigkeit" from the same group, February 1915, both in HSAM 180, LA Mbg, 892; on enrollment in 1914, students at the front, and the number of students killed in battle (580), see Ehlers and Leib, "Marburg—Stadt und Universität," p. 109; vom Brocke, "Marburg im Kaiserreich," p. 538; and Heer, *Marburger Studentenleben*, p. 177.

25. "Kriegschronik der Stadt Marburg," in HSAM 330, Mbg A, II, 51, pp. 328–29.

26. Ibid., pp. 27–61. On women in World War I nationally, see von Gersdorff, *Frauen im Kriegsdienst*, pp. 15–37; for further discussion, see chap. 4 below.

27. "Kriegschronik der Stadt Marburg," pp. 171–72.

28. Compare Reulecke, "Phasen und Auswirkungen der Inflation," pp. 175–87.

29. Friedrich-Wilhelm Henning, *Das industrialisierte Deutschland*, p. 63; furthermore, see Hoffmann, *Wachstum der deutschen Wirtschaft*, p. 801, and Witt, "Finanzpolitik und sozialer Wandel," pp. 403–4. On the decline of urban financial autonomy, see Wells, *German Cities*, pp. 166–71.

30. Comparison of percentages of individuals receiving different types of unemployment compensation in Marburg and all German cities of 20,000–50,000 inhabitants, 1930–32:

| | Types of Compensation | | | |
	Insurance	Crisis Support	Welfare	Total
Marburg	25.1	17.9	57.0	100.0
				N = 2,888
All cities of 20,000–50,000	31.0	25.0	44.0	100.0
				N = 1,055,693

Sources: "Arbeitslose und Arbeitslosenhilfe 1930 und 1931," *SJDS* 27 (1932): 310–20; "Arbeitslose und Arbeitslosenhilfe 1932," *SJDS* 28 (1933): 543–49; and "Arbeitslose und Arbeitslosenhilfe 1934," *SJDG* 29 (1934): 416–21. On Reich benefits for needy Marburg pensioners, see *OZ* 4 September 1930.

31. For a running account of municipal government policy in Marburg after World War I, see "Bericht über die Verwaltung der Stadt Marburg (1918–35)," ASM. The antagonism that city policies aroused in the Republic is well reflected in the meeting of the United Independents in November 1929 where representatives of this nonparty special interest slate criticized the city administration for relying too greatly on tourism and the university instead of attracting industry. See *OZ* 12 and 14 November 1929, and *Volksstimme für Lahn-, Dill-, und Westerwaldgebiet*, 13 November 1929.

32. The mayor claimed that the number of Marburg students was reduced from 4,200 in summer 1931 to 2,700 in summer 1934, a drop of more than 35 percent; see OB to Rektor der Universität, 26 March 1935, in HSAM 305a, Acc 1975/79, 64. The mayor based his figures on city administrative data, which generally gave higher enrollment figures than national statistics did. But there can be little doubt that Nazi economic policy furthered this trend. See *DHS* 4 (1930): viii, 10 (1932/33): 11, and 12 (1933/34): 20. See also Ehlers and Leib, "Marburg—Stadt und Universität," p. 109, which puts Marburg enrollments at a higher level than do national statistics.

33. Willertz, "Marburg unter dem Nationalsozialismus," pp. 622–28. See also the NSDAP Landrat Krawielitzki's five-year report, "Der Landkreis Marburg von 1933 bis 1937," in HSAM, 330 Mbg C, 5613.

34. *OZ* 29 July 1927.

35. *Berufslosen* included all individuals living on their own property, investments, or pensions; schoolchildren, university students, and dependents living away from home; and persons without an occupation or who did not identify an occupation. See Hohorst, Kocka, and Ritter, *Sozialgeschichtliches Arbeitsbuch*, p. 68. For the proportion of *Berufslosen* in other cities, see *SDR* 408 (1931): 105. For student data, see n. 32, this chapter.

36. Percentages for trade, administration, and domestic service in cities of 20,000–50,000 inhabitants were 20.4, 9.8, and 3.6 respectively. See *SDR* 408 (1931): 26–27. The increase in the percentage of the working population involved in agriculture and forestry (from 1.6 in 1925 to 2.7 in 1933) was most likely due to the consolidation of the village of Ockershausen in 1931 and increased employment in gardening resulting from the lack of jobs in industry during the Depression.

37. On the share of particular occupational groups in the labor force in other cities, see *SDR* 408 (1931): 121. For unemployment figures, *SDR* 456 (1936): 25/41.

38. For other cities, see *SDR* 408 (1931): 121. Had the absolute number of independents remained unchanged between 1925 and 1933, the change

in their proportion of the labor force would have been -2.6 percentage points instead of -3.5.

39. On the share of the working population in domestic service in cities of 20,000–50,000 inhabitants, see *SDR* 408 (1931): 121. In 1929 the number of domestic servants per 1,000 of population in Marburg was 40, compared to 24 in Kassel and 21 in Bonn. For women earning the main income of a household, the ratios per 1,000 were 290 in Marburg, 240 in Giessen, and 252 in Kassel. The *Oberhessische* called this level of female employment "unusually high" (*OZ* 23 July 1929).

40. Before 1914 900 marks annually was the cutoff point for nonpayment of income tax; after the war this was raised to 1,200 marks. Computations for the period prior to World War I are based on data from vom Brocke, "Marburg im Kaiserreich," pp. 440–42, and for the postwar years, on *OZ* 19 April 1930.

41. Protokoll der städtischen Kriegskommission, July 1916, I in HSAM 330, Mbg C, 1378, and *OZ* 19 April 1930. For national income structures, see Geiger, *Soziale Schichtung des deutschen Volkes*, p. 29.

42. For general data on consumer prices compiled by the Marburg Housewives' Association, see Marburger Hausfrauenverband, Protokollbuch, 2:76; for the quote and data on meat prices and baked goods, refer to *HT* 4 August 1926, wherein the *HT* commentator wrote that Marburg "shops are completely oriented toward tourists and students who pay in full."

43. For city-size wage differentials, see Bry, *Wages in Germany*, p. 102; for data demonstrating that Marburg artisans earned lower hourly wages than their counterparts in Kassel and Hanau, see Handwerkskammer zu Kassel und Kurhessisch-Waldeckischer Handwerkerbund, *Jahrbuch*, pp. 19–21.

44. For data on savings and the quote, see Kürschner, *Geschichte der Stadt Marburg*, p. 299; for the rest, see *OZ* 11 September 1919, 11 January and 11 February 1922.

45. See Kürschner, *Geschichte der Stadt Marburg*, p. 299.

46. Feldman, "The Political Economy of Germany's Relative Stabilization," pp. 180–81.

47. "Kriegschronik der Stadt Marburg," pp. 344–45.

48. For *Mittelstand* incomes, see Holtfrerich, *Die Deutsche Inflation*, pp. 272–73.

49. *OZ* 11 February 1922, 11 August and 7 November 1923, 4 September 1930.

50. For May 1924, see chap. 2; more generally on savers and the May 1924 Reichstag elections, see Childers, "Inflation, Stabilization, and Political Realignment," pp. 418–24, and Hughes, "Economic Interest, Social Attitudes, and Creditor Ideology," p. 395. On Marburg *Rentner* associations, see *OZ* 4 November 1919; 23 January, 25 September, 10 October, 23 November 1920; 13 March, 1 May, 30 June 1922; 28 December 1923.

51. Eulenberg, "Die sozialen Wirkungen der Währungsverhältnisse," pp.

774–75; Bresciani-Turroni, *Economics of Inflation*, p. 319; on civil servants, see Kunz, "Verteilungskampf oder Interessenkonsensus?," pp. 347–84; on students' conditions, see DSt announcement, SS 1921, in HSAM, 305a, Acc. 1950/9, 635; DSt questionnaire, WS 1924/25, AUWAR I*6, phi 564; Heer, *Marburger Burschenschaft Arminia*, pp. 124–25; WB 53 (19 June 1924), col. 132; 49 (15 May 1920), col. 316; for unemployment, see below, this chapter.

52. Moeller, "Winners as Losers," pp. 255–88.

53. Holtfrerich states that the thesis regarding the *Mittelstand*—again, a very big part of the urban *Bürgertum*—as "the main loser of the inflation is not only arguable because of the undifferentiated character [of the analysis] but also simply false" at the level of aggregation used in previous research. See *Die Deutsche Inflation*, pp. 272–73.

54. See chap. 4 below.

55. On prices, see Bry, *Wages in Germany*, pp. 187–90; on rents, Willertz, "National Socialism in a German City and County," p. 12; on savings, Kürschner, *Geschichte der Stadt Marburg*, p. 299; on the tourist industry, *OZ* 4 January and 12 December 1929, 30 January 1932; on student enrollments, see table 4-3; on building, *OZ* 29 July 1927 Jubiläumsausgabe; on students' economic conditions, DSt questionnaire, WS 1924/25, UAWAR I*6, phi 564.

56. For motor vehicles, see "Hauptübersicht. Aufbau der Bevölkerung, der Finanzen und der Wirtschaft in den Gemeinden mit mehr als 10 000 Einwohnern," *SJDG* 30 (1935): 1–27; on domestic servants, *OZ* 23 July 1929.

57. *OZ* 29 July 1927 Jubiläumsausgabe.

58. On economic conditions before World War I, see vom Brocke, "Marburg im Kaiserreich," pp. 428–50; for the war, see the letter of the Kriegsarbeitsgemeinschaft für das Baugewerbe, Marburg to LR, 24 February 1915, in HSAM 180, LA Mbg, 892.

59. *OZ* 13 January 1919, 19 March 1921, 11 February 1922.

60. *HT* 29 October, 9 and 18 December 1925; on Polish labor, see LR to RPK, 5 January 1928, in HSAM 180, LA Mbg, 3807.

61. *OZ* 14 February 1928; *HT* 30 April 1928.

62. *OZ* 7 September 1931.

63. "Hauptübersicht. Aufbau der Bevölkerung, der Finanzen und der Wirtschaft," pp. 1–27. For further data on unemployment in Marburg, see n. 30, this chapter.

64. See table 4-2.

65. The number of overnight guests in Marburg hotels, 1925–32, was as follows:

1925	34,897	1929	52,873
1926	35,511	1930	51,840
1927	37,406	1931	44,802
1928	45,923	1932	34,665

Source: *OZ* 4 January, 12 December 1929, 30 December 1932. The figures for 1931 and 1932 exclude December.

For students, see table 4-3. Per capita income declined 39.6 percent in the Reich and 37 percent in Marburg in 1929–32. For Marburg my computations are based on *OZ* 13 January 1933, but for the Reich I have used figures from Hohorst, Kocka, and Ritter, *Sozialgeschichtliches Arbeitsbuch,* p. 102, which are different from (and presumably more up-to-date than) those provided in the *OZ* article.

66. Kürschner, *Geschichte der Stadt Marburg,* p. 299.

Chapter 2

1. Barraclough, *Introduction to Contemporary History,* pp. 129, 135–39.
2. Von Gerlach, *Von Rechts nach Links,* p. 171.
3. On the earlier "age of organization," see Nipperdey, "Verein als soziale Struktur," pp. 175–76, and Freudenthal, *Vereine in Hamburg,* p. 180.
4. Naumann, "Neudeutsche Wirtschaftspolitik," *Werke,* 3:104–5, cited in Ritter and Kocka, *Deutsche Sozialgeschichte,* 2:32.
5. Hohorst, Kocka, and Ritter, *Sozialgeschichtliches Arbeitsbuch,* pp. 173–76. All subsequent national electoral statistics for the Second Empire are derived from this source.
6. Mittmann, *Fraktion und Partei,* pp. 67–82; Nipperdey, *Organisation der deutschen Parteien,* pp. 265–392.
7. Nipperdey, *Organisation der deutschen Parteien,* pp. 316–51; on sports and cultural clubs in the turn-of-the-century SPD, see Nolan, *Social Democracy and Society,* pp. 133–35.
8. On the Center as *Fraktionspartei,* see Mittmann, *Fraktion und Partei,* pp. 74–82; on the *Volksverein* and the national context of changes in the Center party, see Blackbourn, *Class, Religion, and Local Politics,* pp. 23–60.
9. Puhle, *Agrarische Interessenpolitik,* and *Politische Agrarbewegungen;* Fricke, "Bund der Landwirte," in Fricke, *Die bürgerlichen Parteien,* 1:129–49; Gerschenkron, *Bread and Democracy.*
10. Quoted from Sheehan, *German Liberalism,* p. 246; for the rest, see ibid., pp. 159–277.
11. For the electoral decline of national liberalism, see Milatz, *Wähler und Wahlen,* pp. 11–28; for the 1890 election, see O'Donnell, "National Liberalism," p. 95.
12. On National Liberal party structure, see Nipperdey, *Organisation der deutschen Parteien,* pp. 86–175.
13. Ibid., p. 175; on the relationship between national liberalism in the Reich and in communities and regions, see Sheehan, "Liberalism and the City," and *German Liberalism;* and White, *Splintered Party.*
14. O'Donnell, "National Liberalism," pp. 109, 111, 130.

15. Friedrich Naumann, "Die Erneuerung des Liberalismus," in *Werke*, 4:281, as cited in Struve, *Elites Against Democracy*, p. 98.

16. Nipperdey, *Organisation der deutschen Parteien*, pp. 176–240.

17. Ibid., pp. 241–64.

18. For the relationship of parties and extraparliamentary organizations generally, see Stegmann, *Die Erben Bismarcks*, pp. 20–58, 113–28; for nationalist *Verbände*, Eley, *Reshaping the German Right*; for the Pan-German League, Chickering, *We Men Who Feel Most German*.

19. For the concept of inventing traditions, see Hobsbawm and Ranger, *The Invention of Tradition*.

20. Gramsci, *Prison Notebooks*, p. 422; Adamson, *Hegemony and Revolution*, p. 150.

21. For examples among German liberals, see Sheehan, *German Liberalism*, pp. 14–17, 150, 233–36; more generally, see Baum, *The Holocaust and the German Elite*, pp. 267–68. Baum refers to an "antipolitics outlook" in nineteenth-century European society. In my opinion this was not a popular antipathy to thinking about power relations as such, but rather a resistance to the development of mass parties.

22. For Bismarck, see Stegmann, *Die Erben Bismarcks*, p. 115; for the veterans' society, see "Das deutsche Kriegervereinswesen," *Jahrbuch des Deutschen Krieger-Bundes. Kalender für 1912* (Berlin, 1912), p. 30.

23. Equating "politics" with "mechanistic-democratic" concepts of the Western state, Mann wrote: "Politics—democracy—is by its very nature something un-German, anti-German. . . ." Of Western forms of democracy he wrote: "Away with the foreign and repugnant phrase 'democratic!' The mechanistic-democratic state of the West will never be naturalized here. We germanize the word and say 'popular' [*volkstümlich*] instead of 'democratic'—thereby saying and thinking the precise opposite: because to Germans popular means 'free' inwardly and outwardly, but it does not mean 'equal,' either inwardly or outwardly." See Thomas Mann, *Betrachtungen eines Unpolitischen*, pp. 254, 270.

24. Sheehan, *German Liberalism*, p. 237; for National Liberal provincial politics as a defense against the national scene, see the instructive discussion of the Heyl-Oriola affair in White, *Splintered Party*, pp. 179–84.

25. For local constituencies and national party politics in English liberalism, see John Vincent, *Formation of the Liberal Party*.

26. Stegmann, *Die Erben Bismarcks*, pp. 451, 455; Robert Ullrich, "Deutsche Vaterlandspartei," in Fricke, *Die bürgerlichen Parteien*, 1:620–28; Karl Wortmann, *Geschichte der Deutschen Vaterlandspartei*.

27. Herbert Schwab, "Nationalliberale Partei," in Fricke, *Die bürgerlichen Parteien*, 2:367–69; Stegmann, *Die Erben Bismarcks*, p. 455.

28. Ludwig Elm, "Fortschrittliche Volkspartei," in Fricke, *Die bürgerlichen Parteien*, 1:805.

29. Lother Wallraf, "Deutschkonservative Partei," in Fricke, *Die bürgerlichen Parteien*, 1:697–700; Dieter Fricke, "Reichs- und Freikonservative Partei," ibid., 2:576.

30. Wolfgang Mommsen discusses the "potential for modernization" of national liberalism before 1914 in "Der deutsche Liberalismus," p. 89.

31. On the failure of *bürgerlich* party unity in the early Republic, see Turner, *Stresemann and Politics,* pp. 3–26. On the DDP, see Werner Fritsch and Heinz Herz, "Deutsche Demokratische Partei," in Fricke, *Die bürgerlichen Parteien,* 1:307, and Reinhard Opitz, *Der deutsche Sozialliberalismus,* pp. 11–17. On the DVP, see Turner, *Stresemann and Politics,* pp. 27–113; for the DNVP, Wolfgang Ruge, "Deutschnationale Volkspartei," in Fricke, *Die bürgerlichen Parteien,* 1:716–23, and Hertzmann, *DNVP.*

32. Milatz, *Wähler und Wahlen,* pp. 114–50. For the broader contours of disunity among *bürgerlich* political parties, see Jones, "Dissolution of the Bourgeois Party System," "Crisis of White-Collar Interest Politics," "The Dying Middle," and "Sammlung oder Zersplitterung?"

33. Childers, "Inflation, Stabilization, and Political Realignment." For three examples of the dissolving links between the *bürgerlich* parties and their allied pressure groups, see Jones, "Crisis of White-Collar Interest Politics"; on the old *Mittelstand,* see Winkler, *Mittelstand, Demokratie, und Nationalsozialismus,* pp. 121–82; for agrarian organizations, Gessner, *Agrarverbände,* pp. 83–267.

34. Childers, "Inflation, Stabilization, and Political Realignment," pp. 423–26.

35. Jonas, *Die Volkskonservativen;* Gunter Opitz, *Der Christlich-Soziale Volksdienst;* Schumacher, *Mittelstandsfront und Republik.* See also Winkler, *Mittelstand, Demokratie, und Nationalsozialismus,* pp. 123–24, for the Economic party and one of its leaders, Johann Viktor Bredt, a Marburg professor.

36. Childers, *The Nazi Voter,* pp. 50–118.

37. Helmuth Croon, "Das Vordringen der politischen Parteien im Bereich der kommunalen Selbstverwaltung," in Croon, Hofmann, and von Unruh, *Kommunale Selbstverwaltung,* p. 54. For the limited Social Democratic challenge to bourgeois parties in two other cities in the Empire, see Hofmann, *Bielefelder Stadtverordneten,* pp. 114–15, and Ilse Fischer, *Industrialisierung, Sozialer Konflikt, und politische Willensbildung,* pp. 273–92, 331–42.

38. For muncipal elections in 1929 and 1933, see "Ergebnis der Gemeindewahlen 1933 in Preussen," *SJDS* 28 (1933): 550–62.

39. Ibid., p. 550.

40. All computations based on ibid., pp. 550–62.

41. Computations for 1929 based on ibid.; for special interest slates, see Wells, *German Cities,* p. 104.

42. *SJDS* 28 (1933): 550–62; for the special interest slates and the Marburg NSDAP, see chap. 6 below.

43. Sheehan, "Liberalism and the City," p. 119.

44. On Schüler's *Stammtisch* at the Seebode, see vom Brocke, "Marburg

im Kaiserreich," p. 415; on Drallia, Stammtisch Käsebrod, *Servus. Käsebrod* (Marburg, n.d.), p. 10.

45. Ibid., p. 13. Though Drallia of Weidenhausen was not the precursor of Käsebrod, the two *Stammtische* enjoyed a close relationship, and Käsebrod incorporated many of the conventions of the older Weidenhausen group. See ibid., p. 10.

46. On the *Stadtrat*, see vom Brocke, "Marburg im Kaiserreich," pp. 420–24. For sources on organizational affiliations, see chap. 4, n. 1.

47. This definition of liberalism is based generally on Wolfe, *Limits of Legitimacy*, p. 4.

48. For data and discussion on the Liberal Association, see vom Brocke, "Marburg im Kaiserreich," pp. 459–61.

49. On cultural custodianship, see Chickering, *We Men Who Feel Most German*, pp. 108–18.

50. Vom Brocke, "Marburg im Kaiserreich," pp. 412–28.

51. I take issue here with Hopwood's argument in "Paladins of the *Bürgertum*," pp. 222–24.

52. Vom Brocke, "Marburg im Kaiserreich," p. 452.

53. *OZ* 1 February 1911, as cited in vom Brocke, "Marburg im Kaiserreich," p. 452.

54. Marshall also stresses the importance of links between university and city for the political life of the community in "Einfluß der Universität," p. 265. Marshall lists three variables that influence a university's impact on city politics: city size, social structure, and level of university integration with the city.

55. See chaps. 3 and 4 below.

56. Hofmann concentrates on the politicizing effects of industrialization in a muncipal setting. See his comments in *Bielefelder Stadtverordneten*, p. 11. Crew finds that industrialization also generated increased involvement of workers in strikes and other forms of collective action, though he is careful to root this process in the specific circumstances of work structures, social organization, employers' interests, and state activity. See Crew, *Town in the Ruhr*, pp. 159–220. Consideration of Marburg counterbalances the majority of local studies of late nineteenth- and early twentieth-century Germany because it demonstrates the growing involvement of townspeople in political life in a community in which large-scale industry did not take hold.

57. On the SPD generally, see vom Brocke, "Marburg im Kaiserreich," pp. 481, 494–513; on the national debate over the agrarian issue within the socialist movement, Lehmann, *Agrarfrage*. In 1903 the officials of the Sozialdemokratischer Wahlverein in Marburg consisted of two printers, one coppersmith, one shoemaker, one carpenter, and one unskilled worker, while its forty-four members were made up of fifteen printers, seven carpenters, six shoemakers, three fitters, two plumbers, two stokers, two unskilled workers, one university instructor, one free professional,

one innkeeper, and four other dependent tradesmen. For the above data, see bylaws and membership list of the Wahlverein, 29 August 1903, and report of Marburg police on Social Democratic assembly, 4 September 1903, both in HSAM 180, LA Mbg, 2318. For academic Marburg and the Socialists, see H. G. Höfschen, "Universität und Arbeiterbewegung." On Michels, see Guttsman, *The German Social Democratic Party*, pp. 264–65.

58. On Böckel, see Dascher, "Der politische Antisemitismus"; Herbert Gottwold, "Antisemitische Parteien, 1879–1894," in Fricke, *Die bürgerlichen Parteien*, 1:36–40; Knauß, "Der politische Antisemitismus," pp. 43–68; Levy, *Downfall of Anti-Semitic Political Parties*; Mack, "Otto Böckel," pp. 113–47; Massing, *Rehearsal for Destruction*, pp. 87–89, 114; Pulzer, *Rise of Political Anti-Semitism*, pp. 107, 190; Schmahl and Seipel, *Entwicklung der völkischen Bewegung*; and Schön, *Nationalsozialismus in Hessen*, pp. 9–15. I was unable to consult Peal, "Anti-Semitism and Rural Transformation."

59. Percentage distribution of total votes for anti-Semitic parties in Marburg city and electoral district (with runoff elections in parentheses):

	City	District without Marburg
1887	42.1	57.9
1890	41.7	68.0
1893	35.4 (70.8)	51.0 (68.7)
1898	12.5 (26.5)	26.7 (57.2)
1903	13.8	17.1
1907	22.7 (31.0)	53.8 (60.5)
1912	7.6 (35.6)	35.0 (61.7)
	6.6	12.9

Source: vom Brocke, "Marburg im Kaiserreich," p. 488. The figures for 1907 and the first set of figures for 1912 represent the vote percentages of the German Social party; the second set of figures for 1912 represents the percentage of the German Reform party.

60. Levy, *Downfall of Anti-Semitic Political Parties*, pp. 43–66; von Gerlach, *Von Rechts nach Links*, p. 170.

61. Schmahl and Seipel, *Entwicklung der völkischen Bewegung*, pp. 22–70; for anti-Semitic youth groups, see 11th Gendarme district, Fronhausen, to Marburg LR, 24 October 1891; statutes of the Deutscher Jugendbund in Lang Göns, 12 April 1891, both in HSAM 180, LA Mbg, 760; and von Gerlach, *Von Rechts nach Links*, p. 170. For an argument that distinguishes late nineteenth-century German anti-Semitism from National Socialist racial policies, see Volkov, "Kontinuität und Diskontinuität."

62. Scheidemann, *Memoirs of a Social Democrat*, pp. 51, 57; police to LR, 26 May and 8 June 1893, both in HSAM 180, LA Mbg, 2318.

63. Vom Brocke argues that "undoubtedly the authorities contributed

most effectively to the decline of the Böckel movement" ("Marburg im Kaiserreich," p. 488). Conversely, Levy discusses the efforts of the "alert administration of Prussian Hesse" but writes that "the resistance to Böckel put up by the state administration was not very successful" (*Downfall of Anti-Semitic Political Parties*, p. 137). On cooperatives, see Raiffeisenverband Kurhessen, *75 Jahre*, pp. 63, 68; on the Marburg Verein zur Abwehr des Antisemitismus, see vom Brocke, "Marburg im Kaiserreich," p. 489; for all the rest, see Schmahl and Seipel, *Entwicklung der völkischen Bewegung*, pp. 99–102; Levy, *Downfall of Anti-Semitic Political Parties*, pp. 107–8, 145–65; and von Gerlach, *Von Rechts nach Links*, pp. 170–71.

64. Von Gerlach, *Von Rechts nach Links*, pp. 170–71; Levy, *Downfall of Anti-Semitic Political Parties*, pp. 43–66.

65. For the "aesthetics" of the new politics, see Mosse, *Nationalization of the Masses*. Von Gerlach wrote that his campaign experiences before 1903 convinced him that "one cannot simply take a rural electoral district as if by a hussar attack; instead one had to occupy it systematically." Von Gerlach's preparation for occupying the Marburg–Frankenberg–Kirchhain district reflected the respect he had developed for country people's self-interested approach to politics. See *Von Rechts nach Links*, p. 172. Of the measured and objective style that Böckel often used in northern Hesse, a follower of the peasant king said: "I never saw Böckel speak with anything but the utmost seriousness. All his speeches were well conceived and rigorous. Always serious and objective" (quoted from Schmahl and Seipel, *Entwicklung der völkischen Bewegung*, p. 23). One must discount the bias of a Böckel enthusiast and the tendency to glorify the peasantry in such quotes, but exaggeration always contains a significant kernel of truth. For Nazi agitators' similar views on the need for addressing country people in measured and rational terms, see chap. 5 below.

66. Böckel is quoted in Knauß, "Der politische Antisemitismus," p. 53; on worker and peasant, see Schmahl and Seipel, *Entwicklung der völkischen Bewegung*, p. 36; for Kirchel, ibid., p. 64. See also Demandt, "Leopold v. Sacher-Masoch."

67. For populism, see Laclau, *Politics and Ideology*, pp. 143–98. The precentage distribution for 144 individuals in the Marburg Reformverein in the 1880s was as follows: craft workers, 38.9; students, 23.6; civil servants, 11.8; craft masters, 8.3; salespeople and retailers, 8.3; workers, 4.9; and academics, 4.2. See Dascher, "Politische Antisemitismus," p. 95. Limited to a particular time, place, and organization, these data provide an incomplete view of Böckel's following. On Böckel's 1893 agitators, see police to RPK, 20 June 1893, in HSAM 180, LA Mbg, 2318.

68. Computations based on vom Brocke, "Marburg im Kaiserreich," pp. 478–79; on propaganda outside the city, see police to Cassel, 21 May 1893, in HSAM 180, LA Mbg, 2318; on the Bauernbund and Agrarian League, Levy, *Downfall of Anti-Semitic Political Parties*, p. 221.

69. *Die Hilfe* 4 (21 August 1898): 5, as cited in Düding, *Der National-*

soziale Verein, p. 95; for the rest, see Düding, *Der Nationalsoziale Verein*, p. 177; von Gerlach, *Von Rechts nach Links*, pp. 170–74; and vom Brocke, "Marburg im Kaiserreich," pp. 492–94.

70. Kürschner, *Geschichte der Stadt Marburg*, p. 278.

71. Despite the presence of nonsocialist workers and the lower middle classes in nationalist associations, available occupational data indicate that the Pan-German League remained isolated within the social circles of the upper middle classes. See Chickering, *We Men Who Feel Most German*, chap. 5. Eley discusses the relative marginality of the nationalist associations in the everyday lives of their members. See *Reshaping the German Right*, pp. 101–59. On Marburg student organizational life, including patriotic societies, see Jarausch, *Students, Society, and Politics*, pp. 294–332.

72. For an example of government alarm at the volatility of Reichstag politics in the district, see police to RPK, 21 May 1893, in HSAM 180, LA Mbg, 2318. For the response of local government agents to conflicts between political parties after the turn of the century, see for the SPD, police reports of assemblies of 21 January and 19 March 1903, both in HSAM 180, LA Mbg, 2318, and assembly of 19 May 1908, in HSAM 180, LA Mbg, 2365; for the National Socials, police reports of 22 January, 11, 24 May, 12 and 16 November 1908, all in HSAM 180, LA Mbg, 2365; and for the German Social Johann Heinrich Rupp, police report of 16 December 1910, in HSAM 180, LA Mbg, 2365. For the comparison with Tübingen, see Koshar, "Two 'Nazisms,'" p. 36; for Tübingen and Württemberg, see Blackbourn, *Class, Religion, and Local Politics*, and "Class and Politics," pp. 220–49; Hunt, *The People's Party in Württemberg*; Simon, *Die württembergischen Demokraten*; and Payer, *Autobiographische Aufzeichnungen*.

73. Vom Brocke, "Marburg im Kaiserreich," pp. 450–94.

74. Ibid.

75. Computations for the National Liberals, left liberals, and Center are based on data for *Wahlmänner* in ibid., p. 472. For Social Democrats and National Socials, see Michels, "Die Deutsche Sozialdemokratie," pp. 489, 501, 509, 510 (n. 61). Refer to the appendix for discussion of my occupational categories.

76. The percentage distribution of occupations was as follows: university professors, 26.1; merchants, 21.9; civil servants and administrators, 11.6; craft masters, 10.3; free professionals, 8.9; bankers and industrialists, 7.5; and miscellaneous, 13.7. "Marburg–Kirchhain–Frankenberg," National Liberal flyer, 1 January 1907, in HSAM 180, LA Mbg, 2365.

77. Ibid., and "Wahlkreis Marburg–Kirchhain–Frankenberg!," National Liberal flyer, 31 December 1906, HSAM 180, LA Mbg, 2365.

78. The 31 December 1906 handout cited in n. 77 was particularly explicit about the sectional groups to which Siebert appealed.

79. Vom Brocke, "Marburg im Kaiserreich," pp. 421, 453, 458–59. In contrast to the Marburg SPD, the Bielefeld SPD ran candidates in the third

class of voters in city elections for the first time in 1889. See Hofmann, *Bielefelder Stadtverordneten*, pp. 90–104.

80. See chaps. 3 and 4 below.

81. Wilhelm II's statement quoted in Pinson, *Modern Germany*, p. 334; for the resolution and statement by Rupp and the Deutsche Fraktion, see *OZ* 24 August 1917; on the composition and motivation of the Fraktion, see Fricke, "Reichs- und Freikonservative Partei," p. 576.

82. For angry criticism by Rupp's coalition partners, see *OZ* 27 August 1917.

83. *OZ* 26 September, 6 October, 19 December 1917, 9 March 1918.

84. For membership, see *OZ* 5 November 1917; for assemblies, "Übersicht über die in den Monaten Februar bis Juni 1918 veranstalteten und verbotenen Versammlungen," LR, in HSAM 180, LA Mbg, 897, Bd.2; for student membership, "Mitgliederverzeichnis der studentischen Gruppe der deutschen Vaterlandspartei," n.d., in HSAM 305a, Acc 1950/9, 203; and *OZ* 12 February 1918.

85. Wehler, *Das Deutsche Kaiserreich*, pp. 212–18; Stegmann, *Die Erben Bismarcks*, pp. 497–522.

86. DVLP advertisement, *OZ* 9 March 1918.

87. On the Student Lodge, see chap. 4, n. 42. On students' disagreement with *Altherren* over the DVLP, see the letter from Marburg Alemannen Ernst Troll to his Marburg fraternity, 11 December 1917, in which he states his reasons for not joining the DVLP. His reasons are not political, he argues, because he "is no politician"; instead, he resists the DVLP "out of purely formal considerations" and urges his brothers to join the Student Lodge. Troll also mentions disagreements over the issue that arose between actives and alumni at a Burschenschaft meeting in Magdeburg. See the letter in NA T-81, 232, 5015643–5015646. For Kopsch and the editorial, see *OZ* 4 December 1917; for a VFV assembly, *HLZ* 15 June 1918; for the moderate and leftist parties, advertisement in *OZ* 15 December 1917 and report on meeting in *OZ* 19 December 1917. On the VFV nationally, see Robert Ullrich, "Volksbund für Freiheit und Vaterland," in Fricke, *Die bürgerlichen Parteien*, 2:794–98. The comments from the Reich headquarters of the Center were reported in *OZ* 17 October 1917 along with the same organization's statement that some Center party members had nevertheless joined the DVLP.

88. Kürschner, *Geschichte der Stadt Marburg*, pp. 292–94.

89. Neusüß-Hunkel, *Parteien und Wahlen*, pp. 17–41.

90. For the Marburg DDP, see interview with former DDP member Perino, 10 March 1980; interviews with former DDP member and *HT* publisher Bauer, 1 April 1977 and 5 March 1980; and list of DDP *Wahlvorstände*, 9 May 1928, in HSAM 330, Mbg C, 2676. On Corell and the Athletic Association, see "Verein für Bewegungsspiele," entry of 15 October 1921, AKMVR, 45.

91. Neusüß-Hunkel, *Parteien und Wahlen*, pp. 32–41.

92. *OZ* 1, 3, 4, 5 June 1920.

93. For the Marburg Economic party, see Bredt, *Erinnerungen und Doku-mente*, pp. 159–66.
94. On the Bavarian VSB, see Stachura, *Gregor Straßer*, p. 32; for Marburg nazism in 1924, see chap. 5 below.
95. Neusüß-Hunkel, *Parteien und Wahlen*, pp. 35, 40. Neusüß-Hunkel argues that VSB success in May 1924 cannot be explained solely by the impact of hyperinflation.
96. For Marburg special interest slates, see "Ergebnisse," *SJDS* 28 (1933): 551–62; *OZ* 2 March 1919, 26 April 1924, 9 November 1929, 2 March 1933; and Neusüß-Hunkel, *Parteien und Wahlen*, pp. 42–45.
97. For the tendency of municipal politics to fall into patterns of alliances based on economic interest, see Bredt's discussion in *Erinnerungen und Dokumente*, pp. 158–61.
98. *OZ* 1 May 1924.
99. On the Civil Servants and the Working Alliance, see *OZ* 3 May 1924; on the United Businessmen, *OZ* 12 November 1929.
100. On attempts to keep the 1919 city elections unpolitical, see *OZ* 25 February 1919. For the Renters' Association, see *HT* 3 May 1924; for the occupations and party affiliations of municipal parliament candidates, *OZ* 25 and 28 February 1919, 26 April 1924, 9 November 1929, 2 March 1933.
101. Data for the occupations of Marburg party members were derived from the sources cited in the preceding note, from *Verein* listings in *MEB* cited in chap. 4, n. 1, and from lists of *Wahlvorstände*, 1925 and 1928, in HSAM 330, Mbg C, 2676–78.
102. Interview with Perino, 10 March 1980.
103. Letter from Lahn–Eder business manager of DVP to party general secretary, 6 March 1933, in BAK, 60 VO 1, Deutsche Volkspartei, film no. 11.
104. Kürschner, *Geschichte der Stadt Marburg*, pp. 293–94; Neusüß-Hunkel, *Parteien und Wahlen*, p. 36.
105. LR to RPK, 12 January 1928, on meeting of County Agricultural Association, in HSAM 180, LA Mbg, 3807. On Marburg county farmers' associations before 1933, see also *HT* 2 February 1928; report of meeting of Marburg Bauernverein assembly and march, 4 February 1928; list of demands from Bauernverein to LR, 3 February 1928, all in HSAM 180, LA Mbg, 3807; *OBZ* 30 March, 20 July 1929, 22 March 1930; protocols of general assemblies of the Bauernverein, 8 February 1921, 23 March 1929, 2 July 1932; protocol of the *Verein* officials, 20 March 1929, all in AKMVR, 61. For 1928 CNBLP support in the district, see Rosemarie Mann, "Entstehen und Entwicklung der NSDAP," p. 336; for the 1930 elections, LR to RPK, 4 October 1930, in HSAM 165, Kassel I, 3884.
106. On the 1919 Allgemeine Studentenausschuß election, see *WB* 48 (12 July 1919), col. 396; for other AStA elections and analysis, Seier, "Radikalisierung und Reform," p. 343; on the Hochschulring, Heer, *Marburger Studentenleben*, p. 184.
107. On the national background of the Becker conflict, see Steinberg,

Sabers and Brownshirts, pp. 65–71, and Zorn, "Student Politics in the Weimar Republic," p. 135. The drive to reorganize student government in the guise of a "private" Allgemeine Marburger Studentenschaft is outlined in a letter from the Marburg chancellor to the Ministry of Science, Culture, and Education, 5 April 1928, in HSAM 305a, Acc. 1950/9, 645. See also *OZ* 24 October 1927. On the distribution of power in the AMSt, see *MAMSt* 1 (1929). The predominance of dueling fraternity members among AMSt representatives led one NSDStB student to remark sarcastically that AMSt meetings resembled Hochschulring assemblies; see letter from Karl-Albert Coulon to Willi Tempel, 28 May 1927, in AUWAR, II/A, 10. For increased student interest in politics, see "Arbeitsbericht des Hochschulrings über WS 1929/30," *MHZ* 2 (3 May 1930): 12; for AMSt election totals, Mann, "Entstehen und Entwicklung der NSDAP," p. 286.

Chapter 3

1. Yeo, *Religion and Voluntary Organizations*, p. 7.
2. The term *Zeit der Vereine* comes from an 1845 statement by Hamburg mayor Kirchenpauer quoted in Freudenthal, *Vereine in Hamburg*, p. 181; see also Nipperdey, "Verein als soziale Struktur," p. 176.
3. Jarausch, *Students, Society, and Politics*, pp. 81–89, 239–62.
4. Kürschner, *Geschichte der Stadt Marburg*, pp. 258–60, 266–70.
5. Yeo, *Religion and Voluntary Organizations*, pp. 85–86, from which the furniture imagery is derived.
6. On Hamburg, see Freudenthal, *Vereine in Hamburg*, pp. 34–39. For a general treatment of Marburg *Vereinswesen* in the nineteenth century, see vom Brocke, "Marburg im Kaiserreich," pp. 523–28; more detail is available in Kürschner, *Geschichte der Stadt Marburg*, pp. 207–32, 252–58; on the word *Verein*, see Schmalz, "Geschichte des Wortes 'Verein.'"
7. On *Gesellschaften*, see Dann, "Anfänge politischer Vereinsbildung," pp. 200–201; on savings banks, see Kürschner, *Geschichte der Stadt Marburg*, p. 249.
8. Ibid., pp. 252–54.
9. Ibid.; for the Marburg Tugendbund, ibid., pp. 207–8; more generally on the Tugendbund, see Schmalz, "Geschichte des Wortes 'Verein,'" p. 300; for Bielefeld sociability, Hofmann, *Bielefelder Stadtverordneten*, pp. 30–31.
10. Dann, "Anfänge politischer Vereinsbildung," pp. 220–21; Schlummbohm, *Freiheit*, pp. 35–38; Nipperdey, "Verein als soziale Struktur," pp. 183–90.
11. Kürschner, *Geschichte der Stadt Marburg*, pp. 252–53. The early social *Vereine* were certainly more specialized than premodern corporate forms and conventions, but the former were also more inclusive than subsequent special interest organizations. For a comparison of *Korporation* and *Verein*, see Habermas, *Strukturwandel der Öffentlichkeit*, pp. 28–41,

82–83, and Nipperdey, "Verein als soziale Struktur," p. 174. For an argument stressing the weakness of voluntary associations in the political theory of early nineteenth-century German liberalism, see Iggers, "Political Theory of Voluntary Association," pp. 141–58.

12. See Köllmann, *Sozialgeschichte der Stadt Barmen*, p. 109.

13. On exclusivity in German *Vereine*, see Mosse, *Nationalization of the Masses*, p. 138, which features a discussion of early bourgeois male choirs. On the egalitarian potential of German *Vereinsleben*, see Freudenthal, *Vereine in Hamburg*, pp. 181, 465.

14. The importance of accessibility is discussed in Habermas, *Strukturwandel der Öffentlichkeit*, esp. pp. 42–60, 144–58. On *Vereine* and the state, see Nipperdey, "Verein als soziale Struktur," pp. 195–204, and Kosselleck, *Kritik und Krise*, pp. 11–39.

15. On secretiveness, see Kosselleck, *Kritik und Krise*, pp. 74–103, and Schmalz, "Geschichte des Wortes 'Verein,'" p. 300. For the Blackbourn quote, see Blackbourn and Eley, *Peculiarities of German History*, p. 226.

16. Freudenthal, *Vereine in Hamburg*, pp. 129, 181.

17. On "critical mass" and social organization, see Claude S. Fischer, *Urban Experience*. pp. 36–37.

18. Kürschner, *Geschichte der Stadt Marburg*, p. 216.

19. For brief remarks on voluntary organizations and the state, see Freudenthal, *Vereine in Hamburg*, p. 142.

20. The data are derived from organizations that survived into the period 1880–1935, but they suggest the actual curve of organization formation. For sources and further discussion on mapping the city's organizational fabric, see the appendix.

21. All data derived from Kurhessischer Kriegerbund, *Geschäftsbericht des Bundesvorstandes* (Kassel, 1904–1909/10), in HSAM 165, Kassel I, 4008.

22. For additional information on the rise of nonnotable occupational associations in Marburg, see vom Brocke, "Marburg im Kaiserreich," pp. 447–50; on Marburg trade unions at midcentury, Kürschner, *Geschichte der Stadt Marburg*, p. 223. Notables' hegemony in representing the economic interests of nonnotable groups eroded throughout the second half of the nineteenth century; it was one of the first areas of social life in which workers and the lower middle classes emancipated themselves from notables' rule. For comparison, see von Saldern, *Vom Einwohner zum Bürger*, p. 365.

23. *OZ* 29 July 1927 Jubiläumsausgabe; vom Brocke, "Marburg im Kaiserreich," pp. 447–50, 494–513; Scheidemann, *Memoirs of a Social Democrat*, pp. 17–74.

24. On the DHV, see Hamel, *Völkischer Verband und nationale Gewerkschaft*, pp. 62–67, 72; on peasants, beside the information in chap. 2 above, see Raiffeisenverband Kurhessen, *75 Jahre*, pp. 7–10, 63; Levy, *Downfall of Anti-Semitic Political Parties*, pp. 60–61.

25. "Verzeichnis der Marburger Vereine," *MEB* (1913), p. 44.

26. Ibid., pp. 43–44. For the Unterbeamtenverein, letter from F. A. Dern-hardt to Marburg LR, 30 October 1897, in HSAM 180, LA Mbg, 760. For Hannover, see Hansjoachim Henning, *Das westdeutsche Bürgertum*, pp. 131–32.

27. For the physicians' association, see bylaws and *Vorstand* members, 21 September 1912, AKMVR, 43; for parallels with medical doctors else-where, see Hansjoachim Henning, *Das westdeutsche Bürgertum*, pp. 440–41; on the fraternity alumni associations, see dated entries listing names, occupations, and residences of group officials in AKMVR, 6, 7, 11–17, 20, 22–23, 25, 27–28, 31–32, 36, 40, 78, 82, 88, 90, 92, 99, 104, 112, 124, 128.

28. Bylaws and board of officers, 31 May 1913, AKMVR, 44.

29. See chap. 4, n. 38. For the national polity, see Bridenthal, " 'Profes-sional' Housewives," pp. 154–55.

30. On the guilds, see *OZ* 29 July 1927 Jubiläumsausgabe. On retailers, see bylaws and board of officers, 8 October 1896, AKMVR, 2; interview with Bauer, 1 April 1977; and, for a discussion of regional and local retail-ers' associations, Gellately, *Politics of Economic Despair*, pp. 58–111. For homeowners, see bylaws and board of officers, 28 April 1922, AKMVR, 79; telephone conversation with former Property Owners' and Landlords' As-sociation member Heinrich Seibel, 25 March 1977; and *Jahresberichte des Marburger Grund- und Hausbesitzer-Vereins* (1914–20), in HSAM 330, Mbg C, 4182.

31. On unions, see vom Brocke, "Marburg im Kaiserreich," pp. 503–13; on retailers, *HT* 7 July 1928.

32. For a contrast regarding economic class differentiation in Wilhel-mine Marburg, see Crew, *Town in the Ruhr*, pp. 103–57.

33. Huerkamp, "Ärtze und Professionalisierung in Deutschland."

34. Nolan, *Social Democracy and Society*, p. 135; Bausinger, "Verbürger-lichung," pp. 24–49.

35. For the Wenck example—and a very different conclusion from the one reached here—see vom Brocke, "Marburg im Kaiserreich," p. 527. For a short discussion of social organizations unable to muffle party conflict, see the example of Lindheim in Demandt, "Leopold v. Sacher-Masoch," pp. 182–83.

36. On the Marburg Museum, see "Offener Brief an die p.t. Studenten-schaft zu Marburg," from Friedrich Siebert, vice-mayor, ca. 1905, in HSAM 330, Mbg C, 2919; Kürschner, *Geschichte der Stadt Marburg*, p. 252; and vom Brocke, "Marburg im Kaiserreich," pp. 525–28. On Freiburg, see Museumsgesellschaft to club members, 21 April 1909, in BGLA 60, 1735. The letter speaks of the "serious situation" and "regression" of the organi-zation. For Tübingen, see Jeggle, "Geld und Geltung," and Kretschmer, "150 Jahre Tübinger Museumsgesellschaft."

37. The gradual alienation of bourgeois dignitaries from clubs in Read-ing, England, a process connected to growing state control and the loss of "localness" as well as to economic factors, is discussed in Yeo, *Religion and Voluntary Organizations*, pp. 105–8, 229–30. Peter Steinbach argues

that Detmold notables became more isolated from organizational life as social differentiation increased in that town. But Detmold also had a larger working-class population than Marburg and, perhaps more importantly, lacked a central institutional force to counterbalance social differentiation like that provided by the university in Marburg. In any case, much more comparative research is required on such aspects of German urban life after the 1880s. We need not accept an argument stressing a simple linear process of increased elite isolation and the "dissolution" of a "public sphere" in towns and regions. See Steinbach, *Industrialisierung und Sozialsystem*, p. 250. Vom Brocke makes an argument similar to that of Steinbach in "Marburg im Kaiserreich," pp. 523–28.

38. See table 4-1.

39. Board of officers and bylaws, 12 November 1904, AKMVR, 19.

40. Board of officers and bylaws of Marburg VF, 26 February 1902; membership numbers (July 1902); and "Dem Vaterländischen Frauen-Verein beigetretene Damen (in Marburg) 1902," all in AKMVR, 10.

41. On the notion of women's *Vereinsfähigkeit*, see Freudenthal, *Vereine in Hamburg*, p. 180. Freudenthal uses the term to describe a process in which women not only formed their own voluntary associations but also participated in organizations that had been the preserve of men. For women's rights in the Imperial era, see Evans, *Feminist Movement*, pp. 9–24.

42. "Dem Vaterländischen Frauen-Verein beigetretene Damen," AKMVR, 10.

43. This estimate does not take into account the fact that many political and occupational associations were also important to the daily sociability of their members. For the number, type, and density of voluntary organizations in 1913, see the appendix.

44. A classic study is Hausknecht, *The Joiners*; more recently for Germany, see Dunckelmann, *Lokale Öffentlichkeit*.

45. See table 5-1.

46. "Verzeichnis der Marburger Vereine," MEB (1913), pp. 43–47, lists about two-thirds of the voluntary groups in the city.

47. Kurhessischer Kriegerbund, *Geschäftsbericht* (1909/10), p. 13.

48. Ibid.

49. Ibid. (1905), p. 11.

50. Computations based on ibid. (1909/10), pp. 72–73.

51. Quoted from Preußischer Landes-Kriegerverband, *Geschäftsbericht* (Berlin, 1907), p. 5, in HSAM 165, 4008.

52. Schützenverein Marburg, *Festschrift zum 50jährigen Bestehen*, pp. 1–18, 25–27, in HSAM 330, Mbg C, 4179.

53. Ibid., pp. 17–18; computations based on ibid., pp. 18–22. For the age qualifications of the Turnverein, see bylaws, Marburger Turnverein 1860, 1894, in HSAM 180, LA Mbg, 760.

54. Schützenverein Marburg, *Festschrift zum 50jährigen Bestehen*, pp. 22–39.

55. The quotes are from ibid., pp. 40–42. I found evidence for the party

affiliations of twenty-eight Sharpshooting Club members in the Republic. Thirty-nine affiliations were distributed in the following manner: special interest slates, fifteen; NSDAP, fourteen; DNVP, three; DDP, three; DVP, three; and Economic party, one. The membership list, dating from ca. 1930, is in HSAM 165, Kassel I, 1061. For sources and methodology on organizational affiliations, see chaps. 4 and 6 and the appendix.

56. For other Marburg sharpshooting clubs, see bylaws and board of officers of Schützenklub 1924, 14 September 1924, AKMVR, 83; bylaws, board of officers, 26 April 1925, Schützengesellschaft Marburg 1897, AKMVR, 91.

57. Schützenverein Marburg, *Festschrift zum 50jährigen Bestehen*, p. 38. The exclusive St. Georgius-Schützen-Verein of Bocholt required an entrance fee of fifteen marks and an annual fee of six marks in 1877. In contrast, the entrance fee of the Schützen-Corps Legden was a half mark and the annual dues only one mark in 1879–85. See Hansjoachim Henning, *Das westdeutsche Bürgertum*, p. 444 (n. 74).

58. Computations based on Schützenverein Marburg, *Festschrift zum 50jährigen Bestehen*, pp. 43–46.

59. Ibid.; for the other Marburg clubs, see n. 56, this chapter.

60. Local retailers continued to be attracted to the Marburg Schützenverein after 1918. Ca. 1930 twenty-three out of forty-four club members for whom I could identify occupations were self-employed storekeepers. See membership list, n.d., in HSAM 165, Kassel I, 1061.

61. Schützenverein Marburg, *Festschrift zum 50jährigen Bestehen*, p. 47.

62. On Marburg Turnvereine, see Kürschner, *Geschichte der Stadt Marburg*, pp. 218, 222–23; for membership lists, correspondence, and bylaws, see HSAM 180, LA Marburg, 760; VfL, *Festschrift*; entries listing boards of officers and bylaws of gymnastics and sports groups in AKMVR 12, 45, 60, 69, 84, 99, 110, 115, 123, 141; and OZ 2 August 1930. On gymnastics clubs nationally, see Eberhard Jeran, "Deutsche Turnerschaft," in Fricke, *Die bürgerlichen Parteien*, 1:605–19.

63. On Schneider, see vom Brocke, "Marburg im Kaiserreich," p. 498; for 1860, OB to Kurfürst. Polizei-Direktion, 10 August 1860, in HSAM 180, LA Mbg, 175.

64. VfL, *Festschrift*, p. 8. The VfL was a consolidation of Marburg sports clubs including not only the Turnverein 1860 (which became the Turn- und Sportverein 1860 in 1920) but the VfB as well.

65. Ibid. Marburg was unexceptional in this regard, as the evidence cited in Steinbach, *Industrialisierung und Sozialsystem*, p. 248, suggests. But Steinbach goes too far. He argues that Lippe *Vereine* "devoted themselves fully to the pursuit of sociability," a process that was nevertheless "superficial" in light of the "participation [of *Vereine*] in nationalist festivals, the incorporation of patriotic songs, and the military drills of gymnastics clubs and volunteer fire departments. . . ." By developing this strict distinction between "sociability" and "politics"—which is viewed in strictly

national terms—Steinbach excludes a broad range of public functions performed by social clubs that enabled them to continue to shape general interests at the local level. It is participation in political life that looks "superficial" if we allow our view to encompass only patriotic songs, festivals, and the like.

66. Bylaws, 1863, in HSAM 180, LA Mbg, 175; bylaws, 1893, in HSAM 180, LA Mbg, 760.

67. For Marburg sports clubs in 1913–14, see "Verzeichnis der Marburger Vereine," MEB (1913), p. 44; on the founding of one of the new specialized sports clubs, the Marburger Fußball-Club 1905, see the description in the entry of 22 January 1934, VfB, AKMVR, 45; on other new clubs, see VfL, *Festschrift*, pp. 11–15, 20–25; for the quote on the Turnverein, OZ 2 August 1930. One caveat: the appearance of specialized sports clubs was not part of a linear process leading toward greater specialization of local organizational life. Some specialized clubs imitated the Turnverein by adding more varied activities to their club agendas as they grew. For instance, the Fußball-Club 1905 changed its name in 1908 to the Verein für Bewegungsspiele 05 "because other kinds of athletic activity had been incorporated in its sports program in the preceding years." In 1924 the latter organization allied with the Sportverein Kurhessen. Finally, in 1933 this club was forcibly merged with the Turn- und Sportverein 1860 by the Nazis. The entire process of amalgamation, however, had originated in the initial segmentation of organizational life decades before. For the examples, see VfL, *Festschrift*, pp. 14–15, and AKMVR, 45, as cited above.

68. Jeran, "Turnerschaft," pp. 612–16; Mosse, *Nationalization of the Masses*, pp. 127–36.

69. Quoted in Jeran, "Turnerschaft," p. 607.

70. For the Turnverein, see list of boards of directors, 2 April and 15 September 1894, 28 October 1897, 25 September 1903, 25 October 1906, all in HSAM 180, LA Mbg, 760.

71. Before 1918 VfB membership included six elites (one dentist, one building contractor, one high-ranking city official, one medical doctor, one factory owner, and one university-educated archivist), two self-employed *Mittelständler* (one storekeeper and one craft master, a roofer), and two employed *Mittelständler* (one city employee and one salesclerk). See AKMVR, 45, entries of 28 June 1913, 28 March 1919, 15 October 1921; VfL, *Festschrift*, pp. 12–16; and interview with Friedrich Bluhm, former VfB member, 30 March 1977, Marburg.

72. VfL, *Festschrift*, pp. 7–11. DT leaders seem not to have considered the possibility that membership in any other group, not just other gymnastics associations, might "contaminate" DT members.

73. See Freudenthal, *Vereine in Hamburg*, p. 181.

74. Turnverein Marburg, *Lieder für die Feier des 50. Stiftungsfestes*, p. 5.

75. For a compatible argument, see Bausinger, "Eher im Gegenteil."

76. The best discussion to date on student organizational life in the Second Empire is Jarausch, *Students, Society, and Politics*, pp. 234–332.

77. Ehlers and Leib, "Marburg—Stadt und Universität," p. 109.

78. Data for student organizations are based on the appropriate folders in HSAM 305a, Acc 1954/16, 1–78. To compute organization formation per thousand students in each decade, I took student enrollment at or near the end of each decade as the base population. The number of student organizations formed by decade up to 1919 was as follows: 1870–79, six; 1880–89, eleven; 1890–99, four; 1900–1909, three; and 1910–19, three. The numbers are small and should be used only to establish an overall impression of the curve of organization formation.

79. For the history of Marburg student organizations, see Heer, *Marburger Studentenleben*, and *Marburger Burschenschaft Arminia*; and Jarausch, *Students, Society, and Politics*, pp. 262–332, which cites a voluminous literature. The standard source for the history of German student associations before World War I is Schulze and Ssymank, *Das Deutsche Studententum*. My estimate for the number of Marburg students in organizations includes inactive fraternity students, a reasonable procedure if we are to focus on social networks that go beyond formal organizational boundaries. Inactive fraternity students were hardly isolated from the smaller groups of actives, and social interchange continued between alumni, inactives, and actives. Focusing only on actives underestimates the extent to which fraternity social life exerted influence throughout the student body and the *Bürgertum*, though for analytical purposes I make the distinction elsewhere in this study. The figure for organized students does not include an estimate of membership in the Freistudentenschaft, for which no formal membership rosters exist, but the figure does include groups like the Akademische Freischar, which was inspired by the Freistudentenschaft.

80. Heer, *Marburger Studentenleben*, p. 163. I divide student organizations into four categories: pure fraternities (dueled and wore colors; includes mainly Corps, Burschenschaften, Turnerschaften, and Landsmannschaften but also some miscellaneous associations), modified fraternities (dueled but did not wear colors, or forbade dueling but wore colors; includes Catholic fraternities), political groups (party and nationalist organizations at the university), and others (a miscellaneous group of sports clubs, religious associations, and women's groups).

81. The eleven organizations were Teutonia, Arminia, Philippina, Normannia, Hasso-Guestphalia, Hasso-Borussia, Schaumburgia, Germania, Alemannia, Hasso-Nassovia, Guestphalia. The percentage of active dueling fraternity students in the total organized student population in Marburg declined from 40.7 in 1873 to 28.3 in 1893 and 18.1 in 1913, according to Jarausch, *Students, Society, and Politics*, p. 296. For Second Empire comparisons of the degree of corporatism at Marburg, Bonn, and Berlin, see ibid.

82. Heer, *Marburger Studentenleben*, pp. 163–64, 207; on Stengel and the philology Verein, see NA T-81, 256, 5047419, 5047428, and Heer, *Marburger Studentenleben*, p. 206

83. In 1913 the modified fraternities included Nibelungia, Marburger Wingolf, Chattia, Akademischer Turnverein Kurhessen, Fridericiania, Thuringia, Akademischer Turnverein, Franconia, Rheinfranken, Palatia, Unitas, Rhenania, Verein Deutscher Studenten, Tuiskonia. There were 581 active and inactive members of these clubs in 1913. For the individual examples, see Heer, *Marburger Studentenleben*, pp. 205–10; additionally, on Marburger Wingolf, see Jarausch, *Students, Politics, and Society*, p. 317. I refer to the latter association throughout this study as Marburger Wingolf to distinguish it from Clausthaler Wingolf, which appeared in Marburg in 1929.

84. On the fraternity "structure of protection and connection," see Kreutzberger, *Studenten und Politik*, p. 82. On Marburg alumni associations, see n. 27, this chapter; for alumni money gifts, see Heer, *Marburger Studentenleben*, p. 167; for a concrete example of the way fraternity networks operated, see the letter of the former Marburg Alemannen M. Stauch, a physician, who arranged to have his brother accepted as a pledge by the Marburg corporation, 19 December 1916, NA T-81, 232, 5015525–5015528; for the classic discussion of the fraternities and the broader social nexus in which they were embedded, see Weber, "National Character and the Junkers," pp. 387–88.

85. Officers of Verband alter Marburger Teutonen, 16 May 1901, AKMVR, 6.

86. Jarausch, *Students, Society, and Politics*, p. 298.

87. For a fictionalized depiction of dueling in Marburg, see Bloem, *Der krasse Fuchs*, p. 20 ff., as cited in Böth, "Talare, Wichs, und Jeans," pp. 38–39. My thanks to Konrad Vanja for sending me this booklet.

88. For Weber's criticism of the pretensions of the dueling fraternities in representing general interests, see his "National Character and the Junkers," pp. 387–89. See also Kreutzberger, *Studenten und Politik*, pp. 81–83, and Jarausch, *Students, Society, and Politics*, pp. 239–62. Some organizations, such as the more exclusive Corps, insisted that they did not want to influence members "with regard to the highest questions of existence, which are expressed in religion, politics, and a worldview." See Neuhaus, *Die Konstitutionen des Corps Teutonia*, p. 88. For insights into the concerns of pure fraternity members in the Second Empire, see the Alemannia minutes in the *Kopierbuch*, NA T-81, 256, 5046353–5046382.

89. On the history of the duel from Empire to Republic, see Kreutzberger, *Studenten und Politik*, pp. 88–91.

90. Jarausch, *Students, Society, and Politics*, pp. 294–332.

91. On intellectual inbreeding, see Weber, "National Character and the Junkers," p. 388; on authority, see Kreutzberger, *Studenten und Politik*, p. 82.

92. On Teutonia, see Heer, *Marburger Studentenleben*, p. 167; on fraternity isolation, see Friedrich Siebert, "Offener Brief an die p.t. Studentenschaft zu Marburg," ca. 1905, in HSAM 330, Mbg C, 2919. For comparative evidence, see n. 36, this chapter.

93. Heer, *Marburger Studentenleben*, p. 168.

94. Wilhelm Fischdick, "Der Marburger Studenten-Ausschuß," *WB* 45 (16 March 1916), cols. 332–35, in HSAM 305a, Acc 1950/9, 224.

95. Information sheet of Deutsche Freistudentenschaft, November 1907, and resolution of Marburg Freistudentenschaft to the chancellor concerning student government, 12 May 1906, both in HSAM 305a, Acc. 1950/9, 225; proposal to establish general student government by Marburg Freistudentenschaft, 9 July 1913, in HSAM 310, Acc. 1975/42, 2190; Heer, *Marburger Studentenleben*, pp. 172–75.

96. On the Külz affair, see vom Brocke, "Marburg im Kaiserreich," p. 528, and Heer, *Marburger Studentenleben*, pp. 168–69; Schulze and Ssymank, *Das Deutsche Studententum*, pp. 357–58.

97. Heer, *Marburger Studentenleben*, p. 168.

98. Fischdick, "Der Marburger Studenten-Ausschuß"; for organizations in the Marburg Korporationsausschuß, see NA T-81, 256, 5046980.

99. Memorandum of Marburg AStA, 11 July 1923, in HSAM 305a, Acc. 1950/9, 635.

100. Jarausch, *Students, Society, and Politics*, pp. 64–69.

101. On the description of Marburg anti-Semitism by former student Isaak Rulf, see vom Brocke, "Marburg im Kaiserreich," pp. 476 (n. 234), 485 (n. 258). On Corps Teutonia, see Neuhaus, *Die Konstitutionen des Corps Teutonia*, pp. 48–60. On the Verein Deutscher Studenten, formed in June 1886, see Heer, *Marburger Studentenleben*, p. 65. But Heer argues that the Marburg VDSt "could hardly exert an impact outside the circle of its own members, as occurred at other larger universities." The activity of a number of Marburg VDSt students in the Böckel movement suggests that this assessment is wide of the mark. See Levy, *Downfall of Anti-Semitic Political Parties*, pp. 58–59, 277 (n. 50). For VDSt students in the Marburg NSDStB, see the appendix. Finally, on the conflicts between Jewish organizations and the fraternities in Marburg, see Heer, *Marburger Studentenleben*, pp. 172–73.

102. For the quantitative dimension of student involvement in nationalist associations, see Jarausch, *Students, Society, and Politics*, table 5-1, pp. 296–97; on the nationalist celebration, see *OZ* 12 December 1906, as quoted in H.G. Höfschen, "Universität und Arbeiterbewegung," pp. 103–4.

103. Jarausch, *Students, Society, and Politics*, p. 386. A "modern student politics" did evolve in Marburg, as Jarausch argues, but it was allergic to direct party activity and remained a minority phenomenon.

104. Vom Brocke, "Marburg im Kaiserreich," p. 529.

105. Fischdick, "Der Marburger Studenten-Ausschuß," col. 333.

106. Ringer, *Decline of the German Mandarins*, pp. 14–80; Jarausch, *Students, Society, and Politics*, pp. 23–77, 160–233; on Marburg, see Seier, "Wahl und Amt des Rektors," pp. 757–79; more generally on professors, see vom Brocke, "Marburg im Kaiserreich," pp. 518–21.

107. Bestimmung der Deputation, 7 June 1913, in HSAM 305a, Acc. 1950/9, 224; Troeltsch to OB, 13 June 1913, in HSAM 330, Mbg C, 2818.

108. Von Sybel to Deputation, 20 March 1907, in HSAM 305a, Acc. 1950/9, 225.

Chapter 4

1. Only individuals who were members of boards of directors (*Vorstände*) of social organizations appear in this list. Political party affiliations are mentioned in the text to convey the breadth of joiners' organizational involvement, but party ties are not counted in table 4-1. The sources are as follows: boards of officers, AKMVR, 1–112, 117–22, 124–40, 142–44; "Verzeichnis der Marburger Vereine," *MEB* (1913), pp. 43–47; "Marburger Vereine," *MEB* (1920), pp. 35–38; "Marburger Vereine," *MEB* (1925), pp. 30–39; "Marburger Vereine," *MEB* (1930), pp. 81–94; "Marburger Vereine," *MEB* (1934–35), pp. 91–106; additionally, see sources cited in reference to individuals' affiliations. Working-class club officials are underrepresented in the Imperial era because city address books were less detailed in listing trade union local branches and leading club officers in this period than they were during the Republic and Third Reich. However, considering that Marburg had a below-average working-class population and that many laborers lived outside the city limits, the data do not seriously underestimate working-class involvement in organizational leadership.

2. This statement is based on an analysis of the occupations of 231 members and 45 officials of two sharpshooting clubs, two cultural *Vereine*, one sports club, one alumni association of a sports club, one fraternity alumni association, and one veterans' society. Whereas only 15.2 percent of all club members came from the city's elite, 51.1 percent of the club officers did.

3. For useful biographies of Marburg professors, see Schnack, *Marburger Gelehrte*.

4. Vom Brocke, "Marburg im Kaiserreich," pp. 518–21; Seier, "Radikalisierung und Reform." Vom Brocke emphasizes that Marburg professors were still more active politically than were their counterparts in Straßburg, Freiburg, or Berlin.

5. On Corell, see VfB, 15 October 1921, AKMVR, 45, and "Für Demokraten," *OZ* 28 February 1919. For Bork, see "Liste Rohde," *OZ* 25 February 1919; Verein alter Marburger Allemannen, 5 November 1911, AKMVR, 36; and *MEB* (1934–35), p. 93. For Ritter, see Verband der Marburger Wingolfsphilister, 21 February 1931, AKMVR, 11, and *WB* 60 (15 October 1931), col. 469. On Plannet, see Philippshaus zu Marburg, 25 February 1920, AKMVR, 19; "Herberge zur Heimat," 2 June 1924, AKMVR, 35; and "St. Jakob" Hilfsverein, 21 February 1919, AKMVR, 50.

6. Yeo, *Religion and Voluntary Organizations*, p. 85.

7. See the appendix.

8. Interviews with Hermann Bauer, 1 April 1977 and 5 March 1980.

9. Meinhold, "Schaefer," p. 327. See also *OZ* 23 February 1918.

10. Ibid., pp. 328–29. On the Retailers' Association, see entry of 8 October 1896, AKMVR, 2.

11. Hansjoachim Henning, *Sozialgeschichtliche Entwicklungen in Deutschland*, pp. 132–33, mentions public involvement of early manufacturers but stresses self-interest rather than ideology.

12. Meinhold, "Schaefer," p. 329.

13. Crew, *Town in the Ruhr*, p. 110.

14. Meinhold, "Schaefer," p. 329.

15. Hessischer Verein für Luftschiffahrt, entries of 15 June 1911 and 7 December 1928, AKMVR, 34; Marburger Ruder-Verein 1911, entry of 5 March 1921, AKMVR, 54; VfL, *Festschrift*, p. 17; "Liste Rohde," *OZ* 25 February 1919; *MEB* (1934–35), p. 98; membership list of the Krieger- und Landwehrverein, September 1922, in HSAM 330, Mbg C, 4179; Meinhold, "Schaefer," pp. 329–40.

16. For the economic situation of the local *Bürgertum*, see chap. 1.

17. On Kuhn, see Zitherkranz, entries of 2 October 1911 and 17 January 1912, AKMVR, 38; Turngemeinde 1885, entry of 19 February 1921, AKMVR, 69; *MEB* (1925), p. 39; and list of municipal parliament candidates, *OZ* 9 November 1929. For Schimpff, see *MEB* (1930), pp. 87, 92; Krieger- und Landwehrverein membership list, September, 1922, in HSAM 330, Mbg C, 4179; and *OZ* 26 April 1924.

18. For a sociological analysis of economic standing and voluntary organization membership, see Hausknecht, *The Joiners*, pp. 15–30.

19. For unregistered retailers, see *HT* 7 July 1928; for Krapf, *MEB* (1913), p. 44, and Schützengesellschaft Marburg, entry of 26 April 1925, AKMVR, 91.

20. On small-scale Marburg retailers, see *OZ* 6 September 1921.

21. For officials and employees in the work force, see table 1-2; for these groups in the NSDAP, see table 6-7.

22. On Fülling, see Kavallerie-Verein, entry of 15 July 1925, AKMVR, 89, and Gesellschaftsverein "Hessen," entry of 10 January 1927, AKMVR, 85. On Merle, see *MEB* (1930), pp. 81, 92, and *OZ* 9 November 1929.

23. On Wißner, see interview with Bauer, 1 April 1977; VfL, *Festschrift*, p. 17; *MEB* (1925), p. 36; and Marburg NSDAP membership list (with membership numbers), n.d., in HSAM 327/1, 5488. For Gils, see Fortbildungsverein, entries of 22 July 1911 and 29 May 1918, AKMVR, 37, and list of State party *Wahlvorstände*, 1930, in HSAM 330, Mbg C, 2676.

24. For Fischer, see Elisabeth-Verein, entries of 27 March 1919 and 3 September 1930, AKMVR, 55, and *MEB* (1913), p. 44.

25. For the early history of the Marburg Social Democratic party, see chap. 3. For Weber, see *MEB* (1930), p. 85, and *OZ* 3 March 1919, 26 April 1924, 9 November 1929. On Emmerich, see Turngemeinde 1885, entry of 10 May 1927; *MEB* (1930), p. 85; and *MEB* (1934–35), p. 102.

26. For Corell, see Verein der ehemaligen Schülerinnen und der Freunde der Elisabeth-Schule, entry of 6 June 1929, AKMVR, 118; for Joseph, "Aus

der 60-jährigen Tätigkeit des Marburger Hausfrauenverbandes e.V.," p. 1 (my thanks to the Marburg Hausfrauenverband for providing me with this information); and "Liste Rohde," *OZ* 25 February 1919; for Hast, *MEB* (1930), p. 83; Hausfrauenverband, entry of 17 September 1930, AKMVR, 125; and *OZ* 26 April 1924, 9 November 1929.

27. For sources on organization formation, see the appendix. For the journalistic response, see n. 47, this chapter.

28. See the appendix for details.

29. For an attempt to estimate the percentage distribution of voluntary organizations in Marburg, see the appendix. For the alumni clubs, see chap. 3, n. 27; for the University Association, see entry of 5 December 1920, AKMVR, 63.

30. An example of the amalgamation of clubs in Marburg is provided by sports associations. The Marburger Fußball-Club 1905 changed its name to VfB 05 in 1908, having incorporated sports other than soccer in the preceding years. In 1924 the VfB merged with the Sportverein Kurhessen to become VfB 05 Kurhessen. In the Third Reich the VfB and Turngemeinde 1885 were merged with the Turn- und Sportverein 1860. But these processes occurred later and more unevenly in Marburg than in larger or more industrialized cities. For comparisons with industrial Reading, see Yeo, *Religion and Voluntary Organizations*, pp. 200–201. For more general discussion of the question of amalgamation, see Bausinger, *Volkskultur in der technischen Welt*, p. 65.

31. For Marburg trade union membership, see *OZ* 29 July 1927 Jubiläumsausgabe. For national comparisons, see Guttsman, *German Social Democratic Party*, pp. 152–53.

32. *HT* 1 February 1929. On working-class sociability and politics, see James Wickham, "Working-Class Movement and Working-Class Life."

33. For the Property Owners' and Landlords' Association, see *Jahresberichte des Marburger Grund- und Hausbesitzer-Vereins*, 6 (1930): 6–7; on the political activity of the association in Marburg after World War I, refer to Bredt, *Erinnerungen und Dokumente*, pp. 158–66. For the hiking club, see *Mitteilungsblatt des Oberhessischen Gebirgsverein*, 1 January, 1 April, 1 October 1932, 1 January 1933. For the veterans, see *OZ* 29 July 1927 Jubiläumsausgabe; for the housewives, see "Aus der 60-jährigen Tätigkeit des Marburger Hausfrauenverbandes," p. 1; for the Volunteer Medical Corps, see *Jahresbericht des Preussischen Landesvereine vom Roten Kreuz. Freiwillige Sanitätskolonne* (1927, 1932); for the Fishing Club, see *OZ* 29 September 1932.

34. These estimates do not include the Freistudentenschaft, but they do include organizations like the Sportvereinigung Marburger Freistudenten, which regularly submitted membership lists to university authorities. I have included inactive fraternity students for reasons discussed in chap. 3, n. 46. If we compare Marburg to Freiburg for winter 1930/31 and eliminate nonactive fraternity members, Marburg students appear less organized: there were 393.8 organized students per thousand enrolled students in the

Hessian university town and 431.2 in Freiburg. However, the percentage of active pure fraternity students in the total student population in 1930/31 was higher in Marburg (18.2) than in Freiburg (15.5). As I have argued in chap. 3, the total membership of the pure fraternities was not as important as their social and political influence in student life—which was considerable. For Kreutzberger's figures on enrollments and student membership in organizations, see his *Studenten und Politik*, pp. 57, 76. Using these figures, the percentage of organized students in the total student population (43.1) in Freiburg is different from that given by Kreutzberger on p. 76, table 6 (42.6). My calculation of the percentage of pure fraternity members in the total student population also differs from that of Kreutzberger (15.3).

35. Marburg Hauptausschuß zur Fürsorge für Kriegsbeschädigte to local *Vereine*, 26 April 1915, in HSAM 330, Mbg C, 2905.

36. On Marburg women's organizations, see *OZ* 29 July 1927, Jubiläumsausgabe, ánd *OZ* 18 January 1917. On the agricultural association, see protocol of the city War Credit Commission, I, 28 February 1917, in HSAM 330, Mbg C, 1378; for bakers, ibid., 27 July 1917; on the building trades, letter of the Kreisarbeitsgemeinschaft für das Baugewerbe to LR, 24 February 1915, in HSAM 180, LA Mbg, 892; on fraternity houses, Heer, *Marburger Studentenleben*, p. 177; on Marburgers selected for enlightening townspeople, LR to District Army Command, Kassel, September 1918, in HSAM 180, LA Mbg, 898.

37. For the Akademischer Hilfsbund, see pamphlet of February 1916, in "Die Universität Marburg im Weltkrieg," UBM collection; and, for the national Bund, Jarausch, "German Students in the First World War," p. 321. For the Vereiningung der Kriegsbeschädigte, see *HLZ* 3 June 1918.

38. For Stumpf, see Protokoll des Kriegswirtschaftlichen Ausschuß, 24 July 1917, in HSAM 330, Mbg C, Bd. III, 1380. For women, see "Aus der 60-jährigen Tätigkeit des Marburger Hausfrauenverbandes." Part of a national development, the Hausfrauenverband initially concerned itself mainly with problems of securing and regulating household help, though its activities widened after the war. For nationwide organization of housewives in the war and Republic, see Bridenthal, " 'Professional Housewives,' " and "Class Struggle around the Hearth."

39. *Ministerialblatt der Handels- und Gewerbeverwaltung* (August 1914); Magistrat to Kassel Handwerkskammer, 29 September 1914; Magistrat to RPK, Kassel, 14 November 1914; all in HSAM 330, Mbg C, 1017.

40. Freudenthal, *Vereine in Hamburg*, p. 328.

41. Postcard dated 28 February 1917 (signature illegible) to Marburg Alemannia, NA T-81, 232, 5015568; E. T. to Marburg Alemannia, 21 November 1917, ibid., 5015637–5015640; letter from Leonhard to "all student associations" in Marburg, 17 February 1917, ibid., 5015540; letter from the student S. to Alemannia, 23 January 1918, ibid., 5015566–5015567. Here we confront another Marburg peculiarity. Jarausch argues

that during the war "only in the oldest corporation strongholds such as Marburg and Göttingen did [student] associations display their colors" ("German Students in the First World War," p. 323).

42. Unidentified newspaper article, ca. summer 1917; letter from H. S. to Alemannia, 8 June 1917; postcard from H. S. (a different student from the sender of the previous letter) to Alemannia, 19 November 1917; all in NA T-81, 232, 5015616–5015663.

43. Letter from the student "Christian" to Marburg Alemannia, 10 August 1917, NA T-81, 232, 5015653–5015660. Emphasis in original.

44. For the veterans' association, see *OZ* 15 January 1917; for the Fortbildungsverein, *OZ* 6 January and 8 September 1917; for Germania 08, *OZ* 6 January 1917.

45. For the quotes on the DVLP, see Wortmann, *Geschichte der Deutschen Vaterlandspartei*, pp. 29, 30. For the Hessenbund, see "Vorläufige Ankündigung—Hessenbund," signed by Braun, Dr. Hitzeroth, Dr. Knetsch, Prof. Dr. Stengel, Prof. Dr. Wenck, Prof. Dr. Wrede, in HSAM 330, Mbg C, 4183 (emphasis in original).

46. For a brief discussion of the relationship between wartime social conflict and postwar upheavals, see Kocka, *Klassengesellschaft*, pp. 131–37.

47. *HLZ* 25 November 1918.

48. Freudenthal, *Vereine in Hamburg*, pp. 328–29.

49. See the appendix for data on the number and type of Marburg voluntary organizations. For the SPD white-collar official, see *OZ* 23 March 1923. For the fraternity member, see Dr. Quaet-Faslem, "Organisation," *DCZ* 36 (15 August 1919): 17.

50. J. R. C. Wright, *"Above Parties,"* pp. 11–12.

51. For the December meeting and Stephan quote, see *HLZ* 9 December 1918; for the rest, *OZ* 15, 27 January, 1 February 1919.

52. Quaet-Faslem, "Organisation," p. 14.

53. Ibid.

54. Ibid., p. 15.

55. *OZ* 1 June 1919.

56. On Liederkranz, which had 200 members and "around" 100 active members in 1929, see *OZ* 29 July 1927 Jubiläumsausgabe, and *OZ* 24 June 1932. For Liedertafel, which had 189 members and 83 actives in 1923, see letter of Verein officials to RPK, 30 July 1923, in HSAM 330, Mbg C, 4082, and *OZ* 24 June 1932. For Harmony, which consisted of 79 (30 active) male and 26 (9 active) female members in 1929, see *HT* 1 February 1929.

57. For discussion of the ingrained exclusivity of the male choirs, see Mosse, *Nationalization of the Masses*, p. 138.

58. On closure, see chancellor to (name illegible), 1 March 1920, in HSAM 310, Acc. 1975/42, 2190. On the 1928 celebration, see Heer, *Marburger Studentenleben*, p. 188. For implosion, see *WB* 58 (15 May 1929), col. 199.

59. For retailers, see *HT* 7 July 1928. On the city association of women's

clubs, see "Satzungen des Stadtverbandes Marburger Frauenvereine (type-script)," ca. 1919, in Marburger Hausfrauenverband, Protokollbuch, vol. 2. For Rheinfranken, see report on winter semester 1929–30, "Rheinfranken-geschichte," NA T-81, 256, 5047458; for a related incident involving contacts between Alemannia and local officers, see the invitation extended to the fraternity by the Officers' Club, 8 February 1925, ibid., 233, 5016068. For Wingolf, see *WB* 56 (15 May 1927), col. 165. For the religious associations, see "Evangelisch-Lutherische Tage in Marburg," *OZ* 15 September 1927, and "Kreiskirchentag in Marburg," *OZ* 20 July 1928.

60. For the legal aspects, see Loening and Loening, "Vereins- und Versammlungsfreiheit," pp. 558–59; for the political context, Rosenberg, *Geschichte der Weimarer Republik,* pp. 5–71, and Diehl, *Paramilitary Politics,* pp. 23–46.

61. *HLZ* 13 November and 16 December 1918; Mai, "Marburger Arbeiter- und Soldatenrat 1918/20," p. 196, and "Marburger Arbeiter- und Soldatenrat 1918–19," pp. 541–57.

62. *HLZ* 21 November 1918.

63. *HLZ* 16 December 1918.

64. *OZ* 5 December 1918.

65. For the national appeal to university students, see Steinberg, *Sabers and Brownshirts,* p. 49. For the quote, see *OZ* 19 March 1920.

66. *OZ* 19 March 1920, extra edition. For further information on Stuko, see Bensch, "StuKoMa," pp. 187–218; Bleuel and Klinnert, *Deutsche Studenten auf dem Weg,* pp. 72–78; Könnemann and Krusch, *Aktionseinheit contra Kapp Putsch;* Lemmer, "Drama von Mechterstädt"; Nipperdey, "Deutsche Studentenschaft," pp. 19–48; Schaumlöffel, *Studentenkorps Marburg;* von Selchow, *Hundert Tage aus meinem Leben;* and Weingartner, "Massacre at Mechterstädt," pp. 598–618.

67. Weingartner, "Massacre at Mechterstädt," p. 602.

68. Schaumlöffel, *Studentenkorps Marburg,* pp. 5–6; the university chancellor later wrote of the "moving impression" that the student corps made when it departed for the field (see his letter to the university commissioner, 31 March 1920, in HSAM 310, Acc. 1975/42, 2190).

69. Quoted in Könnemann and Krusch, *Aktionseinheit contra Kapp Putsch,* p. 414. For von Selchow's background, see Weingartner, "Massacre at Mechterstädt," p. 604.

70. Schaumlöffel, *Studentenkorps Marburg,* pp. 30–32; *HLZ* 30 April 1920; Weingartner, "Massacre at Mechterstädt," pp. 602–3.

71. Koshar, "Two 'Nazisms,'" pp. 36–38; Zorn, "Politische Entwicklung des deutschen Studententums," p. 257; Bleuel and Klinnert, *Deutsche Studenten auf dem Weg,* pp. 72–78; Könnemann and Krusch, *Aktionseinheit contra Kapp Putsch,* pp. 413–15. The testimony of fraternity students is recorded in defense lawyer Luetgebrunne's papers in NA T-253, 28 and 29. For the trial, see Weingartner, "Massacre at Mechterstädt," pp. 610–14.

72. Kreisrat to Oberpräsident, 9 April 1920, in HSAM 165, Kassel I, 1230, Bd. 1; *OZ* 15 March 1920.

73. *HLZ* 30 April 1920; Seier, "Marburg in der Weimarer Republik," p. 572; *OZ* 19 July 1920. On violence between students and workers, see Wachsmuth, "Der Zusammenschluß der Marburger Studentenschaft," *DCZ* 37 (5 October 1920): 137–38. For the largest single instance of collective violence in postwar Marburg, see Seier, "Marburg in der Weimarer Republik," p. 571.

74. Rektor to Kurator, 31 March 1920; Rektor und Deputation to Haenisch, 17 July 1920, both in HSAM 310, Acc. 1975/42, 2190.

75. Rektor to Kurator, 28 September 1920; declaration of Rektor and Deputation, 27 December 1920, both in HSAM 310, Acc. 1975/42, 2190.

76. On Stuko, see LR to RPK, 1 June 1926, in HSAM 165, Kassel I, 1184. For Prussian government efforts to monitor veterans' societies, see RPK to all Kassel district Landräte, 29 September 1927, in HSAM 165, Kassel I, 3846, Bd. 2. Marburg area officials reported to Prussian authorities on changes in social composition and other matters regarding veterans' clubs, as evidenced in LR to RPK, 30 January 1928, in HSAM, 165 Kassel I, 3846, Bd. 2. On authorities' monitoring of small-caliber sharpshooting societies, see "Verzeichnis der Kleinkaliber-Schützenvereine im Kreis Marburg," 1 April 1927, in HSAM, 180 LA Mbg, 3599, and LR to RPK, 20 April 1926, in HSAM 165, Kassel I, 1184. On the leniency of Marburg police officials toward students, see the evidence cited in chap. 5, nn. 61, 64.

77. See chap. 1 for the *Bürgertum* in the years of hyperinflation.

78. Note the contrast with Hopwood's analysis of the effects of the hyperinflation in "Paladins of the *Bürgertum*," p. 228. Hopwood speaks of the "strange wave of enthusiasm and feeling of impending national revival" among *Bürger* groups in the middle of 1923. But he focuses on a limited number of *bürgerlich* organizations; I think a wider view makes it clear that few grass roots organizations could act on such emotions in the difficult days of 1923. Kocka finds similar developments for white-collar workers, whose national associations lost members steadily from 1922 to 1925. See Kocka, *White Collar Workers*, pp. 29–30.

79. Käsebrod, *Servus*, p. 16; *OZ* 1 November 1923; VfL, *Festschrift*, p. 15.

80. Coyner, "Class Consciousness and Consumption," pp. 310–31; Wickham, "Working-Class Movement and Working-Class Life," pp. 335–38.

81. See table 2-4.

82. On Münscher, see *OZ* 26 April 1924; Schützenverein membership list, ca. 1930, in HSAM 165, Kassel I, 1061; and *OZ* 22 June 1933. On Ilk, see *OZ* 26 April 1924; Schützenverein membership list, ca. 1930, in HSAM 165, Kassel I, 1061; Kreishandwerkerbund, entries of 4 November 1921 and 10 November 1930, AKMVR, 74; *MEB* (1930), p. 94; and list of *Wahlvorstände*, 1925, in HSAM 330, Mbg C, 2676. For Stumpf, see *OZ* 28 February 1919, 9 November 1929; Creditreform, entry of 17 May 1920, AKMVR, 1; and Verein der blinden Akademiker, entry of 8 October 1916,

AKMVR, 47. For Wildhack, see *OZ* 26 April 1924; Kreishandwerkerbund, entries of 4 November 1921 and 10 November 1930, AKMVR, 74; and *MEB* (1930), p. 87.

83. Käsebrod, *Servus*, pp. 13–17.

84. Interview with Karl Wilser, former Krieger-Kameradschaft official, 29 July 1976.

85. The political party pluralism of local social organizations in the Republic was not as great as club spokesmen claimed, but enough parties were represented in most clubs to make the image of pluralism convincing. See the evidence for party affiliations of Sharpshooting Club members cited in chap. 3, n. 55. A smattering of Social Democratic party members in the Krieger-Kameradschaft was deemed sufficient by officials of that club to legitimize the argument that their organization was open to "all estates" and that this in turn necessitated strict political neutrality. See the interview cited in the preceding note.

86. For the general situation, see Zorn, "Student Politics in the Weimar Republic," pp. 123–48; for a nuanced discussion of what most non-Socialist university students understood politics to be, see Kreutzberger, *Studenten und Politik*, pp. 144–48. For the Marburg Sozialistische Studentengruppe, see bylaws and program, April, 1919, in HSAM 305a, Acc. 1950/9, 212.

87. See the articles or semester reports contained in *WB* 48 (19 March 1919), cols. 243–44; 49 (9 November 1920), col. 46; 54 (20 May 1925), col. 144; 54 (16 December 1925), col. 376; 55 (15 March 1926), col. 13; 56 (15 May 1927), col. 166; 56 (15 November 1927), cols. 436–40; 57 (15 November 1928), col. 424; 57 (15 February 1928), col. 58. For Marburger Wingolf students' involvement in the Marburg NSDStB, see chap. 6 and the appendix.

88. *OZ* 2 August 1924; *BB* 40 (October 1925): 19; Heer, *Marburger Burschenschaft Arminia*, p. 138.

89. For the AMSt, see chancellor to culture ministry, Berlin, 28 September 1928, in HSAM 305a, Acc. 1950/9, 645. For Genzmer, see Seier, "Radikalisierung und Reform," pp. 347–48; Genzmer's reply to his critics appeared in *Berliner Tageblatt*, 16 July 1929, in HSAM 310, Acc. 1975/42, 2209.

90. On the conflict between the Hausfrauenverband and the Marburg branch of the Reichsvereinigung deutscher Hausfrauen, see Marburger Hausfrauenverband, Protokollbuch, 2:174–82. For the quote from the reader's section of *OZ*, see ibid., p. 182.

91. *HT* 20 April 1926. Büttner, *Hamburg in der Staats- und Wirtschaftskrise*, p. 427, finds similar developments in *Bürgervereine* in late 1930.

92. Mosse, *Nationalization of the Masses*, pp. 143–44.

93. For the veterans' clubs and other organizations participating in the celebration, see *OZ* 19 January 1927; for the university festival, see *OZ* 20 January 1930.

94. Sozialdemokratischer Wahlverein to OB, 22 March 1919, in HSAM 330, Mbg C, 2818. For a subsequent celebration of Bismarck's birthday, see *OZ* 31 March 1925.

95. For *Totensonntag* in Marburg in 1929, see *HT* 26 November 1929. For an example of the lack of interest in the day in Tübingen, see Law and Economics dean to Tübingen university chancellor, 24 November 1931, in UAT 117c/285. The dean noted that university instructors rarely attended Memorial Sunday and asked the chancellor to use his influence to encourage faculty to take part in these ceremonies. For Marburg officials' defense against the *HT*'s charges, see OB to RPK, 10 December 1929, in HSAM 165, Kassel I, 3983, Bd. 10.

96. *OZ* 24 January 1928.

97. For Immanuel, see Karl Wilser interview, 29 July 1976. For the landlords, see the Marburg Property Owners' and Landlords' Association report of a Wiesbaden rally, *OZ* 28 November 1926; for the civil servants, see *HT* 12 March 1928.

98. For fraternity May festivals, see *OZ* 1 May 1923 and 1 May 1925.

99. Seier, "Marburg in der Weimarer Republik," p. 571.

100. *HT* 30 September 1929.

101. Ibid.

102. For the referendum drive, see Rosemarie Mann, "Entstehen und Entwicklung der NSDAP," pp. 303–7; for the formation of the local committee, *OZ* 2 October 1929.

103. For the quote and names of the committee members, see *OZ* 16 October 1929.

104. For the national campaign against the Young Plan, see Eyck, *Weimar Republic*, 2:203–25; for Marburg, see Rosemarie Mann, "Entstehen und Entwicklung der NSDAP," p. 305.

Chapter 5

1. For the first quote, see H. Marckwald to RPK, 8 May 1929, in HSAM 165, Kassel I, 1153; for the second, *Volksstimme* (Frankfurt/Main), 30 August 1929, in HSAM 305a, Acc. 1950/9, 585.

2. For the nationalist network, see SA Brigade 47, *Geschichte der Kurhessischen SA*, pp. 22–25; Lohalm, *Radikalismus*, pp. 16–19; Schön, *Nationalsozialismus in Hessen*, p. 17. On the origins of the Marburg NSDAP, see NSDAP Marburg, *Festschrift*, p. 15, and SA Brigade 47, *Geschichte der Kurhessischen SA*, pp. 22–25.

3. See Merkl, *Political Violence under the Swastika*, pp. 146–47, 207–30.

4. I am thinking particularly of Wolfgang Sauer's influential argument regarding the "military desperadoes" of Fascist movements. See his "National Socialism," p. 411.

5. On military style, see NSDAP Marburg, *Festschrift*, p. 16. On the

"bloodless" bourgeois parties, see SA Brigade 47, *Geschichte der Kurhessischen SA*, p. 23. On military style and nazism generally, see Diehl, *Paramilitary Politics*, pp. 283–85.

6. NSDAP Marburg, *Festschrift*, pp. 15–16; SA Brigade 47, *Geschichte der Kurhessischen SA*, p. 24; Maser, *Frühgeschichte der NSDAP*, p. 345.

7. NSDAP Marburg, *Festschrift*, p. 16.

8. Ibid., p. 42; I leave the psychological arguments regarding these male cliques to Theweleit, *Männerphantasien*.

9. See chap. 4, nn. 78, 79.

10. See chap. 4, nn. 74, 75.

11. SA Brigade 47, *Geschichte der Kurhessischen SA*, p. 24.

12. For the origins of the VSB in Hesse, see Schön, *Nationalsozialismus in Hessen*, pp. 54–62. For the VSB nationally, see Manfred Weißbecker, "Nationalsozialistische Arbeiterpartei," in Fricke, *Die bürgerlichen Parteien*, 2:395–99. For the VSB's success in a regional context, see Hambrecht, *NSDAP in Mittel- und Oberfranken*, pp. 62–84.

13. Interview with Hans Krawielitzki, former Marburg NSDAP leader, 20 March 1980.

14. *OZ* 3 May 1924. For other VSB assemblies, see *HB* 12 and 19 April 1924.

15. *OZ* 3 May 1924.

16. *HB* 12 April 1924; Schön, *Nationalsozialismus in Hessen*, pp. 54–62.

17. *OZ* 3 May 1924.

18. For the Bavarian VSB, see Stachura, *Gregor Straßer*, p. 32; for voting in the city parliament, see table 2-4.

19. For the swastikas, see *OZ* 3 May 1924. According to NSDAP Marburg, *Festschrift*, p. 16, the Marburg SA displayed the swastika on a flag for the first time in 1923, during a local march and protest demonstration against French occupation authorities in the Ruhr, who had executed Albert Leo Schlageter, a nationalist agitator.

20. On Ludendorff and nazism in 1923–24, see Orlow, *History of the Nazi Party*, pp. 45, 50–51, 54.

21. *HB* 19 April 1924.

22. "Aus der völkischen Bewegung," *HB* 10 May 1924. Despite the appearance of two lists in the May 1924 municipal elections in Marburg, the Landrat wrote at the end of the year that "we have so far heard nothing of a Großdeutsche Volksgemeinschaft. . . ." See LR to RPK, 18 December 1924, in HSAM 180, LA Mbg, 2917.

23. For information on party finances, see NSDAP Marburg, *Festschrift*, p. 19; the Marburg Landrat knew very little about how the local NSDAP was financed; see LR to RPK, September, 1930, in HSAM 165, Kassel I, 3846, Bd. 3.

24. NSDAP Marburg, *Festschrift*, p. 19.

25. Krawielitzki vehemently denied this contention and wrote of the "consistently high membership" of the NSDAP around 1928; Krawielitzki

to OB, 5 May 1936, NA T-81, 225, 5005266. Of course, NSDAP leaders themselves doubted the reliability of membership figures in the early years of the party.

26. Membership fluctuations computed from NSDAP Marburg, *Festschrift*, p. 59. The first NSDAP meeting to which the conservative *OZ* sent a reporter occurred on 16 July 1930.

27. Hitler himself conceded that in the early 1920s the NSDAP could not eradicate other organizations but had to infiltrate them and accommodate itself to them tactically. See his discussion of the party and trade unions in *Mein Kampf*, pp. 596–606. But there were many exceptions to the party's tolerance of dual memberships, as Stachura, *Nazi Youth*, pp. 96–103, makes clear.

28. NSDStB membership list, 12 June 1929, in HSAM 305a, Acc. 1954/16, 1.

29. All quotes are from my questionnaire to Fritz Schwalm, 16 September 1980, and telephone interviews with him on 28 September and 5 October 1980. My thanks to Herr Schwalm for his cooperation.

30. For a social profile of Nazi leaders, see Kater, *The Nazi Party*, pp. 169–233.

31. Schwalm's recollections appear to be accurate with regard to the internal democracy of the Marburg *Ortsgruppe*. Krawielitzki told me that until 1931 Nazi party members still elected their city group leader. Interview with Krawielitzki, 21 March 1980.

32. For the quotes regarding Böckel, see NSDAP Marburg, *Festschrift*, p. 14. For a compatible argument, see Hambrecht, *NSDAP in Mittel- und Oberfranken*, pp. 136–42, in which the author refers to a Nazi *homo novus*. Volkov also stresses the differences between the anti-Semitism of turn-of-the-century agitators and that of the Nazi cadres in "Kontinuität und Diskontinuität," pp. 240–43.

33. For Krawielitzki's official biography, see "Lebenslauf," NS Reichsleiter. Personalakte des Obersten Parteigerichtes, n.d., BDC; all quotes are from interviews with Krawielitzki, 20 and 21 March 1980.

34. For von Eltz's biographical data, see "Lebenslauf," Rasse- und Siedlungsamt. Hauptamt SS, ca. 1936, BDC; for von Eltz's approach to the SA and students, as viewed critically by a party rival, see Heinrich Link to NSDStB Reich headquarters, 26 November 1929, AUWAR II/A 10; for the comparison with Göttingen, see Marshall, "Einfluß der Universität," p. 282.

35. Von Eltz to Reich NSDStB, 7 October 1928 and 15 January 1929, both in AUWAR II/A 10.

36. NSDAP Marburg, *Festschrift*, pp. 21–29; *OZ* 19 May 1928; LR to RPK, 7 March 1929, in HSAM 180, LA Mbg, 2917; Rosemarie Mann, "Entstehen und Entwicklung der NSDAP," pp. 303–4.

37. Only Krawielitzki remained in Marburg.

38. I refer here to Scheller, Walz, Wagner, and Jensen. See Willertz, "Mar-

burg unter dem Nationalsozialismus," p. 597.

39. On the lack of Nazi success in the Hessian countryside before 1928, see Schön, *Nationalsozialismus in Hessen*, pp. 91–92. On tensions between county and provincial leaders of the Peasants' Association, see LR to RPK, 5 January 1928, in HSAM 180, LA Mbg, 3807; and protocol of general assembly of county Bauernverein, 23 March 1929, AKMVR, 61. On competition between the Bauernverein and Landwirtschaftlicher Kreisverein, see LR to RPK, 12 January 1928, in HSAM 180, LA Mbg, 3807.

40. Quoted from Bergemann's recollections in NSDAP Marburg, *Festschrift*, p. 22.

41. Landjägerpost Wetter II to LR, 27 February 1929, in HSAM 165, Kassel I, 3866.

42. For Böckel's antiparliamentarism, see Levy, *Downfall of Anti-Semitic Political Parties*, pp. 235–36. A report of the Bauernverein assembly appears in *OZ* 26 March 1928.

43. For membership in the NSDStB see chap. 6, n. 61.

44. Rosemarie Mann, "Entstehen und Entwicklung der NSDAP," p. 304.

45. NSDStB leader Hans Glauning to university chancellor and senate, 21 May 1926, in HSAM 305a, Acc. 1954/16, 1.

46. Link to Reich NSDStB, 26 November 1929, AUWAR II/A 10.

47. On the AMSt, see von Eltz to Reich NSDStB, 7 October 1928, AUWAR II/A 10; on the philistinized fraternities, Ernst Schwarz, Marburg NSDStB leader in summer 1928, to Reich NSDStB, 31 July 1928, AUWAR II/A 10.

48. Von Eltz to Reich NSDStB, 15 January 1929, AUWAR II/A 10.

49. Ibid.; *OZ* 18 January 1929, as cited in Rosemarie Mann, "Entstehen und Entwicklung der NSDAP," p. 283 (n. 155).

50. NSDAP Marburg, *Festschrift*, p. 27; Rosemarie Mann, "Entstehen und Entwicklung der NSDAP," pp. 298–310.

51. Rosemarie Mann, "Entstehen und Entwicklung der NSDAP," pp. 314–17.

52. Tilly defines repression as "the costs of collective action to the contender resulting from interaction with other groups; as a process, any action by another group which raises the contender's cost of collective action; an action which lowers the contender's cost is a form of *facilitation* . . ." (*From Mobilization to Revolution*, p. 55).

53. For SPD vote totals in the county, see Rosemarie Mann, "Entstehen und Entwicklung der NSDAP," tables 1 and 2, pp. 336–37, and tables 4 and 5, pp. 339–40. On city voting, see table 2-4 above. For the Socialist Student Group membership list, see HSAM 305a, Acc. 1954/16, 12.

54. See chap. 1, nn. 30, 59–63, table 4-2, and chap. 4, n. 31.

55. Quoted from bylaws and program, Socialist Student Group, April 1919, in HSAM 305a, Acc. 1950/9, 212.

56. Indeed, identifying enemies was part of the definition of politics for some Germans. See Carl Schmitt, *The Concept of the Political*, pp. 25–37.

57. Bergemann insisted on agitating in locales such as Mellnau, where a strong Reichsbanner group existed. See NSDAP Marburg, *Festschrift*, p. 22.

58. Severing to provincial authorities, 25 June 1930, in HSAM 165, Kassel I, 3838.

59. RPK to Marburg LR and other officials, 21 July 1930, in HSAM 180, LA Mbg, 3543; RPK to Marburg LR, 2 January 1931, in HSAM 180, LA Mbg, 4332; RPK to Oberpräsident, 10 January 1929, in HSAM 165, Kassel I, 1153. For the Kassel meeting, see typed minutes, 26 March 1930, in HSAM 165, Kassel I, 3815.

60. Evidence on police and allegations cited from H. Marckwald to RPK, 8 May 1929, in HSAM 165, Kassel I, 1153.

61. There are numerous complaints of the leniency with which police officials, university authorities, and fraternity alumni associations treated university students in HSAM 165, Kassel I, 1153.

62. *VB* 30 September 1926; *Frankfurter Zeitung*, 6 December 1926; both in BGLA, Cul. Min., 235/4790. Of course the Darmstadt decision was also based on a form of apoliticism: university officials considered the NSDStB to be "basically only political" and therefore inadmissible as a student organization.

63. A concrete example of disunity among professors over Weimar politics: the popular Wilhelm Mommsen's support for the DDP created antagonisms in the history department, which, according to one Marburg instructor, was distinguished by its "conservative, narrow-minded nationalism"; see the written testimony of E. Jaensch on W. Mommsen to the NSDAP, 14 February 1938, NA T-81, 225, 5005725–5005726. See also Seier, "Marburg in der Weimarer Republik," pp. 584–92.

64. Quoted from H. Marckwald to RPK, 8 May 1929, in HSAM 165, Kassel I, 1153.

65. Republikanische Beschwerdestelle to Kurator, 22 February and 28 March 1929; Kurator's response (in which he passes along the demand of Rektor Genzmer that the informant be named), 9 March 1929; Rektor's description of meeting with von Eltz, 21 May 1929, all in HSAM, 305a, Acc. 1950/9, 584.

66. NSDAP Marburg, *Festschrift*, p. 48; Seier, "Marburg in der Weimarer Republik," p. 588; *Volkswacht* (Bielefeld), 18 January 1930; *Generalanzeiger für Dortmund*, 19 January 1930; *Westfälische Landeszeitung*, 18 January 1930, the latter three in HSAM 305a, Acc. 1975/79, 125.

67. See *Volksstimme* (Frankfurt/Main), 29 August 1929, in HSAM 305a, Acc. 1950/9, 585.

68. NSDAP Marburg, *Festschrift*, pp. 23–24.

69. For city totals, see table 2-3 above; for the county, Rosemarie Mann, "Entstehen und Entwicklung der NSDAP," table 1, p. 336; for the municipal parliament, table 2-4 above; for the county parliament, Willertz, "National Socialism in a German City and County," p. 29; for membership to-

tals, NSDAP Marburg, *Festschrift*, pp. 59–61, and Rosemarie Mann, "Entstehen und Entwicklung der NSDAP," pp. 295–97.

70. Articles by NSDStB members appeared with increasing regularity in the student newspaper. See, for example, Lucie Scholtz, "Studentin und Hochschulorganisation," *MHZ* 2 (12 July 1930): 27–28. Scholtz was a member of both the NSDStB and Deutsch-Akademischer Frauenbund. Another example is Fritz Weibezahn, "Der organische Gedanke," *MHZ* 2 (1 December 1930): 34–35. By the winter semester 1930 the NSDStB boasted that it had placed one of its members in the AMSt press office; see *HV* 22 June 1932. For the Stahlhelm student group, see HSAM 305a, Acc. 1954/16, 8.

71. See chap. 6.

72. For sources, see n. 69, this chapter. Electoral participation (in percent of total eligible voters) in Marburg city and county in 1928–33 was:

	City	County
1928	69.0	62.4
1930	73.0	74.1
1932-I	88.0	—
1932-II	84.0	—
1933	90.0	86.1

Sources: Neusüß-Hunkel, *Parteien und Wahlen*, p. 35; Rosemarie Mann, "Entstehen und Entwicklung der NSDAP," pp. 336–40. (Mann's data on the county is incomplete. Her data on voting participation in the city is likewise incomplete, and I have used Neusüß-Hunkel for these totals.)

73. Faust, *Der Nationalsozialistische Deutsche Studentenbund*, 2:140–50.

74. NSDAP Marburg, *Festschrift*, pp. 46–47.

75. AMSt elections, 1931–32:

	1931	1932
Electoral slates	% Votes	% Votes
National Block	25.2	23.3
German-Academic Ring	13.7	—
NSDStB	49.6	62.8
Nonpolitical coalition	7.7	8.4
Ring German Women Students	2.4	4.7
Disqualified ballots	1.4	0.8
Totals	100.0	100.0
	N=3,074	N=2,404

Source: Rosemarie Mann, "Entstehen und Entwicklung der NSDAP," p. 286, n. 181.

76. For sources, refer to chap. 1, nn. 30, 59–63.

77. The Landrat had emphasized the "misery of the farmers" in early

1928 and simultaneously stressed the long-term aspects of such problems as labor shortages in the countryside. See LR to RPK, 5 and 12 January 1928, in HSAM 180, LA Mbg, 3807.

78. An NSDStB advertisement before the 1931 AMSt campaign hardly reflected a predominant concern for economic hardship:

> We demand: the exclusion of foreign races from German universities; only Germans as educators of German youth; doing away with the Versailles Treaty and war guilt lies; a secure future; the intellectual and material strengthening of Germans' capabilities to defend themselves militarily; a chair for military science at each German university; the awakening of Germans' consciousness about folk characteristics; a chair for the study of hereditary and racial teachings at all German universities; the purposive use of all elements of German culture (the press, theater, art, literature and radio) in the struggle for folk-national interests; the struggle of the German student for the German worker! We demand: the unification of the worker of the head and worker of the hand, the national and social liberation of the German people in a true folk community. That's what it's all about in the struggle at the university. German student, do you want what we want? Then vote for the NSDStB list, List 3! (*HV* 4/5 July 1931)

79. See chap. 4.
80. Quoted from *WBe* 20 September 1930.
81. *OZ* 16 July 1930.
82. The organizations were Schaumburgia, Chattia, Saxnot, Normannia, and Akademischer Turnerbund. In addition, the NSDStB assumed that it could count on the support of another forty fraternity students who were not activists but who were loyal to the party. See von Eltz to NSDStB propaganda *Abteilung*, ca. August 1928, AUWAR II/A 10.
83. Gilde Saxnot invited Student League member Werner Gaul to speak at an open house in the summer of 1929. During that semester, Arminia and the Akademischer Turnerbund also invited NSDStB speakers to discussion evenings and informal talks. Due to von Eltz's friendship with Stahlhelm students, the NSDStB and Stahlhelm student group marched together at the 1929 Bismarck Day ceremonies; see letters from von Eltz to Reich NSDStB, 5 June and 22 July 1929, AUWAR II/A 10. For the contact organizations, see Faust, *Der Nationalsozialistische Deutsche Studentenbund*, 2:29–35. For Nazi involvement in nonstudent organizations, see chap. 6 below.
84. For Wißner, see chap. 4, n. 23. For Schweinsberger, see NSDAP membership list, n.d., in HSAM 321/1, 5488; *OZ* 9 November 1929; and minutes of 5 October 1931 Kreishandwerkerbund meeting, AKMVR, 74. For Hübner, see HSAM 305a, Acc.1954/16, 45; report from Landjägerpost Sterzhausen to LR on 15 November 1930 NSDAP meeting (at which Hüb-

ner appears for the first time as a Nazi assembly leader), in HSAM 180, LA Mbg, 2917; and Hübner, "Korporationsstudent und Nationalsozialismus," *HV* 4/5 July 1931.

85. This was partly an effect of continually increasing organization density since World War I. See table A-2.

86. For the continued importance of fraternity culture, see Heer, *Marburger Burschenschaft Arminia*, p. 144. For cutbacks in fraternity social life, see the self-congratulatory letter from Corps Teutonia to Rektor, November 1930 (in which the fraternity writer informs the chancellor that "in consideration of the inauspicious circumstances of the present" Teutonia will drop all social activities in winter 1930/31 except for the upcoming holiday celebration), in HSAM 305a, Acc. 1954/16, 45. For Marburger Wingolf, see semester report, *WB* 61 (10 May 1932), cols. 222–23.

Membership in pure fraternities, 1926–32 (winter semesters):

	Active	Total	Percent Active
1926	397	604	65.7
1928	491	720	68.2
1930	481	732	65.7
1932	370	629	58.8

Source: HSAM 305a, Acc. 1954/16, 1–78.

87. Reprint of speech by Glauning (Germania, Marburg), "Burschenschaft und Nationalsozialismus," *BB* 45 (1930/31): 283.

88. *OZ* 19 and 21 April 1932; *HT* 21 April 1932. For a compatible argument regarding Hitler's appeal as leader of a mass movement rather than as a cult hero per se, see Zofka, *Ausbreitung des Nationalsozialismus*, p. 84.

89. For the schoolteachers' auxiliary, see *OZ* 29 October 1932; for the Factory Cell Organization, NSDAP Marburg, *Festschrift*, pp. 44–45; for civil servants, *HV* 9 June 1932; for the HJ, 2 December 1931 letter from Gunter Ruge to all district HJ, in HSAM 180, LA Mbg, 2917; for women, *HV* 9 June 1932; on NSDStB social programs, *HV* 22 and 29 June 1932, and Rosemarie Mann, "Entstehen und Entwicklung der NSDAP," p. 287; for the increasingly popular tone of NSDAP collective action, Rosemarie Mann, "Entstehen und Entwicklung der NSDAP," p. 315.

90. For Marburg Reichstag elections, see table 2-3. For the AMSt, see n. 75, this chapter. For Tübingen student government elections, see Alf Ludtke, "Vom Elend der Professoren," p. 104.

91. On cell and block attendants, see *OZ* 10 October 1932.

Assemblies, handbills, and posters of political parties in Marburg city and county, June 1931 to August 1932:

Party	Assemblies	Handbills	Posters
		CITY	
NSDAP	37 (35.2)	41 (20.6)	38 (26.4)
SPD	14 (13.3)	12 (6.0)	18 (12.5)
KPD	21 (20.0)	68 (34.2)	48 (33.3)
DNVP	9 (8.6)	20 (10.1)	7 (4.9)
Others	24 (22.9)	58 (29.1)	33 (22.9)
Totals	105 (100.0)	199 (100.0)	144 (100.0)
		COUNTY	
NSDAP	247 (39.9)	19 (26.1)	15 (32.6)
SPD	168 (27.2)	2 (2.7)	10 (21.7)
KPD	101 (16.3)	12 (16.4)	5 (10.9)
DNVP	80 (12.9)	32 (43.8)	11 (23.9)
Others	22 (3.7)	8 (11.0)	5 (10.9)
Totals	618 (100.0)	73 (100.0)	46 (100.0)

Source: compiled from data cited in Rosemarie Mann, "Entstehen und Entwicklung der NSDAP," pp. 320, 326.

92. Participation in student government elections in Marburg, 1919–1932, in percent of total eligible voters:

1919	37.0	1927	77.0
1925	52.5	1931	71.9
1926	68.4	1932	62.7

Sources: Seier, "Radikalisierung und Reform," p. 343; Rosemarie Mann, "Entstehen und Entwicklung der NSDAP," p. 181. The 1927 figure represents the Becker vote. For the Becker vote, see *WB* 56 (15 November 1927), col. 477. For the incident in the theology department, see NSDAP Marburg, *Festschrift*, p. 49.

93. Declarations of political neutrality by organizational leaders were numerous. For two highly visible special interest associations, see the Artisans' Association in *HZKW* 1 February 1932; for the Peasants' Association declaration of neutrality toward the political parties, see *OBZ* 30 July 1932.

94. See data in n. 91, this chapter, for party assemblies, handbills, and posters. For the quote from the Communist party assembly, see the Marburg police report of 27 December 1930, in HSAM 330, Mbg C, 3097. On the relative strength of the KPD in the province, see RPK report to local police officials, 16 November 1930 and, for NSDAP, KPD, DNVP, and others, see RPK report to local officials, 17 November 1931, both in HSAM 330, Mbg C, 3097.

95. Reports of Marburg Polizeiverwaltung, 24 and 25 February 1931, both in HSAM 165, Kassel I, 7015; Schneider, *Marburg 1933–1945*, pp. 20–24; NSDAP Marburg, *Festschrift*, pp. 39–41; *HV* 26 February 1931.

96. On *HT* circulation, see *HT* to Magistrat, 23 December 1925, in HSAM 330, Mbg C, 3074. On the conservative stance of the *OZ*, see RPK

to Marburg LR, 20 August 1927 (in which the former criticizes the newspaper for its contention that only "party politics" dictated Prussian policy), in HSAM 330, Mbg C, 4186. On the comparative effects of public debate in Marburg and Tübingen, see Koshar "Two 'Nazisms,'" pp. 38–39. The clear predominance of one daily newspaper in Tübingen helped to muffle conflict in public life there.

97. For Ockershausen, see *HT* 24 February 1931; for the "Terror and Poison" article, *HT* 17 February 1931. In contrast, the *OZ* was warned by the Oberpräsident that it must be more objective in its reporting after the newspaper criticized Prussian "anxiety maneuvers" and "unprovoked police interventions" when Hitler spoke in Marburg in March 1932; see Oberpräsident to *OZ* publisher and editorial board, 31 March 1932, in HSAM 330, Mbg C, 4186.

98. For the debate between von Eltz and Link, see Link to Reich NSDStB, 26 November 1929, AUWAR II/A 10.

99. Rosemarie Mann, "Entstehen und Entwicklung der NSDAP," p. 315.

100. *OZ* 10 October 1932.

101. See nn. 28 and 29, this chapter.

Chapter 6

1. *VB* 2 August 1930.

2. Kershaw has commented on the importance of local associations "in which nazism was acceptably blended into existing local tradition" in "Ideology, Propaganda, and the Rise of the Nazi Party," p. 172. For interesting but rather impressionistic data on Nazi affiliations in small-town *Vereinsleben*, see Zofka, *Ausbreitung des Nationalsozialismus*, pp. 139–40.

3. For a useful discussion of mass society theory in the context of the historiography of nazism, see Falter, "Radikalisierung oder Mobilisierung?," pp. 441–44, 452–58, and Hagtvet, "Theory of Mass Society." In contrast to my argument, Jamin's comments in *Zwischen den Klassen*, pp. 380–81, revive Arendt's notion that Nazi party adherents were socially rootless, at least with regard to their occupational profile. But this overlooks the possibility that NSDAP members retained social contacts in organizational life despite being upwardly or downwardly mobile.

4. See the appendix.

5. In order to compile a sample group of Marburg's nonstudent ordinary joiners I conducted a systematic sample of heads of household. Seeking to generate a sample for 1930 of about one hundred individuals who had two or more organizational affiliations (and who were thus comparable with Nazi joiners, who had at least one affiliation besides their membership in the NSDAP), I took every seventh name from "Straßenverzeichnis," *MEB* (1930), pp. 107–83. I chose every seventh name on the basis of a conserva-

tive estimate of the number of townspeople for whom I could find at least two organizational affiliations. Using Cochran, *Sampling Techniques,* pp. 206–7, I started with the fourth name in the address roster. For 852 householders, I found 103 who had two or more affiliations with a local voluntary organization. The method and sources for compiling the organizational affiliations of each person were the same as those for Nazi joiners (see the appendix). Because it is impossible to have complete information about the joiners, the data should be considered a conservative estimate of the organizational affiliations of a group of ordinary townsfolk.

6. Nazi students usually belonged to just one other organization at the university and were not strictly comparable with nonstudent townspeople, who might belong to more than one organization.

7. Percent NSDAP members with affiliations to:

	1923–30	1930–33	1933–35
one organization	71.7	81.8	77.2
two or more organizations	28.3	18.2	22.8
Totals	100.0	100.0	100.0
Total numbers	46	154	228

8. Throughout this chapter I refer to 1923–30 for the period that extends from April–May 1923 (the approximate founding date of the Marburg NSDAP) to the 14 September 1930 Reichstag election, to 1930–33 for the period from the Reichstag election to the Nazi seizure of power on 30 January 1933, and to 1933–35 for the period from the *Machtergreifung* to the end of 1935.

9. For the social composition of the Marburg NSDAP, see table 6-7.

10. See student association membership lists, in HSAM 305a, Acc. 1954/16, 1–78. The majority (85.5 percent) of the seventy-six Nazi student affiliations in table 6-2 originated with the Student League. The rest were party memberships. None of the students whose affiliations are reflected in table 6-2 belonged to the other Nazi student organizations in the city: the Arbeitsgemeinschaft nationalsozialistischer Studentinnen, which had twelve members in May 1932, fifty-four in October 1933, and fifty-four in April 1935 (see HSAM 305a, Acc. 1954/16, 13); and the tiny and insignificant Kampfgemeinschaft Revolutionärer Nationalsozialisten, Studentengruppe Marburg (see 17 April 1931 bylaws in HSAM 305a, Acc. 1975/79, 1378).

The findings regarding continued Nazi and non-Nazi affiliations are complicated by the tradition of the "life principle," which supposedly tied students to a single fraternity permanently. It is extraordinarily difficult to gauge the precise effect of this convention, but the life principle speaks to the point developed here in a slightly different way, suggesting that (before 1933) affiliation with a Nazi organization did not significantly alter the notionally permanent ties between an individual and his fraternity. For this reason, I disagree with Konrad Jarausch, who refers to the Nazi Student League as a " 'counterfraternity.' " I believe the league was tied in a variety of ways to both fraternities and nonfraternity organizations by a

fluctuating field of social relationships; it was too closely intertwined socially with the fraternities to be called a "counterfraternity"—unless we
use that term only to define it as it existed in the ideological pronouncements and self-image of NSDStB agitators. For Jarausch's argument, see
his detailed and valuable *Students, Society, and Politics*, p. 421.

11. See the appendix.

12. For the special interest coalitions, see chap. 2, nn. 96–101.

13. Eley, *Reshaping the German Right*, pp. 134–39, and Chickering, *We
Men Who Feel Most German*, pp. 160–67. Despite contrasting methodolo-
gies and aims, both of these accounts stress the narrowness of the social
appeal of the patriotic clubs.

14. For the cartel, see *OZ* 29 July 1927 Jubiläumsausgabe.

15. For comparative examples, see Conan Fischer, *Stormtroopers*, p. 56.

16. See chap. 7, n. 56.

17. *OZ* 13 May 1933.

18. See chap. 3.

19. Interview with former VfB member Friedrich Bluhm, 30 March
1977.

20. I have not been able to generate precise data on the age of Marburg
NSDAP members. But the data contain proxy evidence on the relative
youth of the Marburg NSDAP because of the extensive participation of
university students. However, this reflects the idiosyncracies of social
structure in a university town and/or the particular sociopolitical context
of student actions as much as it addresses the issue of youth per se. For an
argument suggesting that generational analysis is more useful for the
smaller European fascist movements than for the larger movements in
Italy and Germany, which lend themselves more fruitfully to political/
sociological interpretation, see Linz, "Notes toward a Comparative Study
of Fascism," p. 41. But for the application of generational theory to nazism, see Loewenberg, "Psychohistorical Origins of the Nazi Youth Cohort," and, more recently, Kater, "Generationskonflikt."

21. I adopt the phrase from George Melly's *Revolt into Style*, a study of
rock music and youth subcultures. It should be obvious that I do not in-
tend here to draw a parallel between rock subcultures and the social life of
Nazi party members but rather to refer to a general cultural and political
response of youth in contemporary history that takes a multitude of forms
in specific historical contexts. See also Diehl, *Paramilitary Politics*, pp.
211–16, for general discussion of "front ideology" and paramilitary style.

22. For choral groups, see Hans Staudinger, *Individuum und Gemeinschaft*.

23. Kurt Tucholsky, *Zwischen Gestern und Morgen*, pp. 76–77, as cited
in Freudenthal, *Vereine in Hamburg*, p. 427.

24. See chap. 7, nn. 94, 95. On the contradictions between clubs and associations and the NSDAP, see Koshar, "From *Stammtisch* to Party."

25. Of 634 affiliations, student association affiliations number 159, or
25.1 percent of the total.

26. This is an estimate based on the number of Nazi students (party and

league) for whom I have not found evidence of affiliations with non-Nazi organizations. There were 333 of these individuals in a group of 489 Nazi students, or 68.1 percent. These students were certainly not without social ties, and many of them were no doubt members of the diffuse Freistudentenschaft. But their involvement in local networks is less easily demonstrated than is that of members of formal student organizations. In spite of this evidence, we must be careful not to make too much of Nazi mobilization of unaffiliated students. The success of nazism at the university depended on infiltrating the fraternities, and the presence of representatives from these organizations in the NSDAP—against the backdrop of a large number of less formally organized students—made the National Socialist folk community a credible image. Accordingly, Barbara Marshall's argument that the student corporations slowed the advance of the Göttingen NSDStB, which attracted more unaffiliated students than corporation members, may be accurate as far as it goes, but it overlooks the "nurturing" effect that fraternity involvement in the NSDStB had on Nazi mobilization. See Marshall, "Der Einfluß der Universität," p. 289.

27. For the following citations of Nazi joiners from the list mentioned above, I refer to the number in the list (1 through 1,521) first and the membership number second. For estimates of the time of entry into the NSDAP, I have used Kühnl, *Der deutsche Faschismus*, p. 97. See the appendix for complete details. For Müller, see NS list, 921/1,361,307, in HSAM 327/1, 5488; Turngemeinde 1885, entry of 19 February 1921, AKMVR, 69; and HSAM 165, Kassel I, Bd. 2, 5149–5399.

28. Childers, *The Nazi Voter*, pp. 253–57; Falter, "Radikalisierung oder Mobilisierung?," p. 462; Kater, *The Nazi Party*, pp. 22–23, 35–38, 54–55.

29. Hamilton, *Who Voted for Hitler?*, p. 219.

30. Based on fifteen individuals with fifty-five affiliations for Nazi elites and nineteen individuals with sixty-three affiliations for sample elites.

31. For Münscher, see NS list, 929/813,606; Altherrenverband des VfB, entry of 11 August 1920, AKMVR, 60; and Arbeitgeberverband für das Baugewerbe des Kreises Marburg, entry of 12 March 1925, AKMVR, 87. For Braun, see OZ 17 July 1933; chap. 2, n. 83; OZ 25 February 1919, 28 January 1924; Konzertverein, entry of 17 July 1933, AKMVR, 41; Invalidenheim für Jäger und Schützen, entry of 12 December 1923, AKMVR, 46; Oberhessischer Gebirgsverein, entries of 11 December 1930 and 28 June 1934, AKMVR, 126; MEB (1930), p. 84, and (1934/5), p. 94; OZ 15 September 1932; and NS list, 161.

32. On the lower middle classes between a larger bourgeois universe and the working classes, see the comments in Crossick and Haupt, "Shopkeepers and Master Artisans," pp. 4–5.

33. On Schnaut, see NS list, 1,235/484,309; "Herberge zur Heimat," entries of 16 October 1911, 2 June 1924, 19 December 1927, AKMVR, 35; HSAM 165, Kassel I, Bd. 2, 5149–5399; and OZ 9 November 1929.

34. For Wißner, see chap. 4, n. 23.

35. Kater, *The Nazi Party*, pp. 42–43; Caplan, "Civil Service Support."

For the Nazi civil servants' movement in Kurhessen, see Neef, "Entwicklung des Beamtenorganisationswesens," pp. 65–66.

36. For Weitzel, see NS list, 1,454/813,653, and *MEB* (1930), p. 90.

37. Childers, *The Nazi Voter,* pp. 259–60.

38. For Scholtz, see NSDStB list, winter 1929/30–summer 1930, in HSAM 305a, Acc. 1954/16, 1, and Deutsch-Akademischer Frauenbund, summer 1928–summer 1931, in HSAM 305a, Acc. 1954/16, 14. For the general situation of women in the Nazi movement before 1933, see Koonz, "Competition for a Women's *Lebensraum,*" pp. 209–19.

39. On Wadehn, see NS list, 1,410/419,418; Wadehn is listed as being a Reichsvereinigung Deutscher Hausfrauen official since June 1933 in Hausfrauenverband, "Verhandlungsniederschrift," 25 June 1934, AKMVR, 125. For Weintraut, see NSDAP Marburg, *Festschrift,* p. 22.

40. For discussion of neighborhoods in ecological voting analysis, see Hamilton, *Who Voted for Hitler?,* particularly pp. 64–219.

41. For patterns of urban growth in Marburg, see Leister, "Marburg," p. 66; vom Brocke, "Marburg im Kaiserreich," pp. 379–400; and Kürschner, *Geschichte der Stadt Marburg,* pp. 280–81. Despite changes in construction patterns and neighborhoods, the architectural vista of Marburg, partly a product of the city's location in the narrow Lahn valley, remained more uniform than did that of Kassel. See Demandt, *Kassel und Marburg,* p. 5.

42. The three highest-density precincts, with number of Nazis per 1,000 householders in parentheses, were 8 (67.0), 2 (62.9), and 5 (60.3); the three lowest-density precincts were 11 (38.4), 3 (40.4), and 10 (45.7). For sources, see, for electoral precincts, *OZ* 6 September 1930, and, for occupations of heads of household, "Straßenverzeichnis," *MEB* (1930/31), pp. 107–83.

Using every tenth name, and relying on Cochran, *Sampling Techniques,* pp. 206–7, I took a systematic sample of heads of household in the precincts with the three highest and three lowest levels of Nazi recruitment. Elites, the independent lower middle classes, and civil servants are overrepresented in the sample of householders because individuals from these groups tended to be older, disproportionately male, and hence more likely to be heads of household than did workers or white-collar employees such as clerks or elementary school teachers. Workers are also underrepresented in the data because many of them did not live in Marburg but rather commuted to the city from surrounding villages such as Ockershausen. Nevertheless, the value of the comparison *between* above-average and below-average precincts is not diminished.

43. See table 4-1.

44. For the unstable white-collar vote for nazism, see Childers, *The Nazi Voter,* pp. 91, 166–74, 233–43. Childers emphasizes the lack of a consistent Nazi appeal to *Angestellten,* compared with other socioeconomic groups.

45. For craft and skilled workers and the working-class parties, see tables 2-2 and 2-5.

46. For working-class participation in the rank and file of the NSDAP before the seizure of power, see Kater, *The Nazi Party*, pp. 20–23, 34–38, 52– 56.

47. For nonstudent women in the Marburg party, see table 6-7. For women of the *Rentnermittelstand* in the Nazi electorate nationally, see Childers, *The Nazi Voter*, pp. 225–28.

48. Attributed to an unidentified traveler by Kürschner, *Geschichte der Stadt Marburg*, p. 188. Wilhelm von Humboldt, who lived in Marburg in 1788, wrote of it, "Considered as a city, Marburg is the ugliest and most unpleasant place imaginable. Old and ugly houses, unclean streets, crooked and so hilly that in some places where it is too steep people have built steps" (quoted in ibid.).

49. On Weidenhausen, see Görich, "Marburgs Brücken-Vorstadt," pp. 19–26.

50. On Ketzerbach, see Ketzerbach Gesellschaft Marburg, *Hundert Jahre*, pp. 5–64; on festivals, Weber-Kellermann and Stolle, *Volksleben in Hessen*, pp. 72–73, and Heller, *Hessische Volksfeste*, pp. 28–30.

51. Eight of the seventeen came from the Frankfurterstraße alone.

52. There were exceptions: nine professors lived in the Renthofstraße (precinct 1), part of the urban core, in 1930/31. See "Straßenverzeichnis," pp. 155–56.

53. On the northern below-average precincts, refer to Bauer, "Der Afföller," pp. 7–27, and Meschede, "Zur Geschichte des Marburger Nordviertels."

54. NSDAP Marburg, *Festschrift*, p. 42.

55. On fluctuations in party membership, see ibid., pp. 59–61. Most historians have relied on the five-county district data in ibid., pp. 323–33, for evidence of the Marburg NSDAP's social support. See Neusüß-Hunkel, *Parteien und Wahlen*, p. 49, and Rosemarie Mann, "Entstehen und Entwicklung der NSDAP," p. 33. Seier discusses the problems of the NSDAP data and argues that they imply that "*mittelständisch*-academic" Marburg "held back" (*sich reserviert verhielt*) from supporting the NSDAP before 1930. This argument is acceptable only if we adopt the narrower definition of "academic" Marburg that excludes university students. See Seier, "Marburg in der Weimarer Republik," p. 574.

56. Twenty-four of fifty-six DNVP members belonged to the elite, compared with twenty-two of forty-eight in the DVP and eighteen of fifty-one in the DDP. See also table 2-5.

57. For the DNVP the proportion was twenty-one of fifty-six; for the DVP, fourteen of forty-eight; and for the DDP, nineteen of fifty-one.

58. See tables 1-1 and 1-2.

59. Childers, *The Nazi Voter*, pp. 225–28.

60. The percentage of university and advanced high school students among NSDAP entrants nationwide was 3.1 in 1925–32, 1.6 in 1933, and 2.2 in 1934–36. The figures are derived from Kater, "Methodologische Überlegungen," pp. 164–65.

61. Membership in Marburg NSDStB, winter and summer semesters:

WS 1926	9	WS 1930	36
SS 1928	10	SS 1931	48
WS 1928	10	WS 1931	69
SS 1929	28	SS 1932	76
WS 1929	36	SS 1934	256
SS 1930	29		

Source: HSAM 305a, Acc 1954/16, 1.

62. For a comparison of the electoral strength of the Marburg and Tübingen leagues, see Koshar "Two 'Nazisms,'" p. 28. For other schools, we can compare NSDStB members per thousand students before and after the summer of 1931:

Before		*After*	
Halle (WS 1929)	18.7	Würzburg (WS 1931)	28.0
Marburg (WS 1930)	11.2	Marburg (WS 1931)	22.3
Erlangen (WS 1930)	10.4	Göttingen (SS 1932)	17.5
Freiburg (WS 1930)	8.8	Münster (WS 1931)	8.2

Sources: For Tübingen, Uwe Adam, *Hochschule und Nationalsozialismus*, pp. 23–26; for Freiburg, Kreutzberger, *Studenten und Politik*, p. 76; for all the rest, Faust, *Der Nationalsozialistische Deutsche Studentenbund*, 2:147.

63. For Marburg, see HSAM, 305a, Acc. 1954/16, 1. For size of cities listed by students, I used "Hauptübersicht," *SJDG* 30 (1935): 2–27; for the Reich NSDAP, Kater, "Methodologische Überlegungen," p. 164; and for Reich urban population, *SDR* 408 (1931): 26.

There are two reasons for treating a town listed in the Marburg NSDStB membership lists as "hometown" (*Heimatort*) rather than "birthplace" (*Geburtsort*), which is the term used on the forms that all student groups submitted to the university Rektor. First, the compiler of the summer 1931 NSDStB list crossed out "birthplace" and substituted "hometown." Second, the towns listed under "hometown" in the latter list agree with the towns listed as "birthplace" in other NSDStB lists where the same students' names appear again.

64. There were 32 (22.9 percent) students from Hesse-Nassau in the Marburg NSDStB, compared with 691 (21.0 percent) in the Marburg student body. Source: HSAM 305a, Acc. 1954/16, 1; DHS, 1 (1928): 160.

65. Overrepresented majors among NSDStB students in five German universities, 1929–32:

	Law	Medicine	Theology	Arts/ Letters	Natural Science
Marburg	+		+	+	
Erlangen		+	+		
Göttingen			+	+	
Halle	+				
Münster	+		+		+

Sources: for Marburg, HSAM, 305a, Acc. 1954/16, 1; *DHS* 10 (1932–1933): 11–13; for the others, Faust, *Der Nationalsozialistische Deutsche Studentenbund*, 2:146.

66. Kater, *Studentenschaft und Rechtsradikalismus*, chap. 4; Steinberg, *Sabers and Brownshirts*, chap. 2.

67. Faust, *Der Nationalsozialistische Deutsche Studentenbund*, 1:117 and 2:146, rates job prospects in the Republic for university graduates with particular majors this way: theology, favorable to unfavorable; law, unfavorable; arts and letters, bad; natural science, unfavorable to very bad; and medicine, bad to very bad.

Chapter 7

1. NSDAP Marburg, *Festschrift*, p. 61; NSDStB membership list, winter 1933/34, in HSAM 305a, Acc. 1954/16, 1.

2. For Freisler, see *OZ* 2 March 1933. For results of the different elections, see Rosemarie Mann, "Entstehen und Entwicklung der NSDAP," table 5, p. 340; Willertz, "Marburg unter dem Nationalsozialismus," pp. 595, 604–5; and *OZ* 13 March 1933.

3. Rosemarie Mann, "Entstehen und Entwicklung der NSDAP," p. 305.

4. For the comparison between Scheef and Müller, see Koshar, "Two 'Nazisms,'" pp. 39–40; on Müller's firing, Schneider, *Marburg 1933–1945*, p. 48. See Noakes, "Oberbürgermeister and Gauleiter," for a comparative perspective on the situation of big-city mayors after 1933.

5. On the Nazi takeover of city and county offices, see ASM, "Verwaltungsberichte (1935)," pp. 55–57, and Willertz, "Marburg unter dem Nationalsozialismus," p. 595. For a general perspective, see Matzerath, *Nationalsozialismus und kommunale Selbstverwaltung*, pp. 433–34.

6. *OZ* 4 February and 27 March 1933; Schneider, *Marburg 1933–1945*, pp. 44–59. For incidents of persecution of political opponents in the county, see Rauschenberg police to LR, 20 March 1933; Sterzhausen police to LR, 9 April 1933; Cappel police to LR, 19 April 1933; and Sterzhausen police to LR, 4 May 1933, all in HSAM 180, LA Mbg, 4170.

7. For KPD activity in Oberhessen, see Stapo Kassel to Gestapo Berlin, 4 May 1934, in HSAM 165, Kassel I, 3949; Schneider, *Marburg 1933–1945*, pp. 79–92.

8. Cited in Schneider, *Marburg 1933–1945*, p. 60.

9. For massive documentation on the SPD in the Third Reich, see Behnken, *Deutschland-Berichte der Sozialdemokratischen Partei Deutschlands 1934–40*, and Mason, *Arbeiterklasse und Volksgemeinschaft.*

10. Schneider, *Marburg 1933–1945*, pp. 64–65.

11. Interviews with former *HT* publisher Bauer, 1 April 1977 and 5 March 1980. For Nazi opinion of the *HT*, see NSDAP Marburg, *Festschrift*, p. 20. For Bauer's response to Nazi threats to boycott his newspaper, see *HT* 8 April 1933. For Bauer after World War II, see John Gimbel, *A German Community*, pp. 43, 68, 95, 159–61.

12. Schneider, *Marburg 1933–1945*, pp. 49–50. On Jacobsohn's career, see Schnack, *Marburger Gelehrte*, pp. 225–26; on Röpke, ibid., pp. 420–21.

13. *OZ* 31 March 1933. Some townspeople went much farther than observing the boycott. One party member, who signed her letter "A member of her party," (*Eine Anhängerin Ihrer Partei*) informed the NSDAP business office on 30 March 1933 that Carl Haas, a Jew who was formerly a banker in Marburg but went bankrupt in 1930, had caused "unspeakable shame" to many "Christian families" through his business dealings but was now living "in comfort." The unidentified writer made no concrete suggestion as to how this situation might be addressed. See HSAM 330, Mbg C, 5613. On Marburg Jews under the dictatorship, see Rehme and Haase, *Mit Rumpf und Stumpf ausrotten.*

14. For the decrees pertaining to German universities in the first months of the Third Reich, see Faust, *Der Nationalsozialistische Deutsche Studentenbund*, 2:122–23. For the laws governing the enrollment of non-Aryans at the university, see the guidelines from the Prussian education minister to university chancellors, 16 June 1933, in HSAM 305a, Acc. 1975/79, 64. The Marburg chancellor's data indicated that the share of non-Aryan students in total enrollment and incoming students fell far below the statistical ceilings even before the new rulings took effect. In the winter semester 1932/33, for instance, the proportion of non-Aryans among the 3,576 enrolled students was only 0.6 percent. See report of the chancellor, 23 June 1933, in HSAM 305a, Acc. 1975/79, 64.

15. See Hermann Bauer interviews, 1 April 1977 and 5 March 1980. For von Papen's speech, see n. 71, this chapter.

16. For von Soden, see Schnack, *Marburger Gelehrte*, pp. 501–12; for Hamann, ibid., pp. 124–37; for Mommsen, E. Jaensch to NSLB, 14 February 1938; During to NSLB, 22 February 1938; Wolf, *Kreisamtsleiter* to NSLB, 23 February 1938, all in NA T-81, 225, 5005722–5005726. The character references cited above generally defended Mommsen's liberal political background, stating that his support for the DDP was due to either his reaction to the "conservative, ossified nationalism" of the Marburg history department (Jaensch) or his "lack of political insight" (During). But the recommendations clearly are defensive in tone and should be viewed as efforts by Mommsen's supporters to deflect Nazi repression of a man

who, along with Rade and a number of other Marburg professors, was closely identified with the Republic.

17. See n. 13, this chapter.

18. For planning and implementation of National Labor Day, see ASM, "Verwaltungsberichte (1933)," pp. 1–2; and *OZ* 29 April, 3 and 6 May 1933. For a later celebration of the day, see *OZ* 2 May 1935.

19. *OZ* 29 April 1933.

20. Ibid.

21. *OZ* 6 May 1933.

22. For both organizations, see *OZ* 29 April 1933. For further information on the Turnverein in this period, see *OZ* 13 May 1933.

23. Meyer, *Verein im neuen Staat*, p. 15. On the issue of the legal status of sectional interests in the Nazi dictatorship, see Frankel, *The Dual State*, pp. 85–86.

24. Freudenthal argues that there were "gradations" of "coordination." See his *Vereine in Hamburg*, pp. 346–47.

25. For the social clubs, see "Marburger Vereine," *MEB* (1934/35), pp. 93–94.

26. For an overview of which clubs and associations still existed formally in Marburg as of 1 February 1934, see ibid., pp. 91–107. Additionally, see the questionnaires that cultural clubs were required to fill out and submit to the Gauleitung, Abteilung für Volksbildung, in March 1934, in HSAM 330, Mbg C, 4030.

27. Meyer, *Verein im neuen Staat*, pp. 15–23.

28. *OZ* 18 June 1933; list of board of directors, 23 March 1933, AKMVR, 74.

29. *OZ* 19 May 1933.

30. *OZ* 26 April and 5 May 1933. The most useful account of civil servants during the Nazi dictatorship remains Hans Mommsen, *Beamtentum im Dritten Reich*. For interesting insights on the problems of civil servants in German society in 1933–45, see Caplan, "Civil Service Support for Nazism."

31. *OZ* 20 May 1933.

32. Minutes of 12 July 1933 meeting, AKMVR, 61; *OZ* 10 May 1933.

33. *OZ* 13 May 1933. The membership numbers of the six NSDAP members were 622,647; 1,360,899; 2,828,245; 2,828,386; 2,828,530; 2,828,559. See NSDAP membership list, in HSAM 327/1, 5488.

34. *OZ* 26 May 1933.

35. *OZ* 11 May 1933. Board members who were in the NSDAP held membership numbers issued after the seizure of power.

36. Prussian education minister to RPK, 7 and 8 November 1933; Wilke to LR, 28 November and 4 December 1933; Wilke and Friedrichs, adjutant of *Gauleiter*, to NSDAP county and communal officials, 6 December 1933; Schütrumpf to Wilke, 13 December 1933; LR to RPK, 18 December 1933; Schütrumpf to LR, 18 December 1933; Prussian education minister

to RPK, 28 December 1933; Wilke to district Landräte, 15 January 1934; Prussian education minister to LR, 24 January 1934, all in both HSAM 180, LA Mbg, 3585 and HSAM 330, Mbg C, 4078.

37. OZ 27 May 1933.

38. Protocol of 25 June 1934 Hausfrauenverband meeting; letter of attorneys Bock and Böttcher to Amtsgericht, 9 March 1936, both in AKMVR, 125. For a general view of women in German society after 1933, see Koonz, "Mothers in the Fatherland."

39. Quoted from Frau Prof. Strecker's 28 August 1936 description of the final meeting of the Hausfrauenverband on 3 July 1936, AKMVR, 125. A list of participants at the July meeting includes 169 names.

40. Ibid.

41. Faust, Der Nationalsozialistische Deutsche Studentenbund, 2:122–23.

42. For the socialist student group, see HSAM 305a, Acc. 1954/16, 12; for the Catholic students' political group, HSAM 305a, Acc. 1954/16, 17.

43. The membership total breaks down as follows: Corps, sixty-five; Burschenschaften, ninety; Landsmannschaften, sixty-two; Turnerschaften, twenty-nine; and others, forty-three. See HSAM 305a, Acc. 1954/16, 1–78.

44. For the threats of SA students against fraternity members, see letter from Gunter Kranz to Academic Dueling Ring in Berlin, 5 July 1934, AUWAR II/105. For the decision to build Kameradschaftshäuser, see n. 51 this chapter.

45. Based on analysis of affiliations of individuals in NSDStB membership list, 20 November 1933, in HSAM 305a, Acc. 1954/16, 1.

46. Kranz to Dueling Ring, 5 July 1934, AUWAR II/105.

47. "At the 2 May National Labor Day ceremonies the leader of the new student government [Studentenschaft], Kurt Hübner, received from the chancellor the new student constitution. The ceremonies took place in an intimate gathering of students and faculty, whose close association in the new state Professor Mannhardt emphasized particularly strongly in his formal address." See "Aus der Studentenschaft," Mitteilungen Universitätsbund Marburg, 4 (1933), in HSAM 330, Mbg C, 4260.

48. Ibid.

49. Hübner's version of the Manigk incident is related in his letter to DSt officials, 30 November 1933; the SA student Müller's version appears in his letter to Standarte SA J11, 29 November 1933, both in AUWAR I/03 phi 253/V.

50. Chancellor Baur to Reich education minister, 4 May 1936, HSAM 305a, Acc. 1975/42, 2059.

51. Kater, The Nazi Party, p. 98.

52. OZ 7 November 1935.

53. "Even though the student corporations were eliminated, one must understand the psychic aftereffects on Marburg students. The rumor spread that the young student, regardless of his view of nazism, could do

358 Notes to Pages 260–64

better if he studied at a larger urban university, because he would find himself under constant surveillance in a small town." Unsigned report on Marburg university, ca. 1936, NA T-81, 225, 5005326–5005328.

54. The quote is from Chancellor Baur, letter to Reich education minister, 4 May 1936, in HSAM 305a, Acc. 1975/42, 2059.

55. The fraternity Saxonia's complaints appeared in a letter to Dr. Kruger, 31 May 1933, AUWAR I/04/phi 92.

56. Heer, *Marburger Burschenschaft Arminia*, pp. 150–53.

57. Ibid., pp. 160–61. For the chancellor's remark, see Baur to Reich education minister, 4 May 1936, in HSAM 305a, Acc. 1975/42, 2059.

58. This chronology, which conceptualizes 1935/36 as the end point of one period of coordination and the beginning of another, agrees with that of Adam, *Hochschule und Nationalsozialismus*, pp. 206–7.

59. Hans Mommsen, "National Socialism," pp. 193–95.

60. See the evidence cited for 1937 in Willertz, "Marburg unter dem Nationalsozialismus," pp. 620–22. The roots of such disillusionment can be found in the late Republic and early dictatorship.

61. Stapo Kassel to Gestapo Berlin, 4 May, 20 July, 4 August 1934, all in HSAM 165, Kassel I, 3949. For Krawielitzki's onesidedly optimistic account of the economic situation in the county, see his report, "Der Landkreis Marburg von 1933 bis 1937," in HSAM 330, Mbg C, 5613. On the problems of townspeople deprived of rental income by Nazi policies, see unsigned, undated party report, NA T-81, 225, 5005326–5005328. The deleterious economic effects of comradeship houses and reduced rental incomes are also touched on in OB to RPK, 17 September 1934, in HSAM 330, Mbg C, 5612. For comparable but more detailed evidence on dissatisfaction with material conditions in the 1930s, see Kershaw, *Popular Opinion and Political Dissent*, pp. 33–155.

62. For Schwalm, see interviews of 28 September and 5 October 1980.

63. *HV* editor to *KLZ*, 18 January 1934, in HSAM 330, Mbg C, 5613.

64. Jensen to Krawielitzki, 26 May 1936, NA T-81, 225, 5005325; Jensen to Krawielitzki, 10 July 1936, ibid., 5005315–5005316; Krawielitzki to Jensen, 13 July 1936, ibid., 5005323–5005324.

65. Stapo Kassel to Gestapo Berlin, 18 June 1934, in HSAM 165, Kassel I, 3949.

66. Interview with Frau Prof. Luise Berthold, 17 March 1980; Berthold, "Ansprache an ehemalige Marburg Mitbürger," pp. 82–85.

67. Schneider, *Marburg 1933–1945*, pp. 89–91.

68. University Association secretary to chancellor, 22 August 1933 (in which the former passes along an association publication entitled "Marburg, die Universität in der Gegenwart") in HSAM 305a, Acc. 1975/79, 631.

69. Ibid. A form of *Resistenz*, this activity has found effective if uneven documentation and analysis in Broszat et al., *Bayern in der NS-Zeit*.

70. Schneider, *Marburg 1933–1945*, p. 92.

71. All quotes from von Papen, "Marburger Rede."

72. Bracher, *German Dictatorship*, p. 239.

73. Stapo Kassel to Gestapo Berlin, 5 July 1934, in HSAM 165, Kassel I, 3949.

74. Interviews with Bauer, 1 April 1977 and 5 March 1980; Berthold, *Erlebtes*, p. 51; Schneider, *Marburg 1933–1945*, pp. 94–95.

75. Scholder, *Die Kirchen und das Dritte Reich*, 1:239–74; Conway, *Nazi Persecution of the Churches*, pp. 1–66; Bracher, *German Dictatorship*, pp. 379–90; Dickmann, "Der Kirchenkampf 1933/34" (my thanks to Erhart Dettmering for bringing this publication to my attention); Meier, *Der evangelische Kirchenkampf*, 1:3–145; Slenczka, *Evangelische Kirche*; Brakelmann, "Hoffnungen und Illusionen."

76. "Dokumentation zur Kirchenkampf," Vol. 1, pp. 390–91. See also Meier, *Der evangelische Kirchenkampf*, 1:421–28 and Scholder, *Die Kirchen und das Dritte Reich*, 1:566–67.

77. For May 1933 disputes over the Reich Bishop, see Conway, *Nazi Persecution of the Churches*, p. 35; for Berlin–Dahlem and Barmen–Gemarke, see Scholder, *Die Kirchen und das Dritte Reich*, 1:568.

78. Hermelink, *Kirche im Kampf*, p. 51. On Erlangen, see Manfred Franze, *Die Erlanger Studentenschaft*, pp. 184–85. For additional documentation on Marburg theologians and the Aryan legislation, see Liebing, *Marburger Theologen*. See also Balzer, Borschel, and Held, "Evangelische Demokraten." For the Kurhessian Synod, see Scholder, *Die Kirchen und das Dritte Reich*, 1:615–16.

79. Schnack, *Marburger Gelehrte*, p. 506; Berthold, *Erlebtes*, pp. 45–46; Schneider, *Marburg 1933–1945*, pp. 76–77. More generally on ideology, see Bracher, *German Dictatorship*, pp. 384–85.

80. Berthold, *Erlebtes*, p. 53.

81. Berthold interview, 17 March 1980; Schneider, "Widerstand und Verfolgung," p. 234.

82. Berthold interview, 17 March 1980; Schnack, *Marburger Gelehrte*, p. 512; Schneider, *Marburg 1933–1945*, pp. 98–106.

83. Stapo Kassel to Gestapo Berlin, reports of 5 and 19 September and 5 and 22 December 1934, in HSAM 165, Kassel I, 3949.

84. Schneider, *Marburg 1933–1945*, p. 101. Marburger Wingolf dissolved in late 1935. See "Vom Wingolf auf dem Bundestag zu Marburg am 27. Oktober 1935 abgegebene Erklärung," in HSAM 305a, Acc. 1954/16, 49.

85. Schneider, *Marburg, 1933–1945*, p. 104.

86. Ibid.

87. Scholder, *Die Kirchen und das Dritte Reich*, 1:470.

88. Stapo Kassel to Gestapo Berlin, 5 December 1934, HSAM 165, Kassel I, 3949.

89. Berthold to the author, 25 April 1980, and interview, 17 March 1980.

90. Berthold, *Erlebtes*, p. 53.

91. Quoted in Schnack, *Marburger Gelehrte*, p. 510.

92. Conway, *Nazi Persecution of the Churches*, pp. 77–78.

93. Bracher, *German Dictatorship*, p. 381.

94. *OZ* 1 November 1935.
95. *OZ* 8 May 1935.
96. Harro Jensen's instructions in report of 20 October 1936, NA T-81, 224, 5004244–5004245. See also the document reproduced in Willertz, "Marburg unter dem Nationalsozialismus," p. 623, in which Jensen again complains of low attendance, this time at a Nazi instructional meeting of 21 October 1936.

Conclusion

1. Quoted from Bessel and Feuchtwanger, *Social Change and Political Development*, p. 14. The major inspiration for sociopolitical history since the early 1970s has been Hans Mommsen, Petzina, and Weisbrod, *Industrielles System und politische Entwicklung.*
2. Childers, *The Nazi Voter*; Falter, "Wer verhalf der NSDAP?"; Hamilton, *Who Voted for Hitler?*; Jamin, *Zwischen den Klassen*; Kater, *The Nazi Party.*
3. See Tilly, *From Mobilization to Revolution*, pp. 52–142.
4. White, *Splintered Party*, pp. 159–98.
5. Arns, "Grass Roots Politics," pp. 285–392; Zofka, *Ausbreitung des Nationalsozialismus.*
6. Boissevain, *Friends of Friends*, p. 7.
7. Bessel, *Political Violence*; Diehl, *Paramilitary Politics*; Rosenhaft, *Beating the Fascists?*
8. Staudinger, *Individuum und Gemeinschaft*, p. 3.
9. Blackbourn, "The Discreet Charm of the Bourgeoisie," in Blackbourn and Eley, *Peculiarities of German History*, p. 160.
10. Maier, *Recasting Bourgeois Europe.* Concentrating on economic contradictions within agrarian and industrial sectors, Abraham offers a Marxist interpretation of the recasting of sociopolitical alliances at the top of German society in *Collapse of the Weimar Republic.*
11. Geyer, "The State in National Socialist Germany," p. 193. A critical rethinking of the history of the Imperial German state is also presently underway, as evidenced in Eley, "The British Model and the German Road," in Blackbourn and Eley, *Peculiarities of German History*, pp. 127–43.
12. Geyer, "The State in National Socialist Germany," p. 197. A similar argument is implied in Childers, *The Nazi Voter*, particularly pp. 79–80, 126, where the author discusses the realignment of electoral loyalties during the 1920s.
13. The term is from Jamin, *Zwischen den Klassen.*
14. Ibid., pp. 372–73.
15. Thus the argument that Nazis were not "fanatics, or desperadoes, or psychopaths, or quasi-criminals, but ordinary Germans," remains crucial. See Barraclough, "The Nazi Boom," p. 21.

Bibliography

Archives and Public Records

Berlin
  Berlin Document Center
    Akten des Obersten Parteigerichtes
    Akten des Rasse- und Siedlungsamtes. Hauptamt der SS
Karlsruhe
  Badisches Generallandesarchiv
    60   Geheimes Kabinett, Innenministerium
    235 Kultusministerium
Koblenz
  Bundesarchiv Koblenz
    60 VO 1, Deutsche Volkspartei, film no. 11
Marburg
  Amtsgericht Kreis Marburg
    Akten des Vereinsregisters, nos. 1–153, 1899–1945
  Hessisches Staatsarchiv Marburg
    Bestand 165   Preußische Regierung Kassel, Abt. I
            180   Landratsämter. Marburg, 1821–1952
            305a Universitätsarchiv
                  Acc. 1950/9
                  Acc. 1954/16
                  Acc. 1975/42
                  Acc. 1975/79
                  Acc. 1976/19
            310   Universitätsarchiv
                  Acc. 1975/42
            327/1 NSDAP Marburg
            330   Stadtarchive. Marburg
  Stadtverwaltung Marburg
    Berichte über die Verwaltung, 1918–1935
  Universitäts-Bibliothek Marburg
    Document collection: Die Universität im Weltkrieg
Tübingen
  Universitätsarchiv Tübingen
    Bestand 117c

Washington, D.C.
National Archives (Microfilm)
T-81   Rolls 224–25, 232–35, 256
T-253 Rolls 28–29
Würzburg
Archiv der Universitätsbibliothek Würzburg. Archiv der ehemaligen
Reichsstudentenführung und des NSDStB
Abt. I Akten der ehemaligen Deutschen Studentenschaft bzw. der
Reichsstudentenführung (ab 1933)
Abt. II Akten des Nationalsozialistischen Deutschen Studenten-
bundes und der Arbeitsgemeinschaft Nationalsozialistischer
Studentinnen seit 1925

Interviews, Questionnaires, and Correspondence

Hermann Bauer, former editor of *Hessisches Tageblatt,* interviews on 1
April 1977 and 5 March 1980.
Luise Berthold, Professor Emeritus, interviews on 10 and 17 March 1980;
correspondence of 25 April 1980.
Friedrich Bluhm, former member of Marburg VfB and Property Owners'
and Landlords' Association, interview on 30 March 1977.
Hans Krawielitzki, former NSDAP Kreisleiter, interviews on 20 and 21
March 1980.
Theodora Perino, former Marburg DDP member, interview on 10 March
1980.
Fritz Schwalm, former SS Schulungsleiter and Marburg student, question-
naire and telephone interviews of 28 September and 5 October 1980.
Heinrich Seibel, former Property Owners' and Landlords' Association
member, telephone conversation on 25 March 1977.
Karl Wilser, former Kriegerkameradschaft official, interview on 29 July
1976.

Unpublished Hausfrauenverband Records

"Aus der 60-jährigen Tätigkeit des Marburger Hausfrauenverbandes e.V."
N.d. (Typewritten).
Marburger Hausfrauenverband, e.V. Protokollbuch. 2 vols. 1918–1930.
(Handwritten).

Newspapers, Newsletters, Yearbooks, and Association Reports

Burschenschaftliche Blätter
Deutsche Corpszeitung

Geschäftsbericht des Bundesvorstandes des Kurhessischen Kriegerbundes
Handwerkszeitung für Kurhessen und Waldeck
Hessische Landeszeitung
Hessische Volkswacht
Hessischer Beobachter
Hessisches Tageblatt
Jahrbuch des Deutschen Krieger-Bundes
Jahrbuch des Handwerkskammers Kassel und Kurhessisch–Wald-
    eckischen Handwerkerbundes
Jahresbericht des Preussischen Landesvereine vom Roten Kreuz. Freiwil-
    ligen Sanitätskolonne
Jahresberichte des Marburger Grund- und Hausbesitzer-Vereins
Kasseler Neueste Nachrichten
Kurhessische Landeszeitung
Marburger Hochschulzeitung
Mitteilungen. Universitätsbund Marburg
Mitteilungen der Allgemeinen Marburger Studentenschaft
Mitteilungsblatt des Oberhessischen Gebirgsvereins
Mitteilungsblätter für das Einzelhandel
Oberhessische Bauernzeitung
Oberhessische Zeitung
Völkischer Beobachter
Volksstimme (Frankfurt/Main)
Volksstimme für Lahn-, Dill-, und Westerwaldgebiet
Waldecker Beobachter
Wingolfs-Blätter

Statistical References

Deutsche Hochschulstatistik. Vols. 1 (1928), 4 (1930), 10 (1932/33), 12
    (1933/34).
Statistik des Deutschen Reiches. Vols. 405 (1931), 408 (1931), 456 (1936).
Statistisches Jahrbuch Deutscher Städte (after 1934 *Statistisches*
    Jahrbuch Deutscher Gemeinden). Vols. 27–30 (1932–35).
Statistisches Jahrbuch für das Deutsche Reich. Vol. 46 (1927).

Secondary Sources on Marburg and Hesse

Abendroth, Wolfgang. "Fruchtloser Heroismus?—Kampf für die Humani-
    tät." *Marburger Blätter* (November 1965): 4–6.
Arns, David C. "Grass Roots Politics in the Weimar Republic: Long-Term
    Structural Change and Electoral Behavior in Hessen-Darmstadt to
    1930." Ph.D. dissertation, State University of New York at Buffalo,
    1979.

Balzer, Fr.-Martin; Borschel, Angelika; and Held, Axel. "Evangelische Demokraten an der Marburger Theologischen Fakultät." In *Universität und demokratische Bewegung. Ein Lesebuch zur 450-Jahrfeier der Philipps-Universität Marburg,* edited by Dieter Kramer and Christina Vanja. Marburg, 1977.

Bannasch, H., and Lachmann, H. P., eds. *Aus Geschichte und ihren Hilfswissenschaften.* Marburg, 1979.

Bauer, Hermann. "Der Afföller im Wandel der Zeiten." *Afföllergemeinde e.V. Marburg/L. Festschrift zum 10-jährigen Jubiläum.* Marburg, 1961.

Bensch, Udo. "StuKoMa—Oder die unrühmliche Rolle der Marburger Burschenschaften in den politischen Auseinandersetzungen am Beginn der Weimarer Republik." In *Universität und demokratische Bewegung. Ein Lesebuch zur 450-Jahrfeier der Philipps-Universität Marburg,* edited by Dieter Kramer and Christina Vanja. Marburg, 1977.

Berthold, Luise. "Ansprache an ehemalige Marburg Mitbürger in der Woche der Brüderlichkeit." *Hessische Blätter für Volks- und Kulturforschung.* Bd. 9: *Judaica Hassiaca* (1979): 82–85.

———. *Erlebtes und Erkämpftes.* Marburg, 1969.

Bloem, W. *Der krasse Fuchs.* Leipzig, 1911.

Böth, Gitta, ed. "Talare, Wichs, und Jeans. Zur Geschichte der Universitätskleidung in Marburg." Ausstellung anläßlich des 450jährigen Universitätsjubiläums der Philipps-Universität, Marburg, 12. Juni–31. August, 1977.

Bredow, Wilfried Freiherr von, ed. *450 Jahre Philipps-Universität Marburg. Das Gründungsjubiläum 1977.* Marburg, 1979.

Bredt, Johann Viktor. *Erinnerungen und Dokumente von J. Viktor Bredt 1914–33.* Edited by Martin Schumacher. Düsseldorf, 1970.

Brocke, Bernhard vom. "Marburg im Kaiserreich 1866–1918. Geschichte und Gesellschaft, Parteien und Wahlen einer Universitätsstadt im wirtschaftlichen und sozialen Wandel der industriellen Revolution." In *Marburger Geschichte. Rückblick auf die Stadtgeschichte in Einzelbeiträgen,* edited by Erhart Dettmering and Rudolf Grenz. Marburg, 1980.

Dascher, Ottfried. "Der politische Antisemitismus im Marburger Raum 1887–1893." Hausarbeit, Philipps-Universität Marburg, 1960.

Demandt, Karl E. *Geschichte des Landes Hessen.* Kassel, 1972.

———. *Kassel und Marburg. Ein historischer Städtevergleich.* Marburg, 1975.

———. "Leopold v. Sacher-Masoch und sein Oberhessischer Volksbildungsverein zwischen Schwarzen, Roten, und Antisemiten." *Hessisches Jahrbuch für Landesgeschichte* 18 (1968): 160–208.

Dettmering, Erhart, ed. *Kirche und Schule im nationalsozialistischen Marburg.* Marburg, 1985.

Dettmering, Erhart, and Grenz, Rudolf, eds. *Marburger Geschichte. Rückblick auf die Stadtgeschichte in Einzelbeiträgen.* Marburg, 1980.

Dickmann, Friedrich. "Der Kirchenkampf 1933/34 in der Evangelischen Presse Marburgs. Ein Beitrag zur Geschichte örtlicher Publizistik." In

Kirche und Schule im nationalsozialistischen Marburg, edited by Erhart Dettmering. Marburg, 1985.

"Dokumentation zur Kirchenkampf in Hesse und Nassau." Vol. 1. *Jahrbuch der Hessischen Kirchengeschichtlichen Vereinigung* 25 (1974).

Duderstadt, Henning. *Der Schrei nach dem Recht. Die Tragödie von Mechterstädt*. Marburg, 1921.

Ehlers, Eckart, and Leib, Jürgen. "Marburg—Stadt und Universität." In *450 Jahre Philipps-Universität Marburg. Das Gründungsjubiläum 1977*, edited by Wilfried Freiherr von Bredow. Marburg, 1979.

Eriksen, Wolfgang. "Klima und Witterung im Räume Marburg." In *Marburg und Umgebung. Ein landeskundlicher Excursionsführer*, edited by Wilhelm Lauer. Marburg, 1967.

Gimbel, John. *A German Community under American Occupation: Marburg 1945–52*. Stanford, 1961.

Görich, Willi. "Marburgs Brücken-Vorstadt. Zur Entwicklungsgeschichte von Weidenhausen." *Hessenland* 2, no. 25 (1955).

Heer, Georg. *Die Marburger Burschenschaft Arminia*. Marburg, 1951.

————. *Marburger Studentenleben 1527–1927*. Marburg, 1927.

Heinemeyer, W.; Klein, Th.; and Seier, H., eds. *Academia Marburgensis. Beiträge zur Geschichte der Philipps-Universität Marburg*. Marburg, 1977.

Heller, Carl. *Hessische Volksfeste*. Kassel, 1926.

Hennig, Eike, ed. *Hessen unterm Hakenkreuz. Studien zur Durchsetzung der NSDAP in Hessen*. Frankfurt/Main, 1983.

Hermelink, Heinrich, and Kaehler, S. A. *Die Philipps-Universität zu Marburg 1527–1927*. Marburg, 1927.

Höfschen, H. G. "Universität und Arbeiterbewegung vor dem ersten Weltkrieg." In *Universität und demokratische Bewegung. Ein Lesebuch zur 450-Jahrfeier der Philipps-Universität Marburg*, edited by Dieter Kramer and Christina Vanja. Marburg, 1977.

Ketzerbach-Gesellschaft Marburg. *Hundert Jahre. 1859–1959. Ketzerbachfest*. Marburg, 1959.

Keyser, Erich. *Hessisches Städtebuch*. Kassel, 1957.

Knauß, Erwin. "Der politische Antisemitismus im Kaiserreich (1871–1900) unter besonderer Berücksichtigung des mittelhessischen Raumes." *Mitteilungen des Oberhessischen Geschichtsvereins* 53/54 (1969): 43–68.

Knobel, Enno. *Die Hessische Rechtspartei. Konservative Opposition gegen das Bismarckreich*. Marburg, 1975.

Kramer, Dieter, and Vanja, Christina, eds. *Universität und demokratische Bewegung. Ein Lesebuch zur 450-Jahrfeier der Philipps-Universität Marburg*. Marburg, 1977.

Kürschner, Walter. *Geschichte der Stadt Marburg*. Marburg, 1934.

Lauer, Wilhelm, ed. *Marburg und Umgebung. Ein landeskundlicher Excursionsführer*. Marburg, 1967.

Leister, Ingeborg. "Marburg." In *Marburg und Umgebung. Ein landes-*

kundlicher Excursionsführer, edited by Wilhelm Lauer. Marburg, 1967.

Lemmer, Ernst. "Das Drama von Mechterstädt. Erinnerungen aus dem Kapp Putsch." *Hessisches Tageblatt,* 22 February 1930.

Leppla, Rupprecht. "Marburg wird preußisch. Aus Briefen Carl Justis an Otto Hartwig." *alma mater philippina* (1969/70): 33–37.

Liebing, Heinz, ed. *Die Marburger Theologen und der Arierparagraph in der Kirche. Eine Sammlung von Texten aus den Jahren 1933 und 1934.* Marburg, 1977.

Mack, Rüdiger. "Otto Böckel und die antisemitische Bauernbewegung in Hessen 1887–1894." *Wetterauer Geschichtsblätter* 16 (1967): 113–47.

Mai, Gunther. "Der Marburger Arbeiter- und Soldatenrat und die Militärpolitik im Bereich des XI. Armeekorps (Kassel) 1918–19." In *Marburger Geschichte. Rückblick auf die Stadtgeschichte in Einzelbeiträgen,* edited by Erhart Dettmering and Rudolf Grenz. Marburg, 1980.

————. "Der Marburger Arbeiter- und Soldatenrat 1918/20." *Hessisches Jahrbuch für Landesgeschichte* 26 (1976): 149–99.

Mann, Rosemarie. "Entstehen und Entwicklung der NSDAP in Marburg bis 1933." *Hessisches Jahrbuch für Landesgeschichte* 22 (1972): 254–342.

Meinhold, Wilhelm. "Johann Conrad Schaefer." In *Lebensbilder aus Kurhessen und Waldeck 1830–1930,* vol. 6, edited by Ingeborg Schnack. Marburg, 1958.

Meschede, Kurt. "Zur Geschichte des Marburger Nordviertels. Von der 'Wasserscheide' durchs Elisabethentor und über die Lahnbrücken zum Bahnhof." *Hessenland* 10, no. 22 (2 November 1963).

Möker, Ulrich. *Nordhessen im Zeichen der industriellen Revolution.* Cologne, Vienna, 1977.

Nationalsozialistische Deutsche Arbeiterpartei Marburg. *Festschrift zum 10 (12) jährigen Bestehen der NSDAP in Marburg.* Marburg, 1935.

Neuhaus, Helmut. *Die Konstitutionen des Corps Teutonia zu Marburg. Untersuchungen zur Verfassungsentwicklung eines Kösener Corps in seiner 150jährigen Geschichte.* Marburg, 1979.

Neusüß-Hunkel, Ermenhild. *Parteien und Wahlen in Marburg nach 1945.* Meisenheim am Glan, 1973.

Papen, Franz von. "Marburger Rede." In *Reden die die Welt bewegten,* edited by Heinrich Peter. Stuttgart, 1959.

Peal, David. "Anti-Semitism and Rural Transformation: The Rise and Fall of the Böckel Movement." Ph.D. dissertation, Columbia University, 1985.

Raiffeisenverband Kurhessen e.V. *75 Jahre Raiffeisenverband Kurhessen.* Kassel, 1957.

Rehme, Günther, and Haase, Konstantin. *Mit Rumpf und Stumpf ausrotten. . . . Zur Geschichte der Juden in Marburg und Umgebung nach 1933.* Marburg, 1982.

Röpke, Wilhelm. "Marburger Studentenjahre." *alma mater philippina* (1963/64): 1–4.

Schaumlöffel, Karl. *Das Studentenkorps Marburg in Thüringen.* Marburg, 1920.

Schmahl, Eugen, and Seipel, Wilhelm. *Entwicklung der völkischen Bewegung.* Giessen, 1933.

Schnack, Ingeborg, ed. *Lebensbilder aus Kurhessen und Waldeck 1830–1930.* Vol. 6. Marburg, 1958.

_____. *Marburger Gelehrte in der ersten Hälfte des 20. Jahrhunderts.* Marburg, 1977.

Schneider, Ulrich. *Marburg 1933–1945. Arbeiterbewegung und Bekennende Kirche gegen den Faschismus.* Frankfurt/Main, 1980.

_____. "Widerstand und Verfolgung an der Marburger Universität 1933–1945." In *Universität und demokratische Bewegung. Ein Lesebuch zur 450-Jahrfeier der Philipps-Universität Marburg,* edited by Dieter Kramer and Christina Vanja. Marburg, 1977.

Schön, Eberhart. *Die Entstehung des Nationalsozialismus in Hessen.* Meisenheim am Glan, 1972.

Schützenverein Marburg. *Festschrift zum 50jährigen Bestehen des Schützenvereins Marburg.* Marburg, 1912.

Seier, Hellmut. "Marburg in der Weimarer Republik." In *Marburger Geschichte. Rückblick auf die Stadtgeschichte in Einzelbeiträgen,* edited by Erhart Dettmering and Rudolf Grenz. Marburg, 1980.

_____. "Radikalisierung und Reform als Probleme der Universität Marburg 1918–33." In *Academia Marburgensis. Beiträge zur Geschichte der Philipps-Universität Marburg,* edited by W. Heinemeyer, Th. Klein, and H. Seier. Marburg, 1977.

_____. "Wahl und Amt des Rektors der Universität Marburg 1918–35." In *Aus Geschichte und ihren Hilfswissenschaften,* edited by H. Bannasch and H. P. Lachmann. Marburg, 1979.

Selchow, Bogislav von. *Hundert Tage aus meinem Leben.* Leipzig, 1936.

Slenczka, Hans. *Die evangelische Kirche von Kurhessen und Waldeck in den Jahren von 1933 bis 1945.* Göttingen, 1977.

Sturmabteilung Brigade 47. *Handbuch der NSDAP. Gau Kurhessen. Die Geschichte der Kurhessischen SA.* Kassel, 1935.

Turnverein Marburg. *Lieder für die Feier des 50. Stiftungsfestes des Turn-Vereins Marburg.* Marburg, 1910.

Verein für Leibesübungen 1860. *VfL 1860–1950. Festschrift zum 90. Stiftungsfest des VfL 1860 Marburg.* Marburg, 1950.

Vereinigung der Verfolgten des Naziregimes—Bund der Antifaschisten, Kreisvereinigung Marburg–Biedenkopf. *Marburg–Behring–Buchenwald.* Marburg, 1980.

Weber-Kellerman, Ingeborg, and Stolle, Walter. *Volksleben in Hessen 1970.* Göttingen, 1971.

Weingartner, James. "Massacre at Mechterstädt. The Case of the Marburg Studentenkorps." *Historian* 37 (1975): 598–618.

Willertz, John R. "Marburg unter dem Nationalsozialismus (1933–1945)." In *Marburger Geschichte. Rückblick auf die Stadtgeschichte in Einzel-

beiträgen, edited by Erhart Dettmering and Rudolf Grenz. Marburg, 1980.

_____. "National Socialism in a German City and County: Marburg 1933–1945." Ph.D. dissertation, University of Michigan, 1970.

Other Secondary Sources

Abraham, David. *The Collapse of the Weimar Republic: Political Economy and Crisis.* Princeton, 1981.

Adam, Uwe. *Hochschule und Nationalsozialismus. Die Universität Tübingen im Dritten Reich.* Tübingen, 1977.

Adamson, Walter L. *Hegemony and Revolution: A Study of Antonio Gramsci's Political and Cultural Theory.* Berkeley, Los Angeles, 1980.

Allen, William Sheridan. *The Nazi Seizure of Power: The Experience of a Single German Town, 1922–1945.* Rev. ed. New York, 1984.

Anderson, Perry. "The Antinomies of Antonio Gramsci." *New Left Review* 100 (November 1976–January 1977): 5–78.

Barraclough, Geoffrey. *An Introduction to Contemporary History.* Harmondsworth, 1967.

_____. "The Nazi Boom." *New York Review of Books* 26, no. 8 (17 May 1979): 18–21.

Baum, Rainer C. *The Holocaust and the German Elite: Genocide and National Suicide in Germany 1871–1945.* Totowa, N.J., London, 1981.

Bausinger, Hermann. "Eher im Gegenteil: Zum Tübinger Weingärtner Liederkranz und seiner 125jährigen Geschichte." *Tübinger Blätter* 57 (1970): 93–96.

_____. "Verbürgerlichung—Folgen eines Interpretaments." In *Kultureller Wandel im 19. Jh. Verhandlungen des 18. Deutschen Volkskunde-Kongresses,* edited by Günther Wiegelmann. Göttingen, 1973.

_____. *Volkskultur in der technischen Welt.* Stuttgart, 1961.

Behnken, Klaus, ed. *Deutschland Berichte der Sozialdemokratischen Partei Deutschlands 1934–40.* Salzhausen, Frankfurt/Main, 1980.

Berger, Suzanne. "Regime and Interest Representation: The French Traditional Middle Classes." In *Organizing Interests in Western Europe: Pluralism, Corporatism, and the Transformation of Politics,* edited by Albert Hirschman and Charles Maier. Cambridge, 1981.

Bessel, Richard. *Political Violence and the Rise of Nazism: The Stormtroopers in Eastern Germany 1925–34.* New Haven, London, 1984.

Bessel, Richard, and Feuchtwanger, E. J., eds. *Social Change and Political Development in Weimar Germany.* London, 1981.

Blackbourn, David. "Class and Politics in Wilhelmine Germany: The Center Party and the Social Democrats in Württemberg." *Central European History* 9 (1976): 220–49.

_____. *Class, Religion, and Local Politics in Wilhelmine Germany: The Centre Party in Württemberg before 1914.* New Haven, London, 1980.

————. "The *Mittelstand* in German Society and Politics, 1871–1914." *Social History* 4 (1977): 409–33.

Blackbourn, David, and Eley, Geoff. *The Peculiarities of German History: Bourgeois Society and Politics in Nineteenth-Century Germany.* New York, 1984.

Bleuel, Hans-Peter, and Klinnert, Ernst. *Deutsche Studenten auf dem Weg ins Dritte Reich.* Gutersloh, 1967.

Boissevain, Jeremy. *Friends of Friends: Networks, Manipulators, and Coalitions.* New York, 1974.

Bracher, Karl Dietrich. *The German Dictatorship: The Origins, Structure, and Effects of National Socialism.* Translated by Jean Steinberg. New York, 1970.

Brakelmann, Günter. "Hoffnungen und Illusionen evangelischer Prediger zu Beginn des Dritten Reiches: Gottesdienstliche Feiern aus politischen Anlässen." In *Die Reihen fast geschlossen. Beiträge zur Geschichte des Alltags unterm Nationalsozialismus,* edited by Detlev Peukert and Jürgen Reulecke. Wuppertal, 1981.

Braun, Karl, et al., eds. *Das andere Tübingen. Kultur und Lebensweise der Unteren Stadt im 19. Jahrhundert.* Tübingen, 1978.

Bresciani-Turroni, Constantino. *The Economics of Inflation: A Study of Currency Depreciation in Postwar Germany 1914–23.* New York, 1931.

Bridenthal, Renate. "Class Struggle around the Hearth: Women and Domestic Service in the Weimar Republic." In *Towards the Holocaust: The Social and Economic Collapse of the Weimar Republic,* edited by Michael N. Dobkowski and Isidor Wallimann. Westport, Conn., 1983.

————. " 'Professional' Housewives: Stepsisters of the Women's Movement." In *When Biology Became Destiny: Women in Weimar and Nazi Germany,* edited by Renate Bridenthal, Atina Grossmann, and Marion Kaplan. New York, 1984.

Broszat, Martin. "Zur Struktur der NS-Massenbewegung." *Vierteljahrshefte für Zeitgeschichte* 31 (1983): 52–76.

Broszat, Martin, and Fröhlich, Elke, eds. *Bayern in der NS-Zeit.* Vol. 2, *Herrschaft und Gesellschaft im Konflikt,* pt. A. Munich, Vienna, 1979.

Broszat, Martin; Fröhlich, Elke; and Grossmann, Anton, eds. *Bayern in der NS-Zeit.* Vols. 3–4, *Herrschaft und Gesellschaft im Konflikt,* pts. C–D. Munich, Vienna, 1981.

Broszat, Martin; Fröhlich, Elke; and Wiesemann, Falk, eds. *Bayern in der NS-Zeit.* Vol. 1, *Soziale Lage und politisches Verhalten der Bevölkerung im Spiegel vertraulicher Berichte.* Munich, Vienna, 1977.

Bry, Gerhard. *Wages in Germany 1871–1945.* Princeton, 1960.

Büttner, Ursula. *Hamburg in der Staats- und Wirtschaftskrise 1928–1931.* Hamburg, 1982.

Caplan, Jane. "Civil Service Support for National Socialism: An Evaluation." In *Der "Führerstaat": Mythos und Realität. Studien zur Struktur und Politik des Dritten Reiches,* edited by Gerhard Hirschfeld and Lothar Kettenacker. Stuttgart, 1981.

Chickering, Roger. *We Men Who Feel Most German: A Cultural Study of the Pan-German League 1886–1914.* Boston, 1984.

Childers, Thomas. "Inflation, Stabilization, and Political Realignment in Germany, 1924–28." In *Die Deutsche Inflation. Eine Zwischenbilanz,* edited by Gerald D. Feldman et al. Berlin, New York, 1982.

_____. *The Nazi Voter: The Social Foundations of Fascism in Germany, 1919–1933.* Chapel Hill, 1983.

Cochran, William. G. *Sampling Techniques.* New York, 1963.

Conway, J. S. *The Nazi Persecution of the Churches 1933–45.* New York, 1968.

Coyner, Sandra. "Class Consciousness and Consumption: The New Middle Class during the Weimar Republic." *Journal of Social History* 10 (1977): 310–31.

Craig, Gordon A. *The Germans.* New York, 1982.

Crew, David. *Town in the Ruhr: A Social History of Bochum 1860–1914.* New York, 1979.

Croon, Helmuth; Hofmann, Wolfgang; and Unruh, Georg Christoph von. *Kommunale Selbstverwaltung im Zeitalter der Industrialisierung.* Stuttgart, 1971.

Crossick, Geoffrey, and Haupt, Heinz-Gerhard, eds. *Shopkeepers and Master Artisans in Nineteenth-Century Europe.* London, New York, 1984.

Dahrendorf, Ralf. *Society and Democracy in Germany.* New York, 1967.

Dann, Otto. "Die Anfänge politischer Vereinsbildung in Deutschland." In *Soziale Bewegung und politische Verfassung. Beiträge zur Geschichte der modernen Welt,* edited by Ulrich Engelhardt, Volker Sellin, and Horst Stuke. Stuttgart, 1976.

Diehl, James. *Paramilitary Politics in Weimar Germany.* Bloomington, London, 1977.

Düding, Dieter. *Der Nationalsoziale Verein 1896–1903. Der gescheiterte Versuch einer parteipolitischer Synthese von Nationalismus, Sozialismus und Liberalismus.* Munich, Vienna, 1972.

Dunckelmann, Henning. *Lokale Öffentlichkeit. Eine gemeindesoziologische Untersuchung.* Stuttgart, 1975.

Eley, Geoff. *Reshaping the German Right. Radical Nationalism and Political Change after Bismarck.* New Haven, London, 1980.

Eulenberg, Franz. "Die sozialen Wirkungen der Währungsverhältnisse." *Jahrbuch für Nationalökonomie und Statistik* 122, no. 6 (1924): 748–94.

Evans, Richard J. *The Feminist Movement in Germany 1894–1933.* London, Beverly Hills, 1976.

_____, ed. *Society and Politics in Wilhelmine Germany.* London, 1978.

Eyck, Erich. *A History of the Weimar Republic.* Translated by Harlan P. Hanson and Robert G. L. Waite. 2 vols. New York, 1963.

Falter, Jürgen. "Radikalisierung des Mittelstandes oder Mobilisierung der Unpolitischen? Die Theorien von Seymour Martin Lipset und Reinhard Bendix über die Wählerschaft der NSDAP in Lichte neuer Forschungsergebnisse." In *Probleme politischer Partizipation im Modernisie-rungsprozeß*, edited by Peter Steinbach. Stuttgart, 1982.

———. "Wer verhalf der NSDAP zum Sieg?" *Aus Politik und Zeitge-schichte* B28–29 (14 July 1979): 3–21.

Faust, Anselm. *Der Nationalsozialistische Deutsche Studentenbund. Studenten und Nationalsozialismus in der Weimarer Republik.* 2 vols. Düsseldorf, 1976.

Feldman, Gerald D. *Army, Industry, and Labor in Germany 1914–1918.* Princeton, 1966.

———. "The Political Economy of Germany's Relative Stabilization during the 1920/21 Depression." In *Die Deutsche Inflation. Eine Zwischenbilanz*, edited by Gerald D. Feldman et al. Berlin, New York, 1982.

Feldman, Gerald D.; Holtfrerich, Carl-Ludwig; Ritter, Gerhard A.; and Witt, Peter-Christian, eds. *Die Deutsche Inflation. Eine Zwischenbilanz.* Berlin, New York, 1982.

Fireman, Bruce, and Gamson, William. "Utilitarian Logic in the Resource Mobilization Perspective." In *The Dynamics of Social Movements: Resource Mobilization, Social Control, and Tactics*, edited by Mayer N. Zald and John D. McCarthy. Cambridge, Mass., 1979.

Fischer, Claude S. *The Urban Experience.* New York, 1976.

Fischer, Conan. *Stormtroopers: A Social, Economic, and Ideological Analysis 1929–35.* Winchester, Mass., 1983.

Fischer, Ilse. *Industrialisierung, sozialer Konflikt, und politische Willensbildung in der Stadtgemeinde. Ein Beitrag zur Sozialgeschichte Augsburgs 1840–1914.* Augsburg, 1977.

Frankel, Ernst. *The Dual State.* Translated by E. A. Shils. New York, 1941.

Franze, Manfred. *Die Erlanger Studentenschaft 1918–45.* Würzburg, 1972.

Freudenthal, Herbert. *Vereine in Hamburg. Ein Beitrag zur Geschichte und Volkskunde der Geselligkeit.* Hamburg, 1968.

Fricke, Dieter, ed. *Die bürgerlichen Parteien in Deutschland. Handbuch der Geschichte der bürgerlichen Parteien und anderer bürgerlicher Interessenorganisationen vom Vormärz bis zum Jahre 1945.* 2 vols. Leipzig, 1968.

Gamson, William. *The Strategy of Social Protest.* Homewood, Ill., 1975.

Geiger, Theodor. *Die soziale Schichtung des deutschen Volkes.* Stuttgart, 1932.

Gellately, Robert. *The Politics of Economic Despair: Shopkeepers and German Politics 1890–1914.* Beverly Hills, 1974.

Gerlach, Hellmut von. *Von Rechts nach Links.* Hildesheim, 1978.

Gerschenkron, Alexander. *Bread and Democracy in Germany.* New York, 1966.

Gersdorff, Ursula von. *Frauen im Kriegsdienst 1914–45.* Stuttgart, 1969.

Gessner, Dieter. *Agrarverbände in der Weimarer Republik. Wirtschaftliche und soziale Voraussetzungen agrarkonservativer Politik vor 1933.* Düsseldorf, 1976.

Geyer, Michael. "The State in National Socialist Germany." In *Statemaking and Social Movements: Essays in History and Theory*, edited by Charles Bright and Susan Harding. Ann Arbor, 1984.

Gies, Horst. "NSDAP und landwirtschaftliche Organisationen in der Endphase der Weimarer Republik." *Vierteljahrshefte für Zeitgeschichte* 15 (1967): 341–76.

Giles, Geoffrey J. "The Rise of the National Socialist Students' Association and the Failure of Political Education in the Third Reich." In *The Shaping of the Nazi State*, edited by Peter D. Stachura. London, 1978.

———. *Students and National Socialism*. Princeton, 1985.

Gillis, John. "Germany." In *Crises of Political Development in Europe and the United States*, edited by Raymond Grew. Princeton, 1978.

Gramsci, Antonio. *Selections from the Prison Notebooks of Antonio Gramsci*. Edited and translated by Quinton Hoare and Geoffrey Nowell Smith. New York, 1977.

Grill, Johnpeter Horst. *The Nazi Movement in Baden, 1920–1945*. Chapel Hill, 1983.

Groh, Dieter. *Negative Integration und revolutionäre Attentismus. Die deutsche Sozialdemokratie am Vorabend des Ersten Weltkrieges*. Frankfurt/Main, 1973.

Gutman, Herbert C. "Class, Status, and Community Power in Nineteenth-Century American Industrial Cities—Paterson, New Jersey: A Case Study." In *The Age of Industrialism in America: Essays in Social Structure and Cultural Values*, edited by F. C. Jaher. New York, London, 1968.

Guttsman, W. L. *The German Social Democratic Party, 1875–1933: From Ghetto to Government*. London, 1981.

Habermas, Jürgen. *Strukturwandel der Öffentlichkeit. Untersuchungen zu einer Kategorie der bürgerlichen Gesellschaft*. Neuwied, Berlin, 1972.

Hagtvet, Bernt. "The Theory of Mass Society and the Collapse of the Weimar Republic: A Re-Examination." In *Who Were the Fascists: Social Roots of European Fascism*, edited by Stein Ugelvik Larsen, Bernt Hagtvet, and Jan Petter Myklebust. Oslo, New York, 1980.

Hall, Stuart; Lumley, Bob; and McLennan, Gregor. "Politics and Ideology: Gramsci." *Working Papers in Cultural Studies*. Vol. 10, *On Ideology*. Birmingham, 1977.

Hambrecht, Rainer. *Der Aufstieg der NSDAP in Mittel- und Oberfranken 1925–33*. Nuremberg, 1976.

Hamel, Iris. *Völkischer Verband und nationale Gewerkschaft. Der Deutschnationale Handlungsgehilfenverband 1893–1933*. Frankfurt/Main, 1967.

Hamilton, Richard. *Who Voted for Hitler?* Princeton, 1982.

Hausknecht, Murray. *The Joiners: A Sociological Description of Voluntary Association Membership in the United States*. New York, 1962.

Heberle, Rudolf. *From Democracy to Nazism: A Regional Case Study on Political Parties in Germany*. New York, 1970.

Hennig, Eike. "Regionale Unterschiede bei der Entstehung des deutschen Faschismus: Ein Plädoyer für 'mikroanalytische Studien' zur Erforschung der NSDAP." *Politische Vierteljahresschrift* 21 (1980): 152–73.

Henning, Friedrich-Wilhelm. *Das industrialisierte Deutschland 1914 bis 1972*. Paderborn, 1974.

Henning, Hansjoachim. *Sozialgeschichtliche Entwicklungen in Deutschland von 1815 bis 1860*. Paderborn, 1977.

————. *Das westdeutsche Bürgertum in der Epoche der Hochindustrialisierung 1860–1914*. Pt. I, *Das Bildungsbürgertum in den westdeutschen Provinzen*. Wiesbaden, 1972.

Hermelink, Heinrich, ed. *Kirche im Kampf. Dokumente des Widerstandes und des Aufbaues der Evangelischen Kirche Deutschlands 1933–45*. Tübingen, Stuttgart, 1950.

Hertzmann, Lewis. *DNVP: Right-Wing Opposition in the Weimar Republic 1918–24*. Lincoln, Nebr., 1963.

Hirschfeld, Gerhard, and Kettenacker, Lothar, eds. *Der "Führerstaat": Mythos und Realität. Studien zur Struktur und Politik des Dritten Reiches*. Stuttgart, 1981.

Hitler, Adolf. *Mein Kampf*. Translated by Ralph Manheim. Boston, 1943.

Hobsbawm, Eric, and Ranger, Terence, eds. *The Invention of Tradition*. Cambridge, 1983.

Hoffmann, Walther G. *Das Wachstum der deutschen Wirtschaft*. Berlin, Heidelberg, 1965.

Hofmann, Wolfgang. *Die Bielefelder Stadtverordneten. Ein Beitrag zu bürgerlicher Selbstverwaltung und sozialem Wandel 1815 bis 1914*. Lübeck, Hamburg, 1964.

Hohorst, Gerd; Kocka, Jürgen; and Ritter, Gerhard A., eds. *Sozialgeschichtliches Arbeitsbuch. Materialien zur Statistik des Kaiserreichs 1870–1914*. Munich, 1974.

Holtfrerich, Carl-Ludwig. *Die deutsche Inflation 1914–23*. Berlin, New York, 1980.

Hopwood, Robert. "The Bavarian *Kommerzienräte*: Small Town Economic Elites and the Vertical Lines of Authority and Power." In *Proceedings of the Citadel Symposium on the National Socialist Era, 24–25 April 1980*, edited by Michael B. Barrett. Charleston, S.C., 1982.

————. "Paladins of the *Bürgertum*: Cultural Clubs and Politics in Small German Towns 1918–25." *Historical Papers* (1974): 213–35.

Huerkamp, Claudia. "Ärzte und Professionalisierung in Deutschland. Überlegungen zum Wandel des Artzberufs im 19. Jahrhunderts." *Geschichte und Gesellschaft* 6 (1980): 349–82.

Hughes, Michael L. "Economic Interest, Social Attitudes, and Creditor Ideology: Popular Responses to Inflation." In *Die Deutsche Inflation. Eine Zwischenbilanz*, edited by Gerald D. Feldman et al. Berlin, New York, 1982.

Hunt, James C. *The People's Party in Württemberg and Southern Germany 1890–1914*. Stuttgart, 1975.

Iggers, George G. "The Political Theory of Voluntary Association in Early Nineteenth-Century German Liberal Thought." In *Voluntary Associations: A Study of Groups in Free Societies*, edited by D. B. Robertson. Richmond, 1966.

Jamin, Mathilde. *Zwischen den Klassen. Zur Sozialstruktur der SA-Führerschaft*. Wuppertal, 1984.

Jarausch, Konrad. "German Students in the First World War." *Central European History* 17 (1984): 310–29.

―――. *Students, Society, and Politics in Imperial Germany: The Rise of Academic Illiberalism*. Princeton, 1982.

Jeggle, Utz. "Geld und Geltung. Eine historische Analyse und einige subjektive Anmerkungen zur 150jährigen Geschichte der Museumsgesellschaft." *Tübinger Blätter* 58 (1971): 35–42.

Jessop, Bob. "The Political Indeterminacy of Democracy." In *Marxism and Democracy*, edited by Alan Hunt. London, 1980.

Jonas, Erasmus. *Die Volkskonservativen. 1928–1933*. Düsseldorf, 1965.

Jones, Larry. "The Crisis of White-Collar Interest Politics." In *Industrielles System und politische Entwicklung in der Weimarer Republik*, edited by Hans Mommsen, Dietmar Petzina, and Bernd Weisbrod. Düsseldorf, 1974.

―――. "The Dissolution of the Bourgeois Party System in the Weimar Republic." In *Social Change and Political Development in Weimar Germany*, edited by Richard Bessel and E. J. Feuchtwanger. London, 1981.

―――. "The Dying Middle—The Fragmentation of the Bourgeois Parties." *Central European History* 5 (1972): 23–54.

―――. "Sammlung oder Zersplitterung? Die Bestrebungen zur Bildung einer neuen Mittelpartei in der Endphase der Weimarer Republik." *Vierteljahrshefte für Zeitgeschichte* 25 (1977): 265–304.

Kater, Michael. "Generationskonflikt als Entwicklungsfaktor in der NS-Bewegung vor 1933." *Geschichte und Gesellschaft* 11 (1985): 217–43.

―――. "Methodologische Überlegungen über Möglichkeiten und Grenzen einer Analyse der sozialen Zusammensetzung der NSDAP von 1925 bis 1945." In *Die Nationalsozialisten. Analysen faschistischer Bewegungen*, edited by Reinhard Mann. Suttgart, 1980.

―――. *The Nazi Party: A Social Profile of Members and Leaders 1919–1945*. Cambridge, Mass., 1983.

―――. *Studentenschaft und Rechtsradikalismus in Deutschland 1918–1933. Eine sozialgeschichtliche Studie zur Bildungskrise in der Weimarer Republik*. Hamburg, 1975.

Kershaw, Ian. "Ideology, Propaganda, and the Rise of the Nazi Party." In *The Nazi Machtergreifung*, edited by Peter D. Stachura. London, 1983.

―――. *Popular Opinion and Political Dissent in the Third Reich: Bavaria 1933–45*. New York, 1983.

Kocka, Jürgen. *Angestellte zwischen Faschismus und Demokratie. Zur politischen Sozialgeschichte der Angestellten: USA 1890–1940 im internationalen Vergleich*. Göttingen, 1976.

―――. *Klassengesellschaft im Krieg 1914–1918*. Göttingen, 1973.

————. *White Collar Workers in America 1890–1940: A Social-Political History in International Perspective.* Translated by Maura Kealey. London, Beverly Hills, 1980.

Köllmann, Wolfgang. *Sozialgeschichte der Stadt Barmen im 19. Jahrhundert.* Tübingen, 1960.

Könnemann, Erwin, and Krusch, Hans Joachim. *Aktionseinheit contra Kapp Putsch.* Berlin, 1972.

Koonz, Claudia. "The Competition for a Women's *Lebensraum*, 1928–1934." In *When Biology Became Destiny: Women in Weimar and Nazi Germany,* edited by Renate Bridenthal, Atina Grossmann, and Marion Kaplan. New York, 1984.

————. "Mothers in the Fatherland: Women in Nazi Germany." In *Becoming Visible: Women in European History,* edited by Renate Bridenthal. Boston, 1977.

Koshar, Rudy. "Away from the Center: Two Recent Local Studies of Nazism from the Federal Republic." *Social History* 8 (1983): 77–86.

————. "From *Stammtisch* to Party: Nazi Joiners and the Contradictions of Grass Roots Fascism in Weimar Germany." *Journal of Modern History* 59 (1987).

————. "Two 'Nazisms': The Social Context of Nazi Mobilization in Marburg and Tübingen." *Social History* 7 (1982): 27–42.

————. "Vereinsleben und Nazismus. Eine Analyse der Mobilisierung in Marburg a.d.L." In *Hessen unterm Hakenkreuz. Studien zur Durchsetzung der NSDAP in Hessen,* edited by Eike Hennig. Frankfurt/Main, 1983.

Kosselleck, Reinhart. *Kritik und Krise. Eine Studie zur Pathogenese der bürgerlichen Welt.* Freiburg, Munich, 1959.

Krebs, Albert. *The Infancy of Nazism. The Memoirs of Ex-Gauleiter Albert Krebs 1923–33.* Edited and translated by William Sheridan Allen. New York, London, 1976.

Kretschmer, Johanna. "150 Jahre Tübinger Museumsgesellschaft." *Attempto* 39/40 (1971): 74–87.

Kreutzberger, Wolfgang. *Studenten und Politik 1918–1933. Der Fall Freiburg im Breisgau.* Göttingen, 1972.

Kühnl, Reinhard, ed. *Der deutsche Faschismus in Quellen und Dokumenten.* Cologne, 1975.

Kunz, Andreas. "Verteilungskampf oder Interessenkonsensus? Einkommensentwicklung und Sozialverhalten von Arbeitnehmergruppen in der Inflationszeit 1914 bis 1924." In *Die Deutsche Inflation. Eine Zwischenbilanz,* edited by Gerald D. Feldman et al. Berlin, New York, 1982.

Laclau, Ernesto. *Politics and Ideology in Marxist Theory.* London, 1979.

Laqueur, Walter, ed. *Fascism—A Reader's Guide: Analyses, Interpretations, Bibliography.* Berkeley, Los Angeles, 1976.

Larsen, Stein Ugelvik; Hagtvet, Bernt; and Myklebust, Jan Petter, eds. *Who Were the Fascists: Social Roots of European Fascism.* Oslo, New York, 1980.

Lears, T. J. Jackson. "The Concept of Cultural Hegemony: Problems and

Possibilities." *American Historical Review* 90 (1985): 567–93.

Lebovics, Herman. *Social Conservatism and the Middle Classes in Germany, 1914–1933.* Princeton, 1969.

Lederer, Emil. *Die Angestellten vor dem Nationalsozialismus. Ein Beitrag zum Verständnis der deutschen Sozialstruktur 1918–1933.* Göttingen, 1977.

―――. *Die Privatangestellten in der modernen Wirtschaftsentwicklung.* Tübingen, 1912.

Lederer, Emil, and Marschak, Jacob. *The New Middle Class.* Translated by S. Ellison. New York, 1937.

Lee, J. J. "Aspects of Urbanization and Economic Development in Germany 1815–1914." In *Towns and Societies: Essays in Economic History and Historical Sociology,* edited by Philip Abrams and E. A. Wrigley. Cambridge, 1978.

Lehmann, Hans-Georg. *Die Agrarfrage in der Theorie und Praxis der deutschen und internationalen Sozialdemokratie.* Tübingen, 1970.

Levy, Richard S. *The Downfall of the Anti-Semitic Political Parties in Imperial Germany.* New Haven, London, 1975.

Linz, Juan J. "Some Notes toward a Comparative Study of Fascism in Sociological Historical Perspective." In *Fascism—A Reader's Guide: Analyses, Interpretations, Bibliography,* edited by Walter Laqueur. Berkeley, Los Angeles, 1976.

Loening, E., and Loening, O. "Vereins- und Versammlungsfreiheit." In *Handwörterbuch der Staatswissenschaften,* vol. 8. Jena, 1913.

Loewenberg, Peter. "The Psycho-Historical Origins of the Nazi Youth Cohort." *American Historical Review* 76 (1971): 1457–1502.

Lohalm, Uwe. *Völkischer Radikalismus. Die Geschichte des Deutschvölkischen Schutz- und Trutzbundes 1919–1923.* Hamburg, 1970.

Loreth, Hans. *Das Wachstum der württembergischen Wirtschaft von 1818 bis 1918.* Heidelberg, 1972.

Lüdtke, Alf. "Vom Elend der Professoren—'Ständische' Autonomie und Selbstgleichschaltung 1932/33 in Tübingen." In *Wem Gehört die Universität? Untersuchungen zum Zusammenhang von Wissenschaft und Herrschaft anläßlich des 500jährigen Bestehens der Universität Tübingen,* edited by Martin Doehlemann. Lahn/Giessen, 1977.

Madden, Paul. "Some Social Characteristics of Early Nazi Party Members, 1919–23." *Central European History* 15 (1982): 34–56.

Maier, Charles. *Recasting Bourgeois Europe: Stabilization in France, Germany, and Italy in the Decade after World War I.* Princeton, 1975.

Mann, Reinhard, ed. *Die Nationalsozialisten. Analysen faschistischer Bewegungen.* Stuttgart, 1980.

Mann, Thomas. *Betrachtungen eines Unpolitischen.* Frankfurt/Main, 1956.

Marshall, Barbara. "Der Einfluß der Universität auf die politische Entwicklung der Stadt Göttingen 1918–33." *Niedersächsisches Jahrbuch für Landesgeschichte* 49 (1977): 265–301.

Maser, Gerhard. *Die Frühgeschichte der NSDAP*. Frankfurt/Main, 1965.

Mason, Timothy W. *Arbeiterklasse und Volksgemeinschaft. Dokumente und Materialien zur deutschen Arbeiterpolitik 1936–39*. Opladen, 1975.

Massing, Paul. *Rehearsal for Destruction: A Study of Political Anti-Semitism in Imperial Germany*. New York, 1949.

Matzerath, Horst. *Nationalsozialismus und kommunale Selbstverwaltung*. Stuttgart, 1970.

Meier, Kurt. *Der evangelische Kirchenkampf*. 2 vols. Halle, 1976.

Melly, George. *Revolt into Style*. New York, 1972.

Merkl, Peter. *The Making of a Stormtrooper*. Princeton, 1980.

———. *Political Violence under the Swastika: 581 Early Nazis*. Princeton, 1975.

Meyer, Wilhelm. *Der Verein im neuen Staat*. Berlin-Wilmersdorf, 1935.

Michels, Robert. "Die deutsche Sozialdemokratie. Parteimitgliedschaft und soziale Zusammensetzung." *Archiv für Sozialwissenschaft und Sozialpolitik* 23 (1906): 471–556.

Milatz, Alfred. *Wähler und Wahlen in der Weimarer Republik*. Bonn, 1968.

Mittmann, Ursula. *Fraktion und Partei. Ein Vergleich von Zentrum und Sozialdemokratie im Kaiserreich*. Düsseldorf, 1979.

Moeller, Robert. "Winners as Losers in the German Inflation: Peasant Protest over the Controlled Economy 1920–23." In *Die Deutsche Inflation. Eine Zwischenbilanz*, edited by Gerald D. Feldman et al. Berlin, New York, 1982.

Mommsen, Hans. *Beamtentum im Dritten Reich*. Stuttgart, 1966.

———. "National Socialism—Continuity and Change." In *Fascism—A Reader's Guide: Analyses, Interpretations, Bibliography*, edited by Walter Laqueur. Berkeley, Los Angeles, 1976.

Mommsen, Hans; Petzina, Dietmar; and Weisbrod, Bernd, eds. *Industrielles System und politische Entwicklung in der Weimarer Republik*. Düsseldorf, 1974.

Mommsen, Wolfgang. "Der deutsche Liberalismus zwischen 'klassenloser Bürgergesellschaft' und 'Organisierter Kapitalismus.'" *Geschichte und Gesellschaft* 4 (1978): 77–90.

———. *Max Weber und die deutsche Politik 1890–1920*. Tübingen, 1959.

Mosse, George L. *The Nationalization of the Masses: Political Symbolism and Mass Movements in Germany from the Napoleonic Wars through the Third Reich*. New York, 1975.

Neef, Hermann. "Die Entwicklung des Beamtenorganisationswesens zum Nationalsozialismus." In *Almanach der Deutschen Beamten*. Berlin, 1934.

Nipperdey, Thomas. "Die deutsche Studentenschaft in den ersten Jahren der Weimarer Republik." In *Kulturverwaltung der Zwanziger Jahre*, edited by Adolf Grimme. Stuttgart, 1961.

———. *Die Organisation der deutschen Parteien vor 1918*. Düsseldorf, 1961.

_____. "Organisierter Kapitalismus, Verbände, und die Krise des Kaiser-reichs." *Geschichte und Gesellschaft* 5 (1979): 418–33.

_____. "Verein als soziale Struktur in Deutschland im späten 18. und frü-hen 19. Jahrhundert. Eine Fallstudie zur Modernisierung I." In *Gesell-schaft, Kultur, Theorie: Gesammelte Aufsätze zur neueren Geschichte,* edited by Thomas Nipperdey. Göttingen, 1976.

_____. "Wehler's 'Kaiserreich': Eine kritische Auseinandersetzung." In *Gesellschaft, Kultur, Theorie: Gesammelte Aufsätze zur neueren Ge-schichte,* edited by Thomas Nipperdey. Göttingen, 1976.

Noakes, Jeremy. *The Nazi Party in Lower Saxony 1921–1933.* London, 1971.

_____. "Oberbürgermeister and Gauleiter: City Government between Par-ty and State." In *Der "Führerstaat": Mythos und Realität. Studien zur Struktur und Politik des Dritten Reiches,* edited by Gerhard Hirschfeld and Lothar Kettenacker. Stuttgart, 1981.

Nolan, Mary. *Social Democracy and Society: Working Class Radicalism in Düsseldorf 1890–1920.* New York, 1981.

Oberschall, Anthony. *Social Conflict and Social Movements.* Englewood Cliffs, N.J., 1973.

O'Donnell, Anthony J. "National Liberalism and the Mass Politics of the German Right." Ph.D. dissertation, Princeton University, 1974.

Opitz, Gunter. *Der Christlich-Soziale Volksdienst. Versuch einer prote-stantischen Partei in der Weimarer Republik.* Düsseldorf, 1969.

Opitz, Reinhard. *Der deutsche Sozialliberalismus 1917–1933.* Cologne, 1973.

Orlow, Dietrich. *The History of the Nazi Party 1919–33.* Pittsburgh, 1969.

Payer, Friedrich. *Autobiographische Aufzeichnungen und Dokumente.* Göppingen, 1974.

Petzina, Dietmar; Abelshauser, Werner; and Faust, Anselm, eds. *Sozialge-schichtliches Arbeitsbuch III. Materialien zur Statistik des Deutschen Reiches 1914–45.* Munich, 1978.

Peukert, Detlev, and Reulecke, Jürgen, eds. *Die Reihen fast geschlossen. Beiträge zur Geschichte des Alltags unterm Nationalsozialismus.* Wup-pertal, 1981.

Pinson, Koppel. *Modern Germany: Its History and Civilization.* New York, London, 1970.

Poulantzas, Nicos. *Classes in Contemporary Capitalism.* London, 1975.

Pridham, Geoffrey. *Hitler's Rise to Power: The History of the NSDAP in Bavaria 1923–1933.* London, 1973.

Puhle, Hans-Jürgen. *Agrarische Interessenpolitik und preußischer Konser-vatismus im Wilhelminischen Reich (1893–1914). Ein Beitrag zur Ana-lyse des Nationalismus in Deutschland am Beispiel des Bundes der Landwirte und der Deutsch-Konservativen Partei.* Hanover, 1966.

_____. *Politische Agrarbewegungen in kapitalistischen Industriegesell-schaften. Deutschland, USA und Frankreich im 20. Jahrhundert.* Göt-tingen, 1975.

Pulzer, Peter. *The Rise of Political Anti-Semitism in Germany and Austria.* New York, 1964.

Reulecke, Jürgen. "Phasen und Auswirkungen der Inflation 1914–23 am Beispiel der Barmer Wirtschaft." In *Historische Prozesse der deutschen Inflation 1914–24,* edited by Otto Büsch and Gerald D. Feldman. Berlin, 1978.

Rietzler, Rudolf. *Kampf in der Nordmark. Das Aufkommen des Nationalsozialismus in Schleswig-Holstein 1918–1928.* Neumünster, 1982.

Ringer, Fritz K. *The Decline of the German Mandarins: The German Academic Community 1890–1933.* Cambridge, Mass., 1969.

Ritter, Gerhard A., and Kocka, Jürgen, eds. *Deutsche Sozialgeschichte. Dokumente und Skizzen.* Vol. 2, *1870–1914.* Munich, 1974.

Rosenberg, Arthur. *Geschichte der Weimarer Republik.* 17th ed. Frankfurt/Main, 1975.

Rosenhaft, Eve. *Beating the Fascists?: The German Communists and Political Violence 1929–1933.* Cambridge, 1983.

Roth, Guenther. *The Social Democrats in Imperial Germany: A Study in Working Class Isolation and Negative Integration.* Totowa, N.J., 1963.

Saldern, Adelheid von. *Mittelstand im "Dritten Reich." Handwerker–Einzelhändler–Bauern.* Frankfurt/Main, New York, 1979.

————. *Vom Einwohner zum Bürger. Zur Emanzipation der städtischen Unterschicht Göttingens 1890–1920.* Berlin, 1973.

Sauer, Wolfgang. "National Socialism: Totalitarianism or Fascism?" *American Historical Review* 73 (1967): 404–24.

Scheidemann, Philip. *Memoirs of a Social Democrat.* Translated by J. E. Michell. London, 1929.

Schieder, Wolfgang, ed. *Faschismus als soziale Bewegung. Deutschland und Italien im Vergleich.* Hamburg, 1976.

Schlummbohm, Jürgen. *Freiheit. Die Anfänge der bürgerlichen Emanzipationsbewegung in Deutschland im Spiegel ihres Leitwortes.* Düsseldorf, 1975.

Schmalz, Guenter G. "Zur Geschichte des Wortes 'Verein.'" *Monatshefte* 47 (1955): 295–301.

Schmitt, Carl. *The Concept of the Political.* Translated by George Schwab. New Brunswick, N.J., 1976.

Schmitt, Heinz. *Das Vereinsleben der Stadt Weinheim an der Bergstraße.* Weinheim a.d.B., 1963.

Schoenbaum, David. *Hitler's Social Revolution: Class and Status in Nazi Germany 1933–1939.* New York, 1966.

Scholder, Klaus. *Die Kirchen und das Dritte Reich.* Vol. 1, *Vorgeschichte und Zeit der Illusionen 1918–34.* Frankfurt/Main, 1977.

Schulze, Friedrich, and Ssymank, Paul. *Das Deutsche Studententum von den ältesten Zeiten bis zum Weltkriege.* Leipzig, 1918.

Schumacher, Martin. *Mittelstandsfront und Republik: Die Wirtschaftspartei–Reichspartei des deutschen Mittelstandes 1919–1933.* Düsseldorf, 1972.

Sheehan, James. *German Liberalism in the Nineteenth Century.* Chicago, 1978.

―――. "Liberalism and the City in Nineteenth-Century Germany." *Past and Present* 51 (1971): 116–37.

Sills, David L. "Voluntary Associations." In *International Encyclopedia of the Social Sciences.* New York, 1968.

Simon, Klaus. *Die württembergischen Demokraten. Ihre Stellung und Arbeit im Parteien- und Verfassungssystem in Württemberg und im Deutschen Reich 1890–1920.* Stuttgart, 1969.

Stachura, Peter D. *Gregor Straßer and the Rise of Nazism.* London, 1983.

―――. *Nazi Youth in the Weimar Republic.* Santa Barbara, 1975.

―――, ed. *The Nazi Machtergreifung.* London, 1983.

Staudinger, Hans. *Individuum und Gemeinschaft in der Kulturorganisation des Vereins.* Jena, 1913.

Stearns, Peter. "The Middle Class: Toward a Precise Definition." *Comparative Studies in Society and History* 21 (1979): 377–96.

Stegmann, Dirk. *Die Erben Bismarcks. Parteien und Verbände in der Spätphase des Wilhelminischen Deutschlands.* Cologne, Berlin, 1970.

Steinbach, Peter. *Industrialisierung und Sozialsystem im Fürstentum Lippe. Zum Verhältnis von Gesellschaftsstruktur und Sozialverhalten einer verspäteten industrialisierten Region im 19. Jahrhundert.* Berlin, 1976.

―――. "Regionale Parteigeschichte, historische Wahlforschung und moderne Landesgeschichte. Bemerkungen zu einigen Neuerscheinungen." *Hessisches Jahrbuch für Landesgeschichte* 26 (1976): 200–266.

Steinberg, Michael Paul. *Sabers and Brownshirts: The German Students' Path to National Socialism 1918–1935.* Chicago, 1977.

Stephenson, Jill. *The Nazi Organisation of Women.* London, 1981.

Stern, Fritz. "Die politischen Folgen des unpolitischen Deutschen." In *Das kaiserliche Deutschland. Politik und Gesellschaft 1870–1918*, edited by Michael Stürmer. Düsseldorf, 1977.

Stokes, Lawrence D. "The Social Composition of the Nazi Party in Eutin, 1925–32." *International Review of Social History* 23 (1978): pt. 1, 1–32.

―――, ed. *Kleinstadt und Nationalsozialismus. Ausgewählte Dokumente zur Geschichte von Eutin 1918–1945.* Neumünster, 1984.

Struve, Walter. *Elites Against Democracy. Leadership Ideals in Bourgeois Political Thought in Germany 1890–1933.* Princeton, 1973.

Tenfelde, Klaus. *Proletarische Provinz. Radikalisierung und Widerstand in Penzberg/Oberbayern 1900–1945.* Munich, Vienna, 1982.

Theweleit, Klaus. *Männerphantasien.* 2 vols. Frankfurt/Main, 1977.

Tilly, Charles. *From Mobilization to Revolution.* Reading, Mass., 1978.

Tipton, Frank B. *Regional Variations in the Economic Development of Germany during the Nineteenth Century.* Middletown, Conn., 1976.

Tucholsky, Kurt. "Das Mitglied." In *Zwischen Gestern und Morgen. Eine Auswahl aus seinen Schriften und Gedichten*, edited by Mary Gerold-Tucholsky. Hamburg, 1952.

Turner, Henry Ashby, Jr. *Stresemann and the Politics of the Weimar Republic*. Princeton, 1963.

Vincent, John. *The Formation of the Liberal Party 1857–1868*. London, 1966.

Volkov, Shulamit. "Kontinuität und Diskontinuität im deutschen Antisemitismus 1878–1945." *Vierteljahrshefte für Zeitgeschichte* 33 (1985): 221–43.

──────. *The Rise of Popular Antimodernism in Germany: The Urban Master Artisans, 1873–1896*. Princeton, 1978.

Walker, Mack. *German Home Towns: Community, State, and General Estate 1648–1871*. Ithaca, 1971.

Weber, Max. "Die Erbschaft Bismarcks." In *Gesammelte Politische Schriften*, edited by Johannes Winckelmann. 3d. ed. Tübingen, 1971.

──────. "Geschäftsbericht und Diskussionsreden auf den deutschen soziologischen Tagungen." In *Gesammelte Aufsätze zur Soziologie und Sozialpolitik*. Tübingen, 1924.

──────. "National Character and the Junkers." In *From Max Weber: Essays in Sociology*, edited by H. H. Gerth and C. Wright Mills. New York, 1958.

──────. "Der Nationalstaat und die Volkswirtschaft." In *Gesammelte Politische Schriften*, edited by Johannes Winckelmann. 3d. ed. Tübingen, 1971.

──────. "Parlament und Regierung im neugeordneten Deutschland." In *Gesammelte Politische Schriften*, edited by Johannes Winckelmann. 3d. ed. Tübingen, 1971.

Wehler, Hans-Ulrich. *Das Deutsche Kaiserreich 1871–1918*. Göttingen, 1975.

Welch, David, ed. *Nazi Propaganda: The Power and the Limitations*. London, 1983.

Wells, Roger. *German Cities: A Study of Contemporary Municipal Politics and Administration*. Princeton, 1932.

White, Dan S. *The Splintered Party: National Liberalism in Hessen and the Reich 1867–1918*. Cambridge, Mass., 1976.

Wickham, James. "Working-Class Movement and Working-Class Life: Frankfurt am Main during the Weimar Republic." *Social History* 8 (1983): 315–43.

Williams, Raymond. *Marxism and Literature*. Oxford, 1977.

Winkler, Heinrich August. "From Social Protectionism to National Socialism: The German Small-Business Movement in Comparative Perspective." *Journal of Modern History* 48 (1976): 1–18.

──────. *Mittelstand, Demokratie, und Nationalsozialismus. Die politische Entwicklung von Handwerk und Kleinhandel in der Weimarer Republik*. Cologne, 1972.

Witt, Peter-Christian. "Finanzpolitik und sozialer Wandel in Krieg und Inflation 1918–24." In *Industrielles System und politische Entwicklung in der Weimarer Republik*, edited by Hans Mommsen, Dietmar Petzina, and Bernd Weisbrod. Düsseldorf, 1974.

Wolfe, Alan. *The Limits of Legitimacy: Political Contradictions of Contemporary Capitalism.* New York, London, 1977.

Wolff, Robert Paul. *The Poverty of Liberalism.* Boston, 1968.

Wortmann, Karl. *Geschichte der Deutschen Vaterlandspartei 1917–1918.* Halle, 1926.

Wright, J. R. C. *"Above Parties": The Political Attitudes of the German Protestant Church Leadership 1918–33.* London, 1974.

Wulf, Peter. *Die politische Haltung des schleswig-holsteinischen Handwerks 1928–32.* Cologne, 1968.

Yeo, Stephen. *Religion and Voluntary Organizations in Crisis.* London, 1976.

Zang, Gert, ed. *Provinzialisierung einer Region. Zur Entstehen der bürgerlichen Gesellschaft in der Provinz.* Frankfurt/Main, 1978.

Zmarzlik, Hans-Gunter. "Das Kaiserreich als Einbahnstraße?" In *Liberalismus und imperialistischer Staat: Der Imperialismus als Problem liberaler Parteien in Deutschland 1890–1914,* edited by Karl Höll and Günther List. Göttingen, 1971.

———. "Das Kaiserreich in neuer Sicht?" *Historische Zeitschrift* 222 (1976): 105–26.

Zofka, Zdenek. *Die Ausbreitung des Nationalsozialismus auf dem Lande. Eine regionale Fallstudie zur politischen Einstellung der Landbevölkerung in der Zeit des Aufstiegs und der Machtergreifung der NSDAP 1928–1936.* Munich, 1979.

Zorn, Wolfgang. "Die politische Entwicklung des deutschen Studententums 1918–1931." In *Darstellungen und Quellen zur Geschichte der deutschen Einheitsbewegung im 19. und 20. Jahrhundert.* Vol. 5. Heidelberg, 1965.

———. "Student Politics in the Weimar Republic." *Journal of Contemporary History* 5 (1970): 128–43.

Index